WITHDRAWN

PERSPECTIVES ON MEMORY RESEARCH:

Essays in Honor of Uppsala University's 500th Anniversary

Conference on Perspectives on Memory
— Research, Univ. of Uppsala, 1977.

PERSPECTIVES ON MEMORY RESEARCH:

Essays in Honor of Uppsala University's 500th Anniversary

EDITED BY

Lars-Göran Nilsson
University of Uppsala, Sweden

 LAWRENCE ERLBAUM ASSOCIATES, PUBLISHERS
1979   Hillsdale, New Jersey

DISTRIBUTED BY THE HALSTED PRESS DIVISION OF
JOHN WILEY & SONS
New York   Toronto   London   Sydney

Copyright© 1979 by Lawrence Erlbaum Associates, Inc.
  All rights reserved. No part of this book may be reproduced in
  any form, by photostat, microform, retrieval system, or any other
  means, without the prior written permission of the publisher.

Lawrence Erlbaum Associates, Inc., Publishers
62 Maria Drive
Hillsdale, New Jersey 07642

Distributed solely by Halsted Press Division
John Wiley & Sons, Inc., New York

BF
371
c723
1977

Library of Congress Cataloging in Publication Data
Conference on Perspectives on Memory Research, University
  of Uppsala, 1977.
  Perspectives on memory research

  Includes indexes.
  1. Memory—Congresses. I. Nilsson, Lars-Göran,
1944–   II. Uppsala. Universitet.   III. Title.
BF371.C723 1977   153.1′2   78-23461
ISBN 0-470-26586-8

Printed in the United States of America

Contents

Preface *xi*

PART I.   INTRODUCTION *1*

1. **Functions of Memory**
    Lars-Göran Nilsson

    Views on Past and Present   *3*
    Views on the Future   *7*

PART II.   CONCEPTUAL PERSPECTIVES *17*

2. **Memory Research: What Kind of Progress?**
    Endel Tulving

    Introduction   *19*
    Some Glimpses into the Past   *20*
    Growth in Memory Research   *23*
    Limitations and Shortcomings   *26*
    Steps to the Future   *29*
    A Concluding Comment   *32*

3. **On the Descriptive and Explanatory Functions of Theories of Memory**
W. K. Estes

Introduction *35*
Three Modes of Theorizing: An Illustration *35*
Functions of Theories *41*
Routes to Explanation *42*
The Descriptive–Explanatory Dimension:
  Remarks on the Standing of Current Theories *46*
Implications of Memory Models for Strategies of
  Theory Construction *57*

4. **Conscious and Unconscious Cognition: A Computational Metaphor for the Mechanism of Attention and Integration**
D. Alan Allport

Introduction *61*
Production Systems *67*
Preattentive Processes and Conscious Perception *77*

PART III. PERCEPTUAL PERSPECTIVES *91*

5. **Memory Functions in Visual Event Perception**
Gunnar Johansson

Background *93*
About the Term "Event Perception" *94*
Time as a Fundamental Dimension in Visual Motion Perception *95*
Event Perception and The Classification of Perception
  and Memory *97*
Event Perception as "Memory" *97*
Perceptual Effects of Liminal Changes in the Stimulus Flow *98*
Theoretical Consequences for the Perception-Memory Problem *101*
Concluding Remarks *101*

6. **Convolution and Correlation in Perception and Memory**
Bennet B. Murdock, Jr.

Introduction *105*
Convolution and Correlation *105*
Applications to Perception *108*
Applications to Memory *110*
Discussion *116*

7. **Perception, Memory, and Mental Processes**
Donald A. Norman

Introduction *121*
On Cognitive Processing *122*
Representation: Schemes and Descriptions *127*
Processing: Control Structures and Resources *133*
Concluding Remarks *140*

8. **Elaboration and Distinctiveness in Episodic Memory**
Fergus I. M. Craik and Larry L. Jacoby

Introduction *145*
Attention *146*
Rehearsal *149*
Encoding *152*
Encoding and Retrieval *156*
Episodic and Semantic Memory *161*
Memory as "Stage Setting" as Opposed to a Trace System *162*
Conclusions *163*

9. **The Primacy of Perceiving:**
An Ecological Reformulation of Perception
for Understanding Memory
M. T. Turvey and Robert Shaw

Introduction *167*
The Legacy of the Past Five Centuries *168*
An Ecological Reformulation *189*
Some Implications for the Interpretation of Memory *216*

PART IV.   BIOLOGICAL PERSPECTIVES   *223*

10.   Learning as Differentiation of Brain Cell Protein
Holger Hydén

General Considerations   *225*
Some Experimental Considerations   *227*
Synthesis of Messenger RNA at the Onset of Training   *229*
Are Enduring Molecular Changes a Result of Learning
    Mediated by a Transient Specific Problem?   *235*
Remaining Protein Differentiation of Neurons as
    a Function of Experience and Learning   *238*
System Changes in Learning Served by Cell Mechanisms
    That Modulate the Cell Membrane   *241*

**11.   Patterns of Activity in the Cerebral Cortex
Related to Memory Functions**
David H. Ingvar

Introduction   *247*
Technical Consideration   *248*
Discussion   *253*
Summary   *254*

**12.   Neuropsychological Research and
the Fractionation of Memory Systems**
Tim Shallice

Introduction   *257*
The Fractionation of Long- and Short-Term Verbal Memory   *263*
Neuropsychology and the Properties of the Auditory–Verbal,
    Short-Term Store   *267*
General Discussion   *273*

13.   Neuropsychology of Complex Forms of Human Memory
Alexander R. Luria

Introduction   *279*
Neuropsychological Method   *280*
Conclusion   *288*

PART V.   REALITY PERSPECTIVES   *291*

14. **Organization and Repetition:**
    Organizational Principles With Special Reference
    to Rote Learning
    George Mandler

    Theory and Data   *293*
    The Application of Organizational Principles   *315*

15. **Reading Comprehension and Readability in**
    Educational Practice and Psychological Theory
    Walter Kintsch and Douglas Vipond

    Introduction   *329*
    New Directions   *336*
    Conclusion   *362*

16. **Applied Cognitive and Cognitive Applied Psychology:**
    The Case of Face Recognition
    Alan Baddeley

    Introduction   *367*
    Applied Research   *367*
    Face Recognition   *369*
    Conclusions   *385*

    Author Index   *389*
    Subject Index   *397*

Preface

This conference on Perspectives on Memory Research was held at the University of Uppsala, June 20-24, 1977. A main purpose of it was to commemorate the birth of the University of Uppsala in 1477. This was also the purpose of more than 40 other conferences and symposia held in Uppsala during the year of 1977. The celebration of a 500-year-old university provides an excellent opportunity to relate the research and higher education of the past with that of the present and the future. Most of the conferences, inlcuding this one on Memory, took care of this opportunity to look at the inevitable and important historical perspective common to all sciences.

It might seem to be a good enough reason to organize a conference on memory in the context where a university is commemorated. Although it is of course interesting to note that the memory area is represented in an occasion of this sort, that was not the real reason for organizing this conference. Instead, the reason was to get students of memory together to discuss and evaluate the memory research that already has been carried out or that is presently under way and to speculate about the type of research in this area that will be carried out in the future.

The dynamic development the area has undergone during the last couple of decades stands in sharp contrast to the slow and somewhat sterile research that was carried out in the verbal learning tradition during the first half of the century. This recent dramatic development needs careful consideration in many different ways before we can enter meaningful scientific enterprises in the future. What started out as a promising and rather coherent alternative to the behavioristic tradition in the middle of the century has now turned out to be a far too diverging area leading everywhere and possibly nowhere. The dynamics in the multiplexity for research in the area is certainly something to protect, but at the same time it also seems to be a strong need for some overall perspective in the field. Preferably, such perspectives could then serve as guidelines for future memory research. Such a goal is probably nothing you can attain by a single book, but this volume seeks to make a modest start in directing the attention of contemporary students of memory on these problems.

The contributors to the conference and this volume were specifically asked to concentrate on overall theoretical and metatheoretical questions at the cost of empirical problems. There were no instructions to forbid the contributors to talk about data, but when such issues were discussed, they were meant to be illustrations to more abstract questions rather than ends in themselves.

It was a privilege for us to arrange this conference with all these prominent scholars. A few other qualified scientists in the field were originally invited, but for different reasons they were unable to attend the conference. With one exception, all the papers that appear in this book were presented at the conference. Just before the conference a message reached us saying that Professor Luria was unable to attend due to medical problems. A few months later the sad message that Professor Luria had died reached us. The paper by Professor Luria presented in this book thus puts an end to a long and successful career with many important contributions to science.

The conference was made possible by strong moral support from Rector Magnificus of The University of Uppsala, Torgny Segerstedt, and with economical support from the University of Uppsala, the Swedish Council for Social Science Research, the Hierta-Retzius Foundation of the Royal Swedish Academy of Sciences, the National Defense Research Institute, and from the project Pedagogical Investigations concerning the study situation of the visually handicapped (PUSS), Department of Educational Research, School of Education in Uppsala.

I am indebted to the following persons for invaluable help in organizing the conference: Trevor Archer, Robert Karlsson, Kjell Ohlsson, Jerker Rönnberg, Les Shaps, and Björn Åström.

LARS-GÖRAN NILSSON

PERSPECTIVES ON MEMORY RESEARCH:

Essays in Honor of Uppsala University's
500th Anniversary

INTRODUCTION

1 Functions of Memory

Lars–Göran Nilsson
University of Uppsala, Sweden

VIEWS ON PAST AND PRESENT

Ebbinghaus is usually considered the founder of memory research. This is somewhat misleading, for, despite the title of his now classic book *Über das Gedächtnis* (1885), his research was about learning and repetition rather than memory. Although learning and repetition are important aspects of memorization, they represent merely a small part of it.

The verbal learning approach initiated by Ebbinghaus was adopted by the behaviorists and became central to their thinking during the next three-quarters of a century. These students of verbal learning were more interested in studying how different tasks affect performance than in inferring what was going on in the minds of their subjects. Taking into consideration this reluctance to postulate any mental mechanisms intervening between stimulus and response and the complete dominance of behaviorism on the intellectual climate of the time, it is not surprising that memory research as understood today was dormant during this period.

Although there was essentially no memory research at this time, memory did mean something more than a simple acquisition of stimulus–response connections to some scholars. One such person was Freud (1915), who wrote about motivational aspects of memory along lines quite different from those of the behaviorists. According to Freud, memories repressed to an unconscious level could be brought to consciousness by psychoanalytic therapy. Thus, for Freud it was convenient to conceptualize the mind in terms of storage and retrieval of information available in an unconscious state. More "modern" ideas of memory had been put forward even earlier than this.

James (1890), for instance, when discussing consciousness, distinguished between primary and secondary memory; and Bergson (1896) distinguished between bodily and mental memory. According to these views, it was possible through mental effort to retrieve information about past experience currently not in consciousness. Other "modern" views of memory appearing in the literature somewhat later included schools of thought that emphasized the productive nature of memory. This should of course be contrasted with the reproductive character so prevalent in the verbal learning tradition. Such a productive nature of memory was emphasized by the Gestalt psychologists. Katona (1940), for instance, demonstrated this productive nature of memory in several ingenious experiments that emphasized organization and understanding instead of the reproductive character of memory commonly shown in rote learning experiments of the time. Although the productive character of memory was demonstrated very nicely by Katona and other Gestalt psychologists, the most prominent among the early scientists who supported this viewpoint was Bartlett (1932). His use of schema as a central concept has influenced later memory research considerably, although it did not have much of an impact on other students of memory during the first half of this century.

All these different views on memory were indeed promising beginnings, but in no case did they initiate any particular memory research tradition. The simplest explanation of this is probably that of a wrong *Zeitgeist* for this type of work. The enormous dominance of behavioristically oriented verbal learning research was impossible to pierce for individual scholars having alternative views of the human mind.

Approximately 30 years after the publication of Bartlett's book, a new era started in this field of psychology. The concept of schema was brought back in the realm of the information-processing approach, as were most of the other ideas touched upon earlier. Nonetheless, it was not necessarily these ideas alone that determined the birth and later the development of modern memory research. In fact, the tradition for current memory research did not appear until the late 1950s, and it was brought about by two critical factors.

One factor was the particular way of conceptualizing information (e.g., Miller, Galanter, & Pribram, 1960). This view of information, which was based on cybernetics and communication theory, made inevitable the postulation of a memory system capable of holding information from one occasion to another. The cybernetic approach of Miller et al. takes for granted that currently presented information is mapped onto some general memory structure consisting of information stored earlier. The other factor that had a considerable impact on the development of memory research tradition was the application of computer terminology. Helped by this new conceptualization of information, Broadbent (1958) realized that it was possible to regard the flow of information through different subsystems within the organism in a way similar to that in which information is handled by a computer. The concept of memory was translated into computer language; and due to the growing popularity of the computer analogy, memory also became a central concept in human information processing. This led to a conceptualization of memory in spatial terms. Thus, memory was considered to be a location where information could be temporarily kept while appropriate processing was carried out and a location where information could be permanently stored.

The basic reason for distinguishing between a short-term and a long-term memory in such a fashion was that forgetting functions and capacity differed between the two systems. This conceptualization of memory in spatial terms might have been one of the most appealing aspects of the approach; but as was shown later, it created some of the main problems for the information-processing approach.

The computer analogy apparently appealed to a great many scientists in the area. They began working in completely new directions, many new questions were asked, and new methods were produced that opened up paths to new goals. Probably the two most important methodological contributions at this early stage were those put forward by Brown (1958) and by Peterson and Peterson (1959). As time went by, it became evident how easy it was to invent new methods that made sense for all the research questions generated. Most of these questions were inconceivable from a verbal learning point of view. One could easily envisage that the information-processing approach had a conspicuous advantage over the verbal learning terminology with respect to description and explanation of memory phenomena.

The computer analogy promised a great deal to scientists in the area who began to think that memory could be studied in a more meaningful and informative way. The approach gave rise to an enormous amount of research questions, producing empirical findings *en masse*; and the formulation of models and miniature theories became a major preoccupation of the time. Tests of all these theoretical notions in turn produced still more experiments, which required modifications of the theoretical concepts, which resulted in further tests, and so on. The inevitable outcome of all this active research work was a veritable explosion of scientific publications in the area. At first sight this gave an impression of progress and significance, and people saw obvious strategic advantages in this way of conducting research. One was the conviction that the highest degree of precision in description and explanation would be reached with such limited theory pursuits. Furthermore there was assumed to be a clear advantage in studying such a complex subject matter as human memory from different points of view, depending on which aspect of memory one was currently interested in. Because of these important principles, there was indeed important progress made during the early information-processing era. There is no question that research pursuits formulated within the information-processing framework have yielded significant facts of how memory works.

Despite all these epoch-making empirical results, models, and miniature theories, the information-processing approach was found to be dissatisfactory. One obvious reason for this was the lack of any real accumulation of knowledge. That is, although a mass of data and numerous theories had evolved, they existed for the most part as independent entities, incapable of being integrated by even the most clever of theorists. This whole state of affairs seemed to indicate the need for some kind of general theory whereby all or most previous contributions could be brought together. Once such a general theory was formulated, it was understood that it should also provide a basis in which to systematize new findings. Apparently, the original information-processing approach was unsuccessful in this respect, because very little or no accumulation of knowledge occurred in the area.

The work and effort needed to formulate such an overall theory may have had a discouraging effect upon people. There were so many new problems to study when the information-processing approach came along that any "miniature approach" was bound to be the most profitable one for each individual scientist. But besides these fads and fashions, were there any other reasons for scientists not to enter a "general-theory" enterprise? A general-theory notion seems attractive at first sight, but there might be good reasons to question its feasibility on other grounds. Could it possibly be the case that the whole notion constitutes a fundamental misconception of science? From the very beginning, one can readily see that it contained considerable problems. The approach requires that science be regarded as a complex puzzle, where scientists first discover the bits and pieces of knowledge and then insert them in their appropriate locations. If the pieces are put in their correct places, a certain pattern will eventually emerge. After a sufficient amount of time and effort, the pattern would ultimately be consummated for all time, and contentment would reign ever after.

According to Kuhn (1962), there are in fact periods of "normal science" for which it is appropriate to talk about an accumulation of knowledge. Such periods are, however, interrupted by other, "revolutionary" periods, where the pieces of knowledge are not considered to be additive in nature. If one were to decide whether modern memory research should be regarded as "normal" or "revolutionary," the latter would definitely seem to be more appropriate. Apparently, there is no general theory in the making, and there are no single findings terminating any research pursuits. Certain discoveries may of course answer specific questions, but beyond those there are always still more challenging questions that require further study. Thus, as it now stands, there is no real hope for a final general theory in memory research.

The general-theory view of science is of course more common among people in general than among scientists. However, even scientists often hope for a general theory that will be the salvation for a given field; and one might wonder how this view has become so popular. One very likely reason is the way undergraduate courses are usually taught. When we teach these courses, we often seek to present the material in such a general and coherent form that it commonly violates scientific reality. If we would present the material in a way that more exactly reflects the diverging state of affairs in the memory area, it would probably leave the students in a state of bewilderment. Simplication and other pedagogical tricks may be necessary to avoid this state, but it is important to keep in mind that they are made for educational and not for scientific purposes.

Although a general-theory notion may be an effect of a confusion between education and science, there is no reason why we should abandon generality in principle. For instance, it is usually fruitful to look for generality whenever we try to integrate experimental results from different paradigms within a common framework. However, from the integration of data from a restricted number of studies to the incorporation of all knowledge, there is an enormous leap. For the more modest integrations of empirical findings and miniature theories, it is usually possible to formulate a testable theory; whereas for the general-theory approach this cannot be attained. The reason is that we will always find occasions to modify a theory as we proceed in testing its validity. The fact that theories of memory of, say, 50 years ago are not the same as those we are entertaining today is probably the best indication of this. It is also relatively safe to suggest that the theories of the next century will not be the same as those we are concerned with today.

VIEWS ON THE FUTURE

It is probably not a very useful exercise to try to build a general theory from available empirical findings, models, and miniature theories. But what should we do with the diverging empirical findings and theoretical concepts? This book seeks to make a modest start toward the solution of this problem by presenting an alternative to the traditional approach to memory research.

The point of departure is the simple assumption that to understand memory more fully, we have to abandon the idea that memory is some kind of object—a storehouse for holding information—or a process. Again, it is argued that education has played a crucial role in promoting such a view of memory. When trying to define memory for undergraduate students, it certainly makes sense to refer to memory as some kind of "thing" that can be studied in and of itself rather than some abstract quality. From this point of view, it is natural to isolate memory from other cognitive functions. This has actually been done, but in fact, it is not a particularly significant feature of the memory area only. It is a well-established way of scientific thinking used in most areas as a means of obtaining some order of their subject matters.

Separation of specific areas in this way is regarded to be fundamental to scientific thinking and presentation of the areas in introductory textbooks. Simplicity and clarification are the main reasons for maintaining such a classification, and it might indeed be necessary to isolate the different subject areas in psychology so that introductory students are able to grasp the major ideas presented. Nonetheless, such a separation does not help clarify matters for established scholars acquainted with the area. Instead of seeking clarification in this "artificial" way, it might be more profitable to narrow research questions and educational enterprises on the basis of the kind of cognitive functions that subjects use in a given task. If, for instance, it is assumed that the subject will use some linguistic skill in an experiment, it would seem desirable to consider memory from that perspective. If some other function is involved, another perspective would be more appropriate. An important prerequisite for such an approach would be the spending of considerable time and effort to do more careful analyses of the tasks we give to our experimental subjects than is commonly done at present.

The example with psycholinguistics as a particular perspective was not chosen arbitrarily. The specific view proposed here has to some extent already been applied by students of memory working in this area. As shown in contemporary literature, this is an important approach to memory research and will probably continue to be a dominating force in the future. We will not deal with this approach as a separate topic in this volume, mainly because semantic and linguistic perspectives are already involved in most memory research anyway. Consequently, it will automatically be included in several contributions to this volume.

The ideas presented in the present chapter are not the basis for a theory of memory. Rather, one should regard the ideas as suggestive of how future memory research should be conducted. However, in order to talk about the research per se, a few words of how memory is conceived are in order.

The basic notion is that memory is not a "thing" that can be studied in isolation as if it were separated from the other components of the cognitive system. That is, memory is not seen as a specific process or a "place" where information is stored. The term *memory* refers to one aspect of adequate cognitive functioning in a given situation. It follows from this that the formulation of a general theory of memory is not the main objective of research in this area. It is argued that memory cannot be understood in a general sense. Rather, the main goal of memory research is to investigate the *function* of memory in a given situation as one aspect, among several others, of the cognitive system. The basic rationale behind this argument concerns the principle of evolution. The cognitive system has developed as an interactive whole, and therefore it is inadequate to pick out specific functions of the cognitive system such as perception, memory, thinking, etc. and study them as if they were separate entities. The interaction among these cognitive functions is regarded as utterly essential for memory research and for all cognitive research for that matter. At first sight, this might only seem to indicate that instead of studying memory and trying to formulate theories of memory, we should be studying cognition and doing our best to formulate theories of cognition. This is, however, not the case; exactly the same arguments against the formulation of a general theory of memory described earlier would also be applicable to the formulation of a general theory of cognition. Instead, the emphasis on the interaction among different cognitive functions should be regarded simply as a necessary premise for this particular view on memory research.

Actually, the nature of this interaction is the crucial point. Due to environmental demands, the nature of this interaction varies. For example, in some cases perceptual aspects will dominate at the cost of memory aspects, whereas in other situations the reverse will hold. Viewed in this way, our subject matter (i.e., memory function) is an effect of two components—the cognitive system and the environment. Memory function as one aspect of cognition relates to the question of how the system works, whereas memory function as one aspect of the environment relates to the question of what it is to be remembered.

Memory has usually been considered solely as an aspect of the human mind. By shifting the emphasis from memory to memory functions, however, it is necessary to include environmental aspects in our discussion. Nobody would probably object to the notion that certain events are easier to remember than others. There is also good reason to believe that in general the events that are easy to remember are also, in one way or another, biologically important or relevant to remember. One might speculate about the reason for this, but it seems a bit premature to be too specific, other than to say that evolutionary factors probably play a major role. For the time being, the main objective is to convince students of memory that the "memorability" of different environmental events should be taken into account in a more complete picture of functions of memory. To date, such pursuits have been far too sparse. By choosing the experimental situations and the to-be-remembered materials in such a way as to maximize the equipotentiality of events, memory research to date has come to be concerned with a very limited spectrum of memory functions.

Although it is argued here that the *memorability* of an event is important, it should be realized that the term has little value on its own. As a specific property of an event, the memorability of that event receives its meaning only with reference to the individual and its cognitive system. That is, the bridge between the memorability of the environmental events and the cognitive system is the memory function proper.

The fact that we are here emphasizing aspects of memory research somewhat different from those in which people have been engaged previously should not be taken as an indication that earlier research is regarded as having been in vain. On the contrary, these earlier contributions will be inevitable starting points for future research following the approach presented here. We will certainly need all the knowledge gained so far about how the cognitive system proper works. Some of the chapters of this volume are primarily concerned with the question of how the system works, whereas others are geared more to the specific relation between the cognitive system and the environment just described. It is also encouraging to note in this context that the contributions to this volume emphasize the role of memory as a part of a larger, more complex system and not as a separate entity in itself.

The chapters in the present volume should be regarded as a means of communicating the ideas about future memory research presented here, at least to some extent. To some larger degree, the chapters are of course also presented on their own merits. The chapters are organized around four topics. These topics are called *perspectives* to indicate that none of them excludes any other and that they are presented as a first attempt to provide direction for future research in this area. Other perspectives would probably also qualify for this purpose; but given our current knowledge of memory and our potential needs in the future, the present perspectives have been judged to be the most fruitful ones. The four perspectives proposed here are: conceptual, perceptual, bilogical, and reality perspectives.

Conceptual Perspectives

Conceptual perspectives are those concerned with theoretical concepts and metatheory used in the area. When specific theoretical concepts are considered, the basic function of memory is to be an integrative part in a larger cognitive system. At a metatheoretical level, there are two central questions that have to be given priority in any scientific enterprise. These include the nature and the role of the theory.

A conceptual perspective should of course consider the state of affairs with respect to conceptual matters in some detail. This is done in Chapter 2 by Tulving, who presents a critical evaluation of memory research. According to Tulving, progress in memory research has been extremely slow and unstable. In general, we do not know very much more about memory now than we knew years ago. In this respect, memory research differs from research in physics and biology. Needless to say, if such a slow progress had occurred in any of these areas, our lives would have been considerably different. A slow rate of progress in memory research, on the other hand, does not have much effect on our standard of living, for example. We will live about the same kind of life as before, whether or not there is any real progress in memory research. The only important effect of slow progress may be to make us feel a bit uneasy, because we have not contributed to science as much as we would have liked.

This difference between memory research and current research in the physical sciences may have important implications for understanding the current situation in our field. We may conceptualize it as follows: Scientific progress in the natural sciences proceeds at a steady pace, because of the enormous opportunities for application of pure research. The technological inventions can be utilized almost immediately by people in society. In memory research, however, there have been far too few opportunities for such applications. In order for such a "feedback" from applied research in our area to become reality, the concepts used require very careful consideration. The fundamental difference between the natural sciences and contemporary psychology of memory might lead to a too-pessimistic picture of memory research. However, only the future can tell us what will happen, and it is not completely unreasonable to think that a single finding in the memory area might open up new fields that will have an impact on everyday life. Before we have this finding, however, it is impossible to know the nature of that impact.

Quite a different conceptual perspective is taken by Estes in Chapter 3. Estes discusses the question of the role of theories in memory research, with special emphasis given to their descriptive and explanatory role. Needless to say, this is an important problem. Estes is concerned about the massive flood of empirical results in the field, and his contribution is an attempt to bring some oder to the area by organizing the various functions of theory.

Although the information-processing approach is only about 20 years old, there have in fact been some major changes in its orientation during the last few years. With some exceptions, the idea of the computer analogy as a transformation of information between different compartments in memory has been deserted. There are now few investigators who believe that information first enters a short-term store, and, following further processing, passes into a more permanent, long-term store. When people nowadays refer to the computer as an analogy to human memory, the considerations are totally different. One such new approach is called the *computational metaphor*, and its basic assertion is that the human mind can be regarded as a physical symbolic system. Allport describes this radical change in Chapter 4. Allport also gives the reasons why he thinks that research on artificial intelligence should form the basis for the study of the cognitive system. It is important to realize this in a metatheoretical context, because it clearly challenges the usual psychological opinions of what a theory is and what is its purpose. Furthermore, it complicates matters about the role of empirical falsification in psychological research.

Perceptual Perspectives

The second perspective concerns psychological holism (i.e., to find the basis for an integrated view of cognitive functioning). In principle, one should integrate all aspects of cognitive functioning. This is a difficult task indeed, and it might be worthwhile limiting the endeavor to a few aspects at a time.

During the information-processing era, there has been a strong tendency to split up different psychological processes of the human mind, processes that actually should be studied together. One example is the separation of perception and memory. It is hard to see this as a meaningful distinction. In a specific experiment it might be of profit to concentrate on one aspect rather than the other, but in general terms such a distinction seems artificial indeed. Up until now, perception theory has typically ignored memory by viewing perception as a process over time. Memory theory, on the other hand, has tried to minimize the role of perception by locating decision, search, thinking, and other cognitive processes almost at the place of the proximal stimulus. A framework of the sort presented in this book strongly emphasizes the need to integrate the two areas.

In Chapter 5, Johansson informs us how concepts of memory can be applied to research on movement perception. The films presented at the conference by Johansson illustrated his point very clearly. These films also fit well into Norman's line of thinking (Chapter 7). Norman's approach to these problems is a more general one. In addition to his attempt to integrate perception and memory, he also incorporates other mental processes. The main concept in Norman's chapter is schema, which brings back much of the flavor of the earlier tradition of Bartlett.

The main concepts in Chapter 6 by Murdock are convolution and correlation. He presents a thorough review of several areas in perception and memory where these two types of analysis apply, and these applications demonstrate beautifully that perception and memory are not separate entities but two aspects of a whole system. The section about general implications promises a good deal for future memory research. In Chapter 8, Craik and Jacoby present the concepts of elaboration and distinctiveness in episodic memory, which is an interesting extension of the original levels of processing approach. Craik and Jacoby argue very strongly for an interactive system where peripheral and semantic processing influence each other during perceptual and conceptual analysis.

Turvey and Shaw, in Chapter 9, present an ecological approach to research in perception and memory. Their contribution is in line with Gibson's way of thinking about perception and very much at odds with the traditional information-processing approach. This chapter is a provocative one, and it will certainly require careful consideration among scientists in future memory research.

Biological Perspectives

Holism extended to aspects outside psychology could be regarded as the rationale for the third perspective. This perspective stresses the importance of a biological orientation. To date, there have been very few (if any) real discussions about evolutionary principles in memory research. Such an approach has fertilized the debate considerably in other areas of psychology such as perception and learning. There is no a priori reason why such an approach should not be profitable in memory research also.

Most theories of memory are limited to the usual psychological concepts. It is, of course, true that physiological and chemical studies on memory are being conducted, but these studies are mainly concerned with purely biological problems and have little or no connection with psychology. It seems strange that this is so, and one may speculate about the reasons. One common argument among psychologists is that there are such enormous problems with the psychological concepts that one should avoid complicating matters by introducing biological concepts. (Such an attitude is based on the idea discussed and criticized earlier in this chapter—that it is possible to add up facts in order to reach the general theory.) In our view, it is a more reasonable approach to follow the tradition in the literature on neuropsychology. This tradition is represented in this book by Shallice and Luria in Chapters 12 and 13, respectively. It is in line with the perspective view presented here, for it seeks the research problem proper in one of the areas and tries to solve the problem using knowledge from the other or both areas. Thus, the appropriate procedure, according to this approach, is not to study neurophysiology first and later correlate these findings with psychological concepts. Instead, physiological studies should be used as indicators of what to study in psychology.

The papers by Hydén and Ingvar, in Chapters 10 and 11, respectively, present biochemical and physiological research, which can possibly serve as such indicators for future psychological research on memory. The biochemical research presented by Hydén certainly shows that a large gap exists between the physiological and the psychological memory research, as they are typically conducted. It is definitely a challenging task to try to bridge the gap between these two disciplines. The paper by Ingvar presents a new technique to measure blood flow in the brain. This biotechnological invention should prove valuable for many research endeavors in the psychological memory area.

Reality Perspectives

A final perspective concerns the world outside the laboratory. Taking into consideration that almost all current theories of memory are based on laboratory studies, it is remarkable that so little is said in the literature about their relationship to the use of memory in "real life." This is not to say that our theories of memory do not deal with reality. It simply means that more consideration should be given to such questions in current memory research. If one takes a point of view such as the one described here, it follows almost automatically that the function of memory in what Brunswik called representative situations should be a central feature in this area.

The applicability of a certain research pursuit does not necessarily determine its value for the future. Certain problems are simply much more suitable for a laboratory setting and should therefore be pursued under strict laboratory conditions. Other problems should not be studied in the laboratory, as they have much more relevance in practical settings and could profitably be studied there. In other words, the research problem should determine how and where the problem is to be studied.

There is probably not much value in simple applications of experimental findings from the laboratory to the world outside. If one has the intention of first figuring out various things about memory in the laboratory and then applying them to real-life situations, one will sooner or later be very disappointed about the outcome of such an enterprise. In those cases where one really succeeds in applying laboratory findings, one is commonly dealing with trivialities only. In most cases, however, it is not even possible to make applications. An alternative to the "laboratory now–real life later" approach is to start the research project with an idea about the representative situation in mind and then do the appropriate study. Problems related to these questions are given an insightful discussion by Baddeley in Chapter 16. The title of his paper, "Applied Cognitive and Cognitive Applied Psychology," is very much to the point. As an example, Baddeley presents a series of experiments in which he attempts to discover the principles of face recognition.

Classically, rote learning was considered to be one of the most important ways of learning new material. In Chapter 14, Mandler questions this and reformulates the problem of learning in terms of organizational principles. It is interesting to note, as Mandler points out, that students of memory can provide valuable help in debates on socially relevant subjects. Much of the destructive debate about racial differences in learning abilities could have been avoided if alert students of memory had criticized Jensen for questionable methods from the very beginning.

The paper by Kintsch and Vipond in Chapter 15 is an interesting example of the general principle advocated here—that memory should not be studied in isolation but from a certain perspective. In this respect, it is provocative for two reasons. First it presents an interesting new approach to the problems of comprehension and readability. Second, a fairly complex type of learning material is used instead of the usual word lists. Lists of words and other fairly simple types of material might be appropriate for many problems in memory, but an aspiration to cover more complex materials would seem to be desirable.

ACKNOWLEDGMENTS

The author is grateful to Berndt Brehmer, Ronald L. Cohen, William Dockens, and Leslie P. Shaps for helpful comments on earlier drafts.

REFERENCES

Bartlett, F. C. *Remembering: A study in experimental and social psychology.* Cambridge: Cambridge University Press, 1932.

Bergson, H. *Matière et memoire.* Paris: Presses Universitaires de France, 1896.

Broadbent, D. E. *Perception and communication.* New York: Pergamon Press, 1958.

Brown, J. Some tests of the decay theory of immediate memory. *Quarterly Journal of Experimental Psychology,* 1958, *10*, 12–21.

Ebbinghaus, H. *Über das Gedächtnis.* Leipzig: Duncker and Humbolt, 1885.

Freud, S. Repression. In *Collected papers* (Vol. IV). London: Hogarth, 1915.

James, W. *The principles of psychology.* New York: Holt, Rinehart & Winston, 1890.

Katona, G. *Organizing and memorizing.* New York: Columbia University Press, 1940.

Kuhn, T.S. *The structure of scientific revolutions.* Chicago: University of Chicago Press, 1962.

Miller, G. A., Galanter, E., & Pribram, K. H. *Plans and the structure of behavior.* New York: Holt, Rinehart & Winston, 1960.

Peterson, L. R., & Peterson, M. J. Short-term retention of individual verbal items. *Journal of Experimental Psychology,* 1959, *58*, 193–198.

II CONCEPTUAL PERSPECTIVES

2 Memory Research: What Kind of Progress?

Endel Tulving
University of Toronto

INTRODUCTION

Understanding the human mind is an arduous task, rendered especially frustrating because of our intimate familiarity with what we are trying to understand. From personal experience, we know exceedingly well what the mind can do, the broad range of its fantastic capabilities; we are also very much aware of its limitations. Yet its understanding—why and how does it do what it does—has so far eluded us. Countless scholars, sages, and scientists have devoted their lifetimes to the study of the mind in its many manifestations, and they have written countless books and articles about it; but the fruits of their labors have been somewhat less than spectacular. Psychological study of memory, by and large, has shared a similar fate. After over two thousand years of rational speculation and a hundred years of experimental study, we can point to few achievements that promise to be of relatively permanent value. The question may be asked, therefore, as to what kind of progress we have made in understanding memory.

The present essay is an attempt to briefly survey and evaluate the accomplishments of the psychological science of memory, to assess some of its current practices, and to point to some of the sources of its metatheoretical problems. This account is necessarily selective, quite personal, and undoubtedly biased. Its purpose is simply to state an opinion with which others can agree or that they can criticize or reject. The discipline might benefit from the ensuing discussion of some of the more global concerns and strategic issues.

SOME GLIMPSES INTO THE PAST

We begin by taking a few random glances at the vast history of man's observation and thought about memory. What we see can serve as a backdrop against which we can place our more recent activity and then decide how much change there has been and how much progress.

More than two thousand years ago, Plato had an image of the mind as an aviary full of all sorts of birds, "both solitary and in groups, flying anywhere and everywhere." The aviary is empty when a person is young, but the process of learning captures the birds of knowledge and detains them in the enclosure. Today we still find it convenient, and sometimes indispensable, to think of the mind and memory in spatial terms: Memories are retained in and retrieved from the memory store if the search through it is successful.

Zedler's *Grosses Lexicon* (1732–1750) was a monumental compendium of human knowledge published in the first half of the 18th century. In it memory is defined as a special power of human reason to take up and retain ideas. A further distinction is made between memory proper—whose function is the retention of ideas—and remembering—which refers to the reproduction of the retained ideas. The article on memory contains a wealth of information. It includes, for instance, sections about the relation between ease of learning and retention (couched in terms of individual differences), constancy of memory ability throughout life, and conditions contributing to the impairment of memory. On this latter topic, we are told that one cannot meditate or learn if one has a cold or has been drunk the day before. Moreover, we are advised that in general, people who enjoy too much brandy, or smoke or snuff too much tobacco, or partake too much of the "pleasures of Venus" will soon find their memories seriously weakened, because these practices lead to the indolence of the whole body and this also impairs the "inner senses." The *Grosses Lexicon*, however, also tells its readers what to do when their memories are impaired. They are to prepare a balsam containing a number of ingredients such as castoreum, rosemary, lavender, and cuttings of fingernails, dissolved in benzoic acid, and smear it on their foreheads every morning and night. This balsam brings back lost memory and makes it stronger.

We can chuckle about some of the things well-meaning scholars wrote about memory two and a half centuries ago, but we also see that the intellectual distance separating them from us is not overwhelming. Many things of concern to students of memory then are still perfectly sensible by today's standards. For instance, the distinction between storage and retrieval is there, the problem of the relation between speed of learning and ease of retention is of current interest, and the relation between alcohol and memory is an up-to-date topic of investigation (e.g., Birnbaum & Parker, 1977). Only the relation between memory and the "pleasures of Venus" seems to have been neglected in more recent times, and interest in memory ointments has been replaced by research into both facilitating (e.g., Dawson & McGaugh, 1973) and inhibiting (e.g., Barraco & Stettner, 1976) effects of drugs on learning and retention.

As everyone knows, Ebbinghaus did his ground-breaking, quantitative research on learning and forgetting of series of nonsense syllables about a hundred years ago, setting the tone for psychological research on memory for a long time to come. William James' insightful observations about association and memory, made at about the same time, represented the culmination of the quest for understanding of human mental processes through the method of introspection. In the shadow of Ebbinghaus' achievements, these ideas had little impact on the thinking of the developing breed of experimental psychologists. Although Ebbinghaus' influence was diluted by the interesting work soon to be done and reported on the basic processes of learning by Pavlov in Russia and Thorndike in the United States, it took a while for the burgeoning field of learning and behavior theory to put an unmistakable stamp on the study of memory. Research on memory 50 years ago was still a part of the tradition created by Ebbinghaus.

A typical annual volume of the *Journal of Experimental Psychology* at that time contained approximately 40 articles, of which perhaps four were concerned with human learning and memory. In the 1926 volume, for instance, there were two papers by Cason, one concerning backward associations and the other on remote forward associations; one article by Williams on the phenomenon of reminiscence; and one by Pan on the influence of context upon learning and recall. The 1927 volume of the *American Journal of Psychology* contained 36 research articles—one of which was on verbal learning, by Dallenbach and Jenkins on the effect of serial position upon recall. The *British Journal of Psychology* for the same year contained a total of 27 research articles, none of them on memory or verbal learning. Judging by this rather limited sample, we see that the total output of experimental psychologists fifty years ago was rather modest by today's standards and that verbal learning and memory constituted an equally modest component of the total activity. Yet the topics covered were not greatly different from those of interest to students of memory today. The study of context effects is currently a "hot" topic, reminiscence continues to interest researchers (e.g., Buschke, 1974; Erdelyi, Buschke, & Finkelstein, 1977; Madigan, 1976), and phenomena involving serial position effects figure prominently in textbooks (e.g., Crowder, 1976; Murdock, 1974). Only problems entailed in remote backward and forward associations are of less interest today, and Cason's work is unknown. His conclusions did not seem to fit into that Zeitgeist; he used prose passages as learning materials and permitted his subjects to learn these passages under conditions that were similar to the learning situations of everyday life. McGeoch and Irion (1952), in the definitive textbook of the time, mentioned Cason's work only in a footnote, saying that they had omitted it from the general discussion of intraserial phenomena, "because the methods employed seemed to the writers to make [the] results indeterminate [p. 93]."

By the beginning of the 1950s, there was almost no work on memory reported in the literature of experimental psychology, although journals contained a fair proportion of articles on verbal learning. For instance, the *Journal of Experimental Psychology* in 1951 contained a total of 123 articles, of which one was on memory—for pleasant and unpleasant experiences—and 17 on topics that could be classified as verbal learning. Problems investigated were greatly influenced by the general learning theory: discrimination, reinforcement, delay of reward, negative incentives, work decrement, warm-up effects, and the like, as well as transfer, retroactive inhibition, and the effects of intralist similarity in paired-associate and serial learning.

We get another glimpse of the world of memory as it existed twenty-five years ago from the influential monograph by McGeoch and Irion (1952) that provided a review of the whole field. Among other things, McGeoch and Irion identified seven "persistent theoretical problems" and discussed each of these briefly. These were problems concerning the existence of general laws of learning, what is associated when learning occurs, the use of intervening variables, the role of contiguity and reinforcement in learning, the status of the principle of frequency, decremental factors in learning (inhibition and experimental extinction), and the relation between special and general theories of learning. On the question of general laws of learning, the authors offered their belief that a single set of principles of learning "will suffice at the present time," although they recognized that the factors of language and meaning "complicate the study of learning in many ways," making necessary many special, complex concepts. They also expressed the hope that eventually these complex concepts might be derivable from simpler ones. They did not offer any suggestions as to the solution of the problem of what is associated in learning, but they did point out that this problem—probably not solvable by experimental data—essentially reflected the attitude of various groups of theorists that "our words are better than your words" (McGeoch & Irion, 1952, p. 44). On the question of whether contiguity alone is sufficient for producing learning (as against the idea that reinforcement is also necessary), McGeoch and Irion thought that no crucial evidence existed either for or against the hypothesis. The issue of the role of frequency was seen as taking two forms: (1) whether frequency (repetition of the learning situation) is necessary for learning to occur; and (2) exactly what it is that has to be repeated in the learning situation. As with the other persistent theoretical problems, this one, too, appeared to be wide open. Under decremental factors of learning, McGeoch and Irion talked about forgetting and suggested that it is a function of three main factors: (1) altered stimulus context; (2) altered set to perform; and (3) retroactive inhibition. They also made a firm statement against disuse as an explanation of forgetting.

GROWTH IN MEMORY RESEARCH

The few thin slices through the long history we have just seen provide the impression of a treelike growth: From a single, central idea or two the field has branched out in many divergent directions. Over the last couple of decades, this branching-out process has become even more conspicuous and has greatly accelerated. Indeed, perhaps the most compelling impression one gets of the field of memory research today is one of rapid growth and tremendous change. The question of interest to us in this essay concerns the nature of this growth and change, especially as we know that change is a necessary but not a sufficient condition for progress. Five specific ways in which memory research has changed are readily apparent.

First, the sheer volume of research is very much greater than it has ever been before. It is probably not an exaggeration to say that the total amount of experimental and theoretical effort devoted to human memory today exceeds the effort expended in the whole field of experimental psychology only twenty-five years ago. There has been a virtual explosion in the variety of methods, procedures, techniques, and materials that have been used in memory experiments, as well as a massive expansion of established experimental facts and phenomena. Although the significance of many of these facts may not always be clear, the enrichment of our data base most likely will enhance the probability that facts with profound theoretical implications could be identified. Moreover, since it could well be argued that a certain critical mass of active and productive researchers is necessary in any field before much progress can be expected, it may well be that we have either achieved or are approaching this critical mass now.

The second way in which the current scene in memory research differs from the past lies in the existence of more comprehensive theories not only of memory (e.g., Atkinson & Shiffrin, 1968) but also of even larger domains of the human mind (e.g., Anderson, 1976). These theories attempt to integrate many different phenomena of memory, as well as other manifestations of the human mind, and they do so in a rather detailed and elaborate fashion. They thus differ considerably from both the earlier "special theories" described by McGeoch and Irion (1952), as well as from the more general sets of theoretical ideas that are more appropriately thought of as approaches, frameworks, or orientations. Although many workers agree that any finite set of experimental facts can always be accommodated by many different general theories or specific models and that unique specification of the structure and processes underlying mental activity and attendant behavior is therefore not possible (Anderson, 1976), the mere fact that some comprehensive theories have been constructed testifies to both increasing confidence and increasing vigor of theoretical thought.

Third, we have witnessed what could be considered a rather welcome expansion in basic approaches and orientations to the study of memory. In addition to the classical associationistic approach, we now can identify the organizational school of thought, the information-processing view, and levels-of-processing ideas, as well as various combinations of these. Associationism in recent years has assumed a rather different and a very much more sophisticated form than the one that was known, say, to McGeoch and Irion (e.g., Anderson & Bower, 1973). In the classical literature, the associative approach was adopted in the study of acquisition, transfer, and interference of simple associations, whereas its modern extensions encompass many other phenomena, including knowledge and retrieval of general facts and understanding of language. The organizational approach to memory (e.g., Mandler, 1967) can be regarded as an offshoot of classical associationism (Postman, 1972), but it has encouraged students of memory to raise issues and questions that had been neglected before.

The information-processing view of memory had its origin in the analogy between human beings and digital computers as information-processing systems (e.g., Broadbent, 1958; Norman, 1970). The metaphor of a human being as an information processor spawned the theoretical distinction between short-term and long-term memory, permitted the conceptualization of memory in new terms such as coding, storage, and retrieval, and encouraged the study of memory in experimental paradigms (e.g., recognition) that had not fitted readily into either the associationistic or organizational orientation.

The levels-of-processing ideas (Craik & Lockhart, 1972) have provided an important alternative to both associationistic and information-processing views by: (1) emphasizing the continuity between perception and memory; (2) suggesting and demonstrating the tremendous importance of the manner of studying to-be-remembered material for its subsequent retrievability; and (3) providing a powerful analytical device for dissecting the hitherto inscrutable processes underlying learning. The levels-of-processing approach also turned out to be a natural vehicle for further theoretical utilization of the important concept of memory units consisting of collections of features or attributes (Bower, 1967; Underwood, 1969; Wickens, 1970).

The fourth kind of change has to do with the development of the attempts to devise different taxonomies of memory. As recently as 1952, McGeoch and Irion represented the point of view that one and the same set of basic principles and laws of learning would apply in all learning situations and perhaps even for all organisms capable of learning. Earlier students of memory also did not differentiate between different kinds of memory and at least implicitly adopted the view of a unitary memory. We now have several basic distinctions that many students of memory find useful. One such is the distinction between primary and secondary memory (Craik & Levy, 1976; Waugh & Norman, 1965); another one is the distinction between episodic and semantic memory, or episodic and categorical memory (Estes, 1976). In addition to these kinds of distinctions, some theorists have found it useful to postulate different basic types of information handled by the memory system (e.g., Murdock, 1974). Classification systems of this sort may be useful for several reasons. For instance, they naturally lead to questions about interrelations between different kinds of memories or different kinds of information, and the pursuit of these questions may turn out to be quite profitable. Another benefit of the classification lies in the natural boundaries within which theorists can seek generality when trying to make sense out of empirical data. It is easier to come to grips with the phenomena of short-term episodic memory, for instance, than with all phenomena under the rubric of memory.

The fifth change, and in some ways potentially perhaps the most important, concerns the increasing tendency on the part of students of memory to exhibit a critical attitude toward metatheoretical problems. Searching questions have recently been posed about the general strategy of memory research, the basic objectives of the total enterprise, the value of laboratory experimentation, the role that empirical phenomena play in attempts to understand memory, the potential contribution that knowledge gleaned from other fields might make, and even the usefulness of the currently popular memory metaphors. Thus, for instance, Newell (1973) has characterized typical research in cognitive psychology, including human memory, as taking the form of discovery and exploration of specific phenomena and their explanation by "oppositional concepts." Newell does not believe that this is a fruitful strategy. Others have expressed serious reservations about the sterility of laboratory experimentation in memory. For instance, Neisser (1976) says that phenomena that contemporary students of memory are trying to explain are "highly artificial": recall of word lists or nonsense syllables, recognition of unrelated pictures, and memorization of sentences or short prose passages. He suggests that theorizing about memory is premature until more is known about memory in the natural situations where memory develops and is normally used. As a third illustration, Bransford, Franks, McCarrell, and Nitsch (1977), as well as Turvey and Shaw (1977), have questioned the usefulness of the assumption that storage and retrieval of memory traces underlies remembering or mediates the effects of learning. As an alternative to the memory storage and retrieval metaphor, they suggest a "stage-setting" or an "attuned organism" conceptualization of remembering. This view has certain advantages over the existing ideas. For instance, it makes it easier to understand how a person can readily perceive an object as "new"; the memory storage and retrieval metaphor would have to account for the perception of newness in terms of failure to retrieve a particular trace.

One might disagree with Newell and argue that whether or not one wins or loses when playing twenty questions with nature does not depend on the characteristics of the game but on the goodness of questions that one asks. It is also possible to disagree with Neisser and think that what is important is not whether observations about memory are made in the laboratory or in some natural setting, but rather the sense that one can make of the observations, and that there is no a priori reason to suspect that the sensibility of facts depends on the setting in which they are gathered. Similarly, one could question whether the difference between the concept of memory trace and that of an attuned organism, or storing information and setting the stage, is anything more than an instance of "our words are better than yours" (McGeoch & Irion, 1952). But in the present context these are less important points. What is more important is the fact that critical analysis directed at both the grand strategy and specific tactics of research, and at some of the most basic assumptions with which we have worked for a long time, represents a striking change in memory research. Until most recently, such free and open discussion was rare in the literature of experimental psychology and human memory. Although many contemporary students still frown on it, times are changing in this respect, too.

SOME LIMITATIONS AND SHORTCOMINGS

There has been a good deal of change and obvious growth in memory research. How about progress? The answer to this question depends on how we define progress. According to the dictionary, progress is movement toward a goal or to a higher stage; and social scientists think of it as the development of a group in a direction regarded as superior to the previous level. The goal toward which our science moves cannot be specified in advance; therefore it is difficult if not impossible to judge progress in terms of changes that take us closer to the goal. But many students of memory undoubtedly would agree that the enterprise has moved to a higher stage, in a direction that is superior to the previous level. Using the criterion of social agreement, and seeking agreement from the practitioners themselves, we would have to conclude that we have indeed made some progress. Indeed, the contrary argument—that we have made no progress whatsoever—even if it were true in some absolute sense, would be counterproductive; and for these reasons, it is better avoided.

What we can ask, however, is how much progress we have made. To guide our judgment on this issue we need some appropriate, explicitly stated criteria. Probably the single most important relevant criterion for judging progress in a science is the extent to which the results of past work have been firmly welded into a cumulatively developing structure of knowledge. Thus, we must decide to what extent the knowledge we have gained from our research is cumulative and to what extent a relatively permanent structure of knowledge already exists. This structure of knowledge would include hard, empirical facts, a definite set of basic concepts, and theoretical solutions to empirical problems.

We do have many facts and findings in our science of memory, and many of them are reasonably hard. But it is not clear that we know what all these facts and findings mean or what they add up to. The conceptual development of our enterprise has simply not kept up with our ability to design and conduct experiments and to generate data. This is where our difficulties lie. After a hundred years of laboratory-based study of memory, we still do not seem to possess any concepts that the majority of workers would consider important or necessary. If one asked a dozen or so randomly selected, active memory researchers to compile a list of concepts without which they could not function, one would find little agreement among them, particularly if one excluded terms referring to experimental operations and data. Similarly, if one compares different current textbooks of memory, one discovers that there is little overlap among their subject indexes: It seems that important concepts of one author can apparently be easily dispensed with by another. Most of our concepts tend to be esoteric: They are used by small groups of people and either ignored or found confusing by others. There is also a good deal of terminological confusion. One and the same term may be used in rather different senses by different investigators.

Related to the absence of progress in the realm of concepts of memory is another phenomenon: The history of our science knows no generally acknowledged solutions to problems. It is difficult to think of a single instance where a problem, generally perceived to be such by the majority of the practitioners in the field, was explained by one investigator and the explanation accepted by most others. What we have inherited are not solutions but problems requiring solutions. Some readers of the present essay undoubtedly will think that my assessment of the situation is not entirely realistic. All that such a reader needs to do to prove my position untenable is to compose a list—even a short list—of problems that have been solved or explained in a nontrivial or relatively permanent sense. Until such time that someone steps forth with such a list, however, it is difficult to resist the conclusion that ours is not yet a cumulative science, that we have not yet succeeded in constructing a stable foundation of knowledge and understanding of memory, and that the progress we have made in the past, therefore, must be regarded as rather modest.

The psychological study of memory shares many characteristics with other sciences. We accept the important role played by observation, particularly controlled observation, and measurement. We agree on rules by which claims and statements about nature are judged, inferences from observations made, data and theory related, and controversies adjudicated. We also have accepted the ethos of science as a social activity, recognizing the inviolate nature of peer judgment and the sanctity of priority of discovery. In some other matters, however, we are closer to what Thomas Kuhn (1962) referred to as preparadigmatic sciences. We lack agreement and consensus as to the importance of problems and facts; our fact-gathering activity is frequently guided by facts already available (we do experiments on experiments, rather than experiments on problems); the importance of one and the same phenomenon may be perceived differently by different investigators; we sometimes tend to evaluate goodness of research in terms of its adherence to conventional form rather than its promise to tell us something we do not yet know; in evaluating each other's research we frequently invoke philosophers of science; we tend to make a fetish out of certain research tools (for instance, statistics); and we are not always clear in our own minds as to what constitutes a useful explanation of a phenomenon. The form of the present essay does not permit me to elaborate on all of these remarks, but I would like to make a few observations about the last point, the nature of explanation.

Many researchers are fond of explanations of memory phenomena that take the form of a functioning structure that behaves in some respects like the learner or the rememberer. This functioning structure may be presented as a set of verbal statements, a flow diagram, a logic machine, a mechanical model, a set of mathematical equations, a computer program, or a mixture of these. Frequently the explanation describes internal processes in terms of activities such as search, generation, differentiation, decision making, discrimination, comparing, "accessing," locating, transforming, and so forth. The purpose is always the same, to construct a simplified model of the human being in a particular task situation in such a manner that inputs into and outputs from the model and the learner are isomorphic in some specified sense.

Explanations assuming the form of correspondences between observed phenomena and different kinds of functioning structures are very popular in psychology, including psychology of memory; but their usefulness must be questioned. Presumably those theorists who have a penchant for such explanations assume that the correspondence between the human learner and the model of that learner extends to components of the two systems that are not directly observable in the case of the learner. This is not a reasonable assumption, for several reasons. First, in almost all situations the number of different functioning structures that can be brought into some sort of isomorphic relation with a human subject performing a task in a particular situation is virtually unlimited; and the specification of one possible model, even if it is shown that in some sense it is better than a few others, is not particularly informative. Second, we have good reasons to be skeptical of all explanations that postulate various, humanlike activities (searching, locating, discriminating, decision making, etc.) as component processes of the mind, which governs and coordinates similar activities on the part of its possessor. Because of their failure to reduce uncertainty and their typical lack of plausibility, correspondence models do not bring us any understanding of memory or its phenomena. They may provide a sense of accomplishment to their creators and some feeling of closure to those who do not question their rationale, but it is difficult to imagine how they would contribute to conceptual progress in our field. We will return to the problem of the nature of explanation in the next section, considering its more promising forms.

STEPS TO THE FUTURE

The science of memory is still looking for its first genuine Kuhnian paradigm; and there is no doubt that one day, one or more paradigms—for the science of memory or for one or more of its offshoots—will be found. When that day arrives, it would be possible to claim that there has been progress. Is there anything that we can do, individually or collectively, to hasten the pace of progress? I am sure that all active researchers have definite ideas on this question and that in some sense we all act out our convictions in our own work. In keeping with the rest of the picture, it is more than likely that there is a good deal of disagreement on what furthers the cause of progress and what hinders it. In this last section of the essay, I mention some of my own ideas on the topic. Most of the points I make have to do with the nature of explanation and understanding that we should be seeking.

First, it is probably unwise to spend too much effort and energy in developing explanations of things that make sense even without explanation. What we do wish to understand are phenomena, deviations from what is intelligible and reasonable in nature (Toulmin, 1963). For instance, because it makes good sense to believe that a living organism capable of some behavior now is also capable of it on a subsequent occasion, it is not necessary (or even possible within the domain of behavioral analysis) to construct a theory of retention—that is, maintenance of the knowledge about a fact or an event over time. Instead, what may need explanation is the failure of such maintenance—that is, forgetting. What are the natural givens at this time in the science of memory, facts that require no explanation?

Second, it is probably not the optimal strategy to spend too much time in affirming what we already know. There is every reason to believe that all current ideas, interpretations, explanations, and theories are wrong, in the sense that sooner or later they will be modified or rejected. Propping them up, as it were, may simply delay the change that, after all, is a necessary condition for progress. Thus, supporting, retaining, and affirming existing theories longer than necessary more often than not stands in the way of progress. Experiments aimed at existing theories should be designed to find out how, where, and in what sense these theories need revision or why they should be rejected, not to provide additional evidence for them. What theories do we have now that have survived despite the determined efforts on the part of many experimenters to find fault with them?

Third, explanations of individual phenomena, or models constructed to account for the results of single experiments, in and of themselves are not particularly valuable. As I mentioned earlier and as argued by others (e.g., Anderson, 1976), the number of possible explanations that fit individual phenomena or results of single experiments is always extremely large, and therefore describing one represents a technical accomplishment and not a scientific discovery. It is easy to agree with Postman (1975), who—when noting the remarkable proliferation of memory models—thought it fortunate that the ratio of models to experiments is still less than unity. In a trenchant review of the developments in mathematical psychology, Estes rejected the success of fitting models to data as a criterion of progress and stated: "What we hope for primarily from models is that they will bring out relationships between experiments or sets of data that we would not otherwise have perceived" (Estes, 1975, p. 271). The same criterion, of course, applies to all forms of explanatory attempts. I would like to add that another form of promising theoretical activity is analysis of more complex phenomena into their simpler components, whose existence and behavior can be verified and measured experimentally under conditions that do not require long and unwieldy chains of inferential reasoning. These components should remain invariant across different tasks and situations. We should seldom be interested in what happens and why in a particular situation; rather, we should always try to understand how what happens in one situation is related to what happens in another. Thus, we should be looking for invariance in the face of apparent variance (Stevens, 1951).

Fourth, premature formalization of whatever kind may hamper progress by providing a sense of false security. Our intellectual resources are misplaced if they are spent on the construction of elaborate and unwieldy logical and mathematical structures to explain experimental findings in situations in which the facts are soft and the basic concepts still to be invented. Preoccupation with precision of measurement and attempts to discriminate between methods yielding highly correlated measures represent another case of misplaced effort. John Platt (1964) has reminded all scientists:

> Many—perhaps most—of the great issues of science are qualitative, not quantitative, even in physics and chemistry. Equations and measurements are useful when and only when they are related to proof; but proof or disproof comes first and is in fact strongest when it is absolutely convincing without any quantitative measurement [p. 352].

We should keep these words in mind whenever we run into temptations to evaluate our own research efforts and accomplishments by the standards of mature sciences.

Fifth, we would do well to assume a skeptical attitude about theories and explanations of memory that accord with common sense. Just about the only worthwhile lesson that we can learn from the history of science is that almost invariably lasting intellectual achievements take the form of theoretical formulations that are not immediately transparent. It is possible that one of our present sources of conceptual difficulties has to do with our desire to reconcile theoretical ideas with the introspective awareness that we have of the workings of our own minds. We tend to dismiss ideas that jar our personal knowledge of memory, even when they agree with experimental observations. I am not advocating that we automatically discard all ideas that do accord with common sense; but I am suggesting that given the choice between two otherwise equivalent ideas, the one that fits less readily into what we already know may be preferable.

Sixth, it is highly desirable, wherever and whenever possible, to follow the precepts of "strong inference" (Platt, 1964). Strong inference is the name that John Platt gave to the method of inductive inference that originated with Francis Bacon. Platt thought that giving it a special name was necessary, because many scientists make little use of it, although it may be the most important ingredient of scientific progress. There are two critical elements of the method: formulating alternative hypotheses and designing crucial experiments whose outcomes will exclude one or more of the hypotheses. Thus, exclusion is the crux of the matter. In the psychological science of memory, we seldom see crucial experiments; the difficulty usually lies in devising testable alternative hypotheses, rather than in creating methods of distinguishing between them once they exist. Platt says that "in numerous areas that we call science, we have come to like our habitual ways, and our studies that can be continued indefinitely. We measure, we define, we compute, we analyze, but we do not exclude" (Platt, 1964, p. 352). I wonder how things would change in our field if it became an accepted practice for authors of hypotheses and explanations to state explicitly exactly what kinds of empirical facts would refute them.

Finally, we should be willing—perhaps "have the courage" would be a more appropriate expression—to reject ideas and hypotheses that are at variance with the data. Instead, frequently the hypotheses incompatible with the data are maintained or just mended, and mended again when they encounter further difficulties. Mending usually takes the form of adding an additional wrinkle, another qualification, or another parameter or two. If such recurrent modification continues for a while, the explanation may eventually collapse under its own weight; but in the meantime its existence has stood in the way of an active search for a better one.

It is sometimes argued that just because an experimental fact is at variance with a hypothesis or a theory need not lead to its abandonment, or even revision, and that a hypothesis or a theory can only be replaced by a better hypothesis or a theory. Such arguments are supported by the citing of certain celebrated cases from the history of science, such as the phlogiston theory, that provide neat illustrations of the point. These arguments, however, make little sense in a developing discipline such as ours in which even the most popular theories are frequently based on rather flimsy evidence. If we had theories that encompassed many diverse facts and meaningfully interrelated them, we of course would not reject them out of hand at the first appearance of some contrary evidence. Until such theories are developed, however, we would do better to play the game according to the rules of strong inference.

What we need more than anything else at the present time of the development of our science is variety: variety of questions, issues, and problems, variety of methods and techniques, variety of theoretical ideas, and variety of approaches to explanation and theory construction. For the time being, therefore, divergence of methodological, experimental, and theoretical thinking should be actively encouraged. The laws of natural selection can operate more successfully, the greater the wealth of organic—or in the case of our science, intellectual—material on which they act.

A CONCLUDING COMMENT

Jöns Jakob Berzelius, one of the towering figures of 19th-century science and a graduate of the great university whose 500th birthday the present volume helps to celebrate, gave a lecture in 1810 to the Royal Swedish Academy of Science under the title, *The Progress and Present State of Animal Chemistry*. In it he showed full awareness of the problems that would meet the inquiring mind trying to understand biological processes (quoted in Jorpes, 1966):

> If knowledge of the transformation of the blood to other fluids, which in itself is analogous to ordinary chemical phenomena, is so obscure to us, how much more so is the renewal of the solid living parts of the body, which is maintained by the constant exchange of fundamental substances. Even more astonishing is the function of the brain; thought reels at the notion that, even in its most soaring flights or when it penetrates most deeply into the secrets of nature, it depends on a chemical process which precedes it, and the slightest error in which would destroy its coherence, turn it to madness or completely destroy it . . . and yet this is an indisputable fact. But is it likely that man's intellect, the fruit of so much cultivation, which has calculated the laws of motion of far-off worlds, which has come to understand much of the beauty and the strangeness of the nature which surrounds it and which by these advances has come a little nearer to the knowledge of the nature of the Almighty, will one day come to understand itself and its own inner nature? I think not [p. 35].

Memory is an integral part of man's inner nature. Evaluation of the progress that has been made in its understanding therefore provides us with a partial test of Berzelius' prophecy. The main thesis of this essay has been that a century and two thirds later, Berzelius' prophecy still stands.

REFERENCES

Anderson, J. R. *Language, memory and thought.* Hillsdale, N.J.: Lawrence Erlbaum Associates, 1976.

Anderson, J. R., & Bower, G. H. *Human associative memory.* Washington, D.C.: Winston, 1973.

Atkinson, R. C., & Shiffrin, R. M. Human memory: A proposed system and its control processes. In K. W. Spence & J. T. Spence (Eds.), *The psychology of learning and motivation* (Vol. 2). New York: Academic Press, 1968.

Barraco, R. A., & Stettner, L. J. Antibiotics and memory. *Psychological Bulletin,* 1976, *83,* 242–302.

Birnbaum, I. M., & Parker, E. S. (Eds.). *Alcohol and human memory.* Hillsdale, N.J.: Lawrence Erlbaum Associates, 1977.

Bower, G. H. A multicomponent theory of the memory trace. In K. W. Spence & J. T. Spence (Eds.), *The psychology of learning and motivation* (Vol. 1). New York: Academic Press, 1967.

Bransford, J. D., Franks, J. J., McCarrell, N. S., & Nitsch, K. Toward unexplaining memory. In R. Shaw & J. Bransford (Eds.), *Perceiving, acting, and knowing.* Hillsdale, N.J.: Lawrence Erlbaum Associates, 1977.

Broadbent, D. E. *Perception and communication.* London: Pergamon, 1958.

Buschke, H. Spontaneous remembering after recall failure. *Science,* 1974, *184,* 579–581.

Craik, F. I. M., & Levy, B. A. The concept of primary memory. In W. K. Estes (Ed.), *Handbook of learning and cognitive processes* (Vol. IV). Hillsdale, N.J.: Lawrence Erlbaum Associates, 1976.

Craik, F. I. M., & Lockhart, R. S. Levels of processing: A framework for memory research. *Journal of Verbal Learning and Verbal Behavior,* 1972, *11,* 671–684.

Crowder, R. G. *Principles of learning and memory.* Hillsdale, N.J.: Lawrence Erlbaum Associates, 1976.

Dawson, R. G., & McGauch, J. L. Drug facilitation of learning and memory. In J. A. Deutsch (Ed.), *The physiological basis of memory.* New York: Academic Press, 1973.

Erdelyi, M., Buschke, H., & Finkelstein, S. Hypermnesia for Socratic stimuli: The growth of recall for an internally generated memory list abstracted from a series of riddles. *Memory & Cognition,* 1977, *5,* 283–286.

Estes, W. K. Some targets for mathematical psychology. *Journal of Mathematical Psychology,* 1975, *12,* 263–282.

Estes, W. K. The cognitive side of probability learning. *Psychological Review,* 1976, *83,* 37–64.

Jorpes, J. E. *Jac Berzelius—His life and work.* Stockholm: Almqvist & Wiksell, 1966.

Kuhn, T. S. *The structure of scientific revolutions.* Chicago, Ill: The University of Chicago Press, 1962.

Madigan, S. Reminiscence and item recovery in free recall. *Memory & Cognition,* 1976, *4,* 233–236.

Mandler, G. Organization and memory. In K. W. Spence & J. T. Spence (Eds.), *The psychology of learning and motivation* (Vol. 1). New York: Academic Press, 1967.

McGeoch, J. A., & Irion, A. L. *The psychology of human learning.* New York: Longmans, Green, & Co., 1952.

Murdock, B. B., Jr. *Human memory: Theory and data.* Hillsdale, N.J.: Lawrence Erlbaum Associates, 1974.

Neisser, U. *Cognition and reality.* San Francisco: Freeman, 1976.

Newell, A. You can't play 20 questions with Nature and win: Projective comments on the papers of this symposium. In W. G. Chase (Ed.), *Visual information processing.* New York: Academic Press, 1973.

Norman, D. A. (Ed.). *Models of human memory.* New York: Academic Press, 1970.

Platt, J. R. Strong inference. *Science,* 1964, *146,* 347–353.

Postman, L. A pragmatic view of organization theory. In E. Tulving & W. Donaldson (Eds.), *Organization of memory.* New York: Academic Press, 1972.

Postman, L. Verbal learning and memory. *Annual Review of Psychology,* 1975, *26,* 291–335.

Stevens, S. S. Mathematics, measurment, and psychophysics. In S. S. Stevens (Ed.), *Handbook of experimental psychology.* New York: Wiley, 1951.

Toulmin, S. *Foresight and understanding.* New York: Harper & Row, 1963.

Turvey, M. T., & Shaw, R. E. *Memory (or, knowing) as a matter of specification not representation: Notes toward a different class of machines.* Paper presented at the conference on "Levels of Processing," Rockport, Massachusetts, June 1977.

Underwood, B. J. Attributes of memory. *Psychological Review,* 1969, *76,* 559–573.

Waugh, N. C., & Norman, D. A. Primary memory. *Psychological Review,* 1965, *72,* 89–104.

Wickens, D. D. Encoding categories of words: An empirical approach to meaning. *Psychological Review,* 1970, *77,* 1–15.

Zedler, J. *Grosses vollständiges universal Lexicon.* Halle and Leipzig. 1732–1750, 64 volumes.

3 On the Descriptive and Explanatory Functions of Theories of Memory

W. K. Estes
Rockefeller University

INTRODUCTION

Somewhat paradoxically, I have been led to a more than usually self-conscious examination of the functions of theories by the increasing frustration I—and evidently many other investigators of memory—experience in trying to cope with the burgeoning volume of research. One of the principal tactics at our disposal for making sense of the flood of empirical results is to sift them through a criterion of theoretical relevance. But we find the number and variety of models and theories of memory proliferating almost as fast as the empirical findings themselves.

We can doubtless be confident that in the long run the models closer to the truth, or in any event more useful in guiding scientific progress, will tend to survive and the less useful to be discarded. But it would be advantageous in the short run to have at hand some explicit principles that could help determine which models, or which kinds, are worth putting forward for consideration at all.

I don't propose to set forth any new principles for this purpose, but I think something might be accomplished simply by organizing the thoughts many experienced investigators share concerning the functions of theory and by illustrating how they can be brought to bear in specific cases.

THREE MODES OF THEORIZING: AN ILLUSTRATION

Some quite different objectives that may be realized by following different strategies of theory construction can conveniently be pointed up in terms of a specific research example. The sample of data presented in Fig. 3.1 comes

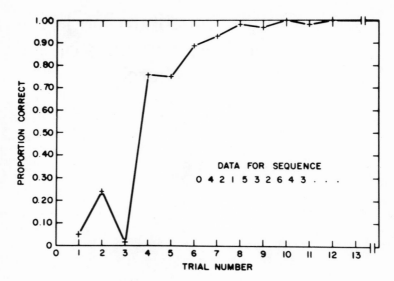

FIG. 3.1 An example of one stimulus sequence presented in Bjork's series-anticipation study, together with the mean learning curve. After Bjork (1968).

from a study of memory in a form of problem solving reported by Bjork (1968). These data were interpreted at the time in terms of one type of theory, but the study is of a kind that one currently finds associated with quite different approaches.

A subject in Bjork's experiment was presented with a sequence of digits, appearing one at a time on a visual display, and had the task of learning to predict each digit in advance of its occurrence by discovering the rule governing a particular sequence. The sequence of digits shown in the figure is typical of one type of sequence used, and it can be seen that the rule for the sequence is not immediately obvious. Nonetheless, the empirical curve shows that subjects learn quite rapidly to anticipate new members of the sequence. How can one provide a theoretical interpretation of the way in which these individuals achieved accurate performance?

If the study had been conducted today rather than a decade ago, an individual steeped in the lore of current information-processing models might proceed almost automatically to sketch a model of the form illustrated in Fig. 3.2. Cognitive operations and structures that might be assumed to be involved in the task are represented by the boxes and the flow of information by the arrows. Thus it might be assumed that initially the subject attends to the visual input, encoding the digit just presented and entering it in short-term memory. Then, after one or more digits have been entered in short-term memory, long-term memory would be consulted for a hypothesis that would generate predictions as to what should have been observed. A comparison would then show whether or not the hypothesis was correct. If not, attention would return to the visual input for more information; but if the hypothesis was verified, then the individual would begin correctly anticipating forthcoming digits, manifesting this ability in his or her sequence of responses.

Although this diagram is typical of many currently appearing in the literature, it may leave the reader feeling somewhat dissatisfied. The principal function of a "white-box" model of this sort—if the flow diagram is implemented no further—is to present a prospectus, so to speak, for a theory that has yet to be constructed. It illustrates relations that are assumed to obtain between various hypothetical mechanisms and processes; but it is inert, like a drawing or snapshot of a mechanical model that leaves one wondering, "Will it work?" In the present instance, one has no way of knowing whether an organism constructed with only the diagram as a guide would actually generate response protocols like those observed. How does one know that the many processes assumed in this model could actually occur without interference? Would they never lead to errors? What kinds of errors would be expected to occur, and how would they depend on properties of the sequence?

Many information-processing theorists would of course recognize the limitations and would take the next step of writing an actual program to represent the sequence of cognitive operations used by an individual in solving the problem. The program would take cognizance of the fact that the sequences presented are generated solely by operations of addition and subtraction (a constraint known to the subjects of the experiment). It would not be difficult to write a program that would readily solve the problem posed by the sequence in Fig. 3.1. The program might begin by entering the first two digits of a sequence into a buffer and ascertaining the positive or negative

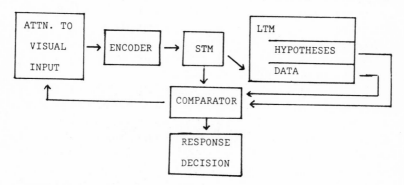

FIG. 3.2 Pseudomodel for the series-anticipation experiment. Mechanisms and processes that might enter into a model are illustrated, but the flow diagram can generate no descriptions or predictions concerning properties of interest in the observed behavior—for example, the course of learning or relative error rates for different stimulus series.

difference between them. Then after reading several additional digits into its memory, the program would scan the sequence to determine the period with which the given increment or decrement occurred. If the period were greater than 1, it would then look at the difference between the second and third terms of the series and again scan for the period of the increment or decrement found there and so on. The program would require only a few trials to solve the problem or other similar ones included in the study, generally fewer trials, in fact, than taken by the actual subjects. This model in the form of a program would be somewhat more satisfying than the diagram, because it would generate descriptions of performance on the part of idealized subjects that would be compared with that of actual subjects. Simon and Kotovsky (1963) have in fact formulated and tested a model for solution of letter-series problems that is very similar to the one proposed here.

A simulation model in the form of a program that can reproduce the main features of the response protocols certainly represents progress toward one of the objectives of theory construction. Unlike the white-box model, a running program can at least yield descriptions or predictions of data. Further, it would be possible to predict in advance something concerning relative difficulty of different sequences, because difficulty should increase with the number of different increments or decrements that occur and with the length of the periods. But we are still short of some desirable goals, for the simulation model is no great help in bringing instructive new relationships out of data or in suggesting what other situations or tasks should be closely related to this one in theory.

In actual fact, when the experiment was done, Bjork took a different tack than either the white-box or the simulation approach. Rather, he noted that information input to the subject at any moment could be interpreted as indicating which of a small number of response alternatives would have been correct, the responses being application of increment or decrement operations. If he could determine how subjects encoded the stimulus situation from trial to trial, he could then interpret learning in terms of the process of associating the permissible responses with the stimulus contexts in which they were correct. This idea led to the analysis illustrated in Fig. 3.3 for the sequence shown in Fig. 3.1 and for another sequence also comprising three rules.

It will be seen that if the stimulus situation at any moment is encoded as a positive or negative difference between the current digit and the one preceding, only three contexts occur in each sequence; and each context is unambiguously associated with one of the permissible responses.

This analysis led to the idea that the protocol for learning of each of these sequences could be decomposed into the learning of the three associations shown in the figure. When the analysis is carried out, the result is three separate learning curves, each representing probability of correct perform-

3. FUNCTIONS OF THEORIES OF MEMORY 39

Three-rule Sequences from Bjork Study

Sequence	Context	Response
0 4 2 1 5 3 2 . . .	(St)	(+4)
	+4	-2
	-2	-1
	-1	+4
0 3 2 3 6 5 6 . . .	(St)	(+3)
	+3	-1
	-1	+1
	+1	+3

FIG. 3.3   Analysis of sample stimulus sequences from the Bjork study in terms of the small sets of contexts that need be discriminated, if the sequences are optimally recoded by the subject, together with the correct response in each context.

ance on the trials when some one of stimulus contexts occurs. These functions look very much like paired-associate learning curves. Further, it was well known at the time that paired-associate learning with short lists and small numbers of response alternatives is generally well described by an all-or-none Markov model. The one free parameter of the model (probability of formation of an association between the stimulus and response terms on any one trial) was estimated for the combined data and the separate learning curves computed, then combined to yield a prediction of the overall course of learning, shown for the pooled data for the two sequences in Fig. 3.4.

The fit of theory to data is about as good as we would expect to achieve with a properly written simulation program. But the model actually constructed has additional implictions. One can predict many relationships among statistics of the data that might not be apparent from inspection of the protocols. As an example, the frequency distribution of total errors during learning for the two sequences is shown in Fig. 3.5 together with the theoretical function computed from the model with the same parameter value used to fit the mean learning curves. The goodness of the prediction is comparable to that routinely achieved by Bower and others for simple paired-associate and verbal-discrimination learning (Atkinson, Bower, & Crothers, 1965).

More questions could be raised concerning this illustrative situation, but we have gone far enough for present purposes—far enough to bring out some of the different functions of a theory relative to interpretation of an experiment and to point up the fact that different kinds of theories may differ

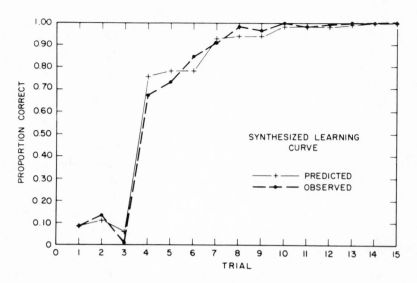

FIG. 3.4 Observed mean learning curve for the two sequences of the Bjork study analyzed in Fig. 3.3 together with predictions from an all-or-none model. Data from Bjork (1968).

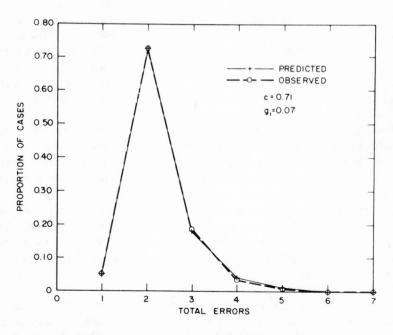

FIG. 3.5 Predicted and observed error distributions for the Bjork (1968) study. (See text.)

greatly relative to their fertility in serving these functions. The implication I propose now to follow up more systematically is that by focusing attention on the functions—rather than on the forms—of theories and models, we may be able to develop a more general framework for evaluating theoretical progress in the various areas of cognitive psychology.

FUNCTIONS OF THEORIES

What, in general, do theories do? They are said to describe, to predict, and to explain the phenomena we deal with. Theories that perform none of these functions may have some heuristic value for particular investigators, but they do not enter into the cumulative systematization of knowledge. The view I am presenting will doubtless shock few readers of this volume, but nonetheless several aspects need some explication.

First of all, one may ask (and some do, e.g., Skinner, 1950) why we should need theories to aid in the description of observations. Data can be recorded as fully as we please by means of cameras, tape recorders, polygraphs. But sheer records of phenomena are of little scientific use. Theories are needed to help distinguish signal from noise, to smooth empirical relationships that in the raw data are perturbed or obscured by uncontrolled sources of error, to help us identify and bring out repeatable regularities. The models of psychophysics, psychological measurement, and scaling theory are our best developed theoretical tools for this descriptive function. In particular, the purely descriptive but nonetheless extremely informative receiver-operating-characteristic (ROC) curve is currently widely used to bring order out of the data of experiments on memory by helping to separate empirical relationships reflecting information storage from those reflecting decision strategies (e.g., Murdock, 1974).

Everyone agrees that theories should also predict observations. But why is the effort desirable? The predictions are not supposed often to be of practical value, because they must nearly always apply only to specially simplified and controlled conditions. Can't we generally afford just to wait for events to occur and then describe them?

The answer in much scientific research is *no*. If we simply wait, the observations needed to advance knowledge will generally never be made. The important predictive function of theories in this connection is not to describe the results of experiments in advance but rather to help us anticipate what will happen in important respects. Then we can prepare to make the necessary observations, to arrange conditions so that phenomena of interest will occur under circumstances that may reveal the processes or mechanisms responsible, to interpret what occurs in relation to the present state of knowledge. No scientific theory is needed in order to enable one to observe an eclipse of the sun when it occurs. But a good descriptive theory is needed to enable one to anticipate the time of occurrence and to arrange and interpret observations that will serve some specific purpose, for example, to determine during the eclipse whether or not light from the sun is bent by the gravitational field of a body intervening between it and the observer.

These functions of theories and models are important enough; but in nearly all theoretical efforts one has in mind a still further objective—the one generally felt to be the loftiest purpose of science—to go beyond description and prediction to the explanation of phenomena. Explanation often carries the implication that one could have predicted the events being explained, but still most prediction does not qualify as explanation. The reason is that most prediction is based simply on regularities that have been observed to occur under specific conditions and that are expected to be repeated if these same circumstances recur. But the concept of explanation goes deeper, including the demand that the phenomenon explained or some aspect of it could have been predicted in advance on the basis of general principles—that is, by virtue of its relationship to other independently obtainable bodies of knowledge.[1]

Like a number of other scientists, I suppose, I thought at one time that I had arrived at this conception of explanation simply by reflecting on what my colleagues and I do. However, many readers will recognize that philosophers of science, who have reflected still longer and harder on similar problems, have arrived at a similar view and have expressed it more formally. For example, Hempel (1965) incisively disposed of the alternative idea that explanation is a matter of achieving familiarity with phenomena:

> Scientific explanation is not aimed at creating a sense of familiarity with the explanandum: "reduction to the familiar" is at best an incidental aspect of it. The understanding it conveys lies rather in the insight that the explanandum fits into, or can be subsumed under a system of uniformities represented by empirical laws or theoretical principles... All scientific explanation involves, explicitly or by implication, a subsumption of its subject matter under general regularities [p. 468].

I will return later to this particular characterization, which I find especially apt for the psychology of memory.

ROUTES TO EXPLANATION

Once models of limited aspects of memory have taken form in relation to specific experimental paradigms and have demonstrated some descriptive utility, how can we seek to proceed toward more explanatory theory? Two

---

[1]E. E. Smith called my attention to the close correspondence between my categories of descriptive and explanatory theories and Chomsky's (1965) distinction between descriptive adequacy and explanatory adequacy of grammars.

routes are available in principle. The one that always offers some prospect of progress is to seek to relate the limited models to other bodies of psychological theory by making use of more general psychological concepts or principles that might have, but in fact have not, entered into the limited formulations. The other route, always beckoning investigators of memory toward deeper explanation but rarely taking them far in practice, leads toward reduction of psychological to the presumably more basic concepts of biological and physical science.

In the case of better developed sciences with longer histories, we are well acquainted with the way assumptions of one theory are constrained or even implied by those of other, generally more fundamental, theories—the familiar motif of reducing the laws of a given science to others lower in the pyramid of sciences. Thus the laws of chemistry are first of all always constrained by general principles of physics such as conservation of energy; but, further, it has come to be understood that perhaps all chemical laws are deducible from the more abstract models of quantum mechanics. We don't expect to find such fully realized examples of theoretical reduction when we look at models of memory, but we may hope to see similar trends. In fact from the earliest days of research on memory, investigators have proceeded on the assumption that any laws or theories they might arrive at could ultimately be reduced to those of biology, especially neuroanatomy and neurophysiology and more recently biochemistry.

Maintaining this working assumption has required considerable faith, however, for perceptible progress toward the explanation of any known phenomena of memory on the basis of neurophysiological or biochemical theory is hard to find. What is not hard to find is evidence of strong and persisting influence of the "lower" disciplines on the form of psychological models for memory. This point can be conveniently, and perhaps instructively, illustrated in terms of two of the oldest and most pervasive concepts in the psychology of memory—those of *association* and the *memory trace.*

Early conceptions of association seem to have taken the form of almost wholly unspecified relations between ideas or images representing previous experiences or actions. But during the same period when experimental studies of human memory were beginning to demand more specific representations, Sherrington and his associates were disseminating a picture of the nervous system that seemed just what was needed to provide a physical basis for theories of association. The portions of the nervous system effectively explored by the microscope proved to consist of concatenations of elementary units, neurons, connected via synapses. This neural model, though based primarily on studies of the peripheral nervous system, was mirrored precisely in the connectionism of Thorndike and his successors in the tradition of functional association theory and in the conditioning theories of Guthrie, Hull, and Spence (see, e.g., Hilgard, 1956).

Even in much current theorizing in cognitive psychology, the influence of the Sherringtonian picture of the nervous system is still apparent. Thus in studies ranging from simple letter recognition (Posner & Snyder, 1975) to lexical decisions (Meyer, Schvaneveldt, & Ruddy, 1975), effects of priming (presentation of a stimulus orthographically or semantically related to the one to which a response will subsequently be made) are interpreted in terms of the activation of associative paths. And in the more elaborate model construction of Anderson (1976), numerous processes having to do with memory for and cognitive operations on propositions are represented in terms of spreading activation of associative linkages between nodes of an associative network.

From my limited explorations into the sparsely recorded history of our subject, a concept akin to our present notion of memory trace has been fundamental to thinking about memory at least since the first formal writings on associationism, but it has changed so much in form from time to time that it is difficult to be sure of continuity. Through the writings of William James and his contemporaries, for example, I can find only mentions of a *mental image*, or copy of an experience. The somewhat more abstract notion of a trace that provides the basis for reconstituting memory of an experience but does not necessarily mirror its form in all detail seems to be associated with the Gestalt psychologists, notably Kohler (1929) and Koffka (1924).

It was always evident, of course, that the mental copy or memory trace of an event must have some basis in the nervous system. The first formal label for this neural counterpart that I have found is Robinson's term *neurogram* (Robinson, 1932), apparently more or less synonymous with the more popular *engram*. The latter term has continued to appear in connection with psychophysiological studies, but the psychological concept of a memory trace lapsed so far into disuse for a long period as to have almost disappeared from theoretical literature, only to return in a much more abstract form as the *image* in Feigenbaum's EPAM model (Feigenbaum, 1963) and as *trace strength* in models for recognition memory (Norman & Wickelgren, 1969).

I attribute the long fall from favor of this concept to two factors. One is the fact that the idea of a trace did not mesh in a natural way with the associationist theories that dominated research on human learning and memory from the first impact of Ebbinghaus (1885) through the crest of "interference theory" in the 1950s (Underwood, 1957). The other is a consequence of Lashley's persistent and well-publicized failure to find any evidence of localization of an engram in the brain (e.g., Lashley, 1929). On the conception of brain function that was current from the time of Sherrington down almost to the present decade, it was quite unattractive to have to think about an important unit of mental functioning that could not be localized somewhere in the brain. With the emergence of such concepts as the holograph, however, it has become apparent that there is no reason whatever in principle why the basis for a unit such as memory trace cannot be widely distributed in the brain but at the same time be well defined and amenable to investigation (Cavanagh, 1976; Pribram, 1971).

An implementation of this new line of thinking by Anderson (1973) in his interactive filter model for memory presents a formalization and way of working with the concept of memory trace that I find particularly attractive. The formal model fits well with the multi-attribute or feature conceptions of memory that are currently becoming popular on purely psychological grounds (Bower, 1967; Underwood, 1969) and at the same time relates these ideas to neurophysiological theory in a way that offers some hope of progress toward a model with explanatory as well as descriptive value.

The basic idea, as developed by Anderson, is that any sensory experience gives rise to a pattern of activity in a large assemblage of neurons in the brain, leading to some response by the organism (the output). This pattern of activity is assumed to leave a similarly patterned trace in the assemblage of neurons—perhaps in the form of altered synaptic conductivities—with the property that if the same sensory input occurs at a later time, the new input will match the trace pattern (the memory trace) and yield a maximum output to the same action pattern that followed the original experience. In contrast, a new sensory experience that differs greatly from the first would set up a pattern of activity that did not match the memory trace and thus would not lead to the same output. In effect, the memory trace thus acts as a gate in the transmission system from input to output.

The process envisaged is illustrated in terms of a simple numerical example in Fig. 3.6. The dimensions of potential neural activity patterns, in principle

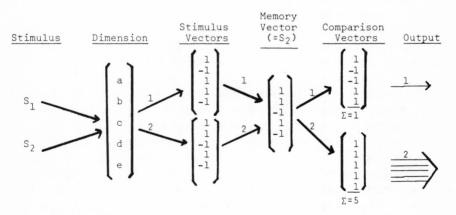

FIG. 3.6 Stimulus input, memory trace, and comparison vectors in the model of Anderson (1973) illustrated for a hypothetical case in which one stimulus (S_2) has been previously experienced, thus giving rise to a corresponding memory trace, and one stimulus (S_1) has not. If either S_1 or S_2 were presented on a recognition test, the comparison of input with memory for S_2 would yield a large output (a positive recognition response), whereas that for S_1 would yield a small output (nonrecognition).

large in number but only five in the example, are denoted by the small letters a-e. In the illustration, we assume that stimulus S_2 has previously been experienced, leaving the memory trace vector indicated, with the value 1 for dimension a, 1 for dimension b, -1 for dimension c, and so on. If now on a later occasion S_2 is experienced again, the pattern of activity set up in the sensory projection area (the lower entry under *Stimulus Vectors* in the figure) has values on each of the dimensions precisely matching those of the memory trace vector for S_2 .

In a quantitative realization of the model, the process of comparing the stimulus to the memory vector is conceived in terms of term–by–term multiplication of the dimension values, in the illustration leading to values of $+1$ in each case and thus a maximum output. If, however, the new experience involved a new stimulus S_1, which gave rise to the upper stimulus vector, the matching process would yield only a small output and therefore much lower probability of the same response as that originally made to S_2.

This model seems to me to capture quite well a number of important ideas characterizing recent multiattribute conceptions of memory and to offer the advantage of permitting us to keep some running check on the extent to which assumptions we are inclined to make about memory on the basis of psychological evidence are compatible with the way in which memory vectors might be expected to behave on the basis of a model that has some support at the neurophysiological level. I suspect that the interactive filter model just may lead to a substantial return to favor on the part of the conception of the memory trace, as evidenced in a small way in some of my own recent work (Estes, 1975, 1976).

THE DESCRIPTIVE–EXPLANATORY DIMENSION: REMARKS ON THE STANDING OF CURRENT THEORIES

In the remainder of this paper I wish to look at some of the most visible lines of theoretical activity in the current psychology of memory from the perspective of these general considerations. In order to bring out the current status of the two principal constructs discussed in the preceding section, I take examples from work on both short-term and long-term (semantic) memory, because in practice the concept of the trace has been more prominent in the former and association in the latter.

The questions I wish to emphasize are not those that receive most space in discussion sections of research reports. There we typically see attention mainly to success in predicting or accounting for results of particular experiments in terms of specific hypotheses or models formulated for the purpose. Here I wish rather to ask how and whether the forms of structural or processing assumptions of descriptive models are dictated by a broader body of theory. My basic premise is that the measure of success in moving toward scientific explanation is the degree to which a theory brings out relationships between otherwise distinct and independent clusters of phenomena.

Models for Short-Term Memory. A highly visible sphere of research in which there has been conspicuous progress toward descriptive theory but perhaps less than we would like toward explanatory theory during the past decade or so is that of human short-term memory. Surely none of us who were at hand when the pioneering studies of Brown (1958) and Peterson and Peterson (1959) were conducted and reported could have foreseen the enormous wave of closely related research that was to ensue. The original basic observation was simple enough on the surface. When human subjects were presented with a few items such as nonsense syllables, but with this input followed by a distracting task such as counting backward so that rehearsal was prevented, the ability to recall the items declined to a very low level within a very few seconds. In contrast, if the individuals were permitted an adequate opportunity to rehearse the input items before the onset of the distracting task, or better yet if the input constituted a meaningful sentence, the items would be retained in memory over a very long period, perhaps indefinitely.

It seemed that the rapid retention loss observed in the Brown-Peterson experiments could not be well accounted for by the kinds of interference effects that had been found to be responsible for much of the forgetting that occurs in experiments conducted over long time spans; hence some new kind of theory seemed called for. The conception that was to dominate research for nearly a decade was of course the Atkinson-Shiffrin model, with its conception of distinct short-term and long-term memory stores (Atkinson & Shiffrin, 1968). In their view it was assumed that the to-be remembered items are read into a limited capacity, short-term store in which they may be maintained in an active state by rehearsal but in the absence of rehearsal are quickly lost without a trace as they are displaced by further inputs.

This theory was most successful in generating and integrating the results of many investigations, but in time the results of new experimental variations suggested by the theory began to overtax the interpretive capacity of the originally postulated theoretical machinery. When in later years investigators (other than the originators of the model) began to accommodate new findings simply by the postulation of new memory stores, it began to appear that some new direction might be needed in order to renew progress toward explanatory theory. Among these reactions, the one that has proven most visible and influential is, perhaps, the proposal of Craik and Lockhart (1972) for a "levels-of-processing" interpretation.

Rather than assuming that items are encoded by the perceptual systems as units and then transferred from one memory store to another, Craik and Lockhart suggested that, depending on the time available and the total processing load, items may be processed to different levels—first only in terms of their sensory attributes, then to higher (or deeper) levels involving semantic attributes. With the further assumption that retention of an item is directly related to the degree of processing, we had an alternative interpretation of the rapid forgetting in the Brown-Peterson experiments. Items are lost because the experimental conditions only permit processing to a very shallow level.

This new approach was refreshing, but within a relatively short time it too has begun to come in for criticism—of a quite foreseeable character(e.g. Nelson, 1977). The assumed relation between depth of processing and retention is descriptive, but it has not been shown to be derivable from any more general or fundamental ideas.

I don't propose to go any further in reviewing criticisms of either of these theoretical approaches. Both have contributed a good deal toward helping us to interpret experiments and to generate more meaningful descriptions of data than we could otherwise have hoped for. Nonetheless, the two approaches share a common limitation, and I have begun to think that attention to it might help us to take another step toward explanatory theory.

The point I wish to make can be conveniently illustrated in terms of a typical trial of an experiment conducted under the Brown–Peterson paradigm, as shown in Fig. 3.7. Here we imagine that an experimental subject is presented with two trigrams, then the number 135 with the instruction to count backward until a recall signal appears, then to report the trigrams as well as possible from memory. How should the contents of memory be represented in a model for this sort of short-term recall? It seems almost compulsory in the spirit of current information-processing approaches, whether of the stores or the levels persuasion, to seek an account of the degree of retention by focusing on properties of the to-be-remembered items themselves. In terms of the Atkinson–Shiffrin model, these items enter short-term store; and if distracting activity prevents their transfer to long-term store, they will be lost from memory and unavailable for recall. In the levels-

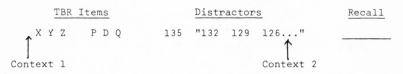

Brown-Peterson Paradigm

TBR Items	Distractors	Recall
X Y Z P D Q	135 "132 129 126..."	_____
Context 1	Context 2	

FIG. 3.7 Illustration of the sequence of events on a typical trial of an experiment in the Brown–Peterson paradigm. The to-be-remembered (TBR) letters are presented visually to the subject, whereas the distractor digits (1 3 2 1 2 9 ...) are generated by the subject in the backward counting task that fills the retention interval.

of-processing approach, the items are assumed to have little resistance to forgetting if they are processed only at a phonetic level but to become more resistant if continued processing reaches a higher level. In each case, the events of the experimental trial illustrated are conceived to be of two quite distinct kinds—the occurrences of *items*, which enter memory, and of *distractors* (the digits produced by the backward counting operation), which do not enter short-term memory but only exert effects on the storage or retrievability of the items.

Models formulated within this framework offer an attractive simplicity and in some instances have shown considerable predictive power within a limited set of experimental paradigms. However, variation in conditions other than properties of the items or their mode of processing do not have natural representations in these models. And as a consequence, the information-processing approach has skirted around substantial bodies of phenomena— for example, the effects (sometimes large) of relations between context during input of items and context at the point of recall (Falkenberg, 1972), of the mode of processing of distractor items (Healy, 1975), and of the temporal distribution or grouping of items within a trial (Lee & Estes, 1977; Shiffrin, 1975).

A Suggested Reorientation of Short-Term Memory Theory. A possibility I would like to examine is that the limitations of the information-processing models owe in large part to a preoccupation with improving descriptive or predictive power relative to a few types of experiments by revising specific assumptions about processing and storage of items. On general principles, we might hope to find a path toward more explanatory theory if instead we consider altering higher level, or more primitive, assumptions in a way that would bring into play more of the ideas that have proven serviceable in other areas of research on memory.

Without meaning to imply that it is the only promising alternative available, I sketch here one specific reorientation (Estes, 1972; Lee & Estes, 1977) that may at least serve to make my proposal on general strategy less abstract.

In the specific model, or family of models, I have been studying, it is assumed that all of the events to which an individual attends during an experimental trial—that is, both the to-be-remembered letters and the distractor digits in the Brown–Peterson paradigm—activate representations in primary memory. Thus these might be termed *event models*, as distinguished from *item models*. By means of a recycling process (perhaps the reverberatory loops posited by Konorski, 1967, and others) the representations are maintained in a state of heightened excitability (availability) so long as input continues from the same background context in which the events occurred. Since the item representations are reactivated with relatively fixed periods, the time relations among them are initially preserved and would continue to be maintained indefinitely if there were no further inputs to the system. In the actual experiments, however, the continuing occurrence of distractor events generates noise in the system, an important consequence of which is to perturb the recycling process. As a result, the reactivations may begin to occur out of their proper order, thus leading to loss of order information; and eventually the recycling process will damp out altogether, leading to a loss also of item information.

If recall is attempted while the event representations are still in an available state, all of the event representations currently undergoing recycling are scanned; and those that meet a criterion, for example possession of the phonetic features of letters that might have appeared in the input, are reported. If the retention test is delayed and the interval is not filled with a sufficiently taxing distractor activity, the same process leads to what has been termed *primary* or *maintenance rehearsal* (Craik & Watkins, 1973; Woodward, Bjork, & Jongeward, 1973). If a long-term retention test is anticipated and conditions of the task permit, the subject may attend to aspects of the experimental context outside of the to-be-remembered items themselves that might be present in a recall situation, in which case representations of these combinations of context and item attributes will be generated. With adequate time and repetition these representations can form units, just as previously established units such as letters or words, and will then be retrievable on later occasions if appropriate constituents of the original context are available as retrieval cues.

This approach has been presented in much more detail by Lee and Estes (1977). Here I would like only to comment on the possibility that it or a similar model could handle the facts that have been especially congenial to the previous short-term memory models, together with others that have been often ignored or by-passed. As in the Atkinson–Shiffrin model, information concerning the order of sequentially occurring events would generally be preserved in short-term memory, with a tendency for the earliest items to be lost first. However, with regard to this last point, the present model would predict, probably correctly, that the serial position function would nearly always be nonmonotone, with lowered recall for items interior to a sequence, provided there is a blank interval at the beginning. Also, as with the Atkinson–Shiffrin model, short-term memory capacity would be limited, the limitations here being a consequence of noise in the system generated by continuing inputs and finite rehearsal time. And under favorable conditions, recoding processes are predicted that would correspond quite closely to Atkinson and Shiffrin's idea of transition to a long-term memory store. As in Craik and Lockhart's interpretation, more extended processing of input items would generally increase retention. However, in the present approach, the level of processing of items in itself would not be predictive, only the level and mode of processing of input items in relation to conditions obtaining during retention intervals and at the point of recall.

In the view of short-term memory here proposed, forgetting is not a matter of an automatic loss of items over time but rather of an increasing difficulty of discriminating the representations of to-be-remembered items from other representations concurrently maintained in the memory system. As a consequence, the model is especially appropriate for handling some kinds of facts that are hardly addressable at all in terms of the "stores" or "levels" models. Examples are the systematic loss of position and order information over the course of a retention interval (Estes, 1972; Healy, 1974; Lee & Estes, 1977), the predictability of order from position information (Lee & Estes, 1977), the role of auditory similarity of items in determining retention of both order and item information (Baddeley, 1968; Lee & Estes, 1977), and the role of relationships between input and recall contexts (Falkenberg, 1972).

Whether or not other investigators agree with me on all specific points of interpretation mentioned, perhaps these remarks will suffice to make the general point at issue here. Although the approaches in terms both of memory stores and of levels of processing have been salutary in many respects, we see that progress toward more adequate explanatory theory is by no means automatic and in fact tends to slow to a halt if there is excessive perseveration on variations of limited experimental paradigms and a restricted population of theoretical concepts. We need continuing and systematic efforts to handle the results of the experimental variations that arise naturally within the framework of memory store or levels-of-processing models, together with others arising within other lines of research. I think that here, as elsewhere, the information-processing metaphor has proven to be double edged—often helping to open up progress on problems that have been refractory to other approaches but at the same time tending to generate models rather sharply cut off from other bodies of potentially relevant theory.

Models for Semantic Memory. Contemporary theoretical treatments of long-term, semantic memory, like those of short-term memory, have been strongly influenced by the information-processing approach; but for the most part they have not departed as sharply from traditional conceptions of associations.

Consider, for example, Fig. 3.8, illustrating a popular current conception of a hierarchical, associative network for semantic memory. Though not copied from any specific source, the diagram is close to the prototype that will have been formed by anyone following the works of Collins and Quillian (1972) or Anderson and Bower (1973). The nodes in the associative network have no internal structure or content themselves but are assumed to correspond in some sense to words or concepts and are connected by conducting pathways. This network differs from the chain of interitem

LEVELS   MEMORY STRUCTURES

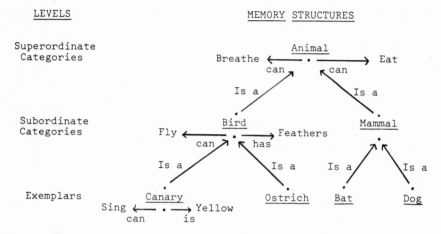

FIG. 3.8 Illustration of the tree structure assumed to describe semantic memory organization in models associated with the approach of Collins and Quillian (1972).

connections characteristic of earlier association models both in the hierarchical arrangement and in the abstract nature of the entities associated.

The hierarchical arrangement was added to accommodate the facts of data on clustering in recall and reaction times in sentence verification tasks rather than as a consequence of any new neurophysiological knowledge. As the quantity and richness of new data generated by current research on semantic memory has strained theorists' ability to handle the findings via simple associative linkages, the trend has been to multiply the kinds of association—thus the "is a" and "has a" associative paths in the model of Collins and Quillian, the linguistically labeled association in Anderson and Bower's model, and so on. These qualitatively distinct varieties of labeled associations certainly bolster the descriptive value of the models, but perhaps at the cost of explanatory power. Newly postulated types of associations account for the facts or intuitions that suggest them but do not necessarily help us see how the facts could have been anticipated from more general principles or from other independent knowledge.

The principal alternative approach to semantic memory is built on a conception of semantic features. In the development by Smith, Shoben, and Rips (1974), for example, the concept corresponding to a word is represented in memory by a list of defining and characteristic semantic features. When an individual is queried concerning the truth or falsity of a sentence—for example, the ubiquitous "A canary is a bird"—the feature lists for the subject and predicate are retrieved from memory by some as yet unspecified process and compared. If a rapid, presumably parallel comparison of the characteristic and defining features of the subject with those of the predicate yields a similarity value exceeding a criterion, a judgment of "true" follows immediately. If not, the defining features are compared one–by–one till a mismatch is found (yielding a "false" response) or till all are found to match (yielding a "true").

I think that the semantic feature models offer some advantages over the network schemes, but I am not persuaded of the necessity of formulating those models in terms of special kinds of features qualitatively different from those entering into other processes of recognition and memory. As the models stand, we seem to face a regress. Meaning is interpreted in terms of features, but the features are defined as properties or constituents of memory representations of word or concepts. We evidently require additional theory to explain how meaning, in the sense of relationship to nonlinguistic entities, accrues to the semantic features.

I hasten to emphasize that in my estimation, research on semantic memory represents one of the most notable accomplishments of cognitive psychology during this decade. It is impressive how much progress has been made on such a complex subject matter. Also it is clear that the progress is due in large part to the role of a few theoretical ideas, notably the hierarchical network and semantic feature models, in generating and guiding research. The only negative aspect of this development, from my view, is that theory construction has been in great part so disjoint from other research and theory on memory. I hope that this is a passing phase and that significant connections between semantic memory models and other theories and models of memory will begin to develop.

Since I have criticized semantic memory theories on grounds of perhaps excessive provinciality, it would be constructive for me at this point to offer some suggestions as to how I think theory development might take a favorable turn.

What basic alternatives can be proposed to those of conceptualizing the meaning of a word either in terms of its relationships to other elements of a network or in terms of semantic markers or features? From the standpoint of more general theories of learning and memory, it seems that the meaning of a word must be interpreted in terms of the contexts in which it is used. I would suggest that two words mean the same thing if they are used in all of the same contexts.

In this view, a characterization of the meaning of a word would consist in a memory trace vector, perhaps of the type conceived by Anderson (1973), the elements corresponding to the attribute values of the contexts in which the word is used.

Thus, for example, on an occasion when an individual heard the word *canary* spoken while a canary was in view, the visual and auditory stimuli would be processed by the perceptual system in terms of attributes or features; then the values of the attributes attended to at the time—both visual and

Presentation of Visual Stimulus

Plus Word

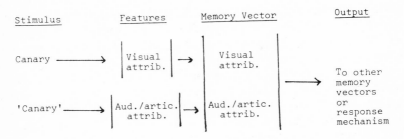

FIG. 3.9   Illustration of the way stimulus features of an object (canary) at which an individual is looking while hearing the name of the object may be stored in a memory trace vector together with auditory or articulatory features of the spoken word. On a later occasion, input of either subset of features would tend to reactivate the memory vector.

auditory—would be stored in a single memory vector as illustrated in Fig. 3.9. Occurrence of either stimulus—the visual appearance of a canary or hearing of the word *canary*—on a later occasion would tend to activate this memory vector and lead to the same output that had occurred on the earlier occasion. The diagram is quite elliptical of course—as, for example, other attributes of the context in which the stimuli occurred might also be attended to and thus incorporated into the memory vector.

Still more importantly, the output of the given memory vector could serve as the input for others. If, for example, in the original episode a speaker had uttered the sentence, "A canary [pointing to the canary] is a bird," then the output of the memory trace vector would be an input to another memory vector incorporating traces of both this input and the input from the spoken word *bird*. Thus, there would be a basis for recall of the word *bird* as well as the word *canary* when an organism with the given attributes was again encountered.

In a model built out of these memory structures, the relationship between different trace vectors that provide the basis for efficient retrieval could be represented formally in a hierarchical tree structure (like Fig. 3.8). However, the connections would not be interpreted as fixed pathways. Rather, any one trace vector might enter into more or less lasting associations with many others as a consequence of its activation in various contexts. However, considering interrelationships among different trace vectors in terms of their values on common attributes, one can generate an orderly structure to picture the relationships between lower and higher-order units. Processing of either verbal or nonverbal stimuli at input would proceed upward through successive levels of units, as illustrated in Fig. 3.10, in a manner remindful of Collins and Quillian's network turned upside-down. Thus if the individual whose memory is portrayed observes an object that eats and breathes, or is told that it eats and breathes, a memory trace would be reactivated that includes attributes of the word *animal*. If, further, the incoming information specifies the outer covering of the object to be feathered and its mode of locomotion to be flying, a trace would be reactivated including attributes of the word *bird*, and so on.

I hasten to add that a diagram of the type of Fig. 3.10 should be taken to represent relationships of commonality and difference among memory traces that provide a basis for category judgments, not a fixed sequence of processing stages. The idea of processing upward through the tree structure via a sequence of operations of memory retrieval and comparison may provide a logical reconstruction of the cognitive processes entering into judgments of word meaning and category membership; but it probably does

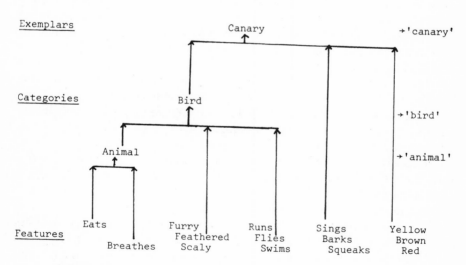

FIG. 3.10   Relationships of commonality among memory trace vectors that might enter into cognitive tasks involving meanings of words at different levels of abstraction. At the bottom of the diagram are representations of relatively unitary features or attributes, at higher levels representations of successively higher order combinations. Note the formal similarity of the structure to those assumed in current models for information processing in reading (Estes, 1975; LaBerge & Samuels, 1974).

not provide a description of cognitive processes occurring in real time, except perhaps under very special circumstances.

The process of activating or determining the meaning of a word would be assumed to follow either of two, not mutually exclusive, routes via: (1) episodic memory—that is, recall of specific contexts in which the word has been used in the individual's experience; and (2) categorical, or semantic, memory in the usual sense—that is, recall of attributes characterizing the set of contexts in which the word is used. The first route would normally be the faster, because when available it would lead directly to a decision or response without necessity for intervening comparison or matching processes.

In the second route, the generation of judgments of category membership, synonymity, etc., is assumed to proceed by comparison of attributes of the given words. Here my proposal is a bit different from current feature models in some details. The features compared are assumed to be attributes of contexts, which may be either linguistic or nonlinguistic in character, rather than being purely linguistic units. The features are conceived as values on dimensions, which may be but are not necessarily sensory continua; and all values, even for binary-valued dimensions (presence vs. absence of some property or entity), are on a par with regard to match–mismatch decisions. The significance of this point is that when the name of a category and the name of a possible exemplar are being compared in a lexical decision task, a single mismatch would suffice to yield a negative decision. Matches on all attributes would yield a positive decision; a mixture of matches on some attributes and ambiguity on others would yield some intermediate probability of a positive decision and, if conditions of the task permitted, a search for additional information.

How would a model of this kind deal with the sentence-verification task, on which the models of Collins and Quillian (1972) and Smith et al. (1974) have made considerable progress? It is not feasible to go into any detail here, but the spirit of the approach is as follows. If a person were asked, "Is it true that a titmouse is a bird?", he or she would in effect first translate the query into a sentence that could be answered on the basis of prestored information [following Smith's (1978) prestorage versus computation distinction]: "Do I remember any relevant experiences?" If this process led to recall of an episode in which a titmouse had been called a bird or in which a dictionary look-up had supplied the answer, the individual could immediately answer "true." If not, the person would—again figuratively speaking—translate the original sentence into the form: "Do titmouses have the same values as birds on their common attributes?" The individual would then recall the attributes stored in memory with the word *bird* and check the values of these against the attribute values recalled for *titmouse*. A mismatch on any one of the common attributes would lead to the answer "false," agreement on all of them to the answer "true." A false sentence such as "A bat is a bird" or "A teacup is a bird" would always have to be answered on the basis of the second question (on the basis of computation in Smith's terms); and in general the second of these sentences would be predicted to be disconfirmed faster than the first, because a mismatch of values on one of the common attributes would on the average be found sooner.

It should be emphasized that such statements as "the individual would then recall particular attributes" are only part of an informal chatacterization of the process assumed. In a model of the kind proposed, probability and speed of recalling an attribute would depend on frequency, recency, and contexts of previous inputs and recalls just as assumed in models for other aspects of memory. The one point I wish to make here is that it may prove possible to retain advantageous properties of current network and feature models for semantic memory while at the same time capitalizing on the resources of other bodies of relevant research and theory to a greater extent than has been recently the mode. If so, we may also see more movement from descriptive toward explanatory theory.

IMPLICATIONS OF MEMORY MODELS
FOR STRATEGIES OF THEORY CONSTRUCTION

Psychologists working on problems of semantic memory should be prepared, above all others, to appreciate the differences between purely descriptive and explanatory theories and to see how to work effectively to move toward the latter. One of the measures of the maturity of a science is the degree to which its facts and empirical laws are all interrelated by higher-order concepts in a way that closely mirrors the retrieval scheme illustrated in Fig. 3.8. For example, the beginnings of a similar schematization for a chemist's knowledge of chemistry might take the form shown in Fig. 3.11. In reasoning about chemical problems, one rarely needs to recall specific facts peculiar to

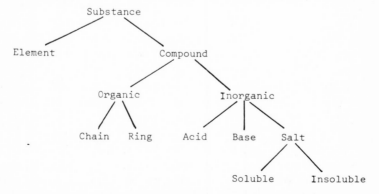

FIG. 3.11 Tree structure representing a hypothetical retrieval organization for knowledge about chemistry, analogous to the associative network portrayed in Fig. 3.8.

specific substances. Nearly all that one might wish to predict as to how a substance will behave follows from knowledge of the categories to which the substance belongs. But to the best of my knowledge, in science as in the individual, organized retrieval structures of this type do not always grow automatically. In fact, excessive efforts to improve one's account of particular facts by adding low level concepts trade off more descriptive power for less explanatory power. Important advances toward explanatory theory must result rather from revisions at higher levels in the network, from which consequences flow for many subsets of phenomena at lower levels.

Thus, for example, in attempting to improve our understanding of the way people perform in sentence-verification tasks, we can hope to make progress either by uncovering new kinds of strategies that people may use in response to particular types of sentences or by attempting to revise more fundamental terms of a theory such as our conception of the memory trace itself. The first tactic, employed with reasonable intelligence, almost guarantees some progress toward better descriptive theory but offers little toward improving higher level integrations. The second tactic offers some chance of getting no result beyond a possibly instructive failure but, in return, also offers some chance of a significant theoretical advance. The choice is with the investigator, but occasional reflection on the purposes of theories and on correspondences between properties of theories and what we know of how our minds operate may aid us in appraising both the risks and the possible benefits.

ACKNOWLEDGMENTS

This chapter is based in part on research supported by Grant MH 23878 from the National Institute of Mental Health. I am indebted to Edward E. Smith for useful comments on my approach to semantic memory.

REFERENCES

Anderson, J. A. A theory for the recognition of items from short memorized lists. *Psychological Review*, 1973, *80*, 417–438.

Anderson, J. R. *Language, memory, and thought.* Hillsdale, N.J.: Lawrence Erlbaum Associates, 1976.

Anderson, J. R., & Bower, G. H. *Human associative memory.* New York: Wiley, 1973.

Atkinson, R. C., Bower, G. H., & Crothers, E. J. *An introduction to mathematical learning theory.* New York: Wiley, 1965.

Atkinson R. C., & Shiffrin, R. M. Human memory: A proposed system and its control processes. In K. W. Spence & J. T. Spence (Eds.), *The psychology of learning and motivation* (Vol. 2). New York: Academic Press, 1968.

Baddeley, A. D. How does acoustic similarity influence short-term memory? *Quarterly Journal of Experimental Psychology*, 1968, *20*, 249–264.

Bjork, R. A. All-or-none subprocesses in the learning of complex sequences. *Journal of Mathematical Psychology*, 1968, *5*, 182–195.

Bower, G. H. A multicomponent theory of the memory trace. In K. W. Spence & J. T. Spence (Eds.), *The psychology of learning and motivation* (Vol. 1). New York: Academic Press, 1967.

Brown, J. Some texts of the decay theory of immediate memory. *Quarterly Journal of Experimental Psychology*, 1958, *10*, 12–21.

Cavanagh, P. Holographic and trace strength models of rehearsal effects in the item recognition task. *Memory & Cognition*, 1976, *4*, 186–199.

Chomsky, N. *Aspects of a theory of syntax*. Cambridge, Mass.: Massachusetts Institute of Technology Press, 1965.

Collins, A. M., & Quillian, M. R. How to make a language user. In E. Tulving & W. Donaldson (Eds.), *Organization of memory*. New York: Academic Press, 1972.

Craik, F. I. M., & Lockhart, R. S. Levels of processing: A framework for memory research. *Journal of Verbal Learning and Verbal Behavior*, 1972, *11*, 671–684.

Craik, F. I. M., & Watkins, M. J. The role of rehearsal in short-term memory. *Journal of Verbal Learning and Verbal Behavior*, 1973, *12*, 599–607.

Ebbinghaus, H. [Memory] (H. A. Ruger & D. E. Bussenius, trans.). New York: Teachers College, 1913. (Originally published, 1885.)

Estes, W. K. An associative basis for coding and organization in memory. In A. W. Melton & E. Martin (Eds.), *Coding processes in human memory*. Washington, D.C.: Winston, 1972.

Estes, W. K. Memory, perception, and decision in letter identification. In R. L. Solso (Ed.), *Information processing and cognition: The Loyola Symposium*. Hillsdale, N.J.: Lawrence Erlbaum Associates, 1975.

Estes, W. K. Structural aspects of associative models for memory. In C. N. Cofer (Ed.), *The structure of human memory*. San Francisco: Freeman, 1976.

Falkenberg, P. R. Recall improves in short-term memory the more recall context resembles learning context. *Journal of Experimental Psychology*, 1972, *95*, 39–47.

Feigenbaum, E. A. Simulation of verbal learning behavior. In E. A. Feigenbaum & J. Feldman (Eds.), *Computers and thought*. New York: McGraw-Hill, 1963.

Healy, A. F. Separating item from order information in short-term memory. *Journal of Verbal Learning and Verbal Behavior*, 1974, *13*, 644–655.

Healy, A. F. Coding of temporal–spatial patterns in short-term memory. *Journal of Verbal Learning and Verbal Behavior*, 1975, *14*, 481–495.

Hempel, C. G. *Aspects of scientific explanation*. New York: The Free Press, 1965.

Hilgard, E. R. *Theories of learning* (rev. ed.). New York: Appleton-Century-Crofts, 1956.

Koffka, K. [*The growth of the mind: An introduction to child psychology*] (R. M. Ogden, trans.). New York: Harcourt, Brace, 1924.

Köhler, W. *Gestalt psychology*. New York: Liveright, 1929.

Konorski, J. *Integrative activity of the brain*. Chicago: University of Chicago Press, 1967.

Laberge, D., & Samuels, S. J. Toward a theory of automatic information processing in reading. *Cognitive Psychology*, 1974, 6, 293–323.

Lashley, K. S. Learning: I. Nervous mechanisms in learning. In C. Murchison (Ed.), *The foundations of experimental psychology*. Worcester, Mass.: Clark University Press, 1929.

Lee, C. L., & Estes, W. K. Order and position in primary memory for letter strings. *Journal of Verbal Learning and Verbal Behavior*, 1977, *16*, 395–418.

Meyer, D. E., Schvaneveldt, R. W., & Ruddy, M. G. Loci of contextual effects on visual word recognition. In P. M. A. Rabbitt & S. Dornic (Eds.), *Attention and performance V*. London: Academic Press, 1975.

Murdock, B. B., Jr. *Human memory: Theory and data*. Hillsdale, N.J.: Lawrence Erlbaum Associates, 1974.

Nelson, T. O. Repetition and depth of processing. *Journal of Verbal Learning and Verbal Behavior*, 1977, *16*, 151–172.

Norman, D. A., & Wickelgren, W. A. Strength theory of decision rules and latency in short-term memory. *Journal of Mathematical Psychology,* 1969, *6,* 192–208.

Peterson, L. R., & Peterson, M. Short-term retention of individual verbal items. *Journal of Experimental Psychology,* 1959, *58,* 193–198.

Posner, M. T., & Snyder, C. R. R. Facilitation and inhibition in the processing of signals. In P. M. A. Rabbitt & S. Dornic (Eds.), *Attention and performance V.* London: Academic Press, 1975.

Pribram, K. H. *Languages of the brain: Experimental paradoxes and principles in neuropsychology.* Englewood Cliffs, N.J.: Prentice-Hall, 1971.

Robinson, E. S. *Association theory today.* New York: Century, 1932.

Shiffrin, R. M. Short-term store: The basis for a memory search. In F. Restle, R. M. Shiffrin, N. J. Castellan, H. Lindman, & D. B. Pisoni (Eds.), *Cognitive theory* (Vol. I). Hillsdale, N.J.: Lawrence Erlbaum Associates, 1975.

Simon, H. A., & Kotovsky, K. Human acquisition of concepts for sequential patterns. *Psychological Review,* 1963, *70,* 534–546.

Skinner, B. F. Are theories of learning necessary? *Psychological Review,* 1950, *57,* 193–216.

Smith, E. E. Theories of semantic memory. In W. K. Estes (Ed.), *Handbook of learning and cognitive processes* (Vol. 6). Hillsdale, N.J.: Lawrence Erlbaum Associates, 1978.

Smith, E. E., Shoben, E. J., & Rips, L. J. Structure and process in semantic memory: A featural model for semantic decisions. *Psychological Review,* 1974, *81,* 214–241.

Underwood, B. J. Interference and forgetting. *Psychological Review,* 1957, *64,* 49–60.

Underwood, B. J. Attributes of memory. *Psychological Review,* 1969, *76,* 559–573.

Woodward, A. E., Jr., Bjork, R. A., & Jongeward, J. Recall and recognition as a function of primary rehearsal. *Journal of Verbal Learning and Verbal Behavior,* 1973, *12,* 608–617.

4 Conscious and Unconscious Cognition: A Computational Metaphor for the Mechanism of Attention and Integration

D. Alan Allport
University of Reading, England

INTRODUCTION

Aims of This Paper

What has the study of artificial intelligence to offer psychology? Much of its contribution, I am convinced, lies still in the future. For the present, this essay attempts to draw out, in a largely illustrative vein and from the viewpoint of one experimental psychologist, some lessons that are already assimilable in the current literature of artificial intelligence.

The design of artificially intelligent systems that operate in anything like the domain of human intelligence, as in the understanding of natural language, is plainly still at an exploratory and relatively primitive stage of development. Nevertheless, some suggestions about rather general design principles, which appear to be important in the effective utilization and integration of large amounts of intrinsically uncertain knowledge, are beginning to be apparent. The aim of this essay is to explore one such principle of organization as a possible metaphor for the architecture of human cognition.

My proposal is sustained, in part, by a view of cerebral information processing as essentially "broad and shallow"—depending on the distributed computation of millions of quasiindependent functions, each one of which individually is highly uncertain and error prone (Burns, 1968). No nonliving device even remotely approaches the multiplicity and complexity of cerebral processing. However, a fundamental design problem that arises for any distributed computational system concerns the way in which the contributions of its individual components are coordinated and integrated. The second, and central, section of this paper (pp. 67–76) reviews what appears to be an increasing convergence of approach, within otherwise quite disparate undertakings in artificial intelligence, toward one possible class of solution. Following this, in the third and concluding section (pp. 77–84), I argue for the possibility of a similar form of organization in human information processing; in particular, I point to some tentative implications for our understanding of the phenomena of attention and of the relationship between phenomenal experience and "preattentive" access to semantic memory.

Before embarking on these two main objectives, I begin by making a few preliminary remarks about the psychological study of memory and cognition and about the possible role of work done in artificial intelligence as a medium for developing conceptual tools for a future theoretical psychology.

Memory and Perception

I take it that "memory" refers to the sum of a person's knowledge acquired throughout life—though of course built on an immensely rich foundation of inherited dispositions—by virtue of which that person is able to interact intelligently with the world and in some measure to understand it. To know how to tell the time or ride a bicycle; to recognize a friend's footsteps or the taste of strawberries or the style of Mozart; to be able to read a book or a map or to tell the way the wind is blowing; all these abilities and thousands more apparently reflect a vast accumulation of very loosely interrelated and certainly incomplete knowledge, little if any of which conforms to the neat and bureaucratic hierarchies imagined by some theorists of "semantic memory."

Seen in this perspective, much the greater part of human memory must be *tacit*: It cannot be introspected or articulated. By contrast, the psychological study of memory (for most of the past 500 years) has concentrated on a person's ability to make *explicit commentaries* on his or her own knowledge, either by attempting to reenact it or to reproduce after a fashion some particular experience or to make judgments on the contextual familiarity of an event when it is presented again. These studies have passed by the fundamental question of how such knowledge, acquired throughout life, can be made use of in everyday intelligent performance, in perception and understanding. The psychological study of memory has been dominated by the metaphor of *storage*: An entity is put in a place and is later "retrieved," even if the entity is thought of as a tag that is attached to an imaginary node or pointer in a semantic network. Only recently has there begun to be active interest on the part of theorists of memory in the way such a mental thesaurus might be *used* in the perception and comprehension of language or of nonlinguistic events; in the way cues in the sensory environment come to address and to be interpreted in relation to prior knowledge; in short, in the process of *assimilation.*

Several factors have contributed to this compartmentalization. One superficial but not less damaging influence is the deceptive ease with which behavioral experiments can be contrived in the neo-Ebbinghaus tradition, requiring the memorization of arbitrary lists of words or similar tokens, a deceptive ease compounded by the simplicity of the criteria for evaluating literal recall or recognition, contrasted with the diverse and ill-defined criteria available for the assessment of comprehension. In practice the field of study recognized as the psychology of "memory" is differentiated from the study of, say, "perception" or "performance," of "language" or "intelligence," predominantly in terms of experimental paradigms, rather than by any more deeply motivated theoretical distinctions, except in the trivial sense that the domain of application of all too many theories is similarly paradigm specific. Yet despite the often acknowledged arbitrariness of the traditional separation between "memory" and "perception," this division continues to be reflected in much of our experimental research effort, in the huge majority of textbooks and monographs, in the courses that are taught, even in the terms of reference of many recently established psychological journals.

The Computational Paradigm

Over the past several years, however, there has emerged what amounts to a radically new approach and a new methodology for psychological or cognitive science, an approach that is not burdened with the same historical divisions of subject matter. Central to this new approach is what has been called the *computational metaphor*—the belief that human cognitive capacity can fruitfully be viewed as some kind of "physical symbol system" (Newell & Simon, 1976).

The methodology hinges on the attempt to design artificially intelligent systems, generally embodied in—or in principle implemented in—the form of computer programs, though some of the most seminal contributions may be a long way from a working computational system and may include little or no actual programmed code (e.g., Charniak, 1972; Huffman, 1971; Minsky, 1975; Moore & Newell, 1974). In taking this approach, the first aim has been to study the potential properties of different representations of knowledge, different process structures, and their interactions and, in so doing, to develop and articulate a repertoire of concepts in terms of which we can think about and describe psychological processes. The second aim—second only in that it is to some degree logically dependent on the first—is to explore the parallels between such principles of possible or effective process and organization as may be discovered by this means and the organization of human cognition. Of course the exploration can begin from both ends. Behavioral phenomena may suggest or constrain possible mechanisms whose properties can be studied computationally, just as computational theories should lead to the search for previously unrecognized behavioral consequences that they imply (or more powerfully, that, if found, would invalidate them as psychological theories). But the approach is not "phenomenon driven" in the way that most current work in experimental psychology is (Newell, 1973a; see also Allport, 1975), certainly including most memory research.

One of its intellectual antecedents, or at least an early collateral, can be seen in the Chomskian approach to linguistics. But the computational approach departs fundamentally from the linguistic tradition in making *process* and mechanism central, in contrast to the linguistic concern with formal derivation as a decision procedure for evaluating well-formedness in language.

Programs and Theories

In understanding the significance of work done in artificial intelligence (AI) for the development of a theoretical psychology, one source of major confusion concerns the relationship between computer programs and (psychological) theories. If the program is held to *be* the theory, it is obvious that innumerable detailed assumptions, which have to be made if the program is to be written at all, cannot be sufficiently justified in terms of known psychological phenomena. Indeed, many of the detailed assumptions may turn out to be demonstrably wrong, although more often it is simply unclear how they could be individually verified. Yet the program can still be a means of formulating, and in one important sense of testing, the theory that underlies it.

For example, many of the programs written by Schank and his colleagues (e.g., Schank, 1975) depend on a theory called *Conceptual Dependency* (CD), which seeks to provide a language-independent representation of sentence or text meaning based on a relatively small number of conceptual primitives. (For an interesting extension, see Russell, 1976.) These programs provide a way of exploring what sorts of things CD representations might enable one to do. They offer a preliminary demonstration, for example, that a conceptual representation of sentence meaning can be derivd from a surface linguistic text by means of almost entirely *lexical*, semantics-driven mechanisms (Riesbeck, 1975). Constructing the programs also reveals deficiencies in the theory and uncovers problems that were not clearly recognized beforehand—such as the problem of controlling the proliferation of inferences that can be triggered from any conceptualization (Rieger, 1975). Confronting this problem pointed to the key status of inferences about unspecified causal connections and incidentally motivated the development of a syntax of causality (Schank, 1973). It also prompted the exploration of "scripts" as one mechanism for establishing the scope of currently possible inferences (Schank

& Abelson, 1977). None of these efforts in any way shows that Schank's particular choice of conceptual primitives is "correct," nor even that translation to conceptual primitives—or for that matter the application of large, scriptlike pieces of knowledge—is essential to linguistic comprehension. But they do at least show that such approaches have some quite impressive capabilities. And they challenge others to propose alternative mechanisms (e.g., Charniak, 1976; Wilks, 1976a).

The computational approach also challenges traditional psychological notions of what a theory *is* or is *for*. Seen as cognitive science, an AI program is not an end in itself but a means toward a better understanding of the theory that motivated it and a better articulation of the problems yet to be understood. This approach vigorously endorses Max Black's view of scientific models as "systematically developed metaphors" (Black, 1962; see also Barbour, 1974). Furthermore, a program could not be a theory, even if it were to pass all Turing tests as a model. According to Winograd (1977):

> If I have a complete blueprint for a complex mechanical device, it is not a "theory" of how that device works. But it would be foolish not to see a blueprint as a valuable part of an "explanation" of that device. Similarly, a program which completely duplicated the processes of human language use would still not be a theory. But any program which is built can be viewed as a hypothesized partial blueprint and can be a step towards understanding [p. 172].

See also an interesting discussion of the role of computational theories in relation to other sciences by Cheatham (1974).

The place of empirical falsification is by no means straightforward when we are dealing with models of very complex interactive systems. Most obviously, there is the problem of attribution—of ascribing a given predicted outcome to individual assumptions of the model. More deeply, there is a problem of discriminating what is central to a given computational model from what is unimportant—baby from bath water.

System Interaction

Winograd in particular has stressed the system-centered approach, which sees behavioral phenomena as emerging from the *interactions* within a system of components rather than as properties of the individual components themselves. According to this view, the *control structure* of an understanding system is itself of crucial theoretical significance. Unless the principles of organization that constrain what intereactions can occur in any large and complex system are understood, that system cannot itself serve as a perspicuous model for understanding human cognition.

This emphasis on organizational principles and systemic interaction is precisely complementary to the currently dominant strategy in experimental psychology. One of the principal goals—perhaps *the* principal goal—of information-processing research over the past decade or more has been the behavioral identification of functionally separable components. The search for different modalities of long- and short-term memory (articulatory, visual, propositional, . . .) is one example of this. In my view this is a goal to which behavioral experimentation is well suited. The neuropsychological literature contains abundant evidence for the grossly modular organization of specialist subsystems in the cerebral cortex, notably in the many varieties of "disconnection syndrome" observed within both linguistic and nonlinguistic capabilities (Geschwind, 1965; Luria, 1976; Marin, Saffran, & Schwartz, 1976; Whitaker & Whitaker, 1976). At a more local level, there is a plethora of behavioral as well as physiological evidence indicating that various attributes of complex stimuli can be processed independently and in parallel by different, specialist analyzers (e.g., Blakemore, Muncey, & Ridley, 1973; Garner, 1977; Hawkins, 1969; Maffei & Fiorentini, 1977; Marcel, 1970; Saraga & Shallice, 1973; Wing & Allport, 1972).

However, when it comes to the analysis of *how* these functionally separable components interact, our present experimental procedures are of severely limited scope. That is, we have methods for ascertaining *that* different subsystems interact but scarcely at all for exploring how, in what way, they do so. And our conceptual repertoire in this respect is if anything even more restricted. If incoming information is analyzed in independent sensory or cognitive subsystems, for example, how is it thereafter reintegrated to construct a coherent world of perception and action?

It is in coming to grips with problems of this order, problems of systemic organization, that the computational approach has most to offer in providing metaphors for psychological organization. They are metaphors in much the same sense that the conception of a linear succession of processing "stages," each stage completed before the next can begin, has been utilized as a metaphor for some aspects of human information processing in terms of which experimental data are interpreted. The metaphor I propose draws its inspiration from the successful adoption, in a number of relatively large-scale artificial intelligence systems, of a control structure that combines in the most thoroughgoing way (at least in its idealized representation) both massively parallel organization and a completely global mechanism of integration, or control-state evaluation. This is the organization known as a *Production System*. The relative success of these computational attempts has even prompted the speculation that AI research, in adapting to the computational demands inherent in something like the "natural" or biological problem domain, may be in the process of rediscovering some of the principles of organization that have also evolved through natural selection in living intelligent systems. That, at least, is to take the "computational metaphor" in its most serious form. It is not in any way evidence for such a conjecture; but at least it provides reason for supposing that these ideas might be worthwhile to explore. Neither is it to assert that any particular, actual production system is presently a satisfactory model of some detailed aspect of human cognition. However, theoretical psychology is not exactly rich in conceptually promising alternatives to the serial recoding model. What is proposed, therefore, is that some features of the *general* architecture of production systems offer alternatives that merit serious consideration.

PRODUCTION SYSTEMS

Modularity

The most striking development in AI activity concerned with modeling ordinary (human?) intelligence over the past 5 years or more has undoubtedly been in the use of modular, active memory units (schemata, demons, templates, frames . . .), where the basic mechanism of thought is seen as a process of *recognition.* This orientation is exemplified in the work of Abelson (1973), Becker (1973), Bobrow and Norman (1975), Charniak and Wilks (1976), Hewitt, Bishop, and Steiger (1973), Minsky (1975), Bobrow and Winograd (1977), and many others. The current enthusiasm in cognitive psychology for the rediscovery of neo-Bartlettian schemata (e.g., Neisser, 1976; Rumelhart & Ortony, 1976) is historically indebted, directly or indirectly, to these developments. Some (e.g., Minsky, 1975; Schank & Abelson, 1977) argue for relatively large-scale units of knowledge, incorporating multiple advice about what other mechanisms to invoke in case of failure. Others (e.g., Wilks, 1976b, 1977) advocate much smaller and simpler structures.

In addition, performance-oriented "expert" systems, not necessarily intended in any direct sense as simulations of human cognition but concerned with the intelligent application of very large amounts of fuzzy or informal knowledge, have increasingly adopted a highly modular, "parallel" form of organization known as a *Production System.* One large program, DENDRAL (Nii & Feigenbaum, 1977; Smith, 1972), which in sheer performance terms has some claim still to be the most "intelligent" AI program and which can outperform postdoctoral chemists in its particular field of mass spectrometry, was entirely rewritten in production system terms when its original, procedural approach proved too inflexible as a basis for continued improvements.

There are, of course, powerful reasons for favoring a modular organization as far as possible in any system that is to be the subject of continuous modifications, either in the course of natural evolution or learning or by human design. If a cognitive system is not organized in this way, with its component parts as nearly independent of one another as possible, any small alteration in one place will inevitably force many other, compensating changes in other places, which may even propagate explosively throughout the system. Where storage capacity is not a limiting factor, as it certainly appears not to be in the human brain, there is a clear advantage in having many overlapping, independent representations of knowledge (cf. Becker, 1973; Brooks, 1976). Error in or damage to even a large proportion of the system should still enable it to maintain some sort of "sensible" behavior, that is to display the graceful degradation of performance that is seen consequent on injury in living creatures (Marr, 1976). Many actual production systems possess this property. Indeed, the corollary of this, the "graceful enhancement" of redundant, modular systems, is the basis of some very promising explorations of cognitive development through the piecemeal addition of simple (production) rules (Baylor & Gascon, 1974; Young, 1977, in press; see also Booth, 1978; Waterman, 1975).

"Pure" Production Systems

Production Systems (PSs) represent a very general class of computational mechanism that, although encompassing a wide range of variations in practice, nevertheless share a clearly recognizable set of design features, which have been admirably surveyed by Davis and King (1976). It is worth emphasizing at the outset, however, a distinction between those features common to what Davis and King (1976) refer to as "pure" production systems on the one hand and the many varieties of system organization that technically conform to PS methodology while departing more or less radically from its "spirit" on the other. This paper is concerned with the former, with certain very simple yet computationally powerful general principles, as a possible framework for human cognitive organization. As such this essay is in no way intended as a review of existing, psychologically oriented simulation programs that adopt a PS format, however interesting.

A Production System (PS) comprises two main components: a set of rules, or "productions," and a data base. In the basic PS, each rule consists of an ordered pair of symbolic structures: a procedure or *action* that can be applied to the data base and a *condition* for applying it (written, *condition* → *action*). The data base can be any collection of symbolic information. In systems designed to model psychological processing, the data base is taken to represent the system's knowledge about the current state of the world, or "working memory," whereas the rules constitute its long-term knowledge.

The simplest conditions call for the literal matching of individual symbols in the data base, and a simple action is one of rewriting: The symbols matched in the data base are replaced with those in the right-hand side (RHS) of the matching rule. More elaborate production rules can include networks of relations between variables, or structural descriptions, as their condition terms and the building of additional network structures in the data base as their resulting action.

In principle, the condition of each rule is evaluated (tested) continuously against the contents of the data base. If a condition is satisfied, its associated action now becomes available for application. In practice, PSs realized on a uni-processing computer need an interpreter that scans the rules in some sequence, one at a time, for matching conditions that may be found in the data base. In some (e.g., Newell, 1973b), the first rule encountered that evaluates successfully is executed at once, and scanning then begins again from the top, so that the ordering of rules is all-important to the system's behavior. (Simple phrase structure grammars are typically of this form.) In this case, a given rule may be applicable only if the conditions tested by rules higher up the list are untrue, although this dependency is not explicit in the rule itself, thus contributing to the "opacity" of the PS. Other systems (e.g., Feigenbaum, Buchanan, & Lederberg, 1971; Lesser, Fennell, Erman, & Reddy, 1974) closer to the spirit of a parallel or multiprocessing PS activate in a "conflict set" all rules whose conditions are satisfied. Priority of execution can then be decided by a variety of different *metarules* (Hayes-Roth & Lesser, 1976). Priority may be assigned on the basis of features of the rules themselves, the confidence assigned to the *condition → action* contingency they represent, their frequency or recency of occurrence, or the kinds of actions they demand. Or it may be evaluated in terms of precedence assigned in many possible ways to the *data* that evoked the rules, or as a function of their goodness of fit, or by selecting the most restrictive or specialized of the matching conditions.

Some of these metarules can be viewed as corresponding to Broadbent's (1970) conceptions of "stimulus set" and "response set" in selective attention, although the theoretical possibilities that can be envisaged in PS terms obviously extend beyond the simple dichotomy that Broadbent proposed. The metarules can themselves also be represented as production rules, different combinations of which may be evoked by different subgoals. The MYCIN system (Davis, Buchanan, & Shortliffe, 1975; Shortliffe, 1976), a consultation program for medical diagnosis, seeks to employ second- and even third-order metarules, rules about rules, that can suggest strategies for selecting potentially useful strategies, and so on.

The rules themselves can ideally be viewed as independent chunks of knowledge, or "demons", each with its own statement of relevance, activated automatically by incoming information. They then compete for (and cooperate in) the assertion or application of their contingent actions via the central data base. In some PSs, such as the MYCIN program, the rules are activated through their RHSs in a goal-directed or top-down manner. Activation of the rule thus initiates an active search for the conditions that would satisfy the goal, in a way that resembles the operation of CONSEquent theorems in PLANNER (Hewitt, 1970). Activation of production rules can be thought of generally as a mechanism for embodying *expectancy*.

Ordered Versus Unordered Production Rules

Newell and Simon (1972) have sought to show, with considerable réclame, how human information processing can be modeled entirely by computations on minimal, serially ordered lists of productions. In addition, Newell (1973b) has proposed that the limitations of attention and of short-term memory (which his model assumes are identical) can be represented simply by restricting the capacity of the data base to 7 ± 2 independent symbols. Although expressed in PS terms, these ideas are in one respect the antithesis of the metaphor that I wish to propose; and a brief comment on the more salient differences is therefore essential.

The behavioral predictions for Newell's model depend crucially on scanning the list of productions strictly in order, one at a time, starting always from the top of the list. The first matching production is executed, and the scan then begins again from the top, so that even a small rearrangement of the order of productions can radically change the model's behavior. Priority of rule evocation, in other words, is entirely top-down and predetermined. There is no place for conflict of any kind, no preattentive access to memory structures, no rule redundancy, no activation of rules that are not executed. "Perceptual" encoding into abstract symbols is simply assumed as some linear processing stage that has already terminated before the "memory" processing represented by the model begins. The possibility of heterarchical interaction between perceptual processes and memory-based expectancies is thereby simply excluded.

Later in this essay I review some behavioral evidence that I believe is profoundly at odds with these assumptions. Most importantly, the evidence appears to force the conclusion that sensory stimuli can gain access to semantic memory —can activate production rules—in parallel and *preattentively* both in the sense of (1) without "attentional" capacity limitations, and (2) without generating any new contents in primary memory or episodic awareness. Given the independent activation of semantic production rules, the phenomena of selective attention can be interpreted in terms of interference and conflict resolution between the *execution* of simultaneously activated, competing productions. Limitations to the division of attention, according to this metaphor, are due to the problems of maintaining disjunct data structures in working memory rather than to any inherent limitations of its informational "capacity."

As Young (1977) has pointed out, the use of ordering in a PS frequently is only a "lazy" way to implement the subgoal structure, and unordered PSs are plainly the more appropriate for psychological models. This becomes particularly relevant where different subsets of production rules, acquired (or written!) independently or in different cognitive environments, are subsequently to be merged or recombined in new ways to meet new task demands, as in many aspects of skill acquisition and cognitive development.

Integration

Thus far, in discussing production rules as a potential metaphor for preattentive semantic memory, I have omitted perhaps the most fundamental characteristic of PS architecture, the restriction on *direct* interaction between rules. In a true PS, all communication between production rules has to be *via* the data base, where each rule may "read" and so act upon the modifications made by all other rules; but no rule may directly invoke another. In a "true" (unordered) PS, therefore, there is both the greatest possible degree of parallelism—in the homogeneous character of the unordered production rules—and the greatest possible degree of central integration—in that all interactions are channeled through one single, global "working memory." As Davis and King (1975/1976) emphasize, the real significance of this organization is that "by choosing each new rule on the basis of the total contents of the data base, we are effectively performing a complete reevaluation of the control state of the system at every cycle [1975, p. 5]. This is in contrast to procedurally oriented or conventional computation, where the appearance of "unintelligent" behavior on the part of the program can often be attributed to control decisions made, perforce, on the basis of the small subset of state variables available to the process making that decision. A global data base also means that the system is maximally interruptable by changes in incoming information from any source, a property possessed in large measure by animals and people and very unlike the relentless undistractibility of conventional computer programs.

This PS structure, with its peculiar combination of an essentially anarchic arrangement of independent s–r rules and a highly centralized mechanism of integration, appears to be particuarly well suited to the domain of application of typically "human" intelligence—that is, to the utilization of very large amounts of only loosely interrelated and uncertain knowledge, accumulated piecemeal, that may be called on in the service of many different contexts from that in which it was originally encoded.

The data-driven, interruptable character of PS operation, its peculiar blend of simultaneously top-down and bottom-up processing, associated with confining all "integrative" processes to one common data base, are particularly clearly exemplified in the speech recognition system, HEARSAY II (Fennell & Lesser, 1975; Lesser et al., 1974; Reddy & Newell, 1974). In HEARSAY II the centralized working memory, known as the *blackboard*, is organized in a two-dimensional space representing, respectively, *time* within the utterance to be recognized and linguisitc *levels* of interpretation. The lowest level contains a parametric (acoustic) representation over time of the speech input. Others, including phonetic, syllabic, lexical, syntactic, and conceptual levels, represent the current solution state in the form of provisional hypotheses asserted in relation to particular temporal segments of that input. Some demons (*Knowledge Sources* or KSs in HEARSAY II terminology) are activated directly by data patterns in the parametric input, others only by hypotheses at one or more higher levels of description. For example, one kind of lexical specialist is invoked by descriptions at the phonetic and secondly at the syllabic level and responds by proposing *lexical* hypotheses to account for them. Another is activated by any new lexical hypothesis and responds by verifying expectations about possible surface-phonemic sequences that should be found if the lexical hypothesis is correct. Semantic KSs are triggered by hypotheses at both lexical and conceptual levels and can respond by proposing additional lexical hypotheses, by confirming or vetoing existing ones, and so on. In each case the KS inserts a new link or links on the blackboard, indicating the dependency between the data pattern that initially invoked the KS and the hypotheses that were asserted or strengthened in consequence and that it thereby "supports." The blackboard also admits lists of alternative or competing hypotheses at each level, ordered on a third dimension that reflects their current credibility or degree of support.

The organization of HEARSAY II is not intended in any direct sense to model human information-processing, despite the peculiarly human capability of speech recognition that it is concerned to reproduce. Nevertheless, many of the design issues that are encountered in its construction suggest interesting parallels or at least raise cognate theoretical choices for a psychological model. One of these that I should not wish to adopt—and that is quite independent of the basic PS metaphor—is the simultaneous assertion in "working memory" of alternative and mutually exclusive perceptual hypotheses. This expedient, moreover, transgresses the important though neglected "Principle of Least Commitment" (Marr, 1976; Sloman, 1977) to the effect that as a condition of fluent performance, nothing should be done that may later have to be undone.

Expectancy Demons and "Understanding"

Much of the current work in artificial intelligence, including much that does not explicitly adopt production system methods, makes use of independent, active knowledge molecules or demons, whose role is characteristically to generate *expectations*. Given the presence of some data pattern that satisfies a particular demon's calling condition, the demon sets up expectations about other patterns, which it continues to look out for. If it finds them, it then asserts some *relationship* linking the pattern that initially triggered the expectation to the new pattern that confirmed it.

This was the role played by KSs in the HEARSAY system, where the relationships for the most part represented inferential "support" links, and the expectations were *explicitly* asserted on the blackboard in the form of provisional, alternative hypotheses, even in advance of any direct evidence to confirm them.

Charniak's (1972) demons used in story understanding are similar to this, except that the expectations generated by his demons remain latent or "preattentive"—outside working memory—until some further confirmatory event occurs. This avoids the presence in working memory of alternative, mutually incompatible hypotheses and reserves it for the current "best bet" beliefs of the system. It also seems at least to agree with introspection, in that people do not appear to be simultaneously aware of alternative interpretations in either linguistic or nonlinguistic perception.

A similar mechanism of expectations is used by Riesbeck (1975) in his conceptual analysis program, which converts minimally parsed natural language texts into a language-free, conceptual-case representation of meaning. In this program nearly all the work is done by independent, productionlike mechanisms contained in a dictionary, directly activated by individual words in the input text. Each word entry in the dictionary consists of an unordered set of expectations ("requests") or *condition → action* rules. Once invoked, the requests remain active, independently looking for their expected pattern in the data base until they can be executed or until some other event causes them to be reset. Their actions typically involve inserting or rearranging pieces of conceptual dependency (CD) network in working memory, to which other requests may then react by asserting further CD relationships, and so on in a collaborative synthesis of the conceptualization.

Expectations of disjunctive or mutually exclusive events can thus be concurrently active—for example, when generated by the separate requests associated with different possible meanings of a lexically ambiguous word. But they remain "preattentive," outside working memory. The verb *break*, for instance, activates separate requests, including one that looks for a physical object of the "breaking" and another that tests for an obligation (a promise, rule, etc.) as its object. Quite different conceptual actions are associated with each of these requests. However, only the request whose expectations are successful will have any effect on the conceptual interpretation of the text that is being constructed in working memory. Expectations associated with the unsuccessful requests remain preattentive; their alternative interpretations never become available to the rest of the system; they are not "perceived."

By contrast, the memory inference program written by Rieger (1975) to interface with Riesbeck's analyzer leans toward the immediate and explicit assertion of all expectations and inferences as soon as they are generated. The inferences in Rieger's program are concerned with the filling in of innumerable missing specifications in the input: unstated objects, locations, causes, enablement conditions, results, motives, intentions, and so on. This "filling-in" process also interacts with and facilitates the solution of anaphoric reference problems, which in turn results in the merging of otherwise separate descriptions in the input. By asserting all hypotheses explicitly in working memory, Rieger argues, potentially useful information is made available to the rest of the system, thereby enabling further inferences and connections that might otherwise have remained undiscovered. This strategy is aimed at the greatest possible breadth of inference, intended to simulate reflexlike, parallel, associative processing performed by independent demons or "inference molecules" without any other goal than to increase the richness of interconnecting relations among the information current in working memory. However, because the inference-making process is directly driven by the occurrence of "missing" components—as defined by the template structures of Conceptual Dependency networks—once a missing specification has been filled in, the system does not continue to propose alternative hypotheses for the same slot. Thus, unlike the HEARSAY scheme, working memory in Rieger's program contains only the system's currently unique "best guesses." If a "contradiction" (that is, more than one candidate specification for what is discovered to be the same conceptual slot) is generated, the inferences leading to one or other of these specifications will have to be "unmade." But the system is intended to avoid this kind of backtracking as far as possible. Where a missing specification cannot be unambiguously inferred, a "fuzzy" hypothesis can be asserted in the form of plausible conceptual features of the missing entity, rather than *specific* disjunctive hypotheses, all but one of which (at best) must be incorrect.

Charniak's (1972, 1976) demons and Rieger's (1975) memory molecules have much in common.[1] In both systems, "understanding" is fundamentally a process of establishing relations between the new and what is known already. In understanding even very simple children's stories, listeners evidently must draw on a vast quantity of knowledge about the world in the form of innumerable, partially interconnected facts or expectancies. Many of the expectancies of common-sense knowledge require multiple conditions. Consider something like:

"If it is raining" and
"If person A is outside," then
→ "A will get wet."

---

[1]Strictly, Rieger's memory molecules correspond to what are called "base routines" in Charniak's system.

(Charniak argues that this is a fact about "rain" rather than about "outside," because many other things happen outside, and getting wet is only a small part of them. Nonetheless, it is one of the most noticeable consequences of rain.) Plausibly, many of the inferences people make in understanding stories (or in perceiving real-world events) depend on simultaneous rules of this sort. In Charniak's proposed system, the occurrence of a statement in the data base to the effect that it is raining will activate (among others) the "GET-WET" demon. This demon at once checks to see whether there is any other information in the data base about someone being outside; it will also remain on the lookout for any *new* information to that effect that may turn up later in the text, so long as the "raining" fact continues to be asserted as true of the current context. If it succeeds in finding that someone is outside, the GET-WET demon will then assert (i.e., add as another new fact about the current context) that the person is likely to be wet and that "rain" is the cause. That is, one or more (here causal) dependency links are asserted between the new information and the old.

Rieger's inference molecules also explicitly record in the memory the *inferential* dependencies between hypotheses, their *reasons* and *offspring*, much as in the HEARSAY system. However, given the often demonstrated inability of subjects to discriminate inferences from original statements (or close paraphrases) of a text shortly after reading or listening to it (e.g., Bransford & Johnson, 1973; Kintsch, 1974), it would seem that such information, if it is ever directly represented in memory, must be short-lived.

Related Approaches

The "understanding" systems based on productionlike schemata discussed in the preceding section have been concerned with *linguistic* understanding. But similar ideas have been applied in many other, nonlinguistic domains. One of the most interesting applications of production system design, for example, has been in the field of medical diagnosis and inference (Davis, Buchanan, & Shortliffe, 1975; Shortliffe, 1976). In a very different domain, a recent model of the discovery process in mathematics (Lenat, 1976) has impressive results to show for a "ruminant" form of production-based inference in many respects similar to Rieger's. Operating with some 250 heuristic production rules and a starting base of about 100 "simple" mathematical concepts, Lenat's program explores different facets of these concepts, discovering new ones and new relations between them as it goes along. It attempts these exploratory tasks in order of their "interestingness," abandoning them when the computational time or effort needed exceeds the expected interest of the results. In the course of its ruminations, Lenat's program more than doubled its initial stock of usable mathematical concepts, including more than a score of "winners" (Goldbach's conjecture that every even number is the sum of two primes, for example), having first had to discover natural and prime numbers from an initial knowledge base containing nothing about them.

In computer vision, the junction labeling and selection rules, which were the minimal units of knowledge in the "model-free" scene-analysis programs of Clowes (1971), Huffman (1971), and Waltz (1975), in essence served the function of local demons whose action was to constrain or veto hypotheses about adjacent picture lines and to assert relationships between different levels of representation—picture lines to three-dimensional edges and corners.

Last, but certainly not least, the meta-DENDRAL program for interpreting protein X-ray crystallographic data, referred to earlier (Nii & Feigenbaum, 1977), has adopted many of the control-structure characteristics used in HEARSAY II. Among others, these are: production rule representation of knowledge, including strategic or "attentional" rules; a globally accessible "blackboard"; and multiple levels of representation of the solution hypothesis.

In neuronal terms, there is good reason to believe that brains are organized in such a way as to construct an enduring record of every contingency (or causal relationship) that is encountered and encoded as such, a record that can subsequently be reactivated by independent, self-addressed "interrogatory pathways" (Uttley, 1976a, 1976b). At the behavioral level, the idea that conditioning or learning is essentially a process of establishing expectancies about the consequences either of environmental events or of an organism's own actions is by no means new but has recently received vigorously renewed attention from learning theorists (e.g., Bolles, 1972; Mackintosh, 1977). Mackay (1956, 1965) has for long argued that propositional knowledge can be represented in behavioral systems as a collection of specifiable "conditional readinesses." Clearly, as a model for "primary process" cognition in living organisms, the uniform representation of knowledge as a vast assemblage of self- or content-addressable production rules has certain promising features.

Summary

To recapitulate, a number of recent approaches in artificial intelligence have included, with varying degrees of transparency, two very simple principles of organization. These are: (1) the modular representation of knowledge ("semantic memory") in the form of independent and unordered condition → action contingencies, or expectancy demons; and (2) the channeling of all interaction between demons through a single, globally accessible, working memory. The remainder of this essay seeks to relate these principles of organization, which have "evolved" or been found to be effective in a number of different domains of artificial intelligence, to certain otherwise paradoxical or at the least puzzling aspects of human perception, attention, and memory. In order to set reasonable bounds on the discussion, however, it is focused principally on linguistic, and particularly lexical, processing.

PREATTENTIVE PROCESSES AND CONSCIOUS PERCEPTION

Some Implications for Linguistic Processing

The principles of organization just summarized lead me to propose the following interpretation of lexical—and semantic—memory and its role in perception.

1. The mental lexicon consists of a vast array of functionally independent demons, which can be directly activated by sensory or other events.

2. Activation of a lexical demon, as in Riesbeck's (1975) analyzer described in the preceding section, sets up numerous referential and syntagmatic expectations, or conditional readinesses, regarding other sensory or conceptual events. These expectations manifest themselves *indirectly* in behavior through their effects on the processing of other linguistic stimuli. However, demon activation remains wholly tacit and preattentive—without resource limitations and without awareness.

3. Every word stimulus reaching the senses (and not subject to peripheral masking or similar data-limiting degradation) will activate its corresponding lexical demon, independently of other concurrent linguistic processing.

4. The perception of sentence meaning, and for that matter the perception of anything, depends on interactions between many such schemata. According to the PS metaphor, interactions between demons can only occur via the constructions that they collaboratively build in a centralized message center, or "working memory." Although activation of lexical demons is assumed to be essentially without resource limitations, synthesis of a conceptualization representing the meaning of the sentence is not. In most instances, it must be presumed, construction of a sentence meaning will involve competing interactions between many alternative demons evoked by the same word forms and will require complex processes of conflict resolution and scheduling, which may themselves compete for limited processing resources.

The following section summarizes some of the psychological evidence relevant to the *preattentive* activation of semantically based expectancies and to some other consequences of the modular organization of functionally independent, specialist processors.

Preattentive Semantic Processing

The experimental literature on reading and listening points to a clear distinction between the semantic processing of isolated words, which occurs with respect to both "attended" and "unattended" lexical stimuli, and the further interactive and necessarily selective processing needed for the construction of sentence meanings and for conscious episodic reports.

Many experimental results testify to the severe limitations on the understanding of more than one sentence presented concurrently, including when they are delivered to different sensory modalities (e.g., Mowbray, 1953; Spelke, Hirst, & Neisser, 1976). In context, subjects seldom perceive the systematic ambiguity of homophones or homographs (Mackay, 1966), yet a variety of behavioral indicators show that both word senses have been activated (e.g., Conrad, 1974; Warren & Warren, 1976). Presented simultaneously with other linguistic stimuli, even unrelated words are seldom available for subsequent direct recall or recognition (Glucksberg & Cowen, 1970); although the concurrent processing of equally demanding *nonlinguistic* information does not have the same damaging effect (Allport, Antonis, & Reynolds, 1972).

In contrast to this there are numerous observations of *indirect*, semantically mediated effects of individual, unattended words. Thus, peripherally presented words that the subject cannot explicitly report nevertheless can bias the semantic interpretation of attended words (e.g., Bradshaw, 1974; Willows & MacKinnon, 1973). Some of the best known results of this kind have been obtained in the dichotic listening paradigm, where words delivered to the unattended ear have been reported to bias the interpretation of words in an attended (orally shadowed) sentence (Mackay, 1973); to delay, or in some circumstances to facilitate, the oral repetition of semantically similar words (Bryden, 1972; Lewis, 1970, 1972; Treisman, Squire, & Green, 1974); and selectively to release autonomic responses previously associated with a given semantic category (Corteen & Dunn, 1974; Corteen & Wood, 1972; von Wright, Anderson, & Stenman, 1975; but see also Wardlaw & Kroll, 1976, for a failure to replicate).

There need be no episodic awareness of the lexical stimuli producing these semantic effects. Some of the most dramatic illustrations of this have been obtained with visual pattern masking, as follows. The associative priming effects studied by Meyer and others (Meyer, Schvaneveldt, & Ruddy, 1975) provide a rather clear example of *expectancy* in lexical processing. In an elegant series of experiments, Marcel has shown that the same associative, semantic effects occur also with respect to pattern-masked words of whose identity, or even presence, the subject remains unaware (Marcel, 1974, and in press; Marcel & Patterson, 1978). The criterion of masking for these experiments was severe: Onset asynchrony between word and pattern mask was adjusted such that performance was at chance level in forced-choice decisions regarding the graphemic constituents of the masked word or even in determining whether on each trial a letter string had or had not been presented prior to the masking stimulus. Yet the effect of semantic association between the masked stimulus and another word presented subsequently for lexical decision was effectively the same as if the priming stimulus had been presented normally. Repeated presentation of priming word and mask increased the absolute magnitude of the facilitation effect without affecting the subject's inability to report the masked stimulus or even to detect its presence. Elsewhere I have reported data of a similar nature, showing evidence of simultaneous semantic access on the part of several words in a pattern-masked array (Allport, 1977). In one experiment the probability of correctly identifying a centrally presented target word was found to increase with the simultaneous presentation of a semantically related, but unperceived pattern-masked word. Because the results depended on the relation of meaning between the two words, evidently some meaning-based interpretation of *both* words must have occurred. In other experiments an array of words was masked such that only *one* word on the average could be explicitly identified from each array. Given a prespecified semantic category, the subjects were able to report *selectively* the one instance of that category in the array, again suggesting parallel access by word stimuli to the semantic domain prior to the stage at which perceptual selection occurs.

Perceptual Integration

These results and many others for which there is not enough space here to review, strongly favor the interpretation of independent lexical demons activated preattentively. What the experimental results just described also very clearly indicate is that *activation of lexical or semantic demons is not in itself a sufficient condition for conscious perception of a word*, or for the control of an explicit naming response. What more is needed?

Considerations of pattern masking led to the suggestion (Allport, 1977) that what is needed is for the outputs of different, preattentive specialist domains of processing (lexical, phonological, orthographic, spatial . . .) to be recombined, or integrated. According to this view, conscious perception of a visually presented word (rather than of a row of squiggles) is contingent on the outcome of this integration process. Thus, unless labeled by lexical or other high-level codes, the visually complex contours of a tachistoscopic word-array cannot be economically represented in terms of visual attributes alone. Consequently, though the subject may detect the presence of complex, letterlike forms, their details will be almost instantaneously forgotten. Conversely, the output of a lexical demon, in the absence of an appropriate visual code and more particularly in the presence of an inappropriate one (resulting, for example, from an after-coming pattern mask), will be vetoed by the integration mechanism. The word is not "seen." In terms of this model, the maximum rate of gain of named or identified items from a multi-item, pattern-masked array is limited directly by the rate at which this process of perceptual integration can operate.

Somewhat related suggestions for a process of perceptual verification have been made recently by Becker and Killion (1977). These and similar proposals and the evidence supporting them have been reviewed elsewhere (Allport, in press). Treisman, Sykes, and Gelade (1977) describe data from visual search tasks suggesting that the detection of arbitrary or unfamiliar *conjunctions* of stimulus attributes requires a spatially sequential integration performed over one object or spatial region at a time. In contrast, where the mapping between compound stimuli and responses is highly practiced and consistent, it appears that spatially parallel, preattentive processes are directly able to initiate a simple overt response (Shiffrin & Schneider, 1977). In a variety of visual search tasks, detection of the target items is found to be faster if the nontargets are drawn from a different symbolic category. In some cases the time to detect a target is independent of the number of nontargets, consistent with spatially parallel, independent access to category information (e.g., Egeth, Jonides, & Wall, 1972; Jonides & Gleitman, 1972, 1976; Schneider & Shiffrin, 1977; but see also Logan, 1978).

Temporal and Spatial Dissociations

If semantic memory is indeed organized as an assemblage of self-activating, asynchronous, parallel processes, we might expect under appropriate conditions to observe temporal dissociations between concurrent domains of processing. Something of this kind appears to be reflected in a phenomenon first reported by Lawrence (1971) and since repeated with interesting variations by Broadbent (1977). In Lawrence's experiment a list of unrelated words appeared on a screen in rapid sequence one after another in the same position in space. One word in the sequence appeared in capital letters, whereas all the rest were in lower case; and the observer attempted to name the capitalized word. Viewed as a search task, the criterion for detecting a target was thus specified in one domain in terms of the characteristics of the letter shape or typography, whereas the subject's overt response depended on the lexical domain of name identity. At rapid rates of presentation, these distinct and *ex hypothesi* functionally independent domains of processing can get out of step, as Lawrence's data testifies. At a presentation rate of 16–20 words per sec, over 70% of all errors made by his subjects consisted of reporting *as the capitalized target item* words that had either closely followed or preceded it in the sequence. The incidence of these displacement errors peaked sharply on the word immediately next in time after the target item, and in this case Lawrence's subjects were apparently quite confident that they were in fact reporting the capitalized word. Evidently, at these high rates of presentation, "category states" depending respectively on typographic form and on lexical identity could not always be correctly integrated, although both were successfully activated independently.

Simultaneous presentation of several adjacent, unrelated words, all of which are pattern masked, can produce dislocation of a different kind between incompletely categorized (graphemic) information on one hand and information about spatial position on the other. In reporting what they have seen in a briefly exposed pattern-masked array of words, subjects commonly describe the appearance in a given position of words or pseudowords made up of letters actually drawn from several different widely separate locations. These wandering letters and letter clusters—products of an incomplete, and erroneous, perceptual integration—still preserve their original segmental status (initial, medial, etc.) in their new, miscegenated union (Allport, 1977; Shallice & McGill, 1978).

Primary Memory and Perceptual Integration

The preceding sections reviewed necessarily briefly and selectively some of the evidence taken chiefly from visual information processing, favoring a view of lexical and semantic memory as a distributed, content-addressable system open to all incoming stimuli, essentially without capacity limitations. Many students of human information-processing from Deutsch and Deutsch (1963) onward, have been led to broadly similar conclusions on the basis of a wide variety of experimental evidence, although not all current theories of semantic memory share these assumptions (Collins & Loftus, 1975, as representative).

Our brief survey also pointed to the crucial status of a mechanism of perceptual integration whereby information generated preattentively in independent processing domains was recombined as a condition of episodic awareness. The products of this integrative process, we proposed, define the contents of current consciousness, or *primary memory*. The evidence that was reviewed indicated very strongly that activation of a unit in semantic memory was not a sufficient condition for perception of the corresponding entity (a word, for example).

This conclusion conflicts radically with a very widely held assumption, namely that the momentarily activated set of structures in semantic memory constitutes, *per se*, the contents of primary memory (e.g., Norman, 1968; Schneider & Shiffrin, 1977, among many). It may be worthwhile, therefore, to recapitulate some of the reasons why this latter view of primary memory, or episodic consciousness, cannot be adequate.

As currently conceived, the principal function of semantic memory is to represent an individual's knowledge about categories of environmental events or objects and their relations and contingencies. The mapping of sensory stimuli into semantic memory, seen in this light, is therefore before all else a process of *categorizing* stimuli, a process that perforce loses information from the sensory domain. Morton's *logogen* model (1968, in press), for example, is intended to schematize such a mapping, from surface linguistic stimuli to lexical and conceptual memory. The output from a given logogen unit (or lexical demon) is always the same abstract "category state," which conveys no further information about the nonlexical sensory attributes of the particular stimulus that excited it. Such a mechanism *by itself* is subject to some peculiarly elementary difficulties even in accounting for the simple naming tasks to which it was originally addressed.

Thus, if two words are simultaneously, briefly displayed, each perhaps in a different color or a different typeface, the system has no mechanism for deciding which of the two activated logogen units relates to a particular location or color or appearance. The same problem arises in the Stroop task, where for example red ink may be used to write the word *blue* and a subject is invited to name the color of the ink. Two nodes are supposedly excited in the logogen system. Both represent color names. But no mechanism exists within the categorizing system to distinguish which of the two specifies the correct name to be produced. Yet subjects can perform these simple tasks correctly.

Similar difficulties are encountered by all models of recognition (or, equivalently, of access to semantic memory) that depend uniquely on a process of feature or category filtering. The prototype of such models is Selfridge's (1959) *Pandemonium*, which has explicitly or implicitly dominated so much psychological and for that matter neurophysiological thinking over the past two decades on recognition. I am not aware that these difficulties have been discussed elsewhere, particularly in relation to primary memory, although a variety of other shortcomings of Pandemoniumlike mechanisms are well documented (Henderson, 1978; Minsky & Papert, 1969). A related and very interesting discussion is given by Treisman et al. (1977).

The problem, put crudely, is this. Once the sensory input has been dismembered into attributes and categories, how to put Humpty together again? For manifestly, the act of recognizing is more than merely assigning a stimulus pattern to a particular category. In subjective experience, as in the evidence of behavior, both sensory and conceptual information from many different domains and levels of abstraction is *integrated.*

One suggestion that has been canvassed is that the activated type-nodes in semantic memory are somehow "tagged" with pointers to the other sensory attributes and concurrently activated categories that are contextually "associated" with them. However, the problem of determining (in anything other than the most factitiously impoverished sensory and cognitive context) *which* among the multitude of concurrently activated categories and attributes *goes with which* appears to raise over again the problem of perceptual integration (or the relationship of episodic to semantic memory) that this suggestion was presumably intended to solve.

An alternative possibility based on the PS metaphor in a sense reverses this suggestion: Lexical and other category states compete to "label" items in current sensory memory. First, that is, the interactions between independent demons depend not on the establishment of individual demon–demon associations but are channeled through one centralized data base. Second, according to the model we are here exploring, the centralized data base is organized in terms of temporal (as in the HEARSAY system) and *spatial* dimensions of the sensory input, either somatotopically or in relation to environmental space (Turvey, 1977). Following the HEARSAY terminology, we can call this centralized data base the "blackboard." All perceptual integration thus converges on and is organized in relation to the sensory input, which is represented initially at the lowest level of the blackboard. Third, perceptual reports, or conscious identification of stimuli, depend wholly on information asserted at the appropriate level *on the blackboard.*

Finally, it seems necessary to assume that the process of integration, in contrast to the activation of independent cognitive demons, involves severe resource limitations.

Division of Attention

Many aspects of selective attention find natural representation in this PS framework in terms of differing priority assignments on demons and their requests and in terms of priorities on specific locations or data structures on the blackboard. Any events activating demons whose actions carry sufficiently high positive or negative value for the organism should be able to interrupt current processing, and thereby obtain global evaluation for themselves.

It is tempting to think of the *limits* of attention as reflecting the total capacity of one, unique blackboard—the hypothetical "working memory" par excellence. However, as against this are several demonstrations of the simultaneous performance of two or more complex, skilled tasks, each of which is being performed at apparently resource-limiting rates, yet without appreciable mutual interference (e.g., Allport et al., 1972; Shaffer, 1975; Spelke, Hirst, & Neisser, 1976). Clearly the capacity limits responsible for setting an upper bound to the rate or fidelity of performance in each of the tasks individually cannot be the same as those that set an upper bound (if one is observable) in their combined performance.

One feature of the particular task-combinations that seems to be critical for successful "division of attention" is that the respective tasks should not compete for the same modalities either in encoding or output (see McLeod, 1978; Shaffer, 1975). Should we then envisage a number of separate, modality-specific blackboards? Manifestly, information proper to different modalities can be integrated in perception and performance. Perhaps we should think therefore in terms of distinct *dimensions* of one global blackboard organized with respect to the different modalities of input and output. I suspect that the difficulties in dividing attention may have at least as much to do with the difficulty of keeping separate two or more disjunct data structures—in terms of which the conflicts and choices of demon–demon interaction can be resolved—as with the limited "space" available on the blackboard or (still less) with any sort of overall limit in terms of bits-per-second. The HEARSAY II program makes use of a number of computational devices of write-locking and tagging to freeze regions of the blackboard while a particular knowledge source is preparing to act on them. If such facilities are denied to biological computation, the only simple way of avoiding global data-base access interference may be by ensuring that the concurrent data demands are disjoint. So long as the input–output and translational demands of concurrent tasks can remain adequately insulated from each other so that no stimuli proper to one task activate schemata pertinent to another and no actions in the response domain of one task are requested by schemata active in the other, there need be no mutual competition. Strict modality separation may be merely part of a conveniently simple recipe for achieving this.

Amnesia

Under certain conditions of "inattention" or of attention to something else, arbitrary or novel configurations of sense data may come and go on the blackboard without any appropriate schemata being combined or synthesized anew to account for them, even though subpatterns in the data may have passively evoked separate demons individually. If the configurations are novel or arbitrary, any expectancies these subpatterns may set up are unlikely to succeed, without being modified, in accounting for the rest of the configuration. Hence there is no "percept," no memory, for the particular configuration, though there may still be for its constituents. Rock, Schauer, and Halper (1976) have described some ingenious and simple demonstrations of exactly this, using random curved and angular forms. Under appropriately manipulated "inattention" on the part of their subjects, they find memory for the constituent *types* of angularity and contour and no memory at all for their *configuration*.

Wishful Thinking

The issue just touched on here, of what is involved in the modification or synthesis of new schemata in order to account for novel events, takes us into what must surely be the most central problem in the whole of psychology, and certainly beyond the scope of this essay. Tulving (this volume) has surveyed the contribution of what might be called the *Ebbinghaus tradition* to our understanding of the learning process. If we restrict ourselves, as he does, to the theoretical advances achieved strictly within that tradition, it is difficult not to concur in his bleak evaluation. Within the computational paradigm, theoretical explorations of learning as anything other than a form of parameter adjustment have begun only very recently (for example, Collins, 1976; Moore & Newell, 1974; Nii & Feigenbaum, 1977; Sussman, 1975; Winston, 1975; Young, in press; cf Smith, Mitchell, Chestek, & Buchanan, 1977). As the theme of this conference invites us to look forward to the next 500 years of psychological research, I offer this conjecture—that work growing out of this as yet small but vigorous start will unlock those theoretical developments in the study of memory for which psychologists in the Ebbinghaus tradition have long ceased even daring to hope.

REFERENCES

Abelson, R. P. The structure of belief systems. In R. C. Schank & K. M. Colby (Eds.), *Computer models of thought and language.* San Francisco: Freeman, 1973.

Allport, D. A. The state of cognitive psychology. *Quarterly Journal of Experimental Psychology*, 1975, *27*, 141–152.

Allport, D. A. On knowing the meaning of words we are unable to report: The effects of visual masking. In S. Dornic (Ed.), *Attention and Performance VI*. Hillsdale, N.J.: Lawrence Erlbaum Associates, 1977.

Allport, D. A. Word recognition in reading. In P. A. Kolers, M. E. Wrolstad & H. Bouma (Eds.), *Processing of visible language 1*. New York: Plenum Press, in press.

Allport, D. A., Antonis, B., Reynolds, P. On the division of attention: A disproof of the single-channel hypothesis. *Quarterly Journal of Experimental Psychology*, 1972, *24*, 225–235.

Barbour, I. G. *Myths, models and paradigms: the nature of scientific and religious language.* London: SCM Press, 1974.

Baylor, G. W., & Gascon, J. An information-processing theory of aspects of the development of weight seriation in children. *Cognitive Psychology*, 1974, *6*, 1–40.

Becker, C. A., & Killion, T. H. Interaction of visual and cognitive effects in word recognition. *Journal of Experimental Psychology: Human Perception and Performance*, 1977, *3*, 389–401.

Becker, J. D. A model for the encoding of experiential information. In R. C. Schank and K. M. Colby (Eds.), *Computer models of thought and language.* San Francisco: Freeman, 1973.

Black, M. *Models and metaphors.* Ithaca, N.Y.: Cornell University Press, 1962.

Blakemore, C., Muncey, J. P. J., & Ridley, R. M. Stimulus specificity in the human visual system. *Vision Research*, 1973, *13*, 1915–1931.

Bobrow, D. G., & Norman, D. A. Some principles of memory schemata. In D. G. Bobrow & A. Collins (Eds.), *Representation and understanding: Studies in cognitive science.* New York: Academic Press, 1975.

Bobrow, D. G., & Winograd, T. An overview of KRL, a knowledge representation language. *Cognitive Science,* 1977, *1*, 3–46.

Bolles, R. C. Reinforcement, expectancy, and learning. *Psychological Review*, 1972, *79*, 394–409.

Booth, D. Language acquisition as the addition of verbal routines. In P. T. Smith & R. N. Campbell (Eds.), *Psychology of language,* New York: Plenum Press, 1978.

Bradshaw, J. L. Peripherally presented and unreported words may bias the perceived meaning of a centrally fixated homograph. *Journal of Experimental Psychology*, 1974, *103*, 1200–1202.

Bransford, J. D., & Johnson, M. K. Considerations of some problems of comprehension. In W. G. Chase (Ed.), *Visual information processing.* New York: Academic Press, 1973.

Broadbent, D. E. Stimulus set and response set: Two kinds of selective attention. In D. I. Mostofsky (Ed.), *Attention: Contemporary theory and analysis.* New York: Appleton-Century-Crofts, 1970.

Broadbent, D. E. The hidden preattentive processes. *American Psychologist*, 1977, *32*, 109–118.

Brooks, L. *Non-analytic concept formation and memory for instances.* Social Science Research Council Conference on Human Categorization, 1976.

Bryden, M. P. *Perceptual strategies, attention, and memory in dichotic listening* (Res. Rep. No. 43). Waterloo, Ontario, Canada: University of Waterloo, Dept. of Psychology, December 1972.

Burns, B. D. *The uncertain nervous system.* London: Edward Arnold, 1968.

Charniak, E. *Towards a model of children's story comprehension* (Tech. Rep. AI-266). Cambridge, Mass.: M.I.T., 1972.

Charniak, E. Inference and knowledge II. In E. Charniak & Y. Wilks (Eds.), *Computational semantics.* Amsterdam: North-Holland, 1976.

Charniak, E., & Wilks, Y. (Eds.) *Computational semantics.* Amsterdam: North-Holland, 1976.

Cheatham, T. E. Jr. The unexpected impact of computers on science and mathematics. *Proceedings of Symposium in Applied Mathematics*, 1974, *20*, 67–75.

Clowes, M. B. On seeing things. *Artificial Intelligence*, 1971, *2*, 79–116.

Collins, A. Processes in acquiring knowledge. In R. C. Anderson, R. J. Spiro, W. E. Montague (Eds.), *Schooling and the acquisition of knowledge.* Hillsdale, N.J.: Lawrence Erlbaum Associates, 1976.

Collins, A. M.,, & Loftus, E. F. A spreading-activation theory of semantic processing. *Psychological Review*, 1975, *82*, 407–428.

Conrad, C. Context effects in sentence comprehension: A study of the subjective lexicon. *Memory & Cognition*, 1974, *2*, 130–138.

Corteen, R. S., & Dunn, D. Shock-associated words in a nonattended message: A test for momentary awareness. *Journal of Experimental Psychology*, 1974, *102*, 1143–1144.

Corteen, R. S., & Wood, B. Autonomic responses to shock-associated words in an unattended channel. *Journal of Experimental Psychology*, 1972, *94*, 308–313.

Davis, R., Buchanan, B. G., & Shortliffe, E. H. *Production rules as a representation for a knowledge-based consultation program.* Stanford, Calif.: Stanford University, October 1975. (AI Memo 266, Computer Science Department.)

Davis, R., & King, J. An overview of Production Systems. In machine representations of knowledge. Dordrecht, Netherlands: D. Reidel, 1976. (Also published as Memo AIM-271, Stanford Artificial Intelligence Laboratory, October 1975.)

Deutsch, J. A., & Deutsch, D. Attention: Some theoretical considerations. *Psychological Review*, 1963, *70*, 80–90.

Egeth, H., Jonides, J., & Wall, S. Parallel processing of multielement displays. *Cognitive Psychology*, 1972, *3*, 674–698.

Feigenbaum, E. A., Buchanan, B. G., & Lederberg, J. On generality and problem-solving: A case study using the DENDRAL program. In B. Meltzer & D. Michie (Eds.), *Machine intelligence* (Vol. 6). Edinburgh, Scotland: Edinburgh University Press, 1971.

Fennell, R. D., & Lesser, V. R. Parallelism in AI problem solving: A case study of Hearsay II. Pittsburgh, Pa: Carnegie-Mellon University, Computer Science Department, October 1975.

Garner, W. R. The effect of absolute size on the separability of the dimensions of size and brightness. *Bulletin of the Psychonomic Society*, 1977, *9*, 380–382.

Geschwind, N. Disconnexion syndromes in animals and men. *Brain*, 1965, *88*, 237–294; 585–644.

Glucksberg, S., & Cowen, G. N. Memory for nonattended auditory material. *Cognitive Psychology*, 1970, *1*, 149–156.

Hawkins, H. L. Parallel processing in complex visual discrimination. *Perception & Psychophysics*, 1969, *5*, 56–64.

Hayes-Roth, F., & Lesser, V. R. *Focus of attention in a distributed-logic speech understanding system.* Pittsburgh, Pa.: Carnegie-Mellon University, Computer Science Department, January 1976.

Henderson, L. Pandemonium and visual search. *Perception*, 1978, *7*, 97–104.

Hewitt, C. PLANNER: A language for manipulating models and proving theorems in a robot. Cambridge, Mass: M.I.T., 1970, AI Memo 168.

Hewitt, C., Bishop, P., & Steiger, R. *A universal modular ACTOR formalism for artificial intelligence.* Proceedings of the Third International Joint Conference on Artificial Intelligence, Stanford Research Institute, Stanford, Calif., 1973.

Huffman, D. A. Impossible objects as nonsense sentences. In B. Meltzer & D. Michie (Eds.), *Machine intelligence* (6). Edinburgh, Scotland: Edinburgh University Press, 1971.

Jonides, J., & Gleitman, H. A conceptual category effect in visual search: O as a letter or a digit. *Perception & Psychophysics*, 1972, *12*, 457–460.

Jonides, J., & Gleitman, H. The benefit of categorization in visual search: Target location without identification. *Perception & Psychophysics*, 1976, *20*, 289–298.

Kintsch, W. *The representation of meaning in memory.* Hillsdale, N.J.: Lawrence Erlbaum Associates, 1974.

Lawrence, D. H. Two studies of visual search for word targets with controlled rate of presentation. *Perception & Psychophysics*, 1971, *10*, 85–89.

Lenat, D. B. *AM: An artificial intelligence approach to discovery in mathematics as heuristic search.* Ph. D. thesis, Artificial Intelligence Laboratory, Stanford University, Stanford, Calif., July 1976.

Lesser, V. R., Fennell, L. D., Erman, L. D., & Reddy, D. R. *Organization of the Hearsay II speech understanding system.* Proceedings of IEEE Symposium on Speech Recognition, Carnegie-Mellon University, Pittsburgh, Pa., April 1974.

Lewis, J. L. Semantic processing of unattended messages using dichotic listening. *Journal of Experimental Psychology*, 1970, *85*, 225–228.

Lewis, J. L. Semantic processing with bisensory stimulation. *Journal of Experimental Psychology*, 1972, *96*, 455–457.

Logan, G. D. Attention in character-classification tasks: Evidence for automaticity of component stages. *Journal of Experimental Psychology: General*, 1978, *107*, 32–63.

Luria, A. R. *Basic problems of neurolinguistics.* The Hague: Mouton, 1976.

Mackay, D. G. To end ambiguous sentences. *Perception & Psychophysics*, 1966, *1*, 426–436.

Mackay, D. G. Aspects of the theory of comprehension, memory and attention. *Quarterly Journal of Experimental Psychology*, 1973, *25*, 27–40.

Mackay, D. M. Towards an information-flow model of human behavior. *British Journal of Psychology*, 1956, *47*, 30–43.

Mackay, D. M. From mechanism to mind. In J. R. Smythies (Ed.), *Brain and mind.* London: Routledge and Kegan Paul, 1965.

Mackintosh, N. J. Conditioning as the perception of causal relations. In R. Butts & J. Hintikka (Eds.), *Logic, methodology and philosophy of science.* Dordrecht, Netherlands: D. Reidel, 1977.

Maffei, L., & Fiorentini, A. Spatial frequency rows in the striate visual cortex. *Vision Research*, 1977, *17*, 257–264.

Marcel, A. J. Some constraints on sequential and parallel processing, and the limits of attention. *Acta Psychologica*, 1970, *33*, 77–92.

Marcel, A. J. *Perception with and without awareness.* Paper presented to meeting of Experimental Psychology Society, Stirling, Scotland, July 1974.

Marcel, A. J. Conscious and unconscious reading: The effects of visual masking on word perception. *Cognitive Psychology*, in press.

Marcel, T., & Patterson, K. Word recognition and production: Reciprocity in clinical and normal studies. In J. Requin (Ed.), *Attention & performance VII.* Hillsdale, N.J.: Lawrence Erlbaum Associates, 1978.

Marin, O. S. M., Saffran, E. M., & Schwartz, M. F. Dissociations of language in aphasia: Implications for normal function. *Annals of the New York Academy of Sciences*, 1976, *280*, 868–884.

Marr, D. Early processing of visual information. *Philosophical Transactions of the Royal Society, B*, 1976, 275.

McLeod, P. Does probe RT measure central processing demand? *Quarterly Journal of Experimental Psychology*, 1978, *30*, 83–89.

Meyer, D. E., Schvaneveldt, R. W., & Ruddy, M. G. Loci of contextual effects on visual word recognition. In P. M. A. Rabbitt & S. Dornic (Eds.), *Attention and Performance V.* London: Academic, 1975.

Minsky, M. A framework for representing knowledge. In P. H. Winston (Ed.), *The psychology of computer vision.* New York: McGraw–Hill, 1975.

Minsky, M., & Papert, S. *Perceptrons: An introduction to computational geometry.* Cambridge, Mass.: MIT Press, 1969.

Moore, J., & Newell, A. How can Merlin understand? In L. W. Gregg (Ed.), *Knowledge and cognition.* Potomac, Md.: Lawrence Erlbaum Associates, 1974.

Morton, J. Consideration of grammar and computation in language behavior. In J. C. Catford (Ed.), *Studies in language and language behavior.* Washington, D.C.: U.S. Office of Education, Progress Report VI, 1968.

Morton, J. Word recognition. In J. Morton & J. C. Marshall (Eds.), *Psycholingustics series II.* London: Elek Scientific Books, in press.

Mowbray, G. H. Simultaneous vision and audition: The comprehension of prose passages of varying levels of difficulty. *Journal of Experimental Psychology,* 1953, *46,* 365–372.

Neisser, U. *Cognition and reality.* San Francisco: Freeman, 1976.

Newell, A. You can't play 20 Questions with nature and win. In W. G. Chase (Ed.), *Visual information processing.* New York: Academic Press, 1973. (a)

Newell, A. Production systems: Models of control structures. In W. G. Chase (Ed.), *Visual information processing.* New York: Academic Press, 1973. (b)

Newell, A., & Simon, H. *Human problem solving.* Englewood Cliffs, N.J.: Prentice-Hall, 1972.

Newell, A., & Simon, H. Computer science as an empirical enquiry: Symbols and search. *Communications of the Association for Computing Machinery,* 1976, *19,* 113–126.

Nii, H. P., & Feigenbaum, E. A. *Rule-based understanding of signals,* Stanford, Calif.: Stanford University, (Tech. Rep. HPP-77-7). Computer Science Department, June 1977.

Norman, D. A. Toward a theory of memory and attention. *Psychological Review,* 1968, *75,* 522–536.

Reddy, R., & Newell, A. Knowledge and its representation in a speech understanding system. In L. W. Gregg (Ed.), *Knowledge and cognition.* Potomac, Md.: Lawrence Erlbaum Associates, 1974.

Rieger, C. J. Conceptual memory and inference. In R. C. Schank (Ed.), *Conceptual information processing.* Amsterdam: North-Holland, 1975.

Riesbeck, C. K. Conceptual analysis. In R. C. Schank (Ed.), *Conceptual information processing.* Amsterdam: North-Holland, 1975.

Rock, I., Schauer, R., & Halper, F. Form perception without attention. *Quarterly Journal of Experimental Psychology,* 1976, *28,* 429–440.

Rumelhart, D. E., & Ortony, A. The representation of knowledge in memory. In R. R. C. Anderson, R. J. Spiro, & W. E. Montague (Eds.), *Schooling and the acquisition of knowledge.* Hillsdale, N.J.: Lawrence Erlbaum Associates, 1976.

Russell, S. Computer understanding of metaphorical verbs. *American Journal of Computational Linguistics,* 1976, *44,* 000–000.

Saraga, E., & Shallice, T. Parallel processing of the attributes of single stimuli. *Perception & Psychophysics,* 1973, *13,* 261–270.

Schank, R. C. *Causality and reasoning* (Tech. Rep. No. 1). Castanola, Switzerland: Instituto per gli studi Semantici e Cognitivi, 1973.

Schank, R. C. (Ed.). *Conceptual information processing.* Amsterdam: North-Holland, 1975.

Schank, R. C., & Abelson, R. P. *Scripts, plans, goals and understanding.* Hillsdale, N.J.: Lawrence Erlbaum Associates, 1977.

Schneider, W., & Shiffrin, R. M. Controlled and automatic human information processing: I. Detection, search, and attention. *Psychological Review,* 1977, *84,* 1–66.

Selfridge, O. G. Pandemonium: A paradigm for learning. In *The mechanization of thought processes.* London: H.M. Stationery Office, 1959.

Shaffer, L. H. Multiple attention in continuous verbal tasks. In P. M. A. Rabbitt & S. Dornic (Eds.), *Attention and Performance V.* New York: Academic Press, 1975.

Shallice, T., & McGill, J. The origins of mixed errors. In J. Requin (Ed.), *Attention and Performance VII.* Hillsdale, N.J.: Lawrence Erlbaum Associates, 1978.

Shiffrin, R. M., & Schneider, W. Controlled and automatic human information processing: II. Perceptual learning, automatic attending, and a general theory. *Psychological Review,* 1977, *84,* 127–190.

Shortliffe, E. H. *MYCIN: Computer-based medical consultations.* New York, Amsterdam, Oxford: Elsevier, 1976.

Sloman, A. Review of D. Marr, Early processing of visual information. *AISB European Newsletter*, 1977, *26*, 17–19.

Smith, D. H. Application of artificial intelligence for chemical inference. *Journal of the American Chemical Society*, 1972, *94*, 5962.

Smith, R. G., Mitchell, T. M., Chestek, R. A., & Buchanan, B. G. A model for learning systems. Stanford Calif.: Stanford University, Computer Science Department, HPP-77-14, June 1977.

Spelke, E., Hirst, W., & Neisser, U. Skills of divided attention. *Cognition*, 1976, *4*, 215–230.

Sussman, G. J. *A computational model of skill acquisition*. Amsterdam: North-Holland, 1975.

Treisman, A. M., Squire, R., & Green, J. Semantic processing in dichotic listening: A replication. *Memory & Cognition*, 1974, *2*, 641–646.

Treisman, a. M., Sykes, M., & Gelade, G. Attention and stimulus integration. In S. Dornic (Ed.), *Attention and performance VI*. Hillsdale, N.J.: Lawrence Erlbaum Associates, 1977.

Turvey, M. T. Contrasting orientations to the theory of visual information processing. *Psychological Review*, 1977, *74*, 67–88.

Uttley, A. M. A two-pathway informon theory of conditioning and adaptive pattern-recognition. *Brain Research*, 1976, *102*, 23–25. (a)

Uttley, A. M. Neurophysiological predictions of a two-pathway informon theory of neural conditioning. *Brain Research*, 1976, *102*, 55–70. (b)

von Wright, J. M., Anderson, K., & Stenman, U. Generalization of conditioned GSRs in dichotic listening. In P. M. A. Rabbitt & S. Dornic (Eds.), *Attention and performance V*. New York: Academic Press, 1975.

Waltz, D. Understanding line drawings of scenes with shadows. In P. H. Winston (Ed.), *The psychology of computer vision*. New York: McGraw-Hill, 1975.

Wardlaw, K. A., & Kroll, N. E. A. Autonomic responses to shock-associated words in a non-attended message: A failure to replicate. *Journal of Experimental Psychology: Human Perception and Performance*, 1976, *3*, 357–360.

Warren, R. E., & Warren, N. T. Dual semantic encoding of homographs and homophones embedded in context. *Memory & Cognition*, 1976, *4*, 586–592.

Waterman, D. A. *Adaptive production systems*. Proceedings of the Fourth International Joint Conference on Artificial Intelligence, Tbilisi, USSR, 1975.

Whitaker, H., & Whitaker, H. L. (Eds.), *Studies in neurolinguistics* (Vols. I–III). New York: Academic Press, 1976.

Wilks, Y. Parsing English II. In E. Charniak & Y. Wilks (Eds.), *Computational semantics*. Amsterdam: North-Holland, 1976. (a)

Wilks, Y. *De Minimis: The archaeology of frames*. Proceedings of Artificial Intelligence and Simulation of Behavior Conference, Edinburgh, Scotland, 1976. (b)

Wilks, Y. *Making preferences more active* (Res. Rep. No. 32). Edinburgh Scotland: Edinburgh, University, Dept. of Artificial Intelligence, 1977.

Willows, D. M., & MacKinnon, G. E. Selective reading: Attention to the "unattended" lines. *Canadian Journal of Psychology*, 1973, *27*, 292–304.

Wing, A., & Allport, D. A. Multidimensional encoding of visual form. *Perception & Psychophysics*, 1972, *12*, 474–476.

Winograd, T. On some contested suppositions of generative linguistics about the scientific study of language. *Cognition*, 1977, *5*, 151–179.

Winston, P. H. Learning structural descriptions from examples. In P. H. Winston (Ed.), *The psychology of computer vision*. New York: McGraw-Hill, 1975.

Young, R. M. Mixtures of strategies in structurally adaptive production systems: Examples from seriation and subtraction (Res. Rep. No. 33). Edinburgh, Scotland: Edinburgh University, Department of Artificial Intelligence, 1977.

Young, R. M. Strategies and the structure of a cognitive skill. In G. Underwood (Ed.), *Strategies of information processing*. London: Academic Press, in press.

PERCEPTUAL PERSPECTIVES

5 Memory Functions in Visual Event Perception

Gunnar Johansson
University of Uppsala, Sweden

BACKGROUND

I come to this symposium on memory not as a theorist in this field but as a student of event perception, especially visual space and motion perception. Admittedly, my reading in the impressive recent development of memory research is both scanty and selective. An important reason for my attempts to keep in touch with this research has been the hope to find, especially in the studies of short-term memory, some new material related to problems met with in my own theoretical work in visual motion perception. I must admit, however, that although this search has given some interesting contact with a field of research with high activity, studies of the type sought have been very rare. It has been hard to avoid the impression that for most students of memory, their research is tantamount to work with alphanumeric material and words. Words, words, and again words. As seen from my own viewpoint these studies deal with a rather special type of memory effects and maybe not with the most essential one. Why concentrate nearly all effort on this highly special and very late manifestation of the biological function termed *memory* and leave perceptual memory outside the sphere of interest? Memory functions in connection with perception probably represent prototypes for the more advanced forms met with in the cognitive sphere of man. My own work in the field of perception has convinced me that there exist highly interesting memory effects in connection with everyday perception. These are possible to study experimentally but represent a field yet hardly more than touched upon. Of course there exist some exceptions to my statement about lack of interest for memory research outside the semantic area—some excellent exceptions, indeed. One such exception is Neisser's (1967) broad perception → memory → cognition approach; another recent one is Turvey's (1977) highly relevant and competent analysis of visual information processing.

The main purpose of my paper is to discuss some problems about relations between event perception and memory. To some extent this discussion has a bearing on the validity of the classification of these functions; thus it touches upon metatheoretical problems. I must admit that another reason for my accepting the invitation to participate in this symposium is the hope of inveigling colleagues on the memory side to pay attention also to memory functions in the perceptual domain.

ABOUT THE TERM "EVENT PERCEPTION"

The title of my paper is *Memory functions in visual event perception.* A short comment on what I mean by the term *visual event perception* may be useful. This term denotes perception of any change of quality, quantity, or position during a chosen interval of time. These intervals may be perceptually very short and the change perceived as stepwise sudden, or the time interval may be longer and the change perceived as being continuous over the interval. The term is not adequate, however, when the rate of stimulus changes is below the perceptual level. For instance, the motion of a shadow caused by the diurnal motion of the sun or the change of daylight caused by the same relative motion do not evoke an immediate perception of change. In such cases, instead, the term *visual event cognition* is more adequate. The organism's information about such long-term changes over time stems from an interplay perception → memory → cognition.

Long ago I introduced the term *event perception* in accordance with the above specification (Johansson, 1950) and studied the perceptual outcome from various types of stimulus changes in various sense modalities. A main result of this investigation was that spatial displacement, i.e., motion, is a highly preferred type of perceptual response. This holds true of course for physically moving stimuli but also for changes in stimulus intensity (brightness, intensity of sound, intensity of pressure, amplitude of vibration, etc.). Spatially separated but temporally coordinated, such changes regularly are perceived as motions, not as changes in intensity; and when it is a question of simultaneous spatial changes, it is the relative displacement that determines the perceptual outcome.

From the above it is evident that stroboscopic motion as studied in our laboratories is regarded as a type of event perception (a sudden change of position) as well as perceived real motion (including movie presentation of real motion).

Because of the biological importance of real motion perception, my interest has been centered about this type of event perception; therefore, my discussion here is mainly restricted to real visual motion.

TIME AS A FUNDAMENTAL DIMENSION
IN VISUAL MOTION PERCEPTION

In physics, time is accepted as a fourth dimension besides the spatial ones; and in our own spontaneous experience as biological organisms, the flow of time stands out as an immediate experience. Strangely enough, however, in the orthodox theory of visual space perception, time never was accepted as a perceptual dimension. This theory originates from Berkeley's analysis of optical information. Berkeley described the visual stimuli as static images projected onto the retinas, and von Helmholtz's theoretical elaborations along the same line gave the theory its well-known orthodox status. In all elementary handbooks it is without exception described as *the* theory.

Because the analyses of space perception with this framework are anchored in description of hypothetical static "images," there generally is no need for the dimension of time in this theory. Consequently, perception was—and still most often is—treated as timeless.

However, motion perception always has brought about great troubles when treated in the framework of the traditional image theory. Usually it was dealt with by describing motion perception as the result of a temporal series of timeless images.

Most students of real motion perception never have been satisfied with this strange and artificial construct. Successively a more and more elaborated alternative type of theory has been advanced. This theory is founded on a description of the visual stimuli in terms of an optical flow rather than as static images. I have in several other connections (e.g., Johansson, 1974, 1975, 1977) treated the flow model as being a far more adequate basis for the theory of visual perception than is afforded by the image model, and here I mainly refer to these publications. The arguments in favor of a flow theory can be summarized as follows.

1. Because of body motions, head motions, and eye movements, the eyes in man and in most other vertebrates seldom are wholly stationary in space.
2. The eye as an optical system has no shutter mechanism like the camera, where it is a necessary device for cutting out images from the optical–spatial flow hitting the lens in a not totally stable camera, working in a not totally static environment.
3. Continuous motion over a receptive field on the retina is followed by a continuous neural response.

4. Technical stabilizing an image on the retina is followed by a rapid fading out of the percept.

These facts in combination indicate that "the retinal image" is a highly artificial construct and that the ordinary visual perception in our daily life is evoked from continuously changing optical stimulation. Therefore, in the following I use the flow model for visual stimulus description and accept a flow theory as a relevant framework for the stimulus → percept analyses.

It is easily understandable that when dealing with problems concerning memory in connection with visual perception, theorists on the memory side have anchored their discussions and theoretical constructs in the traditional static type of perceptual theory. It is understandable from the fact that this theory still forms the framework for most research on visual space perception and is met with in most textbooks. Furthermore, the perceptual material studied in research on memory usually is of image type, like pictures, alphanumeric symbols, or other static forms of pictorial character. As an example, we can choose Neisser's concept "icon." This concept shows that Neisser, in spite of his very promising contributions, also thinks and works in the framework of the image model for visual stimulus description. Therefore, when he touches the problems of motion perception, he must rely on the traditional model and describe motion as a series of "snapshots" integrated by a memory function. In this way perception and memory are separated in accordance with the traditional definitions: The information is *obtained* in series of unchangeable percepts and *stored* and combined by memory acts.[1]

Above I mentioned a recent article by Turvey (1977) as a highly interesting and promising contribution to the discussion of theory in the perception–memory–cognition field. Turvey's position definitely is on the flow theory side, and he gives a number of excellent arguments for this position and against the image type of theory.

At the beginning of this century there was an interesting discussion going on between European psychologists about time and perception. W. Stern coined the term *Präsenszeit* (psychological present) as one denoting certain duration of a percept. This perceptual–temporal effect also was termed *primary memory*, and Stern stressed that the perceptual act should not be regarded as being punctual on the time axis (see a summary in Fröbes, 1923, p. 392 ff.). In studies from these years, the duration of the "psychological present" was maximized to about 5–10 sec. My discussion follows and reflects a position that is related to Stern's.

---

[1]Recently, Neisser (1977) has advanced a theoretical position, not very different from my own, in which he emphasizes that optical transformations due to environmental relative motion must be regarded as a basic correlate to motion perception. Furthermore, he explicitly questions the relevance of the icon concept as related to motion perception (Neisser, 1977, p. 141).

EVENT PERCEPTION AND
THE CLASSIFICATION OF PERCEPTION
AND MEMORY

The traditional classification of the main types of psychological activities says that the organism obtains information from energy impinging on the sensory organs and that this information is retained or stored over longer or shorter periods of time by central processes or in central storages termed *memory*.

The essence of this classification is that these two types of activities in the organism are regarded as mutually exclusive. Such acts must belong either to the perception class or to the memory class, and therefore the snapshot + memory model of processing used by Neisser nicely fits into this traditional scheme. Perceptual "material" is tied together by memory "processing."

When we introduce a flow theory for perception, treating the change itself as a primary stimulus dimension, we find that we meet problems of metatheoretical character concerning the validity of the classical type of definition of perception and memory. If temporal change is a primary dimension of stimulus, it must also be regarded as a dimension of perception itself. This, however, means that we must leave the traditional classification of perception and memory as material contrary to temporal processing and accept—as the concept of *Präsenszeit* indicates—that the spatial information has a temporal extension. Can we accept a memory function "inside" the perception? A positive answer to this question must violate the classification mentioned. From my point of view, however, I can see no alternative; the answer must be "yes." The classical definition of sensory material as a timeless image must be, if not thrown on the scientific rubbish heap, at least locked up in a showcase in the museum for worn-out, scientific tools. In the following section I give some further arguments for this position. Also, the description of short-term memory in terms of storage is hardly acceptable in connection with the perceptual information processing.

EVENT PERCEPTION AS "MEMORY"

Let us start with the phenomenological aspect and an appeal to direct experience. In a demonstration shown at the symposium, a single spot is moving over a video screen and tracing a circle or an ellipse or moving in a more complex, closed path. When the cycle time is very short, say .2 sec, the whole path is seen as a stationary figure but not the spot. The speed of the spot is above the upper temporal resolution threshold of the eye. A cycle time of 2 sec instead gives the percept of a spot moving in the programmed path. We immediately see the form and size of the path, see it without any cognitive inference. What we experience is not a successive remembering and adding of positions passed but just the form of the path of motion. This perception of the form of the path is self-evident when the motion is viewed. The effect is so obvious that in most connections it is regarded as fully trivial.

Such demonstrations of course are demonstrations of Stern's perceptual "present time." The percept has a duration. This is also easily demonstrated when we slow down the speed of the moving dot. At a cycle time of 20 sec the perception of a path has vanished, and we perceive only small, successive parts of the curve.

Such demonstrations can show that within a certain span of angular velocities, simple physical motions evoke a unitary experience. This is an argument for saying that we experience conservation of spatial information over time as a simple perceptual act and that perception in fact is "remembering" as well as "recording." However, a more definite argument for or against the perception-as-memory model should be found in studies about perceptual effects on a temporally liminal level of perceptual recording. Does the nearly instantaneous visual event percept have the character of an icon or an event? In order to get some material for answering this question, I proceed by describing an experiment on tachistoscopic presentations of motion patterns.

PERCEPTUAL EFFECTS OF LIMINAL CHANGES IN THE STIMULUS FLOW

A visual pattern at a certain short moment of time can for the sake of analysis be described as a set of spatial relations between a very great number of optical elements. Such a description represents an "image" when all spatial relations stay constant during this moment of time. This can be said to hold true whether or not the total pattern is displaced during the moment. The essential condition is that the spatial relations within the pattern under study stay constant.

The simplest pattern possible is the set of two elements. It is a well-established fact that when the elements (two or more) are in motion relative to a frame of reference in such a way that the spatial relation between the elements changes simultaneously with their displacements relative to the common frame of reference, the former change is perceived as a within-pattern motion; and the residual component is perceived as a common motion relative to the background. A simple example of this is shown in Fig. 5.1. This perceptual analysis in relative and common motion components is also demonstrated in a film made at the Uppsala laboratory (Maas, 1971).

This effect, which has been described under the term *perceptual vector analysis*, is a totally general effect and the prerequisite for perceiving motion in a rigid world.

FIG. 5.1 Example of perceptual analysis of stimulus motions in common and relative components. *A*. The stimulus pattern. *B*. Diagram of the percept: A vertical line of three dots moves horizontally while one of the dots moves vertically in the line. *C*. A vector analysis of the motion of the second dot corresponding to the percept.

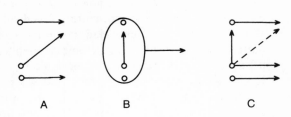

A   B   C

The possibility for the visual system to pick up essential information about even very complex combinations of rigid motions from such nonredundant patterns of elements in motion has been studied, using the motion pattern formed by the human skeleton during walking, etc. Ten to 12 bright spots represented the motion of the main joints of the skeleton (Johansson, 1973; illustrated in Maas, 1971). Such patterns have also been used for a study of the liminal time needed for organization of complex patterns of moving elements (Johansson, 1976). The results of this study have a direct bearing on the present problems.

The typical stimulus pattern in one of the experiments is shown in Fig. 5.2A. Ten moving, bright spots described the motions relative to the

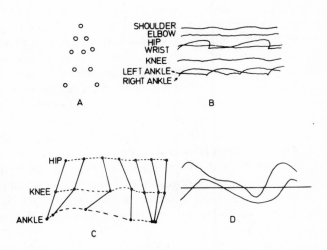

FIG. 5.2 Pattern of element motions representing human walking. *A* shows the typical dot pattern at the moment when both feet are in contact with the floor. *B* is a diagram of the motion tracks of the elements. *C* shows in detail the motions of a leg during one step, and *D* is an example of the pendulum motions of the knee relative to the moving hip and of the ankle relative to the moving knee.

background of the main joints of a man walking in frontoparallel direction. Figure 5.2B shows as an example the motion paths of the hip, knee, and ankle during about 2 sec. The spot pattern was displayed on a video screen during short time intervals, exposing randomly chosen phases of the walking pattern. The series of exposure times chosen was 0.1 sec, 0.2 sec, 0.3 sec, and 0.5 sec presented in this order. The subjects (school youngsters) were totally ignorant about such patterns. Their task was to describe what they saw on the screen during the moment of exposure. As soon as a subject had reported that the motion pattern represented a walking human being, the session was finished and the individual was "stored" in a waiting room till all subjects had passed the experiment. It came out that 40% of the subjects perceived the dot pattern as a walking person at the 0.1-sec interval and no one needed more than 0.2 sec for this perceptual organization of the moving dots. Under the experimental conditions, the displacement of the hip and shoulder spots during 0.1 sec was about 12 min of visual arc (to be compared with the 20/20 visual acuity measure, 1 min).

The outcome of this experiment indicates that the abstracting of (1) relative motions (limb motions) within such a group of moving elements, and (2) common motion representing displacement of the body (a common component motion in all elements relative to the stationary background), must be regarded as an initial perceptual act. It also makes clear that the sensitivity for relative motion within a pattern is very high. (The angular displacement of, for instance, the knee point relative to the hip was of the mean size order of 5–10 min visual angle during 0.1 sec. Therefore the analyses of the experimental results were carried out in terms of vector calculus and hierarchies of moving coordinates systems (see Johansson, 1976). Consequently, perceptual counterparts to vector differentials and their integrals were accepted as adequate constructs on the response side. The instantaneous visual treatment of the interrelations in the stimulus pattern of moving elements, so tremendously complex from a mathematical point of view, hardly can be interpreted in another way. Particularly an interpretation in terms of a primary sensory recording of the positions of the elements and a treatment where each element is remembered as displaced relative to a special reference system in remembered displacements of hierarchies of such systems seems rather absurd. The image + memory model can possibly work only as long as the analysis is limited to the simplest possible type of motion patterns with no relative motion.

When we instead, as I propose, apply the perceptual vector analysis as a descriptive model and accept initial spatio-temporal change as a legitimate description, we have a model for motion perception that at least schematically can cope with the stimulus → percept processes. The consequences for our present problem are evident.

THEORETICAL CONSEQUENCES FOR
THE PERCEPTION-MEMORY PROBLEM

The experiment described strongly supports the hypothesis that continuous relative change over time in the stimulus pattern is the fundamental type of information in space perception. All the motions of the elements are seen as related to each other from the very first moment of presentation or from the onset of relative displacement. The organization of these displacements to a complex figuration in motion seems to be an initial act in the perceptual response. A presentation of the set of light spots without relative motion brings about perception of a meaningless group of such spots. Thus the perception resulting from the relative motions in this set of elements is something more than a memory connection of a sequence of icons. An icon in this stimulus pattern is just the set of spots in a given moment of time, and as already said, this has no resemblance to a walking person. At first, sensory recording of relative spatial *changes* at this moment can bring about perception of walking. Thus, conservation of information over perceptually liminal time is here shown to be a basic characteristic in space and motion perception. Such conservation of information over time is in our traditional vocabulary termed *short-term memory*, and in this meaning perception is memory—memory of spatial relations, not of positions. Only some kind of spatial change over time in a stimulus pattern relative to the retina brings about perception (cf. the fading out of a stabilized retinal image).

In accordance with the perceptual calculus model proposed, we now also assume that the visual system continuously integrates the instantaneous spatial changes over time. The temporal span of this integration is a few seconds, and roughly the "perceptual present" may be regarded as a measure of this span.

We must observe that continuous sensory stimulation is a necessary condition for this perceptual integration. As soon as the actual stimulus flow is interrupted, its event perception ends. Left is only a memory of the perceived event. In this way we get a clear distinction between the perceptual memory function (i.e., perceptual integration) and memory of a percept.

CONCLUDING REMARKS

I started by saying that in my opinion event perception probably would also be a fertile field for memory research. The paper has given my arguments for this position. I have argued that the icon model must be superseded by the flow model. Specifically, I have stressed that a memory component is inseparable from the "material" in visual event perception and that event perception in this meaning *is* memory; I also stress that this perceptual, short-term memory function probably is a basic form of memory and therefore well worth attention from students of memory. Finally, I have said that perception from stimulation that is continuously changing over time is a general type of perception and that ordinarily so-called static perception also is a kind of event perception, because it informs about receiver movements of the head and eyes relative to the stationary surround.

I have anchored my discussion in a treatment of visual event perception. This of course does not imply that I believe that the memory effects treated are limited to vision. On the contrary, we must also assume analogous memory effects in event percepts in other sense domains. Ask another person to trace a simple geometric figure on your palm, and you will find that you are able to recognize the figure if the tracing falls within the span of the "psychological present," just as in the visual demonstration discussed earlier. The recent experiments on tactile vision in Bach-y-Rita's laboratory is also very impressive. In these experiments the subject "looks" at an object or a scene by means of a kind of television camera fixed on spectacle frames. This signal is transformed to a vibrator pattern on a matrix of minute vibrators that are kept in contact with the skin of the abdomen. Spatio-temporal changes in this vibration pattern have been found to carry spatial information about the object or scene "looked" at by the camera. Gibson's "active touch" shows the same effect.

Regarding the field of audition, we can remember a statement from the early study of time perception: the perception of a melody. The continuously changing string of sound from, say, a human voice or a violin represents a close analogy to the continuous spatial change in motion perception. And we all know that these complex variations in tonal quality along the time axis are perceptually integrated to a melody.

REFERENCES

Fröbes, J. *Lehrbuch der experimentellen Psychologie* (Bd. I). Freiburg, West Germany: Herder & Co. 1923

Johansson, G. *Configurations in event perception.* Uppsala: Almqvist & Wiksell, 1950.

Johansson, G. Visual perception of biological motion and a model for its analysis. *Perception & Psychophysics*, 1973, *14*, 201–211.

Johansson, G. Projective transformation as determining visual space perception. In R. B. MacLeod & H. L. Pick, Jr. (Eds.), *Perception: Essays in honor of J. J. Gibson.* Ithaca, N.Y.: Cornell University Press, 1974.

Johansson, G. Visual motion perception. *Scientific American*, 1975, *6*, 76–89.

Johansson, G. Spatio-temporal differentiation and integration in visual motion perception. *Psychological Research*, 1976, *38*, 379–393.

Johansson, G. Spatial constancy and motion in visual perception. In W. Epstein (Ed.), *Stability and constancy in visual perception.* New York: Wiley, 1977.

Maas, J. *Motion perception I, II*. New York: Houghton-Mifflin, 1971. (Films)

Neisser, U. *Cognitive psychology*. New York: Appleton-Century-Crofts, 1967.

Neisser, U. *Cognition and reality*. San Francisco: Freeman, 1977.

Turvey, M. T. Contrasting orientations to the theory of visual information processing. *Psychological Review*, 1977, *84*, 1, 67–88.

6 Convolution and Correlation in Perception and Memory

Bennet B. Murdock, Jr.
University of Toronto

INTRODUCTION

This conference provides an opportunity to see where developments of the past will lead in the future. If we are to look into the future, we can only do so on the basis of present accomplishments. In this paper, I discuss convolution and correlation, two methods of processing information that may be important in human perception and memory. They are methods that have recently found important applications in other areas of information processing (e.g., image processing by computers, holography) and perhaps have relevance to human information processing as well. What I discuss is an abstract model. It may provide a useful way of thinking about how the brain might function.

CONVOLUTION AND CORRELATION

Definitions

Let me start with formal definitions and then try to explain. If we have two continuous functions $f(x)$ and $g(x)$, then the convolution of these two functions may be denoted by the symbol *, and:

$$[f * g] (x) = \int_{-\infty}^{\infty} f(u) \, g(x - u) \, du. \tag{1}$$

The correlation of these two functions may be denoted by the symbol #, and:

$$[f \# g] (x) = \int_{-\infty}^{\infty} f(u) \, g\,(x + u) \, du. \tag{2}$$

If $f(x)$ and $g(x)$ are discrete functions, then for convolution:

$$(f * g)_m = \sum_{i=-\infty}^{\infty} f_i g_{m-i} \tag{3}$$

whereas for correlation:

$$(f \# g)_m = \sum_{i=-\infty}^{\infty} f_i g_{m+i} \tag{4}$$

Useful references are Bracewell (1965) and Borsellino and Poggio (1973).

Basically, convolution and correlation are two ways of combining two different functions. These functions could be any waveforms or frequency distributions, as convolution and correlation may occur in either the temporal or frequency domain. There could be a series of events varying in magnitude from two different sources where these two inputs combine additively in output. Then the resulting output distribution would be the convolution of the two inputs. If we say that the functions to be combined are "events," then in principle it does not matter whether the events are distributed in time or space; nor does it matter whether the events are continuous or discrete. As noted by Bracewell (1965, p. 25), convolution and correlation are sometimes called "functionals" rather than "functions." A function maps one variable into another, whereas a functional maps functions into other functions.

Examples

An illustration from probability theory should be familiar to most psychologists. Suppose $f(x)$ and $g(x)$ are two probability distributions; e.g., $f(x)$ might be the number of 6's occurring when three red dice are thrown, and $g(x)$ might be the number of 6's occurring when two green dice are thrown. Then $(f*g)_m$ gives the combined distribution; i.e., the total number of 6's occurring without regard to color. Two 6's could occur in three different ways: 0–2, 1–1, and 2–0 where the first number is the number of red 6's and the second number is the number of green 6's. Outcomes sum whereas probabilities multiply. In this case, $f(x)$ would be binomial with $n = 3$ and $p = 1/6$; $g(x)$ would be binomial with $n = 2$ and $p = 1/6$; and $(f*g)_m$ would be binomial with $n = 5$ and $p = 1/6$.

A second example comes from a stage analysis of reaction-time distributions. McGill (1963) argued for the importance of a distributional analysis of reaction-time data and showed how moment-generating functions could be used to obviate the necessity for solving convolution integrals. These integrals arise naturally from the stage analysis of reaction-time data; the total reaction time is simply the sum of component stages. The theoretical implications and much experimental data have been summarized and evaluated by Sternberg (1975). Ratcliff and Murdock (1976) have shown that the convolution of two distributions, a normal and an exponential distribution, provides a good empirical fit to data from recognition memory studies using the study-test procedure. In terms of a stage model, if one stage $f(t)$ is normally distributed with parameters μ and σ and the second stage $g(t)$ is exponentially distributed with parameter τ, then the resulting reaction-time distribution (the sum of the two stages) will be the convolution of $f(t)$ and $g(t)$, which is a positively skewed distribution with parameters μ, σ, and τ.

These two examples are intended to make more intuitive and familiar the operations of convolution and correlation; they do not begin to indicate the conceptual importance of these two operations. Continuing in this vein, it is easy to think how one might write a computer program to evaluate convolution or correlation integrals numerically. One simply has an outer and an inner loop. The outer loop is for step position x, the alignment point of the two distributions. Then the inner loop sums the cross-products over the variable u. For convolution (but not correlation), one distribution should be reversed; $g(u)$ becomes $g(-u)$. A better way for convolution is:

```
    DO 1 I=...
    DO 1 J=...
 1  CONV(I+J)=CONV(I+J)+F(I)*G(J)
```

whereas for correlation:

```
    DO 1 I=...
    DO 1 J=..
 1  CORR(J-I)=CORR(J-I)+F(I)*G(J).
```

Here the asterisk denotes the FORTRAN multiplication.

Correlation is familiar to those working with waveform analysis. The cross-correlation function correlates two waveforms at successive displacements of one relative to the other. The auto-correlation function correlates a waveform with itself, again at various displacement points. These are standard methods of analysis when dealing with noisy data.

Let me conclude this section with some examples from other areas. We all know that a measuring instrument has an effect on that which is measured. Perhaps we do not all know that the nature of this effect generally is a convolution, where the input function is $f(x)$ and the impulse response function of the measuring (or recording) instrument is $g(x)$. This applies not only to a light meter or a sound-level meter but also to the lens in a photographic system and the recording head in a magnetic tape recorder.

Terms such as "smoothing, blurring, scanning, and smearing" (Bracewell, 1965, p. 24) or "window, grating, filter, transfer function, dissipative response and feature extractor" (Borsellino & Poggio, 1973, p. 113) convey some idea of the wide applicability (and the potential relevance) of the convolution–correlation concepts.

APPLICATIONS TO PERCEPTION

Optomotor Responses

Optomotor responses are responses to visual stimulation, and in beetles they may be produced by stimulation of adjacent or adjacent-plus-one ommatidia. An analysis by Reichardt (1961) used an experimental apparatus consisting of narrow slits on an inner ring with concentric gray and black–white outer rings to produce different intensity gradients. A linear model with low-pass filters was proposed, and the interaction in the nervous system of ommatidia stimulation was described by convolution and correlation integrals. A test of the model involved variation in the stimulus parameters with predictions about the optomotor responses; as predicted, stimuli that varied only in the phase component of their Fourier transform had no differential effect on the responses at different pattern velocities.

Pattern Detection

Uttal (1975) has studied the detection of dot patterns masked by other random dots. He used a two-alternative forced-choice procedure, and the subject was to report which presentation (first or second) contained the pattern. He used a variety of patterns including lines, squares, triangles, curves, and broken figures; in each case, the pattern was formed by dots and was to varying extents masked by the addition of many other randomly placed dots. Uttal proposed that the information processing was done in terms of a two-dimensional auto-correlation, and this transform of the stimulus pattern provides a means of detecting a visual signal (the pattern) embedded in a noisy background (other dots). Actually, he suggested a figure-of-merit that provided a measure of pattern goodness. He was able to show quite impressive relationships between the pattern goodness measured this way and the detection data from the forced-choice procedure.

Pattern Recognition

Kabrisky, Tallman, Day, and Radoy (1970) have suggested a theory of pattern recognition based on a two-dimensional Fourier transform of the stimulus pattern. In general, the low spatial-frequency components are extracted and stored, and these constitute a form of template. Pattern recognition is a matching process whereby a given stimulus is compared to an ensemble of possible templates and a best match is selected. Although a template-matching view of pattern recognition has been criticized (see, e.g., Neisser, 1967), Kabrisky et al. were able to show in a simulation that this scheme was able to recognized alphabetic letters. Although this model is based on Fourier transforms, it is included here; because Fourier transforms are closely related to convolution. The discrete Fourier transform of a sampled waveform is the convolution (more correctly, the dot product) of these sample values with the sample values of selected sinusoidal frequencies. The results are the amplitude and phase distributions necessary to represent the original waveform. Thus, a Fourier transform provides a different but equivalent mode of representation of the original information. Although it has different properties, there are fixed (generally inverse) relationships between representation in the function domain and representation in the transform domain.

In an analysis of perceptual clarity, Dodwell (1971) suggested that visual information-processing partly consists of computing cross-correlations on the spatial input pattern and that this processing is involved in the growth of perceptual clarity with repetition, extracting signals from noise, and pattern recognition. The cross-correlation (or auto-correlation) is a measure of the overlap between two different patterns (or the same pattern at two different points in time). This could provide a mechanism for the growth of perceptual clarity as reported by Haber (1969); in this study, the probability of correctly perceiving a word increased steadily over 25 trials even though the presentation duration was in the low-millisecond range (about 15 msec). As Dodwell notes, there are many precedents for this type of approach in the artificial intelligence field; see, e.g., the work of Rosenfeld (1969) on picture processing by computers.

Brightness

Apparent brightness is a classical example of how convolution principles can describe one aspect of visual perception. Very briefly, brightness can be understood in terms of the modulation transfer function of a lens. Basically, the modulation transfer function describes the frequency response characteristics of the system. Imagine a striped, repetitive pattern presented for viewing. Such a pattern can be represented in terms of spatial frequencies. The modulation transfer determines how these frequencies are attenuated and, as a consequence, the apparent contrast of the pattern.

The relationship of this to convolution is as follows. The modulation transfer function of the optical system attenuates (i.e., multiplies) the frequency components of the pattern. By transform theory, multiplication in one domain is equivalent to convolution in the other domain. Thus, one could either say that the perceived pattern is filtered by the optical components of the visual system or that the perceived pattern is the convolution of the pattern with the visual receptor system. Mach bands are a well-known example, and there is even a possible physiological mechanism (lateral inhibition). This is one of the few cases I know of in psychology where one has the three necessary ingredients for an adequate scientific explanation; namely, a mathematical description, a physiological mechanism, and behavioral data. For a much fuller account, see Cornsweet (1970).

Pitch Perception

In audition, pitch perception is the counterpart of brightness in vision. Fourier analysis developed in terms of simple auditory stimuli such as sine and square wves; it certainly needs no review here. The theory of pitch perception, however, is not yet a settled matter. The classical Helmholz view is the so-called "place" theory, where location on the basilar membrane is the primary determinant of pitch perception.

An alternative to the place theory is a temporal theory in which the frequency of nervous impulses is considered the critical variable. Much recent work on the missing fundamental has been directed toward these issues. According to a recent review (Green, 1976), the most powerful current theories suggest a modified place theory where the auditory system first does a power-spectrum analysis. It seems indisputable that the auditory system does some sort of spectral analysis; whatever its exact nature, convolution and correlation may turn out to be important explanatory concepts.

APPLICATIONS TO MEMORY

Holography

Holographic models of memory are probably the best-known illustration of the convolution–correlation principle in the memory area. Such models have been proposed by Cavanagh (1976), Pribram, Nuwer, and Baron (1974); and Westlake (1970). Holography is a method of wavefront (as opposed to image) storage and reconstruction and can serve as either an analogy or a model for memory. If it serves as an analogy, one has considerable latitude in how to apply it; but if it serves as a model, then many ancillary details must be specified. The Cavanagh, Pribram, and Westlake models differ in many respects, both in terms of detailed assumptions and areas of application. There is not space to review them adequately here. However, as noted by Gabor (1969), models of this sort share an underlying logic-namely, the mathematical operations of convolution and correlation.

The result is distributed memory. Models for human memory that have recently been popular have—when they have been sufficiently explicit—

generally postulated a localized type of storage. In the extreme, specific items are deposited in specific locations (bins, registers, slots, or boxes), and a major problem in memory is then retrieval. How does one "find" an item when one is looking for it? Is there scanning? Is there direct access? Is the process (or are the processes) serial or parallel? Such questions are a focus of much current research in the memory and information-processing area. They are probably a consequence of our love affair with the computer. Computers do indeed have highly specific localized storage; in fact, if one knows how, one can easily examine a particular location in a computer to determine its contents. There is no assurance that human memory works the same way.

The idea of distributed storage does not necessarily imply that information is physically spread out over a large area. Rather, the key issue is whether memory traces, whatever their nature, are separate or combined. With localized storage, each trace is separate; so whether it is boxes or bins, there is one trace per location. Distributed memory takes the opposite position, where combined (superimposed) traces can be stored and there is no individual representation for a given item. Perhaps the major contribution of holographic models of memory is to show how this is possible. Psychologists may find it hard to imagine how one can have combined but mutually noninterfering information storage, but the holographic models show how it can be done.

Convolution and Correlation Models

There have been proposed a number of memory models that have, in one way or another, been based on principles of convolution and correlation. Anderson (1968) proposed a storage model utilizing spatial correlation functions, which handled in a simple but impressive way some basic findings in recognition and association. Subsequently, he proposed a neural network model (Anderson, 1972); and with the assumption of an "attention filter," he was able to explain some of the standard Sternberg findings on scanning (Anderson, 1973; Sternberg, 1975). Most recently, he and his colleagues have attempted to deal with categorical perception and probability learning (Anderson, Silverstein, Ritz, & Jones, 1977).

There have been other important contributions, too; see, in particular, Kohonen (1977). However, what I would like to do in the remainder of this paper is to discuss CADAM, a particular version of convolution and correlation models developed by Peter Liepa at Toronto. The acronym CADAM (Liepa, 1977) stands for *content addressable distributed associative memory*. Although CADAM is very similar to previous work (particularly that of Anderson), it is quite simple and straightforward to understand and makes contact with a number of current research problems in the memory area.

CADAM

In most memory experiments, we deal with lists of items. Suppose we represent an item as a vector, say $\mathbf{f}$, where

$$\mathbf{f} = (\ldots, f_{-2}, f_{-1}, f_0, f_{+1}, f_{+2}, \ldots) \tag{5}$$

Leave aside for the moment what this vector represents, but remember that each different item is a different vector. Encoding information into memory involves storing these vectors, and retrieving information from memory involves operating on this stored information to generate some response. We store and retrieve different kinds of information. I have suggested there are at least three distinguishable types identified to data; namely, item information, associative information, and serial-order information (Murdock, 1974). CADAM works differently for these three, so it is necessary to consider each in turn.

Item Information. When a list of items is presented for subsequent recognition, a memory vector $\mathbf{M}$ is constructed. This memory vector is simply the sum of the individual items; namely,

$$\mathbf{M} = \sum_{i=1}^{n} \mathbf{f}_j \tag{6}$$

where the items are the vectors $\mathbf{f}_1, \mathbf{f}_2, \ldots, \mathbf{f}_n$. Retrieval consists simply of correlating the probe (test item) with the memory vector. The result is

$$(\mathbf{f} \# \mathbf{g})_0 = \left\{ \begin{array}{l} d', probe = \text{old} \\ \\ 0, probe = \text{new} \end{array} \right\} \tag{7}$$

That is, there are two cases. In the first case, the probe is an old item (one that had appeared in the list), in which case the expected value of the correlation is d', where d' is the standard "strength" measure from signal-detection theory (see, e.g., Murdock, 1974). In the second case, the probe is a new item (one that had not appeared in the list), in which case the expected value of the correlation is 0.

There are two assumptions necessary for this model to work as described. First, each item should be "noiselike;" that is, its auto-correlation should be a delta function (see, e.g., Bracewell, 1965). Second, the items should be orthogonal; the cross-correlation of any two items should be 0. Also, what we are called "correlation" here is really a poor man's correlation-namely, the dot product at the zero index.

It is generally accepted that recognition memory consists of two components, a memory component and a decision component. This scheme provides only a memory component. It must be augmented by some decision rules to convert the output from $(f \# g)_0$ into an observable response. However, there is ample precedent for this type of approach (e.g., Wickelgren & Norman, 1966).

This model exemplifies distributed storage in that there is no separate representation in memory for each item. There is simply the memory vector **M**, which is the pooled representation of the individual items. As in holographic models, there is the assumption of linear combination; the item vectors combine additively.

The outcome of the correlation (Equation 7) is the classical signal-detection situation, illustrated in Fig. 6.1. When the probe is new, there will be a distribution around 0 (pooling, of course, over a number of tests). When the probe is old, there will be a distribution around d' (again pooling over tests). I have symbolized the mean of the old-item distribution as d' to help make contact with more familiar concepts. This scheme is very similar to the matched filter of Anderson (1973); and as he notes, the signal-to-noise ratio (what I am calling d') is equal to k/n, where k is the number of elements in the vectors and n the number of items in the list.

To make this description more concrete, let me discuss briefly a few Monte Carlo simulations I have done on the computer. I simulated a simple study–test, recognition–memory paradigm; see, e.g., Ratcliff and Murdock (1976). In the first simulation, there was a 16-item study list followed by a 32-item test list, half new and half old. Each (study and test) item was a k-element vector, obtained by sampling randomly from a uniform distribution (range -1 to $+1$) for each element of each item. Each vector was then normalized to 1 (i.e., normalized so the dot product of a vector with itself would be 1); then the memory vector **M** was constructed by "presenting" the 16 study items (Equation 6). Then all 32 items were tested, with separate tallies for the cross-correlation (Equation 7) of old and new items. Finally, I ran five such trials

FIG. 6.1 Illustration of the outcome of probe-recognition tests (Equation 7) to show the old- and new-item distributions for the correlation of the probe with the memory vector **M**.

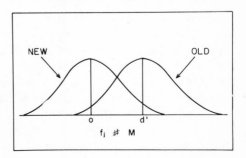

with k values of 5, 10, 15, 30, and 60 (k being the number of elements in the vectors). The resulting d' values were 0.87, 0.62, 1.91, 1.93, and 4.60, respectively. (The d' value was calculated as the mean difference between old and new items divided by the standard deviation of the new-item distribution. As k increased, the main change seemed to be that the standard deviation decreased; for $k > 5$, old- and new-item means were close to 1 and 0, as they should be with this normalization.)

In other simulations (all rather cursory), d' decreased as the number of study items increased. This result, and the previous result, also held (it seemed) when: (a) the uniform distributions were replaced by unit normal distributions; and (b) the vectors were not normalized. Actually, these simulations do not prove very much other than to demonstrate that computers can be made to act as if they had distributed memory. They are primarily intended to reassure those who distrust mathematical theorizing.

Associative Information. Here we must go to a paired-associate format, where pairs of items are presented and "associations" formed. Again represent each item as a vector, and the associative operation is convolution. For a list of items, a memory vector **M** is again constructed, and

$$\mathbf{M} = \sum_j \mathbf{f}_j * \mathbf{g}_j \tag{8}$$

That is, pairs of items are associated by convolving them; and as each new convolution is formed, it is simply added to the common store (i.e., **M**). As in item information, with associative information there are no separate and distinct associations. There is simply the common store.

The retrieval operation is correlation, and the surprising result is:

$$\mathbf{f}_j \# \mathbf{M} = \mathbf{g}_j \tag{9}$$

That is, correlating the probe $\mathbf{f}_j$ with the memory vector **M** produces the associated item $\mathbf{g}_j$, and it is also the case that:

$$\mathbf{g}_j \# \mathbf{M} = \mathbf{f}_j \tag{10}$$

In more familiar terms, with a list of **A**–**B** pairs, probing with one item generates the other; and this is recall—not recognition. Further, associative symmetry obtains in that probing with **A** yields **B** whereas probing with **B** yields **A**. This follows from the properties of convolution and correlation; **A** # (**A** * **B**) = **B** and **B** # (**A** * **B**) = **A** (Borsellino & Poggio, 1973).

In Fig. 6.2 I have given a detailed example to illustrate the principle that convolution of a pair of items followed by correlation with one member of the pair yields the other item. Assume for the sake of simplicity that the two items

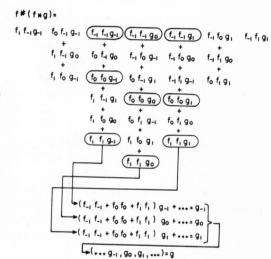

FIG. 6.2 Illustration to show the recall of associative information. The two associated items are **f** and **g**, each portrayed as three-element vectors. The five-element vector, **f*g**, shows the convolution of **f** and **g** that results from associating them. The seven-element vector, **f#(f*g)**, shows how the probe **f** correlated with the memory trace **M** (here consisting of only the one pair), according to Equation 9, yields the associated item **g**.

are each three-element vectors; thus $\mathbf{f} = (f_{-1}, f_0, f_{+1})$ and $\mathbf{g} = (g_{-1}, g_0, g_{+1})$. Then the convolution $\mathbf{f} * \mathbf{g}$ is a five-element vector, and the correlation of the probe **f** with this five-element vector yields a seven-element vector within which the target item **g** may be found. The critical components are circled, and the algebraic sum is the target item **g**. If you are puzzled as to why the remaining (uncircled) components are apparently disregarded, remember the basic assumption about the items; namely, they are orthogonal, so the dot products of f_i and g_j are zero when $i \neq j$. This example may also help one appreciate intuitively the fact that memories of this sort work better, the bigger they are (Anderson, 1973).

Serial-Order Information. Serial-order information is the information necessary to remember a string of items. There are several possible CADAM representations, but the one chosen by Liepa is as follows. Suppose the string of to-be-remembered items is denoted **A–B–C–D–E**. As before, there is a memory vector **M**, and:

$$\mathbf{M} = \mathbf{A} + \mathbf{A} * \mathbf{B} + \mathbf{A} * \mathbf{B} * \mathbf{C} + \mathbf{A} * \mathbf{B} * \mathbf{C} * \mathbf{D} + \mathbf{A} * \mathbf{B} * \mathbf{C} * \mathbf{D} * \mathbf{E} \qquad (11)$$

That is, the memory vector is constructed as follows. When the second item (**B**) is presented, it is convolved with **A** and added to **M** (which at that point contains only **A**). When **C** is presented, it is convolved with **A*B** and added to **M**, etc. (Convolution is commutative, so one could equally well represent Equation 11 as **A +B*A +C*B*A +**... This rewriting makes the CADAM representation of serial-order information more like the nesting model I have suggested; see Murdock, 1974, Fig. 10.12, p. 294.)

Retrieval works as follows:

$$d\#M = A \qquad (12a)$$
$$A\#M = B + d \qquad (12b)$$
$$(A*B)\#M = C + d \qquad (12c)$$
$$(A*B*C)\#M = D + d \qquad (12d)$$
$$(A*B*C*D)\#M = E + d \qquad (12e)$$
$$(A*B*C*D*E)\#M = d \qquad (12f)$$

Here **d** is the delta function, which as a vector is $(\ldots 0 \quad 0 \quad 1 \quad 0 \quad 0 \ldots)$. Perhaps it functions as a terminator, both initiating recall (because **d#M = A**) and signaling when recall is finished (because **[A*B*C*D*E]#M = d**). Also, it shows up at each step in recall, but somehow it must be disregarded so the individual items may be recalled in turn. A slightly different interpretation, suggested by Liepa, is that **d** is "context."

An alternative way of storing serial-order information might be to construct the memory vector as:

$$M=A*B + B*C + \ldots \qquad (13)$$

This scheme would be a string of pairwise associations. However, because of the property of associative symmetry, this would not be satisfactory. As Liepa has noted, this would interfere with the required ordering of recall. Experimental evidence from studies of transfer of training speaks against this possibility as well (Murdock, 1974, p. 293).

DISCUSSION

In this paper I have tried to review some of the applications of convolution and correlation to perception and memory. The applications to perception are of course already well known, and I have simply tried to highlight them here for the sake of completeness. The general point is of course the possible communality of opperations in two different areas of human information processing. The applications to memory are both less well known and more provisional. Consequently, let me confine the discussion to the memory area.

What exactly are the advantages of CADAM-type models? They have been clearly stated in Anderson's writings, but let me summarize some of them here. First, they work. As computer simulations can demonstrate, these schemes are capable of storing and retrieving information imperfectly. Their accuracy level is not unreasonable. Second, the physiological mechanisms required are not extreme. In fact, as many have argued, quite plausible physiological models can be constructed to perform the necessary operations. Third, we can get reliable performance from unreliable elements, and local damage need not have global effects.

These are very general points. Let me try to be more specific about the contribution to our understanding of memory. First, these models in general and CADAM in particular serve to unify item information, associative information, and serial-order information. These are different types of stored information, and now at least we have some operations to interrelate them. Second, these models give a richer and more realistic picture of the nature of an association. Despite the important role associations have had and continue to have in our history, our theoretical conceptualizing of them could not be much more impoverished. To call them a connection, a link, a pairing, a tagged pathway, or even a relationship is essentially saying nothing more than that they exist. To say that associating two items is to convolve them gives a much richer picture. Third, we now can explain why a signal-detection analysis of recognition memory is appropriate. A signal-detection approach is quite well accepted these days, but it is simply assumed ad hoc. Now it is possible to derive it from more basic principles. Fourth, we now have a way of conceptualizing recall–recognition differences. The retrieval operations are similar, but the stored information is different. Quite speculatively, it might even be that CADAM could explain the surprising recognition failure of recallable words recently reported by Tulving (1976); compare Equations 6 and 8.

However, caution should still be exercised. At best CADAM is an approximation, and how good an approximation it is remains to be seen. For one thing, a fundamental assumption is that the human information-processing system is a linear system. Both from sensory physiology and from psychophysics we know this is certainly not completey true and in certain specific cases not even approximately true. For another, we simply do not know how well the rigorous assumptions of linear algebra are represented in the functioning of the human information-processing system. Third, though CADAM-like models can explain simple aspects of human memory, the recent developments in cognitive psychology tell us there is much more. Perhaps distributed memory models could be a useful base on which to build.

Finally, there is one question that has been avoided and should be considered briefly in closing. If items are to be represented as multielement vectors, what are the elements of these vectors? What is the nature of the stored information? It seems unlikely that they are raw, unanalyzed, sensory information (e.g., waveforms in audition or intensity gradations in vision).

There is too much redundancy in the stimuli we see and hear. Some processing occurs early in the sensory systems; so the elements of the vectors could be abstracted or processed physical features. However, this is only one kind of feature, and we know that many types of features are important. Further, recent work by Craik (1973) has provided impressive evidence for the differential effectiveness of different types of features. Perhaps we must entertain the possibility of a multiplicity of features; such a view has been outlined by Kintsch (1970).

In conclusion, convolution and correlation are powerful operations for information processing in a wide variety of areas. They have clearly demonstrated their value in many scientific areas outside our own. They have an important role to play in the human perceptual processes. It may be that the same is true for memory.

ACKNOWLEDGMENTS

This work was supported by Research Grant APA 146 from the National Research Council of Canada and OMHF 164 from the Ontario Mental Health Foundation. I would like to thank Peter Liepa, whose work contributed greatly to this paper.

REFERENCES

Anderson, J. A. A memory storage model utilizing spatial correlation functions. *Kybernetik*, 1968, *5*, 113–119.

Anderson, J. A. A simple neural network generating an interactive memory. *Mathematical Biosciences*, 1972, *14*, 197–220.

Anderson, J. A. A theory for the recognition of items from short memorized lists. *Phychological Review*, 1973, *80*, 417–438.

Anderson, J. A., Silverstein, J. W., Ritz, S. A., & Jones, R. S. Distinctive features, categorical perception, and probabiity learning: Some applications of a neural model. *Psychological Review*, 1977, *84*, 413–451.

Borsellino, A., & Poggio, T. Convolution and correlation algebras. *Kybernetik*, 1973, *122*, 113–122.

Bracewell, R. *The Fourier transform and its applications.* New York: McGraw-Hill, 1965.

Cavanagh, P. Holographic and trace strength models of rehearsal effects in the item recognition task. *Memory & Cognition*, 1976, *4*, 186–199.

Cornsweet, T. N. *Visual perception.* New York: Academic Press, 1970.

Craik, F. I. M. A "levels of analysis" view of memory. In P. Pliner, L. Krames, & T. M. Alloway (Eds.), *Communication and affect: Language and thought.* New York: Academic Press, 1973.

Dodwell, P. C. On perceptual clarity. *Psychological Review*, 1971, *78*, 275–289.

Gabor, D. Associative holographic memories. *IBM Journal of Research and Development*, 1969, *13*, 156–159.

Green, D. M. *An introduction to hearing.* Hillsdale, N.J.: Lawrence Erlbaum Associates, 1976.

Haber, R, N. Repetition as a determinant of perceptual recognition processes. In R. N. Haber (Ed.), *Information processing approaches to visual perception.* New York: Holt, Rinehart & Winston, 1969.

Kabrisky, M., Tallman, O., Day, C. M., & Radoy, C. M. A theory of pattern perception based on human physiology. In A. T. Welford & L. H. Houssiadas (Eds.), *Contemporary problems in perception.* London: Taylor & Francis, 1970.

Kintsch, W. Models for free recall and recognition. In D. A. Norman (Ed.), *Models of human memory.* New York: Academic Press, 1970.

Kohonen, T. *Associative memory: A system-theoretical approach.* Berlin: Springer-Verlag, 1977.

Liepa, P. *Models of content addressable distributed associative memory (CADAM).* Unpublished manuscript, University of Toronto, 1977.

McGill, W. J. Stochastic latency mechanisms. In R. D. Luce, R. R. Bush, & E. Galanter (Eds.), *Handbook of mathematical psychology* (Vol. 1). New York: Wiley, 1963.

Murdock, B. B., Jr. *Human memory: Theory and data.* Hillsdale, N.J.: Lawrence Erlbaum Associates, 1974.

Neisser, U. *Cognitive psychology.* Englewood Cliffs, N.J.: Prentice-Hall, 1967.

Pribram, K., Nuwer, M., & Baron, R. The holographic hypothesis of memory structure in brain function and perception. In D. Krantz, R. C. Atkinson, R. D. Luce, & P. Suppes (Eds.), *Contemporary developments in mathematical psychology* (Vol. II). San Francisco: Freeman, 1974.

Ratcliff, R., & Murdock, B. B., Jr. Retrieval processes in recognition memory. *Psychological Review*, 1976, *83*, 190–214.

Reichardt, W. Autocorrelation, a principle for the evaluation of sensory information by the central nervous system. In W. A. Rosenblith (Ed.), *Sensory communication.* Cambridge, Mass.: MIT Press, 1961.

Rosenfeld, A. *Picture processing by computer.* New York: Academic Press, 1969.

Sternberg, S. Memory scanning: New findings and current controversies. *Quarterly Journal of Experimental Psychology*, 1975, *27*, 1–32.

Tulving, E. Ecphoric processes in recall and recognition. In J. Brown (Ed.), *Recall and recognition.* London: Wiley, 1976.

Uttal, W. R. *An autocorrelation theory of form detection.* Hillsdale, N.J.: Lawrence Erlbaum Associates, 1975.

Westlake, P. R. The possibility of neural holographic processes within the brain. *Kybernetik*, 1970, *7*, 129–153.

Wickelgren, W. A., & Norman, D. A. Strength models and serial position in short-term recognition memory. *Journal of Mathematical Psychology*, 1966, *3*, 316–347.

7 Perception, Memory, and Mental Processes

Donald A. Norman
University of California, San Diego

INTRODUCTION

Today I speak of mental processes, most especially of the interaction between knowledge and processing structures. My charge was to speak of "memory and perception," not of these other things; but I will try to show you that it is not possible to limit the task, for I do not believe that the human mind takes much note of the distinctions made by psychologists. I cannot believe that the human mind is divided up into little compartments—this one doing perception, that one memory, this one emotional, that one rational. We are integrated, wholistic organisms, functioning in a complex, diverse environment. Of course it is impossible to speak of everything at once, even if we had sufficient knowledge to do so. So it does make sense to take a particular view of mental processing and to speak of mental processes from the *perspective* of perception or from the *perspective* of memory. The mental structures do look different when viewed with different perspectives.

I draw together work from several areas. I borrow from studies of memory, learning, attention, and perception as well as from the field of artificial intelligence. I attempt to understand the processing mechanisms that underlie intelligent perceptual performance, and to do this I must attempt to understand a wide range of phenomena. This chapter should be viewed as an illustration of the problems and methods. This is not the appropriate place to discuss the technical details of processing structure or of representation. Hopefully, my demonstrations will amuse you, even if they do not convince you. I think that psychology needs some new approaches and some new techniques. If I were to take the opportunity of the 500th anniversary of the

University of Uppsala to wonder about the progress of the next 500 years, I would speak of the need for a new science of cognition: *cognitive science.* Indeed, I do take the opportunity—but at the end of the chapter.

ON COGNITIVE PROCESSING

In this section I follow a global-to-local approach. First, I present some of the phenomena of perception that I find compelling illustrations. Then I go into more detailed discussion, including a specific example of descriptions and schemas. The entire discussion is probably at the wrong level, for the global, general sections will be at too high a level to be new or useful, and the local, detailed sections will be too specific, too detailed, and therefore either wrong or irrelevant. Still, by my discussion of the extremes, you can determine what I am trying to do and fill in your own versions of the missing levels. Let me start by considering three examples:

1. In perception, it has long been known that expectations can improve performance. But expectations are often set up by those same perceptions that are improved through expectations: One cannot perceive the whole without perceiving the parts, yet the perception of the parts is guided by the perception of the whole.

2. The ability to recall something depends on the activity that is performed at the time of learning. But what is done at the time of learning depends on one's perceptions of the event, and this is of course guided by many factors, including one's memories of similar, related events. I argue later that both the initial perception and the encoding that is done on the information stored depend on finding an adequate "description" of the event.

3. When a skilled task is performed, it takes a certain amount of attentional capacity. If the skill is at all complex, it may occupy all of a person's attentional resources while it is being learned. But when that skill is well practiced or overlearned, then it seems to require little attentional capacity. Thus, novel tasks or unexpected aspects of familiar tasks demand conscious attention. Whenever demands are placed on conscious processing resources, there tends to be severe interference with whatever cognitive task is going on at the same time.[1]

These phenomena are related through considerations of two issues: how the information is processed and how the information is represented. Actually,

---

[1]In this chapter I do not discuss this third principle—that with practice and increasing skill, fewer processing resources seem to be required to perform a task. Nonetheless, I leave the example in the list, for I believe that it is very important, illustrating a principle that must be accounted for both within the representational structures and the processing structures. Some of the implications of this point are discussed in Norman (1976).

there is a trade-off between representation and processing, so that the two must be considered together. The phenomena of memory and perception (and of thought, language, and problem solving) result from processes that operate on knowledge structures; and because only the outcome of the processing is observable, psychological studies cannot distinguish between structure and process. Thus, often we are limited to consideration of the joint operations of possible representations and processes.

Representation

Despite the difficulties of separating structure and process, studies of the representation of knowledge are of critical importance. How can we speak of memory or of perceptual recognition if we do not know what is represented in that memory or what is being recognized perceptually? Both perception and memory involve matching prior knowledge with the current situation. How does one make the match; what knowledge is available; how complete is our recollection of the past; how much does prior knowledge influence current use? All these questions need to be raised, and answered. Moreover, certain questions about representation can be asked—and hopefully, answered—even if one is not sure whether the answer results from the processes that operate upon the representations or from the representations themselves. Thus, rules of classification of arriving sensory information will depend on the representational structure. Possible inferences that can be drawn from perception or from memory depend on the properties of "inheritance" and on the manner in which "default" values of knowledge are applied. Then, there are important issues such as whether we store only specific instances or whether we might reason from general principles. Recent debates on representation have considerably enhanced our sophistication about these topics. For example:

1. There need not be a single, uniform representation of knowledge. Different formats seem suited for different purposes. But of course there must be good interfaces among the different representations, so that knowledge can be interchanged (see Bobrow, 1975; Brown & Burton, 1975).

2. Human classification may not follow a system with rigid criteria but rather may be flexible (and "fuzzy"), with current concepts judged according to their distances from prototype concepts (see Rosch, 1973).

3. Debates about the differences between propositional (verbal) coding and analogical (image) coding may be only of secondary interest, with the real distinctions in representation being the extent to which a given system has "intrinsic" or "extrinsic" knowledge (see Palmer, 1978).

4. Differences between "declarative" and "procedural" knowledge are important. We must have both knowledge *about* things (declarative knowledge) and knowledge for *doing* things (procedural knowledge), but

there need not be fundamentally different representations for these aspects of knowledge. It is possible, however, that some of our knowledge about things is not easily accessible, being only imbedded within procedures that apply the knowledge (see Winograd, 1975).

Representing Perceptual Knowledge. If a perceptual event is to be recognized or interpreted with regard to past events, then there must be some match between the information stored within the memory structures and the information undergoing perceptual analysis. This implies, among other things, that the format of the two forms of information be sufficiently related that a meaningful comparison can take place. Thus, either perceptual information and memorial information must have the same representation, or the interface between the two forms must be such that each can refer to and use the other during perceptual analysis. Moreover, although it is possible for the memory structures to contain many different forms of representation of information—some in a form relevant to perceptual processing, others in a form relevant to other needs—these different representations must also interact with one another; so they, too, must have either some common format or some standardized interface or translation rule.

My view is that there are large numbers of memory units—*schemas*—that organize knowledge. I assume that past experience has created a vast repertoire of these structures or schemas. The problem faced by the perceptual processes is to determine which previously acquired schemas match the present occurrences. Obviously, the past never repeats itself exactly, so the match must be at a level of abstraction that I call a *description*; and any discrepancies must be accounted for either by specific hypotheses or by an adequate "excuse."

I believe that descriptions serve as an important intermediate step between the analysis of newly arriving sensory information and its eventual encoding and storage as schemas. In addition, descriptions serve as an intermediary step between the specification of the information sought from memory and the actual retrieval of the relevant schemas. Descriptions describe memory schemas. Even when they characterize the immediate perception of the world, they do so through the organization and interpretations provided by existing memory structures that serve as prototypes.

Processing

The science of information processing is young. Technology has just begun to produce powerful computational devices, and knowledge about processing in general only leads the technological developments by a slim margin. Nonetheless, we have made considerable progress in our knowledge since the earlier years of simple Boolean switching logic and then of simple sequential machines and then more complex, computational structures with multiple processors, complex intercommunication structures, and active memory structures.

When we attempt to apply what is known today about process to our understanding of brain structures, the result is limited. The brain exhibits evidence of great sophistication in processing. For example, Bobrow and I have suggested the "principle of graceful degradation" as an important aspect of mental processing (Norman & Bobrow, 1975, p. 45). By this, we mean that as components become heavily loaded, make errors, or fail, the system performance simply tends to become slightly degraded. This is to be compared with almost all contemporary computational devices, which fail most ungracefully with even the slightest of problems. Now it is true that error-correcting encoding circuits exist that allow for limited failures with minimal effect and that some computer networks do simply degrade their service as usage becomes high or as redundant links fail, but these are exceptions to the rule. How the brain manages its extreme reliability of operation is not understood.

Psychological theories have not used some of the more recent processing principles. There are some valid reasons why this is so, but I think we have limited ourselves beyond reason. This point comes up again, first in the section on processing and later at the end of the chapter. Here, I simply point out that a number of new processing structures have been developed that allow multiple processes to operate simultaneously and cooperatively to enhance computational power. Thus, the "blackboard" models of speech recognition (Reddy & Newell, 1974) and the "demon" models of computation that are floating around the artificial intelligence community are useful concepts to consider (see Bobrow & Raphael, 1974). I recommended Rumelhart's book (1977) for a useful introduction to some of these ideas from the psychological point of view.

Processing Models of Perception. The common view of processing is that it proceeds in reasonable fashion, performing a sequential series of analyses of the information. In general, most psychological models of processing have this character. Two different directions of flow have been considered. One starts with the receipt of information at the sense organs, extracts perceptually relevant features, and pieces together an interpretation of the sensory phenomena. This can be called a data-driven, bottom-up analysis of the information. The other direction of analysis starts with contextual knowledge and expectations and works its way down the stages of processing, searching for sensory data that are consistent with the prior knowledge. This can be called top-down or conceptually guided processing. There is considerable evidence to support both these directions of processing. I believe that both are necessary but that neither is sufficient.

I propose that perceptual analysis is guided by the overall goal of establishing an integrated interpretation of the events of the world. This requires active construction of internal models of the environment, all the while seeking information that will allow confirmation or elaboration of the model. Serious discrepancies from the model (for which satisfactory excuses cannot be found) force reconsideration or reconfiguration of the model.

The sequential approach does make a good deal of sense, especially for the class of tasks that have been studied in the experimental laboratory. In these tasks, one presents a particular stimulus item to an observer and studies the nature of the recognition process—the assignment of a label to the stimulus item. A good deal of information about the early steps of processing has been revealed by clever manipulation of presentation parameters, the task requirements, the presentation of other signals (and maskers), and so on. But real perception does not always have this characterization. Certainly we must recognize previously experienced objects, but they are usually imbedded in a complex scene with many other things present at the same time, with the items in new configurations, seen from new views, sometimes partially obscured by the surround. The problems of recognition within a complex scene—where the elements are continually shifting, where new and old elements are intermixed—these problems are simply outside the scope of contemporary theorizing.

Today's difficulties are not recognized. Gibson has long advocated a different approach to the problem of understanding perception, arguing that it is essential to study rich, naturalistic settings and that the study of cartoon figures and illusions is, well, illusory. Much more recently, Turvey (1977) has argued persuasively that current views of perceptual processing assumed the analysis of static "snapshots," as if the visual scene were stopped by an intense stroboscopic flash, thoroughly analyzed (by the feature extraction method), and then compared with the next "snapshot." Successive comparisons of snapshots then produce our interpretation of the scene. Turvey then argues that this approach is doomed to failure, for the problem of integrating the independently analyzed snapshots is much more complex than heretofore realized.

Coincidently with the writing of this paper, I received two papers in the mail. Both dealt with the processing principles of human perception; both have influenced the thoughts described here. One paper came from Israel (Navon, 1977b), the other from England (Fox, 1977). When I add these papers to new developments in our understanding of processing structures, to new developments in psychology in the study of language and semantic memory representations, and to such recent papers as those by Turvey (1977) and Bregman (1977), I feel greatly encouraged about the start of a new direction of theorizing and new advances in knowledge.

REPRESENTATION: SCHEMES AND DESCRIPTIONS

Descriptions and Perceptual Phenomena

To find out about mental processes is a difficult task. We have few tools at our disposal. Consider Fig. 7.1, which shows a photograph of La Jolla, California. There is nothing remarkable about the picture. Certainly, there is nothing noteworthy about the process of perception required to view the picture. That is my point. Our analyses of the world occur unconsciously, and there is nothing for the experimental psychologist to study.

The obvious way to proceed is to slow up the process of perception or perhaps to confuse and befuddle it. Thus, we turn to degraded images, or impoverished ones, or simply to misleading ones. This method has its problems; but before I worry about them, let me illustrate some possible virtues. Consider Fig. 7.2, where I show you a drawing. To most of you (I

FIG. 7.1   A photograph of La Jolla, California. The University of California is located just off the top of the photograph. Normal perception occurs so rapidly and effortlessly that the processes are not revealed. (Photograph by Robert Glasheen, Copyright 1966, Glasheen Graphics.)

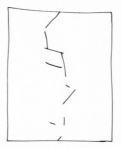

FIG. 7.2 A demonstration that apparently unrelated perceptual phenomena gain in cohesiveness and structure once provided with an adequate description. In this case, the figure shows a cartoon rendition of a face, drawn upside-down. The word *face* provides the proper memory schema with which to interpret the drawing. The phrases *upside-down* and *cartoon* provide further specification (and "excuses") for the particular nature of these data compared with those normally expected by the schema for *face*.

hope), the drawing is at first simply a meaningless combination of lines. But if you view it as a cartoon drawing of a face printed upside-down, you should be able to make sense of it. The description *face* provides an organizational structure: Each of the parts now fits together, and there is structure and cohesion to the image. I believe that the interpretation of this type of figure requires several different things. First, there must be a *prototype schema* in memory that provides the organizing structure for interpreting the sensory information. Second, there must be *further specification* of the schema to specify how it applies to the current event. Finally, the further specification provides *excuses* for the discrepancy between the actual data and those that are normally expected for the schema.

Let us do another exercise: Consider Fig. 7.3. The top half of the figure is relatively unintelligible. Even if I say that it is the word *work*, you will have difficulty seeing how the elements fit together: Telling you the proper

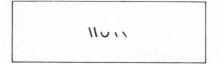

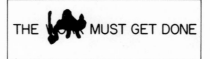

FIG. 7.3 The left-hand part of the figure shows a partial fragment of the letters "WORK." The right-hand part of the figure shows those very same fragments, plus surrounding context and an inkblot. The context "suggests" the schema for "work" as an appropriate candidate for analyzing the letter fragments. The inkblot provides an "excuse" for the mismatch of the fragments and the normal appearance of the word. The word "WORK" is normally more clearly perceived in the left part of the figure than the right, even after this explanation has been read. This demonstrates that cognitive knowledge is not always sufficient to guide the perceptual processing: the knowledge must be in a form appropriate for the perceptual analysis. (The figure is from Lindsay & Norman, 1977, and was based on a suggestion by Rumelhart.)

interpretation is not always an aid to perception. But if you look at the bottom part of the figure, then it becomes much easier to perceive the word *work*. The line segments of the word that are visible are identical in both the left and right parts of the figure. The difference is that the right adds context and an excuse. The inkblot provides an excuse for the missing elements of the word *work*.

Notice that conscious knowledge of the fact that the word is *work* does not really help much in the left part of the figure. I believe that such knowledge must be in a form usable by the schemas involved in the processing. The inkblot of the right figure does provide usable knowledge—it provides the necessary excuse for the particular configuration of data. This illustration, therefore, also serves to remind us that knowledge may exist at many different levels within the human; it is not necessarily the case that the different levels can interact directly with one another. There has been a long history of studies of the interactions of "cognitive processes" with perceptual processes—some demonstrating powerful effects, others failing. I believe the variability can be explained if we examine the situations carefully to see whether the cognitive knowledge could provide information to the perceptual processes in a usable form.

Johansson's Phenomena.   I believe that perception—indeed, most of human experience—requires the development of an adequate *description* of the experience; that description can then provide a unifying, organizational framework for interpreting the world. But a description must not only account for the data that is observable; it must also account for the absence of data that would normally be present. Hence, the requirement for an "excuse" in viewing Fig. 7.3.

Consider the work of Johansson (1973). The viewer sees what appears to be a random set of lights upon the screen. Suddenly the lights begin to move. A mathematical description of the path of the lights is horrendously complex, as is any attempt to verbally describe the paths of the individual lights. But there is one simple description that captures it: The lights are attached to a person who is moving. The perception of a moving person is accurate and quick. About one second of viewing time seems adequate (and I suspect that even less time is really needed). Moreover, when there are distortions in the pattern (produced by such strategies as rotating a mirror in front of the camera lens while taking the photographs) or when the cues are ambiguous (forward motion of the walking person is eliminated by proper panning of the camera), then the perceptions include "excuses" for these aspects. Here are some quotations from Johansson (1973) describing the reports of his subjects (Ss):

[When the camera followed the moving person so that there was no forward motion of the image] some of the Ss also spontaneously described the event as a walking on some kind of moving belt. The (invisible) ground then was experienced as moving backward [p. 209].

[When the experimental image was placed at the rear of a tunnel, but with no distance cues for the observer] some Ss reported seeing the walking pattern as a real, little manikin walking in the back part of the tunnel [p. 209].

[When the image was transformed by rotation (being viewed with a rotating mirror in front of the camera lens)] all Ss also said that the walker moved in a highly strange, "wavy" way [p. 210].

I believe it possible to discuss these and other results of Johansson's work in terms of the perceiver's attempt to find an adequate description of the perceptual phenomena (e.g., Johansson, 1964). The observer has two problems. First, a prototype schema must be found with which to characterize the perceptual experience. Second, there must be justification (excuses) for the differences between the schema and the percept. Both these problems require nontrivial processing. To find the prototype schema requires a memory search based on the fragmentary sensory data that are available. To account for the discrepancies requires a comparison of the schema with the percept and then a memory search for a schema that can account for the differences. Unfortunately, the framework of analysis that I am proposing is not yet sufficiently detailed to show how these processing steps are performed.

Michotte's (1963) work on perceived causality yields similar descriptions of perceptual phenomena (Michotte, 1963; a number of descriptions are available in the dissertation of Millar, 1977).

All these phenomena are clear examples of the observer's need for a description based upon some existing model, modified to account for the discrepancies. Obviously, verbal reports need to be interpreted with some suspicion, because they may reflect the observer's attempt to justify the results of the perceptual experience rather than the mechanics of arriving at the experience. Still, the phenomena are very compelling. Moreover, there is no need for the search and justification processes to take place at a conscious level; I presume these processes are done automatically without the need for conscious control (and sometimes despite such control).

What Is a Schema?[2]

Schemas are the organizational units of memory. New information acquired by memory enters into schemas, each new schema patterned after existing ones. The previous schema acts as a *prototype schema*. Prototype schemas facilitate access to different types of related information.

---

[2]The material in the next few sections is adapted from a rough manuscript on memory retrieval written by Daniel Bobrow and me (Norman & Bobrow, 1979).

Important characteristics of schemas include their ability to be structured according to a prototype but changed according to the "perspective" under which the prototype is viewed, perhaps with "further specification" of the prototype. Memory schemas also have four other properties:

procedural information
inheritance
default values
organizational structure

The first property—*procedural information*—allows for active memory structures, with encoding of actions as well as of concepts, percepts, experiences, and ideas. The second property—*inheritance*—is a standard one for semantic network structures and a necessary aspect of any representation. It provides for properties of the prototype to be "inherited" by instances of that prototype. Hence, if it is known that Sweden is in Europe, it is not necessary to encode that Uppsala is in Europe: The information is derivable if needed from the knowledge that Uppsala is in Sweden and from the property of inheritance.

The third property of records—*default values*—is related to inheritance. Basically, particular features and particular values are assumed to apply to instances of a prototype unless otherwise specified. Thus, in the United States, it is well known that people in Sweden jump into snow banks or icy water immediately after bathing in saunas. Thus, the encoding of a new instance in memory of a particular Swedish person does not require encoding the information about the person's behavior after saunas; it can be assumed, by default, to be like that of the generic Swede. Default values and inheritance can be overridden by further specification of a schema, so that a particular Swedish person can be further specified as disliking either saunas or icy plunges. The fourth property of records—*organizational structure*—provides cohesiveness to knowledge, pulling together into some formal structure otherwise disparate descriptions and relationships.

What Is a Description?

We experience some perceptual event; perhaps it is simply a picture flashed on a screen, perhaps it is a complex environment with many participants and much activity. Whatever the experience—if we are to interpret it, we must make some contact with existing memory schemas that can serve as prototypes on which to base the current encoding. That the past influences the perception of the present is well established. In earlier years the phenomenon was called "apperception." There are numerous illustrations, some of which I present later. Elsewhere (Norman & Bobrow, 1979), I have argued that in order to retrieve information from memory, one must first characterize the information that is sought (else, how would you know where and how to look, and how would you recognize the proper information once it had been found?) I call the initial characterization a *retrieval description*. This description helps to guide the memory search, for it attempts to specify what is known about the memory schemas being sought. Hence, descriptions describe schemas.

The Structure of Descriptions

The view of descriptions presented here comes from work performed with Bobrow (Norman & Bobrow, 1979), and it derives from earlier ideas described in Bobrow and Norman (1975) and Moore and Newell (1974) and partially implemented in the computer language *KRL* (Bobrow & Winograd, 1977). Bobrow and I postulated three essential components of a description: *prototype, perspective,* and *further specification*. Suppose some perceptual event, E, has been experienced and is being encoded. We suggest that the encoding identifies some existing memory record as the organizational framework upon which to interpret E. This existing record is the *prototype*; call it P. Thus, the start of a description is identification of a prototype:

  1. E isa type of P.

But any new experience (such as E) will not match any previous experience in all ways. Sometimes it differs in details, sometimes in point of view. Thus, the description can be elaborated to specify the perspective with which the prototype schema is being viewed. Specification of the perspective requires identifying the component parts of both E and P and specifying what roles and parts of E play in the prototype specified by P. Finally, a description must *further specify* the roles of the component parts. Thus, because memory record P—the prototype record—has certain characteristics that may or may not apply to event E, further specification of the description is necessary. First, there may be particular aspects of E that must be specified. Second, some of the values of P may not apply to E. Third, several prototypes may be required to describe E more precisely:[3]

  2. E isa type of P
      with a perspective in which:

---

[3]These examples are deliberately simplified in order to give a simple picture of descriptions. For a more complete approach, see the paper by Norman and Bobrow (1979). Also, see the formal notation described by Bobrow and Winograd (1977). (The use of *further specification* was suggested by the work of Moore & Newell, 1974). Descriptions may be embedded within descriptions, so one description may serve as a component part of another. In addition, a single description may use several different prototypes.

P26 is replaced by *E1*;
the object of P is given by *E2,* which isa type of *Q*;
except that *P33* is obscured by the object left-of *S*;
the height of *P10* is-greater-than the height of the object of *R*.

. . .

Note that by our structure of descriptions, there are many possible *levels of description.* Information can be described in terms of its sensory features or in terms of various prototype descriptions, and it can be more or less further specified. The level of description is a function of the amount of processing resources put to the task and of the surrounding environment that might suggest different descriptive structures.

Navon (1977a) has argued that visual perception starts with *global* analysis of the scene and then proceeds toward local analysis but only as far as time, processing resources, and need permit. Global processing first implies that the overall framework is first established and the details are filled in later. Note that global-to-local processing is not the same dimension as data-driven and conceptually driven: This is an orthogonal notion. Broadbent (1977) has suggested a similar idea. These arguments would seem reasonable for perception in general, not just for vision. If true, they suggest an interesting development of descriptions; descriptions are first global, and then—as processing continues—they become continually better specified. In perception, Navon's work implies that the very first description of a scene is something like:

3. "this" isa type of "scene,"
   further specified by:
      number-of "object" = 3
      relationship of objects is—

   . . .

As analysis continues, the identification of the scene as a group of "objects" in some particular spatial relationship is elaborated, so that the objects become more differentiated and better specified. The configuration may change, and new identifications are made. All this can be done primarily by embellishments upon the existing description (with exceptions occurring where a global description is found to be incorrect after further analysis).

PROCESSING:
CONTROL STRUCTURES AND RESOURCES

What type of processing structures comprise the brain? Suppose we agree that schemas control the analysis and interpretation of perceptual and memorial information. Suppose that the task of perceptual analysis is to piece together a structure that accounts for the present experience, guided by previous knowledge. How is this accomplished?

The barest beginnings have been made toward understanding the processing control structures that are appropriate for perceptual analyusis. Until recently, our knowledge of control structures was limited, and we understood well only the sequential, serial processing mechanism. Today, we are beginning to understand how multiple processing structures can interact—each independently doing its specialty, yet interacting in controlled fashion with other active processes. Much of this progress in understanding control structures has resulted from the development of new languages and structures for artificial intelligence (see Bobrow & Raphael, 1974). Marr (1975), Fox (1977), and Navon (1977b) have described approaches to the study of perceptual processing. Marr has been concerned with the first stages of processing and with development of the descriptions of surfaces and contours, especially the light gradations that accompany shadings, textures, and perspectives. Fox has attempted to use Marr's work to show how the system could make the link between the initial stages of analysis and the final schemas. Navon has been interested in closely related matters, especially how the overall processing is scheduled.

Processing Directed by Active Schemas

Let me illustrate some processing strategies. First, let me illustrate a reasonably conventional structure for analyzing words; I show both data-driven and conceptually driven processing. Figure 7.4 shows two rows of letters; the top row is easier to read in the visual noise than the bottom row. The reason is well known: The top row consists of a word (*hospital*); the bottom row consists of the same letters scrambled in meaningless order (*iptaoslh*). (This particular illustration does not control well for a number of confounding factors; but the phenomenon is well documented by numerous people including Estes, Mandler, and Tulving, to cite members of this symposium.) I am interested in studying the processing structure. Consider what mechanisms might look like to produce the phenomenon shown in Fig. 7.4.

The initial analysis must be data driven, because initially there is nothing else but the data to go by. Consider, therefore, the processing sequence shown in Fig. 7.5. Here I show random letters being presented to the system along with a processing structure that consists of a sequence of stages. Thus, the

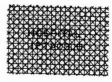

FIG. 7.4 Letters that form a word (the top row) are easier to read than the same letters arranged randomly (the bottom row), when both are partially obscured by noise.

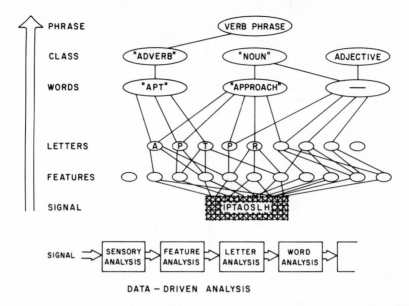

FIG. 7.5   The flow of processing when data-driven. Processing is initiated by the arrival of sensory data (at the bottom of the figure) and then proceeds in a logical sequence of stages upward. This is the direction of processing most frequently studied in the literature on perceptual processing and pattern recognition. It is a necessary form of processing, but it is not sufficient for all situations.

incoming sensory data drive the system, causing each stage of analysis to pass its results to higher stages. Sensory data go to feature analyses, which pass information to letter unit, then word units, then word class, and yet higher level units. This is the spirit of the standard data-driven models that have characterized numerous models of perception (especially of reading). The details have differed, but the principle is the same. This form of model is quite appropriate for many situations.

Now consider what happens when there is a good deal of contextual information but poor data, as in Fig. 7.6. Suppose the following contextual information has arrived: "The patient in the _ _ _ _ _ _ _ _ bed." There is noise around the one word represented by the eight dashes. Thus, there is contextual information and some information about the word itself (for example, some of its features and its length), but the word is not known. Here, the analysis must be primarily top-down, conceptually driven, guided by the contextual information. Figure 7.6 illustrates how this might be accomplished. The bottom part of the figure shows the conventional analysis in a form similar to that of Fig. 7.5, except that the flow of processing proceeds from right to left. Semantic and syntactic information is used to derive word-analysis information, which suggests letters and then features that are to be

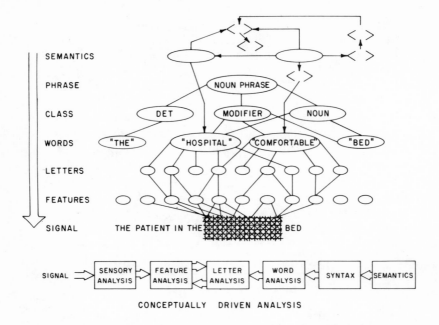

FIG. 7.6 The flow of processing when conceptually driven. Processing is initiated by the context (at the conceptual analyses shown at the top of the figure) and then proceeds by guiding the expectations of the lower stages of analysis. This is the direction of processing guided by expectations and prior knowledge. It is a necessary form of processing, but it is not sufficient for all situations.

looked for. At the same time, there is some data-driven analysis going on, with the visual input undergoing sensory analysis and perhaps some letter analysis. But the primary analysis of the missing word must come from the context. There are many situations in perception where such conceptually guided processing plays an overwhelming role in the perceptual process, sometimes to the extent that the observer is unaware that the information perceived was obscured by noise.

In most normal situations, both data-driven and conceptually driven analyses operate simultaneously. Figure 7.7 is an example of such a situation. The arriving information passes through sensory, feature, letter, and word analysis in turn. At the same time, semantic and syntactic analyses make suggestions about their expectations, causing lower level stages of analyses to examine the data in a directed fashion. The process is thereby both data driven and conceptually driven.

The overall process is one of continual feedback. The initial sensory features suggest a set of possible candidate words. Similarly, the initial conceptual analysis suggests some possible candidates. Suppose (as is shown in Fig. 7.7) that the sensory analyses are consistent with two words: *hospital* and *hotel*. These two possibilities guide further analyses, for they guide processing by suggesting particular letters and features. The suggestions from the data and from the context develop hypotheses that can then be further tested against those same data. This feedback process eventually causes one hypothesis to receive sufficient confirmatory evidence to be selected.

I propose, therefore, that the data initially suggest a number of possible memory schemas to which they might conform; then each of those schemas inquires to see whether or not it can be confirmed. A schema is confirmed if sufficient supporting evidence exists or if there is another schema that provides an excuse for the lack of supporting evidence. Whenever there are conflicting possible interpretations, the one with the strongest excitation (or support) is selected.

From this point on, the efficiency of processing improves, for the number of possible interpretations that need be considered keeps decresing. Moreover, once a schema has been selected to guide the processing, new information is efficiently organized into the structure provided for it. As the

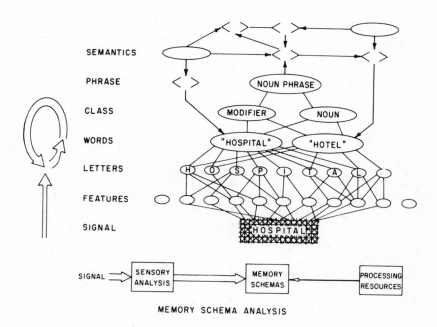

MEMORY SCHEMA ANALYSIS

FIG. 7.7 The flow of processing that is simultaneously data driven and conceptually driven. Data-driven analysis starts from the bottom of the figure and flows upward, attempting to identify the sensory information on the basis of the features present. Conceptually driven analysis uses the preliminary results of the data-driven analyses to make suggestions about possible patterns, guiding the efforts of the data-driven processes. Thus, both directions of processing occur together in complementary fashion, ech supplementing the other.

number of possible schemas decreases, we get a positive feedback loop. Each reduction in candidates frees more computational resources for use in analyzing the remaining possibilities. The extra resources speed up the analysis and rejection of erroneous possibilities. Each new rejection speeds the process even further.

Schema-Driven Analysis

Let me make clear the type of computational system that I am discussing. The processing system is assumed to consist of an autonomous collection of schemas, each acting as an independent processing structure. The normal view of processing as "analysis by sequential stages" becomes "analysis by a pool of memory schemas." Stages of proceing disappear. Schemas play an active role in guiding the flow of information-processing activities, and the flow cannot be characterized as traveling in any particular direction. Moreoever, because the literature on attention suggests that there is a limit to the total amount of processing resources available to a human at any moment, it appears that each schema does not have computational power by itself but rather must draw on some central computational resource. This means that all active schemas share from a common pool. Hence, the more schemas active at any time, the less processing resources remaining for the rest and the more slowly each schema can pursue its activities.

Several other assumptions about processing are necessary. One is what Bobrow and I have called "the principle of continually available output" (Norman & Bobrow, 1975, p. 45). This assumption must be coupled with an understanding of how the various schemas communicate with one another. Although we lack evidence about these structures, we assume that the schemas can communicate with one another in a reasonably direct fashion. They can do this either by direct interconnection, or by each communicating with some common structure, or by direct communication with their physical neighbors who in turn can communicate with their neighbors until the whole pool of relevant schemas has been reached. The assumption of continually available output seems necessary to explain some of the observations of human performance. In particular, this assumption says that as a schema starts the process of analysis, it continually makes available its partial resultants, so that other schemas can make use of the analysis even as it proceeds. Let me illustrate with a mathematical example: Suppose a schema were computing the answer to the problem of determining 3 factorial (3!). The partial outputs might look something like this:

The answer is greater than or equal to:

1

3

6

The answer is equal to:

6

Thus, other schemas are in a position to use the partial information about the value of the factorial as soon as possible. If, for example, a schema needs a value that is specified as being less than 3, it will have sufficient information without waiting for the completion of the factorial schema's computation. Continually available output seems an essential component of any complex processing system (such as a human) where many processes take place at once, where competition for resources is commonplace, and where approximate answers are often as useful as complete ones.

Suggestions and Inquiries

Now let us look at a particular proposal for yielding data-driven and conceptually driven processing from a pool of schemas. Navon (1977b) proposes that active schemas communicate with one another as they analyze the perceptual scene. The communications are of two forms: "suggestions" and "inquiries." A "suggestion" is issued whenever a schema recognizes that the input data are appropriate to its own structure. In analyzing my figure of the upside-down cartoon face (Fig. 7.2), where several types of line segments and intersections are present, the schemas associated with those visual features become activated and send messages to other schemas suggesting that they make use of this information. The T-intersection (where the mouth hits the side of the face) might thus be signaled by the "T-schema" broadcasting:

To: everyone
Suggestion:
"Note that a T-intersection is present at location L."

Those schemas for whom T-intersections are valid accept the suggestions and then do three things. First, they request processing resources in proportion to the number of suggestions they have found relevant to their structure. Second, they send their own suggestions to other schemas suggesting that they, too, are present. Third, they issue "inquiries" of other schemas. Suggestions are the mechanism for data-driven processing in Navon's approach.

Inquiries are requests for verification of data structures. Thus, if the suggestion of a T-schema got received by a FACE-schema as a possible component, the FACE-schema would suggest to others (weakly at first) that maybe a face was present; but it would also inquire whether other facial parts were present:

To: data analyzers
From: FACE—schema
Inquiry:
   "Is a nose present?"

To: BODY-schema
From: FACE-schema
Inquiry:
   "Is a body present below L?"
   . . .

The schemas that receive inquiries use some of the resources of the inquiring schema to answer the questions posed to them. The answer either occurs directly (if it is known at the time of inquiry) or else triggers a request to other schemas for information. Eventually, feature-level schemas respond about the presence or absence of data, and the answers get passed back up the system. Inquiries, therefore, are Navon's method for producing conceptually guided processing of perceptual inputs.

Navon explains how by making appropriate assumptions about resource limits and resource allocation, one final interpretation can be reached. As higher order schemas received more and more confirmation, they would also receive increasing amounts of the resources until the most strongly supported schema would get all the resources, thereby completely inhibiting all competitive interpretations. Thus, Navon shows how a large pool of mutually communicating schemas produces both data-driven and conceptually driven processing. He also shows how suggestions and inquiries lead to the selection of an appropriate prototype schema for the analysis of a perceptual scene. Navon does not deal with "excuses" or the complete analysis of a novel percept. Rather, he has concentrated on the first problem: finding the appropriate prototype schema.

CONCLUDING REMARKS

Memory and perception are intimately related. Perception can be viewed as the process of matching the sensory representation of the world with memory structures. In addition, one could argue that the processes that operate upon memory are closely related to (or are identical with) the processes that operate upon sensory information. Indeed Rumelhart and I have argued (privately) about whether the *process of perceiving* is identical to the *process of retrieving.*

That there is an analogy between the process of memory and that of perception cannot be doubted. Both processes seem to employ a constructive approach to determining the interpretation or nature of their source data.

Thus, in perception, the viewer abstracts selected features of the environment and from these attempts to construct an internal model of that environment. The selectivity seems governed by characteristics of the visual scene as well as by the set or attentional strategy of the viewer. Similarly, in retrieval of information from memory (especially information that has not recently been used), a constructive process seems to be involved.

There is virtue in considering the relationship between the internal synthesis that occurs in perception with the similar synthesis of memory retrieval. Common processing functions could very well be involved; the understanding of one could enhance the understanding of the other. However, it is also important to consider the differences.

A major difference between memory and perception lies in the source and nature of the basic data that are to undergo analysis. The source of data for the perceptual system is usually the environment. Light, sound, odor, body position, movements, and other physical and chemical signals impinge upon the many sensory receptors and provide the excitatory force for the transformation into neurological codes. The human perceiver can move the body or the sense organs in ways that affect the quantity and quality of the initial information processing. Still, most of the sensory data are not much influenced by the observer. In addition, the initial sense data are essentially raw: unanalyzed, uninterpreted. The results of analyses and interpretation are what we call perceptual data.

The sources of data for the memorial system differ considerably. Two sources can be identified: internal and external. Much of the information within our memory structures originated externally with the perceptual analysis and indeed is the stored representation of that analysis. In addition, human thought processes can operate upon both perceptual data and memorial data to produce new conceptualizations that can themselves be stored within memory: This is an internal source of data. Most modern approaches to the study of memory assume that only interpretations of arriving sensory data are stored within memory (as opposed to storage of raw, uninterpreted data). Hence, perceptual information stored within memory differs considerably from sensory data that arrive at the organism. The difference lies in the interpretive, constructive nature of perception.

It might be possible to characterize the process of perception as that of providing interpretation to the arriving sensory information. In similar fashion, one might characterize the process of memory as that of recovering those interpretations.

Cognitive Science

This chapter has touched briefly upon a number of different areas, with special emphasis on representation and processing. I wish to conclude by speculating about the direction of research in future years within psychology.

Recently, a faculty colleague commented on a paper on representation (Palmer, 1977) that he didn't understand what the issue was; the paper did not lead to any new experiments. His criterion of value in psychology, he told me, was how many good experiments an idea will induce.

I disagree fundamentally with this criterion. I want to judge an idea by how much new understanding I get, not how many experiments I can do. Experiments that do not bear upon important issues have negligible value, for they detract from the proper pursuit of understanding. Experiments should be pursued with a purposeful goal in mind, a goal that leads to increased understanding.

We know very little about cognitive functions and of the mechanisms that might be responsible. We know little about intelligence or about the general class of intelligent mechanisms and systems. I believe that psychology will not make progress until it learns to ask the correct questions and that this will not occur until we learn more about the properties of intelligence and cognition in general. Thus, I would like to see a new science of cognition, one that deals with all cognitive proceses—whether real or imaginary, concrete or abstract, human or machine. I want to understand what it takes to be intelligent. What processes can perform what operations? What are the limits and powers of different representations and processing structures? I need to understand the range of possibilities in order to tackle the problem of discovering the cognitive structures of the human in an effective, informed way.

Along the way, I hope that the problem of consciousness will be studied from many different points of view. Humans are conscious beings, and the phenomenon of consciousness is so fundamental to our mental lives that it seems strange that experimental psychologists have ignored it so conclusively. What does it mean for a system to be conscious? What does it mean for a human to perform things automatically, without conscious awareness? Why the difference? Is consciousness necessary for learning or for high level planning? We don't know.

I predict that we will not understand memory or perception until we come to understand representation, processing, and control structures. And I predict that we will not fully understand processing and control structures until we understand the role of conscious and subconscious control and the role of self-awareness. Moreover, I believe this statement to apply to any intelligent system, whether it be man, or machine.

ACKNOWLEDGMENTS

Although the topic of this talk deals with perception, a good deal of the work results from my studies of the learning process. Thus, the central concept of the paper is that of "descriptions," and this notion first was developed from studies of learning. I have benefited tremendously from my co-workers; the concepts in this paper were developed with the aid of David Rumelhart and Daniel Bobrow and by the work of my students (now colleagues) who have studied visual perception: David Navon (now at the University of Haifa), Steve Palmer (now at The University of California, Berkeley), and Al Stevens (now at Bolt Beranek and Newman, Cambridge, Massachusetts). I thank Julie Lustig for her careful reading of the paper and for her patience.

Support for the research on learning was provided by the Advanced Research Projects Agency and the Office of Naval Research and was monitored by ONR under contract number: N00014-76-C-0628.

REFERENCES

Bobrow, D. G. Dimensions of representation. In D. G. Bobrow & A. Collins (Eds.), *Representation and understanding: Studies in cognitive science.* New York: Academic Press, 1975.

Bobrow, D. G., & Norman, D. A. Some principles of memory schemata. In D. G. Bobrow & A. M. Collins (Eds.), *Representation and understanding: Studies in cognitive science.* New York: Academic Press, 1975.

Bobrow, D. G., & Raphael, B. New programming languages for artificial intelligence research. *Computing Surveys,* 1974. *6,* 153–174.

Bobrow, D. G., & Winograd, T. An overview of KRL: A knowledge representation language. *Cognitive Science,* 1977, *1,* 3–46.

Bregman, A. S. Perception and behavior as compositions of ideals. *Cognitive Psychology,* 1977, *9,* 250–292.

Broadbent, D. The hidden preattentive process. *American Psychologist,* 1977, *32,* 109–118.

Brown, J. S., & Burton, R. R. Multiple representations of knowledge for tutorial reasoning. In D. G. Bobrow & A. Collins (Eds.), *Representation and understanding: Studies in cognitive science.* New York: Academic Press, 1975.

Fox, J. *Continuity, concealment, and visual attention.* Unpublished manuscript, 1977.

Johansson, G. Perception of motion and changing form. *Scandinavian Journal of Psychology,* 1964, *5,* 181–208.

Johansson, G. Visual perception of biological motion and a model for its analysis. *Perception & Psychophysics,* 1973, *14,* 201–211.

Lindsay, P. H., & Norman, D. A. *Human information processing* (2nd ed.). New York: Academic Press, 1977.

Marr, D. *Early visual processing.* AI Memo No. 340, MIT Artificial Intelligence Lab, 1975.

Michotte, A. [*The perception of causality*] (T. R. Miles & E. Miles, trans.). London: Methuen, 1963.

Millar, D. B. *Perceptual cohesion in simple motion configurations.* Unpublished doctoral dissertation, La Jolla: University of California, San Diego, 1977.

Moore, J., & Newell, A. How can MERLIN understand? In L. W. Gregg (Ed.), *Knowledge and cognition.* Potomac, Md.: Lawrence Erlbaum Associates, 1974.

Navon, D. Forest before trees: The precedence of global features in visual perception. *Cognitive Psychology,* 1977, *9,* 353–383.

Navon, D. *On activation, evaluation, cursory verification, and other processing principles in visual recognition.* Unpublished manuscript, 1977. (b)

Norman, D. A. *Memory and attention: An introduction to human information processing* (2nd ed.). New York: Wiley, 1976.

Norman, D. A., & Bobrow, D. G. On data-limited and resource-limited processes. *Cognitive Psychology,* 1975, *7,* 44–64.

Norman, D. A., & Bobrow, D. G. Descriptions: An intermediate stage in memory retrieval. *Cognitive Psychology, 1979, 11.*

Palmer, S. E. Fundamental aspects of cognitive representation. In E. Rosch & B. B. Lloyd (Eds.), *Cognition and categorization.* Hillsdale, NJ: Lawrence Erlbaum Associates, 1978.

Reddy, R., & Newell, A. Knowledge and its representation in a speech understanding system. In L. W. Gregg (Ed.), *Knowledge and cognition.* Potomac, Md.: Lawrence Erlbaum Associates, 1974.

Rosch, E. H. On the internal structure of perceptual and semantic categories. In T. E. Moore (Ed.), *Cognitive development and the acquisition of language.* New York: Academic Press, 1973.

Rumelhart, D. E. *Introduction to human information processing.* New York: Wiley, 1977.

Turvey, M. T. Contrasting orientations to the theory of visual information processing. *Psychological Review*, 1977, *84*, 67–88.

Winograd, T. Frame representations and the declarative–procedural controversy. In D. G. Bobrow & A. M. Collins (Eds.), *Representation and understanding: Studies in cognitive science.* New York: Academic Press, 1975.

8 Elaboration and Distinctiveness in Episodic Memory

Fergus I. M. Craik
University of Toronto

Larry L. Jacoby
McMaster University

INTRODUCTION

In keeping with the general theme of the Uppsala Conference on Memory, this chapter gives a broad overview of our current ideas about human memory and related processes. The ideas stem more or less from the "levels of processing" view of memory advanced by Craik and Lockhart (1972). More directly, however, the present views develop the notions discussed by Lockhart, Craik, and Jacoby (1976) and by Jacoby and Craik (1978).

The chapter gives our views on some factors that we believe to be necessary for an adequate description of human memory at a behavioral level. Our description is in terms of hypothesized processes, and it is a *cognitive* view in that it stresses necessary interactions among attention, perception, memory, comprehension, and action. We argue that memory is not a separate entity but is one aspect of the total system. That is, the basic tasks of cognition are to comprehend and to formulate appropriate actions; memory is viewed as the record of the perceptual–motor operations carried out throughout the behavioral sequence. Such a view is inimical to an understanding of cognitive processes in terms of a succession of independent stages; rather, we endorse the arguments of Rumelhart (1977) and others for an interactive system in which sensory and semantic aspects of processing influence each other during perceptual and conceptual analysis. In light of this approach to the study of cognitive processes, it may not be profitable to dissect cognition into a series of stages, to attempt to understand each stage in isolation, and then finally to assemble the stages into an overall view. The "interactive" viewpoint suggests rather that a fuller understanding may be achieved by first formulating an adequate broad characterization of the system and then by refining that description through experiments. This latter strategy is exemplified by the present approach.

One further general theme running through the chapter is the contrast between dichotomies and continuities in descriptions of information processing. As descriptions of cognition become more sophisticated, it is undoubtedly useful to highlight new concepts by framing them as black-or-white alternatives. In most cases, however, as the concepts become familiar, it seems more useful to treat such factors as continuous processes—with one processing mode shading off into another—rather than to insist on the original "either-or" formulation (Newell, 1974). We believe that *some* discontinuities may play a useful theoretical role (for example, discontinuities obviously exist between input modalities and may exist between primary and secondary memory; Craik & Levy, 1976), but in general it seems necessary to move from dichotomies to continuities and their interactions as our understanding grows. Arguments for continuities are given throughout the chapter.

In the following sections, the processes of attention, rehearsal, and encoding are examined; and the distinctions between encoding and retrieval, between episodic and semantic memory, and between memory as stage setting versus memory viewed as a system of traces are discussed in the framework of a processing view of cognition.

ATTENTION

A major controversy in theoretical descriptions of selective attention has concerned the locus of selection in the flow of information through the organism. In Broadbent's (1958) theory, wanted stimuli were selected for further processing quite early in the processing sequence. For classes of stimuli defined physically, this posed no problem; but the theory had some difficulty explaining how semantically relevant stimuli on unattended channels captured attention and conscious awareness. The problem was solved in two different ways. Treisman (1964) modified Broadbent's original filter theory by suggesting that stimuli were subjected to successive levels of analysis and that the level reached by a particular stimulus depended both on physical characteristics of the stimulus and on current biases and expectations existing in the analyzing system. Treisman's modifications were endorsed by Broadbent (1971) in later versions of his model. Despite the role played by semantic factors, the Treisman-Broadbent theory is still an "early selection" model because unattended stimuli are analyzed in terms of their physical features only; typically, they do not proceed to semantic levels of analysis.

The second class of solutions to the problem of semantic analysis involves the suggestion that all incoming stimuli are fully analyzed for meaning and that only after this full analysis are the most important stimuli selected for further processing and for conscious awareness. Such "late selection" models were put forward by Deutsch and Deutsch (1963) and by Norman (1968), among others.

However, several recent theorists have rejected the either/or dichotomy of early versus late selection theories and suggested instead that selectivity takes place throughout the continuum of processing. For example, Erdelyi (1974) postulated that "selectivity is pervasive throughout the cognitive continuum, from input to output [p. 12]." Erdelyi also quotes from Kafka's *The Trial*: "The verdict is not suddenly arrived at, the proceedings only gradually merge into the verdict [p. 1]." In a sense, the verdict is a summary of the proceedings but at a different level of description; in other words, the verdict prescribes appropriate action on the basis of the evidence. Similarly, in cognition, the action taken subsequent to analysis of a stimulus sequence "summarizes" the analytic proceedings. However, in the legal example, records of the court proceedings exist as well as the trial's outcome, and these records may be re-examined later. Again, this is analogous to information processing in our view—that is, cognitive analysis is constrained by procedural rules; it leads to appropriate action and leaves a record of the analytic operations performed throughout the proceedings.

If selectivity takes place throughout processing, what factors determine selection or rejection for particular stimuli? In his notions of stimulus set and response set, Broadbent (1971) essentially suggested that the system could adopt either an early or a late selection mode, depending on the task. For example, if the wanted stimuli are defined physically (e.g., red letters among a mixed array of red and black letters), then "stimulus set" conditions hold, and the targets can be picked out without full analysis of all stimuli. On the other hand, if targets and nontargets do not differ physically (e.g., digits from an array of digits and letters), then "response set" conditions hold, and all stimuli must be analyzed to the level where they are identified as letters or digits.

This line of thinking has been extended by Erdelyi (1974), Keren (1976), and Johnston and Heinz (1976), although these later workers have stressed the continuity of processing and selection rather than the notion of two processing modes. The basic idea is that analysis proceeds along the early–late continuum as far as is necessary to decide whether the stimulus is wanted or not. The amount of processing is thus very much determined by the current task—including both stimulus aspects and aspects contributed by the organism. In the first category, salient stimuli and stimuli that are highly compatible with the analyzing system (e.g., common words and pictures) will receive greater amounts of processing; and in the second category, processing will be modified depending, for example, on whether the subject is proofreading or reading for meaning. By the present view, memory is a record of the processing carried out, and the memory trace will thus reflect both the amount and the qualitative nature of the analyses originally performed. If the perceptual processing necessitated a description of the stimulus in semantic terms, then the memory record will also reflect these semantic qualities. In an effort to relate the qualitative nature of processing to retention, Craik and Lockhart (1972) postulated that stimuli processed to "deeper" semantic levels were associated with higher levels of retention in a subsequent memory task.

The interplay of attentional and memory factors is nicely illustrated in a study by Johnston and Heinz (1976). In the relevant experimental conditions, two lists of words were presented binaurally; subjects were required to shadow the target list, which in one condition was defined physically (words spoken in a male voice, whereas nontarget words were spoken in a female voice) and in a second condition was defined semantically (e.g., animal names as opposed to male first names). In addition to the shadowing task, subjects performed a reaction-time task—they pushed a button in response to a light signal that occurred randomly throughout the shadowing trials. It was argued that reaction time (RT) indexed the amount of residual processing capacity left from the shadowing task; the more attentional capacity consumed by shadowing, the longer the RT. Finally, a recall test was given for the rejected words. The results showed that shadowing was more accurate and RTs to the light signal shorter under early selection conditions—that is, where subjects could select target words by voice quality. Thus, in general, early selection is easier and consumes less processing capacity. However, in the later retention test, it was found that memory for nonshadowed words was superior under late selection conditions—that is, where a semantic analysis was necessary. Finally, in one experiment, nonshadowed words were repeated, and it was found that repetition was associated with larger increments in recall under semantic-selection conditions.

The Johnston and Heinz (1976) results demonstrate the flexibility of attention; the authors reject the early–late dichotomy in favor of a processing continuum. They conclude that as the task necessitates "later" semantic analysis, more attentional capacity is required but also that memory for all stimuli is enhanced. One result that at first sight raises a problem for the notion that semantic analysis is associated with high levels of retention is the finding by Potter (1975) that when subjects monitor a rapidly presented sequence of pictures for a previously described target picture, subsequent recognition memory for nontarget pictures is rather poor. Because the targets are described in semantic rather than physical terms (e.g., "a boy fishing"), it seems that all pictures must be processed semantically and thus that they should be well remembered. However, this argument assumes that semantic analysis is all-or-none, and this is surely untrue; a picture can be rejected as not being of a boy fishing without a very extensive analysis of what it *is*. Analysis presumably proceeds from global to more specific features until a sufficient number of critical characteristics of the target are either confirmed or violated. If a picture can be rejected after a very general, cursory analysis, then memory for the picture will be correspondingly poor.

A further example of flexible processing and its consequences for memory, is Kolers' (1975) observation that increased skill at a difficult reading task (and presumably less extensive analysis of the material) is associated with poorer retention of the material read. The Kolers result shows that memory is not a simple function of how early or late the processing was or of the depth of processing reached but that extensiveness of processing (degree of elaboration) is also of primary importance. It seems preferable to characterize stimulus analysis not as an unvarying sequence of stages with processing stopped at a certain level, but rather as a process in which a variety of possible operations are weighted differentially depending on stimulus characteristics, task demands, and the subject's degree of skill.

REHEARSAL

The question addressed in this section is whether the effects of repetition on memory and learning differ systematically as a function of the mental operations involved in the repetition. The distinction between two types of rehearsal—maintenance and elaborative processing—has been made by several writers (Craik & Lockhart, 1972; Jacoby, 1973a; Mandler, 1978; Woodward, Bjork, & Jongeward, 1973). Although these various authors used different descriptive terms, the central distinction is similar in all cases— namely, that one function of rehearsal is to maintain items in conscious awareness for ready access and that a second function is to perform further cognitive operations on the items to enhance their later memorability. Craik and Lockhart (1972) made the rather extreme suggestion that maintenance rehearsal had *no* beneficial effects on subsequent retention, because memory was held to be a function of depth of processing and in maintenance rehearsal the subject was apparently repeating operations at a depth already attained. This prediction has been confirmed by some authors for recall (Craik & Watkins, 1973; Jacoby, 1973a; Woodward et al., 1973); but when retention is measured by recogntiion, maintenance rehearsal is typically associated with increments in performance (Glenberg, Smith, & Green, 1977; Woodward et al., 1973). Thus apparently Craik and Lockhart's suggested dichotomy between two sets of effects was too simple.

With regard to recognition, Glenberg et al. (1977) have suggested that maintenance rehearsal enhances performance by the addition of frequency or context tags to the item's representation and that these tags facilitate discrimination of old from new items in a subsequent recognition test. Mandler (Chapter 14, this volume) discusses the same issues; he agrees with the empirical outcome but attributes the beneficial effects of maintenance processing to increased integration or coherence of the item.

In at least two studies, beneficial effects of maintenance processing on recall have also been reported (Dark & Loftus, 1976; Darley & Glass, 1975). The reasons for the discrepancy between these studies and experiments showing no effects on recall are not immediately obvious; but in one study (Darley & Glass, 1975), subjects had to compare the maintained item with a succession of other items, so clearly the subject was performing more than simple maintenance operations. Dark and Loftus (1976) presented three or five words at a rapid (1-sec) rate before the retention interval; it seems very possible that the presentation rate left little time for elaborative processing of the word string during presentation and that again subjects did more than maintain items during the subsequent rehearsal interval. However, both sets of authors agree with the present analysis that final retention depends on the operations performed during the rehearsal interval rather than on the number of repetitions per se. Thus Dark and Loftus suggest that overt rehearsal may show maintenance or elaborative properties in different situations; also, both they and Darley and Glass suggest that rehearsal will increase in effectiveness to the extent that attention is involved.

A related issue concerns the relative effectiveness of repetitions at different levels of processing. The results of Johnston and Heinz's experiment described earlier suggest that the effect of repetitions interacts with depth in the sense that repetitions of an item are associated with greater increments in retention performance at greater depths of encoding. For example, if an item is encoded semantically, repetition will have more effect than if the item is encoded phonemically. This interaction between repetition and depth was also reported by Craik and Tulving (1975, Exps. 3 & 4), by Jacoby, Bartz, and Evans (1978), and by Anderson and Reder (1978). On the other hand, both Nelson (1977) and Chabot, Miller, and Juola (1976) reported no interaction between repetition and depth of processing; the reasons underlying this discrepancy are unclear at present.

Nelson (1977) has objected that the finding of an effect of repetition on recall by Craik and Tulving (1975) and others contradicts the notion that maintenance processing has no effect on later recall, because in these experiments items were processed at the same level on each of two presentations. It must be agreed that repetitions do enhance recall even in situations where the item is subjected to the same qualitative type of processing on successive trials, and in this sense Craik and Lockhart's (1972) original suggestion regarding Type I processing (that repetition must lead to deeper processing before retention is improved) is disconfirmed. However, a distinction should perhaps be made between *maintenance processing*—where subjects maintain an item continuously in mind by rehearsal—and explicit *repetitions* of the same nominal item—in some cases after quite lengthy intervals. In the former case, it is likely that the subject indulges in little new processing on each successive rehearsal cycle; but in the latter case, it is probable that the item is treated somewhat differently on successive presentations, especially if the presentations are spaced (Jacoby & Craik, 1978). In addition, spaced presentations may involve spontaneous retrieval of the previous encoding of that item, and this too may augment recall (Lockhart, 1973). Thus there may be little conflict between the cases reported by Nelson in which repetition of an item is associated with enhanced recall and the suggestion discussed earlier that "pure" maintenance rehearsal has essentially no beneficial effect on recall. It seems quite possible that the effects of massed and spaced practice (e.g., Hintzman, 1974) are attributable to the same processes that underlie maintenance and elaborative processing. This possibility is discussed by Jacoby and Craik (1978).

However, it seems that again a simple dichotomy should yield to a continuity. In this case the distinction between maintenance and elaborative processing should perhaps be replaced by a continuum representing the degree to which repetitions lead to different encodings on successive presentations; to the extent that the existing encoding is elaborated, retention will be enhanced. The question of whether repetitions do or do not interact with the type of processing involved to produce increments in retention must await further empirical and conceptual anlaysis before it can be resolved. One recent suggestion by Anderson and Reder (1978) is that deeper levels of analysis provide much greater scope for elaborative processing; thus repetitions at deeper levels of processing have at least the potential for allowing the formation of rich, elaborate encodings, which in turn enhance the item's memorabiity. This suggestion, together with the notion of a maintenance–elaborative continuum, leads to a more complex view of rehearsal; namely that the operations performed during rehearsal can vary both in the extent to which they change or remain the same from cycle to cycle (the maintenance–elaborative dimension) and also with regard to the qualitative nature of the operations carried out (depth of processing). Whereas maintenance-processing operations may be performed at any level of processing, truly elaborative processing will only be possible at deeper levels where the potential for richer encoding exists. In any event, it seems clear that the effects of rehearsal on memory will only be understood once we attain a clearer conceptualization of the constituent mental operations and their interactions. Further related ideas on the interaction of repetitions with depth of processing are discussed by Jacoby et al. (1978).

ENCODING

In this section, we discuss the factors we believe to be important for effective encoding in memory; in the next, the interactions between encoding and retrieval processes are discussed. The factors discussed in the previous two sections under the headings *Attention* and *Rehearsal* are clearly also relevant to the encoding problem. Formation of an elaborated encoding involves extensive or elaborative processing and consumes more attentional capacity (Johnston & Heinz, 1976). Following Bower (1967), Craik and Lockhart (1972), and others, it is argued that the memory trace reflects those operations performed at input for the primary purposes of perception and comprehension. In overview, our position is that elaboration of the perceived event leads to the formation of a distinctive encoding; in turn, this distinctiveness facilitates specification of the wanted encoding at retrieval. This point of view is discussed more fully by Jacoby and Craik (1978); here we restrict ourselves to commenting on several questions that might be asked about such a view. We should also mention that many of the arguments advanced here are similar, at least in part, to the views of other workers (e.g., Eysenck, 1978; Klein & Saltz, 1976; Kolers, 1975; Lockhart, Craik, & Jacoby, 1976; Moscovitch & Craik, 1976; Norman & Bobrow, 1977; Wickelgren, 1977).

What is the relation between elaboration and depth (or type) of processing? We argue that extensive processing of shallow (i.e., sensory) information will not usually benefit later memory performance. For example, prolonged study of complex but meaningless patterns is not associated with good recognition of the patterns (Goldstein & Chance, 1971), whereas very brief exposures of meaningful pictures is associated with high levels of later recognition memory (Potter, 1975). However, it would be wrong to conclude that "sensory" processing inevitably leads to poor memory; experience in discriminating one person's voice from others or in tasting wines or in differentiating samples of handwriting can all lead to excellent memory for a particular pattern. In these cases, the sensory surface features of the stimulus have become rich and meaningful through the gradual build-up of a cognitive structure to differentiate subtly different stimuli (Gibson & Gibson, 1955). In this sense the sensory/semantic distinction is also a continuum rather than a dichotomy. A further correlate of depth is the degree of organization of the system; it is postulated that deeper, more meaningful structures are more highly articulated and thus afford greater possibilities for reconstructive retrieval.

Thus greater depth of processing is characterized by qualitative differences (greater meaningfulness), by a greater number of possible elaborations, and thus, typically, by richer descriptions and more distinctive encodings of events. However, this description of depth is clearly vague; as Nelson (1977) and others have pointed out, it would be far preferable to have an index of depth independent of retention level. Are we any nearer to achieving an independent index of depth? Processing time often correlates with depth defined intuitively, but this relation is not a necessary one; complex, shallow encodings take a long time to achieve but are not well remembered (Craik & Tulving, 1975, Exp. 5).

Residual processing capacity is another possibility; if deep encodings consume more attentional capacity, less will be left to perform a second, concurrent task. Johnston and Heinz's (1976) results, described earlier, are in line with this supposition, as are results of an unpublished study by E. Simon and F. I. M. Craik. In the latter experiment, subjects monitored a rapidly presented series of visual words for target words defined either structurally, by rhyme, or by semantic category; at the same time, a series of seven pairs of digits was presented auditorily, followed by a probe pair for recognition. (The subject's task was to decide whether the probe pair was a member of the series just presented.) The results showed that auditory recognition performance declined as a function of the depth of processing required by the visual monitoring; also, in a subsequent recognition test for the visually presented words, recognition levels were highest for words processed semantically. Although at present, concurrent processing capacity offers a possible way to measure depth, further work must establish the limits of this relationship. It is possible, for example, that processing capacity, like processing time, may be sensitive to complexity as well as to depth.

It is argued that depth of processing and degree of elaboration combine to yield an encoding of greater or lesser distinctiveness. If distinctiveness is the crucial factor underlying memory performance, it might be asked how this dimension differs from the more traditional dimension of trace strength. In our view, distinctiveness is unlike strength, primarily because distinctiveness is necessarily a relational, rather than an absolute, concept. That is, the distinctiveness of an object or event is always relative to a particular context. Because this is so, it follows that for a distinctively encoded event to be discriminable and distinctive again at retrieval, it must be contrasted with the same contextual items that accompanied the event at encoding. That is, the original encoding context must be reinstated. This line of argument stresses the necessity of taking into account the relationship between encoding and retrieval conditions; this topic is treated in a subsequent section.

What are the effects of practice at encoding a class of events on later memory for the events? Following Kolers (1975), we believe that practice makes encoding easier and more efficient; redundant operations gradually drop out. Thus practice is good for the primary task; but because memory is a positive function of the nature and number of operations performed at encoding, it follows that as practice increases, retention of the encoded events will decrease. Note that these remarks do not apply to practice of a single episodic event but rather to practice of a class of events. The notion is nicely illustrated by the results reported by Kolers (1975); he had subjects engage in extensive practice at reading samples of transformed text and found that subsequent recognition memory for the passages read declined as subjects became more practiced at the novel reading operations.

Finally, in this section it may be asked whether distinctiveness is the *only* principle necessary for an understanding of memory functioning. Our answer is that other factors are also necessary; two such factors are briefly discussed. First, the compatibility or congruity between the encoded event and other aspects of the encoded context is important—especially those aspects of the context later used as retrieval cues for the event. This point was illustrated by Jacoby and Craik (1978, Exp. I). On each trial, subjects were shown a card that had one word printed on one side (the focus word) and two words printed on the other side. The task was to decide as rapidly as possible which one of the two words on the reverse (the target word) was more closely related to the focus word. The words on the reverse were either high associates, low associates, or unrelated to the focus word and were arranged in various pairings: high–high, low–low, high–unrelated, and so on. In a second phase of the experiment, the focus words were presented as cues for the chosen target word; or the focus words, followed by the target words, were presented for recognition.

It was expected that difficult initial decisions (for example, when both words on the reverse were high associates, both were low associates, or both were unrelated) would necessitate more analytic operations and would thus lead to formation of a more distinctive trace and higher levels of retention. It might also be expected that the a priori relation between focus and target word would also affect the level of cued recall. The results are shown in Fig. 8.1. For cued recall, the strength of associative relationship (high, low, unrelated) is clearly a major determinant of performance, but within each degree of relationship the difficulty of decision also has an effect. For recognition, neither variable affects performance to the same extent. The major point to be taken from this experiment is that the associative relationship between cue and target, as well as the amount of work performed on the event at encoding, are both important determinants of recall.

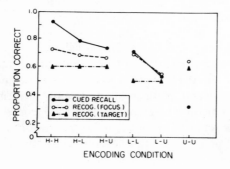

FIG. 8.1   Cued recall and recognition as a function of degree of association between focus and target words. (From Jacoby & Craik, 1978.)

A second and somewhat related factor to be taken into account by any overall theory is the nature of the retrieval test. It seems possible that recall relies more heavily on reconstructive processes than does recognition; if this is so, then an encoded item that is congruent with semantic memory structures should be more easily recalled then one that is not. On the other hand, recognition performance may be less affected by this degree of congruity. A second experiment by Jacoby and Craik (1978) illustrates the point. In this study, subjects were asked about semantic category membership of single words presented briefly. The category question was asked first (e.g., "Is the word an animal name?"); then the word was presented, and the subject decided "yes" or "no" as rapidly as possible. Subjects understood that the experiment was investigating decision latency. Of the 72 trials, 24 led to "no" responses and are not considered further. In the remaining 48 trials, 16 categories from the Battig and Montague norms were used, with three words being drawn from each category. Of the three, one was a high-ranking (common) exemplar, one was drawn from the middle of the normative list, and the third was a relatively uncommon exemplar of the category. It was assumed that subjects would have to carry out more processing before reaching a decision on low-ranking exemplars, and this supposition was borne out by the longer decision latencies associated with low-ranked words. Arguably, this more extensive processing should lead to relatively elaborated, distinctive encodings, which would then be more memorable than high-ranked words. In a second phase of the experiment, subjects were given either a cued-recall test (the category names served as cues) or a recognition test.

The results are shown in Fig. 8.2. Recognition performance was highest for low-ranking exemplars, whereas in cued recall, high-ranking exemplars were associated with the highest retention levels. Jacoby and Craik concluded that although the greater difficulty associated with initial classification of uncommon category members led to formation of a more elaborate encoding—which benefited subsequent recognition—this factor was over-ridden in cued recall by the greater ease with which relatively common

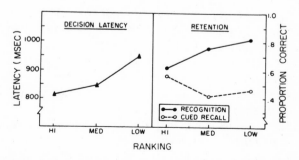

FIG. 8.2 Decision latency, recognition, and cued recall as a function of exemplar ranking. (From Jacoby & Craik, 1978.)

exemplars could be reconstructed from the category name. Again the general conclusion is that whereas trace elaboration and distinctiveness are major determinants of retention, they are not the only factors to be taken into account.

To summarize, we argue that attention, rehearsal, degree of practice, number of repetitions, the extensiveness and qualitative nature of the encoding processes converge to give rise to a memory trace that is more or less distinctive from other traces in the system. By "memory trace" we mean the record of those cognitive operations crried out initially for the purposes of perception, comprehension, and decisions concerning action. Whereas in general, distinctive traces are associated with high levels of retention, other factors—such as the congruity of the target event with the episodic context or with permanent semantic strutures—are also held to be important. Two illustrations of such factors were given, but it should be stressed that the examples are intended to illustrate interactions with other variables rather than to serve as a complete list of relevant factors. The examples showed that it is necessary to take both encoding conditions and retrieval conditions into account before performance can be adequately described; in the following section we put forward some views on the interactions between encoding and retrieval.

ENCODING AND RETRIEVAL

Encoding and retrieval processes have never been viewed strictly as a dichotomy; nevertheless, they have traditionally been regarded as rather separate components of memory. More recently, the work of Tulving and his colleagues has been instrumental in establishing the view that it is the *interaction* between encoding and retrieval, rather than either set of processes taken separately, that is crucial to an understanding of memory performance.

In this section we wish to emphasize the strong similarity between encoding and retrieval; we will argue, in fact, that they are essentially identical processes, although having somewhat different goals. That is, just as at input the stimulus event is processed in certain qualitative and quantitative ways depending on the stimulus, task demands, and so forth, so the information provided at retrieval is processed more or less deeply and elaborately depending on the subject's set, the compatibility of the retrieval cue with the analyzing system, and the demands of the current task as perceived by the subject. At input, encoding operations are carried out and are recorded as a memory trace; it is postulated that the pattern of retrieval operations is automatically matched with such records of past operations and that remembering of a past event occurs when some critical proportion of operations reflected in the trace is repeated in the current set of operations. Some theorists (e.g., Kolers, 1973; Restle, 1974) have argued that the concept of the memory trace is unnecessary and that remembering is simply a function of repetition of the operations themselves. By this view, familiarity is a function of the degree of skill with which the analyzing operations are performed by the system. Although we concede that such a dynamic view of remembering has much to recommend it over the rather static notion of collections of memory traces, it seems to us that the repetition of operations viewpoint has some trouble in explaining the recall or recognition of specific episodic occurrences. If the original event did not leave a record of its occurrence, what underlies the subject's feelings of recognition on the second presentation? To say that the operations are executed more fluently on the second occurrence hardly seems sufficient, as often the event in question comprises well-known elements (words, faces, objects) in novel patterns or surroundings. What is the correlate of the feeling that the event has occurred previously? Finding no answer to this question, we prefer to say that the operations leave a record and that recognition is a function of how completely the record is matched by operations carried out on the event's second occurrence. Also, successful recognition will depend on the uniqueness or distinctiveness of the target event's encoding; if the encoding record is highly similar to the record of many other past events, then even a high degree of overlap between target information and cue information will not be associated with successful recognition, because a distinctive encoding/ retrieval combination cannot be achieved. In metaphorical terms, the retrieval information "resonates" with too many traces for the target trace to be successfully isolated (Lockhart, Craik, & Jacoby, 1976).

What determines how retrieval information is treated? In particular, what determines whether or not the cue is elaborated extensively by the processing system? Some "retrieval encodings" will be formed relatively automatically or spontaneously from the cue, just as stimuli typically induce their "habitual" percept; but other encodings will be formed only in response to task demands. For example, in situations where the subject is aware of having experienced the event previously, he or she will take more trouble to carry out further processing of the cue. Similarly, whereas a casual glance at a person's face may not lead to recognition, if the person proceeds to greet you in a friendly fashion, further information is typically generated in an attempt to remember where you have met the person before. Such self-induced reconstructive processing is presumably utilized much more extensively in recall; in recognition, however, where retrieval information is usually richer, the processing follows more directly from the retrieval cue itself. Thus, in overview, we are arguing that retrieval processing, like input encoding, is under strategic control; the type and amount of elaborative processing carried out on the information provided will depend on a variety of features of the stimulus and task. Some processing occurs relatively spontaneously, and some must be directed by task demands (Jacoby & Craik, 1978).

We postulate that retrieval will be successful to the extent that retrieval processing matches encoding processing. On the other hand, the possibility of retrieving a particular event will be reduced to the extent that the target encoding is similar to other traces in the system. As suggested above, one possible reason for the higher levels of retention typically associated with semantic encodings, compared with phonemic or structural encodings, is that semantic encodings have a greater potential for distinctiveness; in turn, this implies that if the conditions of encoding are adequately reinstated at retrieval, the retrieval encoding thus formed will specify the target trace unambiguously and so lead to successful remembering of the event.

Since naturally occurring events are usually multidimensional in nature, it follows that the encoded trace will reflect many of these component dimensions. It seems possible that the effectiveness of a particular unidimensional cue will depend on how similar the target event is to other encoded events on that particular dimension. Thus, if the dimensions are differentially overloaded, it is possible that one cue would be highly effective whereas a second would be relatively ineffective for a particular target trace. This notion is illustrated in an unpublished pilot experiment carried out by F. I. M. Craik and E. Tulving. In this study, distinctiveness was manipulated by varying the number of other similar items presented. In addition, items were encoded on two major dimensions—sound and meaning—and the distinctiveness of the two dimensions was manipulated independently. Specifically, subjects were presented with a list of 72 words; each word was presented twice, on one occasion with a rhyming word and on the other with its semantic category name. The 144 presentations were randomized; thus the lag between first and second presentation was random. Also, the first presentation of a word was with a rhyme in approximately half the cases and with a category name in the other half. The rhymes and category names were later used as cues for the recall of the words. Each cue was used either 1, 4, or 8 times throughout the set, and the number of words nested under each rhyme cue (1, 4, or 8 words) was combined orthogonally with the number of words nested under each semantic cue (1, 4, or 8 words). There were thus 9 phonemic–semantic cue combinations (1–1, 1–4, 1–8, 4–1, etc.) with 8 words in each of the 9 combinations. Thus, for example, the 8 words in the 1–1 group each had a unique rhyme and a unique category; whereas the 8 words in the 1–8 group each had unique rhymes (i.e., no other word in the list rhymed with any one of them), but all 8 belonged to the same semantic category. After all words had been presented twice, subjects were given either all phonemic cues or all category cues and were asked to recall as many words as possible. After 10 minutes on this task, subjects were given the second group of cues for a similar

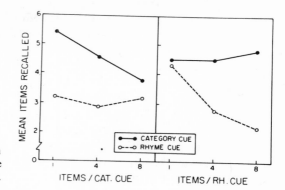

FIG. 8.3 Cued recall as a function
of number of items per category cue
and number of items per rhyme cue.

recall period. The point of the study was to explore whether word retrieval could be manipulated within two independent dimensions. It seemed possible that a word might be inaccessible via one cue but readily accessible via another (cf. Tulving & Thomson, 1973).

The results are shown in Fig. 8.3. The figure shows that as more words were nested under each category name (left-hand panel), the category cues declined in effectiveness whereas the rhyme cues were unaffected; correspondingly, when more words were nested under each rhyme (right-hand panel)(, the rhyme cues declined in power but the category cues did not. The pattern of results illustrates the cue overload effect (Watkins & Watkins, 1975). Also, the design and results of the present study are quite similar to experiments with sentence material reported by Anderson (1974) and by Bransford, McCarrell, Franks, and Nitsch (1977).

A further result concerns the effectiveness of the second cue given that the first was ineffective. Table 8.1 shows first that second cues were associated with quite high recall levels (even though recall had failed on the first attempt) and second that again recall declined as more items were nested under each cue.

Forgetting is thus highly cue dependent (Tulving, 1974), and retention level is a function of the distinctiveness of the encoding along the dimension utilized at retrieval. Thus, as stressed above, distinctiveness is not an absolute quality but is relative to the background of other relevant encodings.

TABLE 8.1
Cued Recall on Second Test Given Nonrecall on First

	Items per Cue		
	1	4	8
Category cue	.63	.33	.23
Rhyme cue	.42	.19	.10

Distinctiveness can be manipulated "episodically" by varying the similarity of other encodings in the same experimental situation; presumably, distinctiveness can be made less localized by inducing encodings that differ from all previous encodings.

A further factor of major importance in retrieval is the congruity of the target encoding with the structure of the system. The organized structure of the system constrains and guides processing of retrieval information; so that if an event was compatible or congruent with the system on first presentation, it is likely that the resulting encoding can be reconstructed relatively easily during retrieval, thereby allowing remembering to occur. There is a paradox inherent in this view, in that commonly occurring or expected events will be encoded easily by the system but will also leave traces that are highly similar to those of many past events; thus accurate reconstruction can occur at retrieval, but performance will be reduced by the cue-overload effect. Optimal retention apparently occurs first in situations where an unusual event is encoded and excellent retrieval information is provided, as in the recognition of rare words (Gregg, 1976; Schulman, 1967) or of low-ranking category exemplars (Jacoby & Craik, 1978; Schnur, 1977). Retention levels are also high when the event can be analyzed by a highly organized section of the cognitive system, which arguably permits fine-grained differentiation of encoded events and guides reconstructive retrieval (Gibson & Gibson, 1955; Saltz, 1971). In this second category could be placed the mnemonic feats of master chess players (De Groot, 1965) and the excellent remembering of events with high emotional or personal implications (e.g., Keenan, MacWhinney, & Mayhew, 1977; Rogers, Kuiper, & Kirker, 1977).

Finally, in this section we endorse the importance of the interactions between encoding and retrieval operations stressed by Tulving and his colleagues (e.g., Tulving & Thomson, 1973). Fisher and Craik (1977) have shown that words encoded semantically are best retrieved by semantic cues, whereas words encoded phonemically are best retrieved by phonemic cues—a result illustrating Tulving's encoding specificity principle. However, they also found that retention levels were substantially higher in the case of semantic encoding/semantic cue than with phonemic encoding/phonemic cue. Fisher and Craik thus argued that both input–output compatibility and the nature of the code were necessary to describe the results fully, although this conclusion has been questioned by Tulving (1978). In the case of word recall, it is possible to compare retention levels between different encoding–cue combinations, but in other tasks such comparisons may be meaningless. To give a rather bizarre example, if two groups of naive Martians were presented with bicycles and one group was set to learn to ride them while the second group's task was to study the bicycles' shape by making drawings, it is reasonable to suppose that subsequent testing would reveal that the "learn to ride" group could ride better than members of the "learn to draw" group and vice versa. However, it is just not possible to compare the riding skill of the "learn to ride" group with the drawing skill of the "learn to draw" group. In terms of memory research, it follows that the criterial memory task must be appropriate for the specific learning operations carried out initially (Bransford, Franks, Morris, & Stein, 1978; Jacoby, 1973b). Whether or not it is meaningful to compare different encoding–retrieval combinations may depend on the level of description adopted by different theorists.

Two further important distinctions have recently been drawn in memory research; the distinction between episodic and semantic memory (Tulving, 1972) and that between memory viewed as a system of traces and memory viewed as global "stage-setting" changes in the system (Bransford, McCarrell, Franks, & Nitsch, 1977). We comment on these distinctions briefly from the viewpoint adopted in this chapter.

EPISODIC AND SEMANTIC MEMORY

Tulving (1972) introduced these terms to distinguish memory for specific autobiographical events tied to a particular time and place (episodic memory) from a person's general knowledge of the world (semantic memory). We find this distinction a useful one but again argue that a conceptual continuity may be more useful than the implied dichotomy of episodic and semantic memories. For example, although it is clear that meeting a new person briefly in a certain setting constitutes an episode, how do we classify our memory of the person's face viewed from several different angles or the gradual build-up of knowledge about the person as we meet her or him in different surroundings? It seems clear that "pure" episodic memories shade off into generalized semantic memories through learning and into memories that are specific, for example, to one object viewed in different surroundings.

One way of characterizing the episodic–semantic continuum is as a hierarchy, with episodes in specific contexts forming the bottom nodes and information comon to several episodes represented by nodes at the next level up. Thus higher levels of the hierarchy would represent increasingly generalized information about relatively wide classes of specific events. In fact, the information represented by higher nodes could be termed *learning*, whereas the lowest nodes would be typically termed *memories*. It is immediately clear that such a hierarchical representation is unsatisfactory if it exists on one plane only; information common to Nodes a, b, c, and d may be represented by a higher Node, x; but there may well be some other dimension of similarity between Nodes a, c, g, and h represented by Node α lying on a different plane.

It seems generally agreed by present-day cognitive theorists that the generalized knowledge abstracted from many episodic experiences subsequently functions as an interpretive system to analyze and comprehend further events. By this view, higher levels of the hierarchy proposed earlier would be utilized relatively often, whereas terminal nodes would be accessed and activated only when a specific episodic memory was retrieved. Speculatively, higher level general procedures may be relatively easy to access and utilize, whereas episodic representations may require more effort and precise guidance from input stimulation before they can be activated. It is an interesting question whether the ability to reactivate episodic memories arose later in developmental and evolutionary history than the ability to utilize general procedures. It seems likely that one major evolutionary advantage enjoyed by man is the ability to reactivate episodic memories and thus be able to *reflect* on specific past events as opposed to merely being able to *utilize* past experience in a relatively general way.

MEMORY AS "STAGE SETTING" AS OPPOSED TO A TRACE SYSTEM

Bransford et al. (1977) have argued that memory should not be viewed as a system of records but rather that the whole system is in some degree modified by successive events, so that when an event recurs it is dealt with differently on its second occurrence than it was on its first. By this view, "learning" consists of modifications to the cognitive system that allow the system to differentiate between stimuli in a finer grained fashion (cf. Gibson & Gibson, 1955; Saltz, 1971), and "memory" reflects the system dealing with events in a skillful fashion. Thus memory is to be understood as the system "setting the stage," or acting as a background for the interpretation of novel and familiar events. Similar views have been put forward by Kolers (1973) and Restle (1974). As discussed earlier in the *Encoding and Retrieval* section of the present chapter, we agree that such a view can provide a basis for feelings of familiarity but do not see that it allows a description of memory for specific episodes.

The main point of the present section, however, is to argue that a controversy between memory as stage setting and memory as a system of records is unnecessary. One way of integrating the two approaches is to postulate that the cognitive system can work in a variety of modes ranging from "comprehension"—in which past learning serves as the background and attention focuses on the incoming events—to "remembering"—in which case new inputs (retrieval cues) act as the background and the attentional focus is on reactivation of some encoded aspect of past experience. In the latter case, the reactivation can be of relatively general information—as in question-answering—or of context-specific information—remembering a particular event.

CONCLUSIONS

In this chapter we have attempted to paint a rather broad picture of the factors important for an understanding of human memory processes. We believe that such a global approach may be useful at present; once many theorists agree on the general outlines of a satisfactory theory, the notions can be refined by a variety of means including experimentation, mathematical formalization, simulation, and further conceptual analysis.

Although the present ideas have arisen indirectly from the work on levels of processing (Craik & Lockhart, 1972; Craik & Tulving, 1975), it is obvious that many features of these earlier models have been de-emphasized or dropped. The notion of a linear sequence of processing stages has gone, for example. Elaboration or extensiveness of processing is more emphasized, but we still stress that some types of encoding are more beneficial for memory than are others: namely, encodings (either "sensory," pictorial, or linguistic) that are rich in associative potential and are encoded in highly structured parts of the cognitive system. Also we have attempted to integrate notions of input processing to the ideas of encoding/retrieval interactions developed by Tulving and his associates.

Our central argument is that an elaborated stimulus leads to a distinctive encoding; distinctiveness is not absolute, however, but is relative to a background of other encoded events on one or more encoding dimensions. The event will be well retrieved to the extent that the retrieval cue can be elaborated in turn to reconstruct the specific target encoding and not other, similar encodings.

Is learning then a matter of differentiation and distinctiveness as argued by Gibson and Gibson (1955), Saltz (1971), and others? To some extent, we are endorsing this notion, although we also wish to incorporate some ideas of the type of encoding and to stress the notion of memory as the record of perceptual analyses and ideas of compatibility between encoding and retrieval processes. A further way in which we differ from the Gibsons' position is that we do not see differentiation as being in competition with reconstructive elaboration; in our view, they are two sides of the same coin. Where the Gibsons (1955), and other theorists who have adopted their viewpoint, talk of the organism becoming attuned to the richness of the stimulus array or educated to pick up information from the light, we are asking what is the nature of that attunement or education; how might we describe the changes in the processes inside the head? Presumably, *something* must correlate with changes in attunement and education. Our description is in terms of elaborative processes and their relations to retrieval conditions.

ACKNOWLEDGMENTS

This chapter was written while the first author was on research leave in the Department of Psychology, Stanford University. The research reported was supported by grants from the National Research Council of Canada to both authors. We are grateful for helpful comments on an earlier draft from Betty Ann Levy and Edward E. Smith.

REFERENCES

Anderson, J. R. Retrieval of propositional information from long-term memory. *Cognitive Psychology*, 1974, *6*, 451–474.

Anderson, J. R., & Reder, L. M. Elaborative processing of prose material. In L. S. Cermak & F. I. M. Craik (Eds.), *Levels of processing in human memory*. Hillsdale, NJ: Lawrence Erlbaum Associates, 1978.

Bower, G. H. A multicomponent view of the memory trace. In K. W. Spence & J. T. Spence (Eds.), *The psychology of learning and motivation: Advances in research and theory* (Vol. 1). New York: Academic Press, 1967.

Bransford, J. D., Franks, J. J., Morris, C. D., & Stein, B. S. Some general constraints on learning and memory research. In L. S. Cermak & F. I. M. Craik (Eds.), *Levels of processing in human memory*. Hillsdale, NJ: Lawrence Erlbaum Associates, 1978.

Bransford, J. D., McCarrell, N. S., Franks, J. J., & Nitsch, K. E. Toward unexplaining memory. In R. Shaw & J. Bransford (Eds.), *Perceiving, acting, and knowing*. Hillsdale, NJ: Lawrence Erlbaum Associates, 1977.

Broadbent, D. E. *Perception and communication*. London: Pergamon Press, 1958.

Broadbent, D. E. *Decision and stress*. New York: Academic Press, 1971.

Chabot, R. J., Miller, T. J., & Juola, J. F. The relationship between repetition and depth of processing. *Memory & Cognition*, 1976, *4*, 677–782.

Craik, F. I. M., & Levy, B. A. The concept of primary memory. In W. K. Estes (Ed.), *Handbook of learning and cognitive processes*, (Vol. 4). Hillsdale, NJ: Lawrence Erlbaum Associates, 1976.

Craik, F. I. M., & Lockhart, R. S. Levels of processing: A framework for memory research. *Journal of Verbal Learning and Verbal Behavior*, 1972, *11*, 671–684.

Craik, F. I. M., & Tulving, E. Depth of processing and the retention of words in episodic memory. *Journal of Experimental Psychology: General*, 1975, *104*, 268–294.

Craik, F. I. M., & Watkins, M. J. The role of rehearsal in short-term memory. *Journal of Verbal Learning and Verbal Behavior*, 1973, *12*, 599–607.

Dark, V. J., & Loftus, G. R. The role of rehearsal in long-term memory performance. *Journal of Verbal Learning and Verbal Behavior*, 1976, *15*, 479–490.

Darley, C. F., & Glass, A. L. Effects of rehearsal and serial list position on recall. *Journal of Experimental Psychology: Human Learning and Memory*, 1975, *1*, 453–458.

De Groot, A. D. *Thought and choice in chess*. New York: Basic Books, 1965.

Deutsch, J. A., & Deutsch, D. Attention: Some theoretical considerations. *Psychological Review*, 1963, *70*, 80–90.

Erdelyi, M. H. A new look at the new look: Perceptual defense and vigilance. *Psychological Review*, 1974, *81*, 1-25.

Eysenck, M. W. Depth, elaboration, and distinctiveness. In L. S. Cermak & F. I. M. Craik (Eds.), *Levels of processing in human memory*. Hillsdale, NJ: Lawrence Erlbaum Associates, 1978.

Fisher, R. P., & Craik, F. I. M. The interaction between encoding and retrieval operations in cued recall. *Journal of Experimental Psychology: Human Learning and Memory*, 1977, *3*, 701-711.

Gibson, J. J., & Gibson, E. J. Perceptual learning: Differentiation or enrichment? *Psychological Review*, 1955, *62*, 32-41.

Glenberg, A., Smith, S. M., & Green, C. Type I rehearsal: Maintenance and more. *Journal of Verbal Learning and Verbal Behavior*, 1977, *16*, 339-352.

Goldstein, A. G., & Chance, J. E. Recognition of complex visual stimuli. *Perception & Psychophysics*, 1971, *9*, 237-241.

Gregg, V. H. Word frequency, recognition and recall. In J. Brown (Ed.), *Recall and recognition*. London: Wiley, 1976.

Hintzman, D. L. Theoretical implications of the spacing effect. In R. L. Solso (Ed.), *Theories in cognitive psychology: The Loyola Symposium* Hillsdale, NJ: Lawrence Erlbaum Associates, 1974.

Jacoby, L. L. Encoding processes, rehearsal, and recall requirements. *Journal of Verbal Learning and Verbal Behavior*, 1973, *12*, 302-310. (a)

Jacoby, L. L. Test-appropriate strategies in retention of categorized lists. *Journal of Verbal Learning and Verbal Behavior*, 1973, *12*, 675-682. (b)

Jacoby, L. L., Bartz, W. H., & Evans, J. D. A functional approach to levels of processing. *Journal of Experimental Psychology: Human Learning and Memory*, 1978, *4*, 331-346.

Jacoby, L. L., & Craik, F. I. M. Effects of elaboration of processing at encoding and retrieval: Trace distinctiveness and recovery of initial context. In L. S. Cermak & F. I. M. Craik (Eds.), *Levels of processing in human memory*. Hillsdale, NJ: Lawrence Erlbaum Associates, 1978.

Johnston, W. A., & Heinz, S. P. *Attention: An integrative conceptual framework*. Paper presented at the annual meeting of the Psychonomic Society, St. Louis, November 1976.

Keenan, J. M., MacWhinney, B., & Mayhew, D. Pragmatics in memory: A study of natural conversation. *Journal of Verbal Learning and Verbal Behavior*, 1977, *16*, 549-560.

Keren, G. Some consideration of two alleged kinds of selective attention. *Journal of Experimental Psychology: General*, 1976, *105*, 349-374.

Klein, K., & Saltz, E. Specifying the mechanisms in a levels-of-processing approach to memory. *Journal of Experimental Psychology: Human Learning and Memory*, 1976, *2*, 671-679.

Kolers, P. A. Remembering operations. *Memory & Cognition*, 1973, *1*, 347-355.

Kolers, P. A. Memorial consequences of automatized encoding. *Journal of Experimental Psychology: Human Learning and Memory*, 1975, *1*, 689-701.

Lockhart, R. S. *The spacing effect in free recall*. Paper presented at the annual meeting of the Psychonomic Society, St. Louis, November 1973.

Lockhart, R. S., Craik, F. I. M., & Jacoby, L. L. Depth of processing, recognition and recall: Some aspects of a general memory system. In J. Brown (Ed.), *Recall and recognition*. London: Wiley, 1976.

Moscovitch, M., & Craik, F. I. M. Depth of processing, retrieval cues, and uniqueness of encoding as factors in recall. *Journal of Verbal Learning and Verbal Behavior*, 1976, *15*, 447-458.

Nelson, T. O. Repetition and depth of processing. *Journal of Verbal Learning and Verbal Behavior*, 1977, *16*, 151-171.

Newell, A. You can't play 20 questions with nature and win. In W. G. Chase (Ed.), *Visual information processing*. New York: Academic Press, 1974.

Norman, D. A. Toward a theory of memory and attention. *Psychological Review*, 1968, *75*, 522–536.

Norman, D. A., & Bobrow, D. G. *Descriptions: A basis for memory acquisition and retrieval* (Tech. Rep. No. 74). University of California, San Diego: Center for Human Information Processing, 1977.

Potter, M. C. Meaning in visual search *Science*, 1975, *187*, 965–966.

Restle, F. Critique of pure memory. In R. L. Solso (Ed.), *Theories in cognitive psychology: The Loyola Symposium*. Potomac, Md.: Lawrence Erlbaum Associates, 1974.

Rogers, T. B., Kuiper, N. A., & Kirker, W. S. Self-reference and the encoding of personal information. *Journal of Personality and Social Psychology*, 1977, *35*, 677–688.

Rumelhart, D. E. Toward an interactive model of reading. In S. Dornic (Ed.), *Attention and performance VI*. Hillsdale, NJ: Lawrence Erlbaum Associates, 1977.

Saltz, E. *The cognitive bases of human learning*. Homewood, Ill.: Dorsey, 1971.

Schnur, P. Testing the encoding elaboration hypothesis: The effects of exemplar ranking on recognition and recall. *Memory & Cognition*, 1977, *5*, 666–672.

Schulman, A. I. Word length and rarity in recognition memory. *Psychonomic Science*, 1967, *9*, 211–212.

Treisman, A. M. Monitoring and storage of irrelevant messages in selective attention. *Journal of Verbal Learning and Verbal Behavior*, 1964, *3*, 449–459.

Tulving, E. Episodic and semantic memory. In E. Tulving & W. Donaldson (Eds.), *Organization of memory*. New York: Academic Press, 1972.

Tulving, E. Cue-dependent forgetting. *American Scientist*, 1974, *64*, 74–82.

Tulving, E. Relation between encoding specificity and levels of processing. In L. S. Cermak & F. I. M. Craik (Eds.), *Levels of processing in human memory*. Hillsdale, NJ: Lawrence Erlbaum Associates, 1978.

Tulving, E., & Thomson, D. M. Encoding specificity and retrieval processes in episodic memory. *Psychological Review*, 1973, *80*, 352–373.

Watkins, O. C., & Watkins, M. J. Buildup of proactive inhibition as a cue-overload effect. *Journal of Experimental Psychology: Human Learning and Memory*, 1975, *104*, 442–452.

Wickelgren, W. A. *Learning and memory*. Englewood Cliffs, NJ: Prentice-Hall, 1977.

Woodward, A. E., Bjork, R. A., & Jongeward, R. H., Jr. Recall and recognition as a function of primary rehearsal. *Journal of Verbal Learning and Verbal Behavior*, 1973, *12*, 608–617.

9

The Primacy of Perceiving: An Ecological Reformulation of Perception for Understanding Memory

M. T. Turvey
University of Connecticut,
and Haskins Laboratories

Robert Shaw
University of Connecticut

INTRODUCTION

In what way do perception and memory relate? Self-evidently, an answer to this question depends a good deal on how the two terms in the sought-after relation are construed. It is equally self-evident that the two terms, *perception* and *memory*, are so intimately bound that given a definition of one, the interpretation of the other is necessarily constrained.

We present an overview of kernel themes that collectively provide the contemporary orientation to perception. These themes have at their source, or so we claim, an overarching dualism that conceives of the animal and its environment as logically independent. This collection of themes is the perceptual theorist's legacy of (at least) the last 500 years; and given the interdependence of the conceptions of perception and memory, it follows that the understanding of perception induced by this legacy conditions our understanding of memory in the large, and not just its relation to perception. It is our major intent to contrast the traditional themes with themes of a radically different kind that have as their base animal–environment synergy (or reciprocity). Collectively, these themes identify what might be called an ecological orientation to perception. Viewed ecologically, perception takes an unconventional form: It appears to be a property of the ecosystem rather than of the animal as such; its laws seem to require a three-term logic for their expression; and it does not appear to be propositional and mediated—to the contrary, perception is nonpropositional and direct. The ecological reformulation of perception offers a new framework in which to pursue the puzzle of memory.

In keeping with the charge of this conference, we propose that the contrast between animal–environment dualism and animal–environment synergy is that between two departure points—one that has determined the direction of thought on matters of perception and memory for the past five centuries (or more) and one that might provide a new direction of thought on these matters for the future.

THE LEGACY OF THE PAST FIVE CENTURIES

Animal–Environment Dualism

The dualism with which we are most familiar is that drawn by Descartes between mind and body. The hegemony of this separation in philosophy, psychology, and physiology needs no comment. Nevertheless, a case can be made for an even more pervasive and influential dualism of which the Cartesian kind is merely one of several significant manifestations. This overarching dualism is that drawn between the animal and the environment: The animal, as perceiver and as actor, is construed as logically independent of the environment, which it perceives, with respect to which it acts, and together with which it evolved. What is denied is the organizational wholeness of the animal–environment system (cf. Fitch & Turvey, 1978; Lombardo, 1973).

A primary consequence of animal–environment dualism has been the promotion of the animal as the proper unit of analysis for psychology. In its ideal form (cf. Lombardo, 1973), the focus of this methodology is strictly on entities whose locus is either obviously the animal or deemed to be the animal as a matter of convention. In reference to perception, consider the three varieties of psychology in the past half-millennium: physiological, mentalistic, and behavioristic. The brain most obviously is in the animal and so, it necessarily follows, must be the brain's constituents. The mind is less obviously *in* the animal, but it has become a matter of convention to speak as if it were and to regard its constituents—the mental processes—as bounded by the skin. Behavior, though not in the animal as such, is often localized in the animal in the form of surrogate, mediating responses. Whether the analysis be in terms of physiology, mentalism, or behaviorism, questions of perception are read as questions of what the requisite animal-localized entities are and how they relate.

We see, in short, that the ideal methodology has been to examine the perceiver as distinct from the environment—a methodology that is consonant with the following two subthemes. First, it is popular to identify the percept as the terminus of a unidirectional causal chain that begins in the world. In this conventional view, the perceiver and world, the animal and its environment, are causally separate. The causal theory of perception (Russell, 1927) suggests that the *proximal cause* for perceptual experience is not the environment as such but one of the links in the cause–and–effect chain that connects the perceiver to his or her surroundings. In short, and this is the second subtheme, "knowledge by acquaintance" is interpreted not as knowledge of something happening in the environment but as knowledge of something happening *inside* the animal. The animal does not perceive the environment as such, but rather an animal-analogue (more familiarly, a homunculus) perceives a representation of the environment.

If an animal and its environment are logically independent, then one is encouraged to speak about certain epistemic entities as being proprietary to the animal or to the environment and to liken the animal–environment relation to an economic transaction. The problem of the ascription of meaning is commonly pursued in the context of an economic metaphor. The conventional practice is to hold distinct what some environmental arrangement *is* and what that environmental arrangement *means*. The former is said to be in the physical or in the environmental domain and the latter in the mental or in the animal domain. Thus follows the view that neural, or mental, or mediating response processes give meaning to meaningless sense data or, more generally, that the animal gives meaning to the environment. The economics of the situation is that the environment supplies the signs and the animal supplies the significances.

There are many more manifestations of the animal–environment dualism —some of which are fleshed out in the remarks that follow. For the present it would be valuable to shore up the claim that mentalism and behaviorism *both* adhere to the methodological ideal fostered by the dualism. Behaviorism would seem to lay great store by the environment; at least behaviorism's explanations of psychological phenomena are environmentally tinged to the degree that mentalism's explanations are not. Moreover, logical (Ryle, 1949), methodological and radical behaviorism (cf. Skinner, 1974) reject mind–body dualism; whereas by and large, the various forms of mentalistic psychology have, over the ages, courted Descartes's separation. Indeed, the commonplace understanding is that mentalism and behaviorism are mutually exclusive; and we should argue in consequence that if mentalism endorses the methodological ideal of animal–environment dualism, then behaviorism most surely cannot. A brief deliberation, focused on the concept of environment, is sufficient to disarm such arguments and to lead us to the important conclusion that theories that distinguish on the issue of mind–body dualism may be indistinguishable on the issue of animal–environment dualism—a conclusion that points to the latter dualism's overarching status.

The term *environmentalism* is not uncommon in behavioristic psychology. It is a synonym for past experience with the environment and is meant to do explanatory duty similar to, but distinguishable from, nativistic abilities on one hand and mental processes on the other. But just as appeals to innate capabilities as explanatory principles are often gratuitous, with the nature of the capabilities left largely unanalyzed, so are appeals to environmentalism.

The term *environment* is used interchangeably with the terms *stimuli* and *reinforcement contingencies*. One interpretation of this commutativity of terms is that the environment is an independent variable in relation to the dependent variable that is the animal's behavior. This unidirectional relation is reminiscent of the causal chain theory of perception, and it is congruent with the methodology of animal–environment dualism. A further interpretation of the commutativity of *environment* with *stimuli* and *reinforcement contingencies* is that the environment is conceived of in a very general sense. Let us explain.

Contemporary behaviorism shares with its intellectual predecessors the beliefs that learning is a general capability and that the laws of learning will hold uniformly across all species. It is the case, however, that each species occupies a different niche where species and niche are defined relative to each other. In brief (and anticipating a larger point of this paper), environments are specific to species, and learning as a facultative adaptation (Williams, 1966) ought to be specific to environments. We may well suppose, therefore, that learning is not a general process differing only quantitatively from one species to another; rather, it is a special ability that differs *qualitatively* from species to species, paralleling the qualitative differences in their environments.

There is no recognition of the fundamental species-specific aspect of the concept of environment in behavioristic psychology. For that psychology, in both its past and present forms, the methodological axiom has been to construct surroundings for an animal that can be reliably and easily controlled by an experimenter. The environment has been experimenter-specific rather than species- or animal-specific. And to this methodological axiom are added the selection of a "representative" animal for the investigation of the laws of learning and the selection of a (piece of) behavior for investigation according to the criteria of reliability and ease of measurement (cf. Skinner, 1957). Collectively, these axioms define the behaviorist methodology, and they are clearly in keeping with the ideal method of animal–environment dualism. If one were to summarize current feelings toward the laws of learning, the summary would bespeak a relativistic rather than uniform view: Learning depends in important (coimplicative) ways on the animal doing the learning, the behavior being learned, and the situation in which the learning is occurring (cf. Bolles, 1975). But this, as remarked, is to anticipate our argument. The section that follows is more pedestrian. In it we identify the doctrines that have been the bedrocks of perceptual theory in the present and past centuries.

The Inadequacy of Stimulation and
the Need for Epistemic Mediators

The received status of proximal stimulation is that it relates poorly, equivocally, to its distal referent, the environment. The retinal image has long been taken as the apposite optical basis for visual perception; yet it is by traditional definition a bidimensional, inverted, distorted, and temporally frozen image of the environmental layout at which the eye is directed. Moreover, under traditional analysis, the same retinal image can result from an indefinitely large number of distal stimuli, and vice versa. To quote Koffka (1935): "for each distant stimulus there exists a practically infinite number of proximal stimuli; thus the 'same stimulus' in the distant sense may not be the same stimulus in the proximal sense; as a matter of fact it seldom is [p. 80]."

Not unrelatedly, the descriptors of light and sound as provided by physics have been taken as the received descriptors for the purpose of perception. Thus, an acceptable description of light is that it is radiant energy in the form of quanta (photons, for visible light) that can vary in mass and energy. From the perspective of the retinal mosiac, light rays are distinguished only by intensity and wave length; and the ageless mystery, then, is how the rich vocabulary of visual perception is induced from the impoverished vocabulary of the light.

In short, the past and current claim is that the energy distributions at the receptor surfaces are insufficient in richness and precision to account for perception. If the energy distributions underdetermine perception, then mechanisms must be proposed to redress the imbalance. Putatively, the animal as perceiver must bring to bear sources of knowledge such as memories and concepts and intellectivelike operations, such as hypothesis testing and inference, in order to achieve an adequate perception of its environment. Perception, in the conventional view, is epistemically mediated (Shaw & Bransford, 1977; Turvey, 1977).

Let us express the fundamental premise guiding theoreticians in the past half-millennium as follows: The relation between proximal stimulation and environmental properties is intractably equivocal or nonspecific. To this doctrine of intractable nonspecificity, should be added the following doctrine: the independence of perception from stimulation. The often-cited evidence is that where proximal stimulation is fixed, perception may vary (e.g., the Necker cube); and where proximal stimulation is varying, perception may be unchanged (e.g., the retinal orientation of an object in the frontal plane varies with head movement, but the perceived orientation does not). In accepting these doctrines as identifying the initial conditions for perception, it follows that insofar as perception is veridical, insofar as the animal and its environment relate adaptively, *the animal as perceiver must embody a theory of the environment and a theory of how the environment structures energy distributions.* Whatever epistemic mediators are proposed, if they are to be taken seriously, they must subsume as a minimal requirement *both* theories. Nothing less will suffice as a basis for discerning the meaning of the light at the eyes, of the pressure waves at the ears, of the molecular distributions at the nose, etc.

The thorny issues to which the conventional view is heir have never been resolved satisfactorily. These issues, at their core, are questions of origin. It is well and good, perhaps, to postulate mediational mechanisms that are essentially embodiments of knowledge about the world if one can present a sensible means by which that knowledge is made possible. Echoing Pattee (1970), one cannot divorce the mechanism question of "How does it work?" from the origin question of "How did it arise?" And it can be argued (and is, later) that neither empiricism nor nativism have responded convincingly or even seriously to the latter.

In view of the problems it gives rise to, why have scholars (both past and present) accepted the traditional analysis of the physical basis of perception as sufficient for their purposes? Faced with the erstwhile doctrines, the student of perception has had two options. Figuratively speaking, one option is to pack whatever *epistemic* entities are needed between the proximal stimulus and the percept so as to derive the self-evident perceptual complexity and consistency from the imputed physical simplicity and equivocality. This option, as intimated, has been virtually the universal choice for the past half-millennium. The other option is to assume that the doctrines are false and (pursuing the figure of speech) to pack whatever *physical* entities are needed into the physical basis for perception so that it and perception are of the same order and are compatible. This option has been almost universally ignored. The choice of option, we believe, has been dictated by the implicit acceptance of animal–environment dualism.

The point about the dualism, in this respect, is that it fosters tolerance for discrepancies between animal-related statements and environment-related statements. If animal and environment are thought of as logically independent, then it is not upsetting nor especially surprising to learn that the descriptors of one do not fit the descriptors of the other (as the classical descriptors of the light reflected from the environment do not fit the descriptors of visual experience). If the animal and its environment do not comprise an organizational whole and if the animal is taken as the relevant unit of analysis, then the idea of a nonspecific, orderless medium (e.g., the light) is tolerable and the conferring upon the animal of capabilities for imparting specificity and order is a relatively simple, and natural, theoretical gambit.

With respect to the options noted, then, there is a further but related aspect of animal–environment dualism that would hamper pursuit of the second option and reinforce choice of the first option. Essentially, it is the issue of reductionism. This issue most commonly focuses on the animal: Can mental processes be reduced to material processes? Can life be reduced to physics? At the heart of the issue is the understanding that there is more than one level at which an animal can be described and that these levels range from very fine-grained descriptors to very coarse-grained descriptors—for example, subatomic particles to the contents of consciousness. It is similarly the case, however, that proximal stimulation and the environment can be addressed at a number of descriptive levels. The issue of reductionism is no less an issue for proximal stimulation and the environment than it is for the animal, but there is a conspicuous asymmetry of concern in favor of the latter. For present purposes, we need only note that given animal–environment dualism, a theorist can deny vigorously a reductionist argument for the animal as a perceiving agent and yet accept unquestioningly a reductionist argument, say, for the optical support of visual perception (see Fodor, 1975, for a contemporary example). More commonly, a theorist can choose one grain size of description—often coarse—for the animal and another grain size of description—often fine—for stimulation. Although a theorist is willing to remark that the light, after all, is nothing but photons (see Boynton, 1975), he or she would presumably be less willing to remark that the animal, after all, is nothing but atoms.

At all events, given the two aforementioned doctrines, let us proceed to assess the classical stances of empiricism and nativism with reference to the origins of the knowledge needed for perceptual efficiency.

The Problem of Origin: The Solution from Empiricism

The difficulty with assessing the empiricist's approach to the origin question is that empiricism is never pure. A rule of thumb says scratch an empiricist and you will find a rationalist. Thus it is more accurate to describe Aristotle as a "less extreme rationalist than Plato" than it is to describe him as an empiricist. Locke refuted innate knowledge in general but allowed the concept of substance and admitted experience-free and question-begging operations such as reflection and judgment. And the great 19th-century empiricist, von Helmholtz, saw fit to propose explicitly a "law of causation" as a law of thinking prefatory to experience and more generally to presume the laws of inference.

Berkeley (1709/1964) devised an enormously influential empiricism with reference to vision. His favored metaphor was that vision was like language in that the variables of light had no more meaning for an experientially naive observer than would a word in Russian have for a non-Russian-speaking person. For Berkeley, the ascription of meaning to the variables of light was achieved by association with the products (ideas) of specific tactile or kinesthetic experience. But Berkeley's solution is a notorious nonsolution to the origin questions and for a number of reasons. Most blatantly, it is a solution that both accepts *and* denies the doctrine of intractable nonspecificity; the doctrine is accepted for vision (hence the ascription of meaning problem in that modality) and denied for haptic perception (hence the rationalizing role imputed to tactile and kinesthetic ideas). The hidden claim is that haptic perception cannot itself be mediated epistemically if it is to epistemically mediate vision in the manner desired (Mace, 1977; Turvey, 1977). Clearly, the fundamental inconsistency of Berkeley's solution makes it undesirable. At the very least, it raises the heretical question, for conventional theory, of why even one modality should not suffer from nonspecificity of stimulation and not require any kind of epistemic mediation. Nevertheless, we should note that the Berkeleyean (non)solution was promoted by scholars in the last century (e.g., Helmholtz, 1911/1925) and continues to be invoked by scholars in the present century (e.g., Gregory, 1969).

Let us press empiricism's solution to the origin question a little further so as to reveal more of its inconsistency. Recall that epistemic mediators must minimally subsume a theory of the environment and a theory of the way in which the environment structures energy distributions. Is it possible that a specific-association mechanism, such as that proposed by Berkeley and championed illustriously by Helmholtz, could achieve in principle this minimal requirement? Helmholtz spoke as if he meant for rules or algorithms to be applied and as if he assumed the internalization of the theories in question; it is true, nevertheless, that he described no mechanism other than specific associations. A blunt result of 20th-century science is that a device constructed in strict accordance with specific associations is inept at rule acquisition and by extension at theory construction. The proof rests with showing that finite state automata, formally equivalent to specific-association mechanisms, are limited to the acceptance of Type 3 languages[1] (Hunt, 1975).

We may justifiably claim that with regard to the origin of minimally sufficient epistemic mediators, a specific-association mechanism will not do. Let us therefore take the liberty of proposing a different acquisition mechanism but one that is continuous with the commonplace empiricist emphasis on perception as a matter of hypothesis testing. Let us propose that the minimally sufficient epistemic mediators are acquired through a process of projecting and confirming hypotheses.

---

[1]That is to say, one-sided (right or left) linear grammars. Put differently, finite-state automata are incapable of the rules that underly the multiple embeddings of natural-language sentences.

A representative example of the rules or algorithm that Helmholtz had in mind and one that is a popular choice of neo-Helmholtzians (e.g., Epstein, 1973, 1977; Rock, 1975) is the size–distance invariance hypothesis: A given proximal extent determines an invariant ratio of perceived size to perceived distance. The size–distance invariance hypothesis emphasizes covariation of percepts; thus, the perception of size takes into account perceived distance, and the perception of distance takes into account perceived size. This hypothesis can be said to entail knowledge about environmental properties and about how the environment structures proximal stimulation in that it relates to the fact that if the metrical distance of an object from an observer increases, its metrical size must also increse if the metrical size of the retinal image corresponding to the object is to remain unchanged. Let us refer to the size–distance invariance hypothesis as the size–distance invariance *concept*, the reason being that we wish to view acquisition as a process—of projecting and confirming hypotheses—that eventuates in some useful conception of the environment. Can an animal, in principle, acquire the size–distance invariance concept?

Let the animal be in the following conjectural state with respect to the environment: "If an object O projects a proximal extent (visual angle) s and is perceived at a distance d (from me), then O's size is given by: $S = sd$." This hypothesis would be confirmed by the algorithm being consistently correct in an (indefinite) number of instances. Let us worry about consistency and correctness, separately. A minimal assay of the consistency of the algorithm would be given by comparing estimates of S at two distances (d_1 and d_2) and therefore necessarily at two times (t_1 and t_2). The comparison is shown in Fig. 9.1. If $S = s_1 d_1 = s_2 d_2$, then this constitutes minimal confirmation of the consistency of the hypothesis. However, since we cannot compromise the doctrine of intractable nonspecificity, a number of ancillary assays must be conducted in order to guarantee the legitimacy of the comparison. It is worth pausing at this point to see what is at stake.

When the object goes to d_2, there is a change in the proximal stimulation. In order to conduct the comparison in good faith and to protect iself against false conclusions, the animal needs to know whether the change in the proximal stimulation is due *solely* to displacement. Suppose that the two estimates of S do not agree. Is the disagreement due to the fact that the algorithm is incorrect, or is it due to other undetected changes that accompanied (causally or otherwise) the displacement? According to the

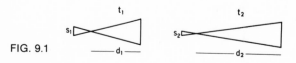

FIG. 9.1

nonspecificity doctrine, the proximal stimulus is ambiguous with reference to the distal object per se and with reference to the *changes* undergone by the distal object. Empiricist theorizing is permitted no *fait accompli*; given intractable nonspecificity, nothing is given.

The point is simply this: To test the consistency of the algorithm, the animal must be assured that only the variables of the algorithm have changed between tests. It must determine, in short, (and much like the scientist) the constancy of the irrelevant variables. To assess the consistency of $S = sd$ entails answers to (at least) the following questions:

1. Has O been preserved over time and displacement? That is, is the O at t_2 (or d_2) the same O as at t_1 (or d_1)? This identifies the problem of *constancy of identity*. If the evidence is that O at t_2 is not the same O at t_1, then the comparison of s_1d_1 and s_2d_2 is invalid.

2. Has O's size been preserved over time and displacement? That is, is the S at t_2 (or d_2) the same S as at t_1 (or d_1)? This identifies the problem of *constancy of size*. If the evidence is that the size has changed, then the comparison is invalid. Unfortunately, the point of acquiring the size–distance invariance concept is to achieve size constancy.

3. Has O's orientation been preserved over time and displacement? That is, is the orientation at t_2 (or d_2) the same orientation as at t_1 (or d_1)? This identifies the problem of *constancy of object orientation*. If the orientation has changed, then the comparison is invalid, because proximal extent is a function of the slant of the object, as Fig. 9.2 demonstrates.

4. Has the animal's orientation to O been preserved over time and displacement? That is, is the orientation of the animal at t_2 (or d_2) the same orientation as at t_1 (or d_1)? This identifies the problem of *constancy of perceiver orientation*. If the animal's orientation has changed, then the comparison is invalid, because proximal extent is a function of the eye's orientation to O.

5. Has O's shape remained the same over time and displacement? That is, has O undergone a nonrigid transformation from t_1 (or d_1) to t_2 (or d_2)? This identifies in part the problem of *constancy of shape*. If O has undergone a nonrigid transformation, then the comparison is invalid, as Fig. 9.3 suggests.

We take the conclusion of this line of reasoning to be that if there is a set A of algorithms to mediate the set C of perceptual constancies, then determining the consistency of any one algorithm, a_i (to mediate the constancy, c_i), requires that the set A be at the disposal of the animal. This conclusion is clearly contradictory to the aims of empiricism.

FIG. 9.2

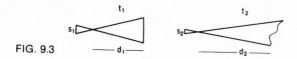

FIG. 9.3

Assuming, nevertheless, that consistency could be established in a manner consistent with empiricism, we ask: Would it be sufficient? If an animal (or a theorist) were content with phenomenal descriptors—that is, descriptors relating solely to how things looked—then consistency might be a sufficient criterion for confirming hypothesized algorithms. It would matter only that for a given distal object or property, the said algorithm would consistently yield the same phenomenal descriptors; on such consistency, stable discriminations could be drawn and category labels reliably ascribed. In the extreme, it is imaginable that a distal object X, by virtue of a given algorithm, would look like Y. That is, X could consistently be given a phenomenal description that is not consonant with the properties of X but with the properties of some other object, Y. Filling in the dummy variables, X could be a saber-toothed tiger and Y a tropical flower. If an animal (or a theorist) were content with phenomenal descriptors, then the physical and behavioral dissonance between tiger and flower would matter little. It would, on the other hand, matter a great deal if the animal (or a theorist) were not content with how things looked but needed to know, in terms of activity, how things related to it and how it related to things.

For any activity to be realized, the material design of the animal and the material design of the environment must be consonant. This mutuality in material design is the support for activity; for example, locomotion by ambulation is possible only if the ground surface can supply reactive forces complementary and equivalent to those forces supplied by the animal. This mutuality, of course, is a matter of physics and cannot be compromised. It follows, then, as a reasonable claim, that for the realization of actions, perception in the service of action cannot simply be consistent; it must be correct. At least it must be correct in the following sense: The animal must veridically perceive the physical nature of the environment in reference to its own physical nature if it is to behave adaptively; algorithms that consistently miscalculate or misrepresent distal objects in reference to the animal will invite physically unrealizable activities and behavioral chaos. The point we are guilty of belaboring is an obvious one: A perceptual theory restricted to an account of the *phenomenal* contact between animal and environment is considerably less constrained and more arbitrary than a theory that respectively includes an account of the *physical* contact between animal and environment.

At all events, the preceding suggests that in reference to confirming a projected algorithm, consistency is insufficient. If, in addition to consistency, correctness (as minimally defined) is required, how might it be determined?

Suppose that a visual algorithm a_i consistently miscalculated the environmental property p_i, which is relevant to the control of some activity. Now according to the official doctrines, proximal stimulation is not specific to the distal object and perception is independent of the proximal stimulation. It follows, therefore, from the official doctrines that the percept "p_i" does not correspond to p_i itself but to a surrogate for p_i—namely, the end product of the algorithm. If the animal could determine the degree to which p_i was consistently miscalculated—that is, the degree to which the property and the percept were at odds—then it could, in principle, make compensatory adjustments to ensure an adaptive relation to p_i. This strategy, however, presupposes that the animal can become apprised of the dimensions of p_i through some means that is independent of the algorithm a_i. For reasons cited above, we cannot allow that haptics is this alternative, independent means if it is intended that haptics makes this appraisal directly. We might allow a comparison of the property p_i as calculated by the algorithm a_i with the property as calculated by a haptic algorithm. But the comparison in question would be of two percepts corresponding to two internal representations (namely, the products of the visual and haptic algorithms), and neither can lay a greater claim to legitimacy than the other.

The muddle that arises is owing to a failure to uncover, within the framework of empiricism, any legitimate kind of knowing that is epistemologically unquestionable. It has been suggested (Fodor, 1975), however, that such epistemic incorrigibility is not really needed. All that *is* needed is that some kind of knowing—in the context of the present argument, some algorithmic consequences—be unquestioned rather than unquestionable. But this solution bears the traces of legerdemain; an unquestioned but incorrect algorithm as a bench mark could hardly guarantee that other algorithms will be adjusted in the direction of a truer fit to reality.

Let us summarize to this point. The question was raised of whether an animal could, in principle, acquire the size–distance invariance concept (as exemplary of the concepts that mediate constancy of perception). The answer appears to be "no" even when the animal is assumed to have the remarkable acumen to propose hypotheses that bear closely on the nature of the environment and the relation between the environment and the light it structures. This acumen, of course, expresses more than just a shade of rationalism; moreover, it invokes nativism. Empiricism's solution to the question of origin, the question of how the animal can come to embody the knowledge needed to achieve perception, reduces to an appeal to a priorism.

We soon inquire whether mechanisms for achieving constancy could have evolved. Our immediate concern is to pursue the comparison between empiricism and rationalism, for most fundamentally, rationalism sought to impugn—on logical grounds—the validity of perception as an instrument of knowledge.

The Primacy of Reason Versus the Primacy of Perception

Rationalism rejects the empiricist's claim that all forms of knowledge can be reduced to just one—namely, perceptual knowledge. Moreover it rejects with equal vigor the notion that perception has primacy over other "faculties of mind." Typically, rationalists have so distrusted the senses as a source of knowledge about the world that they have disavowed any knowledge that does not arise either *de novo* by logical inference or by logical induction from the sparse evidence that the senses on occasion may yield about the world.

The skepticism toward empiricism leads rationalism to distinguish the appearances of the perceived world (phenomena) from the reality that lies behind such appearances (noumena), a reality that is knowable only by rational construction or induction that goes beyond any form of experience. Often in this regard, the fruits of theoretical science (e.g., invisible microbes, unobservable particles, or hidden stellar energy sources) are taken as evidence for skepticism regarding the extent to which human experience can, even in principle, reveal nature's hidden face. For instance, the Copernican revolution and the eventual rejection of the flat-world hypothesis are often cited as significant examples of where our senses have misled us into believing something that reason was eventually able to reveal as patently false. The fact from appearance that the sun rises and sets was replaced by the rational conclusion that it is the earth that moves around the sun rather than vice versa. And although the earth appears to be relatively flat, reasonable arguments to the contrary were launched and embraced by the scientific community centuries before astronauts were able to provide corroborating perceptual evidence. In like vein, the objects of the earth such as rocks, tables, metal rods, and crystal balls appear as densely packed, static solids; however, physical theory, in contravention of the senses, informs us that these perceived solids are in reality clouds of swirling particles whose interstices contain more void than mass. On this line of argument, appearance and reality are largely distinct; and where they are at odds, reason is the final arbitrator.

It is therefore no great leap to the conclusion that theoretical (rational) science has dealt a severe, perhaps fatal, blow to the hypothesis that perception is primary and, in so doing, has undercut the foundation of *any* type of empiricism. But the cogency of this implicit argument against the primacy of perception rests with the legitimacy of distinguishing appearance from reality, a conceptual dichotomy that is a variant of animal–environment dualism.

Let us proceed to the arguments often cited by empiricists for a theory of indirect perception. For interestingly (or ironically) enough, the arguments on which empiricists postulated inferred entities to stand between the knower and the knower's world are the very same arguments that invited rationalists to separate appearance and reality.

The Argument from Illusion (or the Argument from Failure of Specification). Taken to its necessary conclusion, the argument from illusion is generally thought to provide the skeptic with an unassailable position from which to chide empiricism. More positively, the argument is used to buttress a belief in phenomenalism (Ayer, 1940) or in subjective idealism (Berkeley, 1713/1964).

The plausibility of the argument from illusion derives from the fact that things sometimes appear different to different people or to the same person under different circumstances. The early empiricists (like Locke) and later ones (like Moore and Russell) concluded from the fact of variant appearances that some sensible qualities (sometimes called "secondary" qualities) such as colors or odors do not really belong to the objects. Rather, objects are to be identified only with their so-called primary qualities such as shape. Therefore, secondary qualities, such as color, because they do not necessarily belong to the object, must belong to some intermediary entity—an epistemic mediator (e.g., a retinal image or brain-state) that intercedes between the perceiver and his or her world. Such mediating epistemic constructs were usually called "sensa" or "sense data." Significantly, in the postulating of intervening sense data, empiricists ally themselves with a realism that is indirect rather than a realism that is direct.

The dogmatic rationalist often argues that this same argument reveals a chink in the perceptual armor of empiricism, because it can just as well be legitimately used to cast plausible doubt upon the veridicality of so-called primary qualities. Just as an object that is green may appear blue under yellow light, so an object that is circular may appear elliptical from a different perspective. Therefore, one must "perceive" sense data (phenomena) in all cases rather than the actual objects (noumena), so that phenomenalism rather than realism is the only possible contribution of perception. In short, there is a failure of referentiality or specificity in that the patch of color fails to index uniquely a distal *object*. Moreover, because *any* properties perceived may be on some occasion "*p*" and on other occasions "not-*p*," it is impossible to trust perception as a true source of knowledge; surely such a logical contradiction can only inhere in appearance and not in reality; no *real* properties would show such inconstancy. For this reason, it can be argued (e.g., Berkeley) that the primary–secondary property distinction is an invalid contrast. One can no more perceive the true shape of things than one can perceive their true color.

Thus, empiricism was and is hoisted on the twin petards of its implicit dualism: On one hand, empiricism is confounded by the dilemma that if it repudiates the notion of secondary qualities and claims that *all* perceived qualities of objects are primary, then it is guilty of naive realism—thereby exposing the theory to serious attack from the skeptic who uses the argument from illusion. On the other hand, if empiricism seeks to parry this thrust of the skeptic by holding firm to the distinction between primary and secondary qualities, then the argument can be used to infirm not only the usefulness of secondary qualities but that of primary qualities as well. Assuming its validity, the rationalist can wield the argument as weapon, forcing the empiricist to yield up realism to phenomenalism. What begins as a slight retreat of empiricism from naive realism to the apparently more defensible fall-back position of indirect realism ends in a full-fledged route of empirical realism.

The Argument from Incomplete Specification.   Assuming it to be valid, the argument from illusion leads inevitably from the somewhat timid admission by empiricists that some perceived qualities may not be real to the terrible confession that *no* perceived qualities may be real. The argument from incomplete specification has equally dire consequences for empiricism as realism. Following Anscombe (1965), the argument can be summarized as follows:

A hunter aims his rifle and fires at a dark brown patch seen through the green foliage of the forest. Later he discovers much to his dismay that he has unintentionally killed his friend rather than a stag. In this example, the brown patch seems to serve two contradictory perceptual functions—one as an *intentional* object (the stag) and one as a *material* (or referential) object (his friend). To avoid this apparent contradictory outcome, which defiles perception by allowing it to be a source of error rather than of knowledge, it seems advisable to give up a theory of direct perception in favor of an indirect one. From the fact that perception can serve either an intentional function or a material function, to avoid contradiction we must conclude that a sense datum (e.g., a dark brown patch) exists as a perceptual mediary that serves simultaneously as a partial specifier for the intentional object (e.g., the stag) and the material object (e.g., the friend). Error arises because imagination (i.e., invalid inference) can sometimes lead to a fallacious perceptual judgment.

The possible role of imagination in perceptual judgment must be assumed by the traditional empiricist so as to leave unbesmirched the reputation of perception per se as a source of knowledge. For if the empiricist assumes that no imagination is ever involved in the process leading to perceptual judgment, then it would follow that no real difference should exist between intentional and material objects of perception. But such an admission would force empiricism into either of two equally untenable positions: Without imagination as a part of the perceptual judgment process, no errors should ever occur from our perception of the world; or, if it is admitted that imagination can sometimes elaborate sense data to construct intentional objects, then how can it be guaranteed that imagination does not do so in every case, so that perception may always be of appearances and never of reality?[2]

The contrast between empiricism and rationalism is most easily drawn with reference to two distinct questions. First, what is the source of an animal's knowledge? And second, what is the backing for it? Empiricism answered both questions in essentially the same way—"observing events." Rationalism on the other hand answered the first question by an appeal to innate capabilities, an answer referred to as "nativism," and answered the second question by an appeal to reason. The argument from illusion and that from incomplete specification appear to contravene the empiricists' claim that observation or perception is a privileged source of knowledge about the environment and a privileged means for justifying what is known. On these arguments the requisite epistemic mediators—knowledge of the environment and how it structures energy—cannot arise a posteriori. Let us, therefore, consider the claim that they are innately given.

The Problem of Origin: The Solution from Nativism

We will be reading the solution from nativism as the solution from evolutionism. At issue is the question of whether or not the knowledge reputedly needed to achieve perception could have evolved, given the boundary conditions defined on perception by the doctrine of intractable nonspecificity and the doctrine that perception is independent of stimulation (or, conversely, that perception is dependent on internal representation).

---

[2]As the title of this chapter implies, we are clearly of the belief that *an* empiricism is needed. What the conundra identified here suggest, however, is that the establishment of a tenable empiricism will require a radical reconceptualization of perception (and a most careful assessment of the notion of error) so as to take "perception" out of the propositional domain in which it can be said to be either right or wrong and to relocate it in a nonpropositional domain in which the question of whether perception is right or wrong would be nonsensical. Is it that the proper domain of perception is ontology rather than logic or epistemology? If it were, then perception would be characterized as a state of affairs, and like other states of affairs that constitute the facts of the world (such as galaxies, water, living things, etc.), it would be necessarily true by force of existence rather than possibly true by force of argument.

In addition, and closely related, the conundra identified here suggest that the establishment of a tenable empiricism requires that an understanding of "reality" be sought, which for any given animal dissolves the dichotomy of appearance and reality, or the dichotomy of intentional object and material (or referential) object. In part, this dissolution demands a single vocabulary of terms that are symmetric and reflexive, a vocabulary in which animal-focused descriptions are always in reference to the environment and environment-focused descriptions are always in reference to the animal. These thorny issues for a tenable empiricism, in which perceiving is *the* incontrovertible source of knowing what is real, are touched upon in the present chapter and are the subject of a considerably more adventurous treatment elsewhere (Shaw, Turvey, & Mace, in press).

In Neo-Darwinian theory, random variation is affected through mutation defined as change in a chromosomal gene; selection is of those mutants that are most prolific; and what matters is that the gene pool undergoes continuous change.

Let us inquire about the evolution of the size–distance invariance concept. As before, we may take this concept—or algorithm—as representative of the kind of knowledge that would make for stable perception in the face of equivocal and ever-changing stimulation. And the significance of this kind of knowledge to the conventional account of perception should not be underestimated: "The perceptual world without constancies would be a bewildering experience that would make the acquisition of adaptive behavior extremely difficult" (Epstein, 1977, p. 6).

It is not unreasonable to conceive of learning as a speeded-up version of evolution in the sense that learning is a means by which an adaptive relation between animal and environment can be established in a relatively short period of time. When learning intervenes, an animal can be said to know something at a later point in time that it did not know at an earlier point in time. Similarly, it can be said of an evolving species that if one of its members possesses some property at a later point in time (t''), there was an earlier point in time (t') at which an ancestor of the said member did *not* possess that property. Let the property in question be the size–distance invariance algorithm. Now it is necessarily assumed that at t' the ancestor and its environment were *relatively well adapted*. The ancestor at t' was able to multiply in sufficient numbers so as to provide the variability on which natural selection could act to produce the better adaptation at t''. It follows, therefore, that for the adaptive relation to have existed at t', the ancestor must have possessed a goodly number of the constancy algorithms. Without these algorithms, the experiences of the ancestor would have been bewildering and its behavior with reference to its environment essentially chaotic. Consider the following (nonexhaustive) features of the environment that with reference to the control of behavior ought to be perceived as constant despite variations in proximal stimulation: Object and surface properties such as position, size, slant, shape; event properties—more precisely, styles of change that can be participated in by a large variety of different objects such as starts, stops, collisions, touches, breaks, approaches, retreats, falling, rotations, etc.; and relatedly, animal actions such as the behavioral displays that mark aggression and courting. The latter two classes are often ignored as constancy problems, but they are as deserving of consideration as the constancies of object properties. After all, if it is claimed that stimulation is equivocal about object properties such as size and shape, it must also be claimed that stimulation is equivocal about styles of change and the behavior of conspecifics.

Consider now an ancestor at an evolutionary point earlier than t'. Presumably, by the above reasoning, the ancestor did not possess some of the constancy algorithms at t that the later ancestor possessed at t'. But given that natural selection always assumes a reasonably efficient perception–action capability in that it presupposes the means of self-preservation and reproduction, then it must always assume constancy algorithms of some kind at any earlier evolutionary point that we choose. Unfortunately, this last sentence touches upon the issue that makes some scholars (e.g., Bertalanffy, 1969; Moorhead & Kaplan, 1967) skeptical of the theory of evolution in its current form. Natural selection acting by way of differential reproduction presupposes the essential attributes of life (e.g, self-maintenance, reproduction, adaptability), thereby making circular the argument that these attributes are the *effects* of natural selection. While admitting to the inadequacy of natural selection as a directive force in evolution, one should not at the same time construe constancy algorithms as being entities of the same conceptual status as adaptability, reproduction, etc.

A constancy algorithm always *presupposes* sensitivity (however crude) to the surrounding medium. If the surrounding medium is not modulated by the organism's environment in ways that are specific to the environment, then the organism's sensitivity cannot register, and the organism cannot become sensitive to, the specifics of the environment with respect to which adaptation occurs. Consequently, there can never be a perceptual origin for the kind of knowledge that is said to mediate perceptual constancy. We are led to conclude either that some minimal set of constancy algorithms was available a priori—that is, extraevolutionary—or that the problem of the constancies has been ill conceived.[3] The former conclusion is indefensible, and the latter conclusion may draw support from the earlier discussion of what *acquiring* a constancy algorithm would entail.

---

[3]With respect to the animal as perceiver, there are two logically separable demands put on evolution by the assumption of intractable nonspecificity. One demand is to make the animal sensitive to the basic descriptors of at least one, but generally several, forms of energy. The other demand is to provide the animal with the kinds of knowledge needed to make correct inferences about (or to project correct hypotheses about, or to construct a correct representation of, etc.) survival-relevant properties of the world from the basic energy descriptors. The latter demand is what we have referred to previously as the problem of origin for traditional perceptual theory; more poignantly, the *mystery* of where the requisite knowledge comes from. But suppose (as we do in the pages that follow) that contrary to traditional understanding, an energy medium as structured by an environment is *specific* to the properties of that environment (such as surfaces of support for locomotion, enclosures, behaviors of conspecifics, etc.). On this supposition, evolution's task with respect to the animal as perceiver is eased and, we believe, made feasible. The *single* task is that of making animals sensitive to the invariant relationships in the structured energy media that are specific to the properties of the world relevant to their survival. Sensitivity to some invariants embodied by structured energy *is* sensitivity to or knowledge of some properties of the world. We submit that the origin of this sensitivity is a tractable scientific problem unlike the origin of knowledge in the traditional theories of perception, which looks like an insoluble mystery.

Indeed, from an evolutionary point of view, the traditional accounts of perception that propose epistemic mediators and the nonprimacy of perception look more than a little curious. First, there seems to have been an implicit assumption that the eye as an organ evolved prior to the means by which the eye's images might be interpreted. It is not an exaggeration to claim that the focus of visual perception theory in the past five centuries has been on the mechanisms that operate on the retinal image and convert it into a meaningful "cerebral image." In evolutionary terms, it is as if visual scholars conceived the adaptation of interest as that between retinal image and cerebral image (or whatever one wished to call the terminal, internal representation) rather than that between animal and environment. Implicitly, the assumption has been that the structure and function of the eye are disassociated in evolution from the structure and function of the mechanisms by which visual perception is achieved.

Second, and in very much the same vein, the ageless point of view that perception proceeds from elementary sensory variables (corresponding to basic physical variables) seems to have peculiar evolutionary implications. Specifically, it might be taken to imply that the earliest life-forms evolved as sense-data devices (sensitive solely to energy *as such*) and only subsequently did relatively higher life-forms emerge possessing the capability to ascribe meaning to the sensory variables. Although this implication cannot be ruled out completely due to the paucity of understanding of prebiotic evolution, there are good reasons for believing it to be unlikely.

At its most primitive, life seems to be deserving of Dennett's (1971) definition of rationality—an optimal design relative to a goal or optimally related collection of goals and a set of constraints. Additionally and cognately, life at its most primitive exhibits *discrimination by significance* (Dennett, 1969); situations are distinguished by the behaviors they do or do not permit the organism to perform. Discrimination by significance is to be contrasted with the kind of discrimination often discussed with reference to pattern recognition where the focus is whether or not some device is capable of providing outputs (whatever they might be) that co-occur with energy kinds or energy distributions at its surface.

Monstera gigantea is an arboreal vine whose seeds germinate on the ground subsequent to falling from the parent plant. Soon after germination, the seedling grows in the direction of the nearest tree, contacts the tree, and ascends, losing its roots in the process. The seedling's adaptive behavior may be characterized as a positive skototropism—that is, a tendency to move toward darkness (Strong & Ray, 1975). In fact, the seedling always grows in the direction of the darkest sector of the horizon.

We may say of the seedling that it detects a climbable object. A climbable object may be defined by certain properties, some of which would be strength, rigidity, and surface texture. In the environment in which the plant has evolved, these properties have been invariant with dark sectors on the horizon. Because of this invariant, the seedling does not and need not detect the individual properties that we, as scientists, would propose as the distinguishing features of a climbable object for a vine. Moreoever, the darkest sector invariably corresponds to that climbable object that can be reached with a minimum of horizontal growth. The plant exhibits discrimination by significance.

The behavior of *Monstera gigantea* is especially illuminating in reference to the traditional emphasis on the distinction between appearance and reality. It is easy to imagine an environment in which the distribution of light does not relate to the locations of trees. Strong and Ray (1975) used the open ends of opaque tubes to produce dark sectors in the seedling's horizon; the seedlings grew (maladaptively one *might* say) into the open ends of the tubes. There are two points to be emphasized. One point is that from an evolutionary point of view, it cannot be said that the plant's sensitivity (perception?) was in error.[4] The individual plant detected and grew toward the dark sector of its horizon; it did that which it had evolved to do. The other and more general point is that from an evolutionary point of view, perception suffices when it reveals sufficient information about an organism's environment to support self-preserving and reproductive behavior.[5] Both points bear significantly on the appearance–reality dichotomy: *It is not clear from an evolutionary stance how presumed differences between the appearance of things and their description as determined by physics and human reason are differences that*

---

[4]This point is worth belaboring for it bears on our subsequent claim that perception cannot err. The plant's sensitivity is to dark interruptions of an otherwise light horizon. An opaque tube causes such an interruption, and it is detected by the plant. The plant, however, cannot detect those features of the source of this dark sector that are at odds with its upward growing behavior. That is to say, the plant can and does detect that information that specifies support for upward growth, but it cannot detect that information that specifies *non*-support for upward growth. Therefore, it is wrong to say that the plant's sensitivity, its perception, is in error; rather, it should be said that the plant's *lack* of sensitivity, lack of perception, results in its going astray. A similar argument can be made for the complementary case where the inadequacy lies not in the animal or organism's sensitivity but in the information made available. Consider the bird that flies into the plane glass window. Owing to the conditions of illumination and to the absence of irregularities in or on its surface, a window may fail to reflect the light in ways that a substantial surface would normally reflect the light. Because there is no information in the light about the plane glass window, we cannot expect the bird to visually detect the presence of the glass window. The bird perceives the environment that is "broadcast" in the light; its perception is not in error. It flies into the window because of a lack of perception (in regard to the substantial surface) owing to a lack of information.

[5]Which is to say that the description of reality relevant to any given organism or animal is not a description that is true in any absolute or metaphysical sense, but a description that is true in a pragmatic sense as perhaps captured in Plato's concept of *doxa* (see Shaw, Turvey, & Mace, in press).

make a difference in regard to the adaptive relation between animal and environment.

Consider a further primitive life form, the bacterium.[6] The bacterium is a single-cell organism that swims about in a medium consonant with its metabolism through the use of flagella attached to the wall of the cell. The swimming is of two kinds, "runs" and "tumbles" (Adler, 1976); runs are rectilinear motions, and tumbles are random changes in direction. The movement of a bacterium through the medium is essentially a random walk in which the length of the runs is inversely proportional to the frequency of tumbling. When a bacterium is in a gradient of a chemical "attractant," the frequency of tumbling decreases as the bacterium moves up the gradient and increases as it moves down the gradient. The opposite relation holds for a chemical "repellent." The chemical gradient modulates the locomotor styles of the bacterium, guaranteeing (within the environment to which the bacterium is adapted) movement toward nutritious substances and movement away from potentially harmful substances.

A chemical gradient is a "complex" variable in the conventional understanding. Where the stimulation relevant to some behavior is spread over time as well as space, it has been traditional to conceive of the stimulation as being registered in terms of more "basic," discrete variables whose sensory consequences are then preserved in a storage medium for the perusal of inferential mechanisms. On this account, the bacterium's behavior is mediated by a process that computes differences between stored representations of chemical concentrations at successive moments in time.

The logical difficulties with the popular interpretation of temporally extensive, perceptual information have been aired elsewhere (Gibson, 1966a; Humphrey, 1933; Shaw & Pittenger, 1977; Turvey, 1977). Here it is sufficient to make the less formal observation that the bacterium's unicellular material design does not appear to have the complexity needed to support the kinds of processing that have been traditionally implicated. Very much the same argument can be made for *Monstera gigantea*, for the absence of any sense organs rules out a sensation-based account of the plant's discriminative behavior. But if neither bacterium nor *Monstera gigantea* are devices that register the significant properties of their environments through the mediary of the sensory consequences of basic physical variables, then what kind of devices are they? They are, in a simple phrase, "smart" devices (Runeson, 1977a)—that is to say, devices that register complex particulars of adaptive

---

[6]Our thanks are extended to Tim Johnston for bringing both of these examples to our attention and for giving us the benefits of his perspective on them.

significance in an elegantly simplistic fashion, nonmediated by simple particulars.[7]

The polar planimeter measures directly the area of any regularly or irregularly shaped plane figure, and it provides a delightful example of a smart instrument (Runeson, 1977a). The planimeter consists of two rods, say, A and B. Rod A (the tracer arm) connects an index to a measuring wheel, and Rod B (the pole arm) connects Rod A (between the index and the wheel) to a fixture on the surface on which the plane figure is to be measured. The index is moved around the boundary of the figure. As the index traces out the profile, the measuring wheel skids and rotates such that the total angle of rotation consequent to a complete circuit of the figure is directly proportional to the area of the figure. The instrument is a simple mechanical expression of rather abstract mathematical principles (see Runeson, 1977a, for more details).

With regard to reputedly more basic variables, the planimeter is not especially efficient; it does not permit the straightforward measurement of, say, lines and angles, and such measurements may prove to be relatively inaccurate. But to be dismayed at the fact that the instrument is unreliable with regard to these supposedly basic variables would be missing the point. The polar planimeter exemplifies smart devices in this sense: It is a special-purpose instrument tailor-made for a particular kind of task and a particular kind of situation. Such being the case, its construction can take full advantage of the special features of the task it is to perform and the circumstances in which it is to operate (cf. Fowler & Turvey, 1978; Gel'fand & Tsetlin, 1962).

Apart from bringing into question the hypostatizing of the basic variables of physics, the preceding examples and arguments are of importance in the following final respect. The suggestion is that the evolution of perceptual systems may be understood as the compiling of special-purpose, smart devices to directly register higher order variables or complex particulars. This would contrast with the understanding that evolution manufactured a few types of basic components, each computing a basic physical variable or simple particular, and achieved the computation of more complex variables through programs defined over the basic components.

We might go further, and further than we have room for here, to delimit and evaluate the conceptual bequest of the preceding five centuries as it bears on the nature of perception. But what has been deliberated to this point must suffice; and in the contrast drawn in the last few paragraphs we have caught a

---

[7]We believe it prudent to avoid where possible the concrete–abstract distinction, where *concrete* refers to particular things and *abstract* to nonparticular things. In the view that we wish to promote, animals always perceive particulars. Some of these particulars may, as a matter of convenience, be deserving of the label *complex* in comparison with other particulars, but they are, nevertheless, particulars and thus ought not to be conceived of as reducible in the way that abstract amorphous entities might arguably be reduced to concrete particular entities. We thank Ed Reed for introducing us to this conception of *particular*, although our usage is somewhat different from his.

glimpse of a different conceptual basis and one that we now try to develop. As postulated at the outset, the stock concepts of traditional and conventional perceptual theory follow from the assumed dualism of animal and environment. The promissory note to be cashed in is that an assumed synergy of animal and environment yields an orthogonal collection of concepts and in consequence a radically different understanding of perception.

AN ECOLOGICAL REFORMULATION

The Principle of Mutual Compatibility

There is a contemporary understanding with which animal–environment dualism and the doctrine of intractable nonspecificity seem to be graphically at odds. It is that the universe is finely balanced with reference to life (Trimble, 1977; Wheeler, 1974). Characterizable in terms of a relatively small number of properties, it is becoming increasingly evident that the universe's hospitality to life depends on these properties having just the particular values they have, and no others. A fairly minor change in either a fine-grain property or a coarse-grain property of the universe, and life would be impossible. Thus, at the fine grain, a lowering of the electromagnetic force that regulates the structure and interactions of atoms and molecules would release electrons from their bondage to atoms, thereby making chemical reactions impossible; at the coarse grain, a rise in the rate of expansion of the universe would rule out the forming of galaxies and induce a uniform spread of matter (see Trimble, 1977). We recognize, therefore, the fitness of the universe for life. But more than this we will recognize that the universe and life are coimplicative: They have coevolved and they are codesigned. For the 17th-century philosopher, Leibniz, it could not have been otherwise.

Leibniz believed that substances could not interact. That which passes for causal interaction among substances was interpreted by Leibniz as a parallel coordination of state changes; the coordination arising from the inexorable unfolding of natural laws according to symmetry among substances. In his "principle of sufficient reason," Leibniz advocated that only those things may coexist—only those things are possible—that satisfy certain fundamental compatibility relations. By this principle—which we will refer to as the "principle of mutual compatibility"—compatibility relations among logically possible structures is the defining criterion of existence.

We see, in short, that for Leibniz there must be a good or a sufficient reason for anything to exist. Darwin's theory of evolution and other evolutionary theories (e.g., cosmological theories) all begin by assuming the existence of a collection of things that evolve, but they do not address the issue of why *that* collection—or any other, for that matter—should exist at all. Leibniz sought a deeper understanding: Whatever exists does so because it is mutually compatible with more things than something else. Thus he sought to derive the existence of things from a logically more primitive and simpler notion, namely, that of compossibility, or what we have chosen to call *mutual compatibility*. Hence the Leibnizean argument for existence is not circular; it does not derive existence from existence, but from something else.

There is a good deal (of what we take to be necessary future endeavors) foreshadowed in Leibniz's intuitions. Looming large is the necessity to develop a logic of synergistic relations among natural systems—a logic that does not shy away from the image of natural law relentlessly fashioning reality. In what follows we reiterate and embellish a sketch of the desired logic as given by one of us elsewhere (Shaw & McIntyre, 1974).

Adjunctive Logic, and Natural Law

The Stoic philosophers distinguished several kinds of logical propositions: among them the *hypothetical, causal,* and *adjunctive*. The hypothetical or conditional proposition takes the form: "*If x*, then *y*." This can be contrasted with the causal proposition: "*Because x*, then *y*"; and the adjunctive proposition: "*Since x*, then *y*."

The hypothetical proposition is invalid whenever the premise is true and the conclusion is false, and valid otherwise. It can be said to be conditionally true or correct if the opposite of its conclusion contradicts its premise (i.e., by *modus tollens*). However, the opposite of the conclusion (e.g., not *y*) is not necessarily inconsistent with the premise (e.g., *x*). For instance, "If this is Monday, I go to work." However, it may indeed be Monday, but I may not go to work simply because it is a holiday. In short, the consequent does not disconfirm the premise.

In general, hypothetical propositions constitute a poor model for natural laws, primarily because there are too many ways in which they can be invalid. Additionally, they fail to provide a necessary relationship between premises and conclusions. The reason why these limitations make the hypothetical proposition an inappropriate model for natural laws becomes apparent as soon as one attempts to fit these laws to this propositional schema.

Let the initial and auxiliary conditions that define the domain of application of the natural law correspond to the premise of the proposition. The valid outcome predicted by the natural law will then correspond to the consequent of the proposition. A principle is considered to be a natural law: (1) if the denial of its prediction or consequent is necessarily inconsistent with the premises; and (2) when its premise can be shown to be true (i.e., when its initial and auxiliary conditions can be shown to be satisfied). In brief, a natural law is a principle that predicts true outcomes whenever it can be shown to validly apply.

It clearly violates what we mean by a natural law to say that the law validly applies but does not predict the outcome. In such a case, either we would not accept the principle in its stated form as being a valid law, or else we would deny that the conditions for its application had actually been satisfied. In sum, a law cannot validly be applied to any situation where its premises are not true, but a hypothetical proposition is valid, by definition even when its premises are false. It is not difficult to see how attempts to interpret laws as hypothetical propositions lead to paradoxes. In particular, what is conventionally and intuitively accepted as the function of scientific theory evades formal confirmation. Thus, Popper (1959) and others have shown that when stated in hypothetico-deductive form, neither natural laws nor theories are logically verified simply because their predictions are confirmed. Affirming the consequent of a hypothetical proposition does not affirm the premise. Hence, if law x predicts outcome y, given that y is true does not imply that x is true.

Unfortunately, Popper's attempt at an alternative evaluation of scientific laws and theories fails in like fashion. His argument is that even though laws or theories cannot be verified directly they can be evaluated by showing that their predictions do not hold. The falsifiability procedure is based on the time-honored and valid argument schema known as the *modus tollens*: If law x, then outcome y, but not y, therefore, not x.

It is quite unlikely, however, that falsifiability is ever achieved in practice (Lakatos, 1970), because the premises for a law or theory are such a complex of variables that it often proves impossible to determine which one has been falsified. The onus, therefore, falls upon the theorist to decide whether a major or a minor assumption of the theory is at fault. Given the potential arbitrariness of this choice, it would be imprudent to reject a law or the core of a theory that had been developed carefully and arduously.

On learning that Eddington's measurement of light bending around the eclipsed sun agreed with the predictions of his theory, Einstein replied: "But I knew that the theory is correct." When asked how he would have responded if the predictions had not been confirmed, Einstein candidly countered: "Then I would have been sorry for the dear Lord—the theory is correct" (Clark, 1971, p. 369). The point on which argument and vignette converge is this: The validation of theories and laws appear to be logically impossible. Thus it is important to note that it is not that logic makes no difference in theory evaluation (and a law is, of course, just an accepted consequence of a theory), but rather that logic makes so little difference. The fruitfulness of a theory in explaining anomalies and bringing general consistency into science is more important than either logical verification or falsification. In other words, the degree to which a new law applies symmetrically across a wide domain of natural phenomena and relates other laws is the highest criterion of its worth. It is also a realistic measure of the resistance scientists will show in abdicating it.

At all events, we should pursue logical forms other than the hypothetical proposition. What is sought is a logical form that is consonant with the aforementioned facts about theory evaluation. In this perspective, consider the Stoics' conception of causal propositions.

A causal proposition begins with a true premise and ends with a necessary consequence; for example: "Because it is day, then it is light." The causal schema more appropriately expresses the form of laws; by contrast we are reminded that the hypothetical proposition is still valid if its premises are assumed false. For instance, consider the following hypothetical: "If it is night, it is light," then whether night or day, it follows that "it is light"—a valid logical argument but scientifically false.

The causal proposition, however, does not permit such a trick to be performed on our scientific intuition. A causal proposition is incorrect (by definition) if it begins with a false premise or ends with a conclusion that does not follow from it. Thus, unlike hypothetical forms, the causal interpretation demands that the premise and conclusion correspond.

Although the schema for natural laws seems to be satisfied by causal propositions, the intuitive notion of causal relation cannot be effectively captured in formal statements. Moreover, it can be argued that invariance laws (Wigner, 1970), laws that characterize the symmetry relations existing among natural laws, do not seem to fit the schema for causal propositions (see Shaw & McIntyre, 1974).

There seems to be a fit among the varius phases of matter that permits some kind of macro-determinism to hold among their distinct phenomena, but that does not permit (nor does it require) the micro-deterministic relations necessary to the concept of causal interaction (Shaw & McIntyre, 1974). On this point the adjunctive propositional form offered by the Stoics, although essentially ignored by history, seems more promising.

An adjunctive proposition begins with a true premise and ends with a necessary consequence. For example: "Since it is day, then the sun is shining." This proposition is incorrect when it either begins with a false premise or ends with a consequence that need not follow. The adjunctive proposition professes both that the second member follows from the first and that the first member is true. Adjunctive logic requires a commitment to one's premises, and it is this propositional schema that we believe is consonant with the sense of natural laws.[8]

---

[8]Our experience is that the adjunctive propositional form is not so easily grasped as the more familiar propositional forms. The following example sometimes proves helpful. Mendeleev predicted the existence of elements on the basis of a profound belief in the symmetry of the periodic table of chemical elements. Or, as we might say here, Mendeleev believed that *since* the elements that were known to exist did in fact exist, then elements x, y, z, etc., must also necessarily exist. Clearly, it was not a matter of Mendeleev believing in a hypothetical relation that *if* the elements known to exist did exist, then x, y, z, etc., exist. Nor (and perhaps more significantly) was it a matter of his believing in a cause–effect relationship such as: Those chemical elements known to exist *caused* those not known to exist—say, x, y, z, etc.—to come into existence. The point is that the adjunctive entailment of one thing by another is a manifestation of an underlying principle of symmetry and that the existence of either one of the things in question is inconceivable without the other.

If we analyze the "adjunctive proposition, "Since x, then y," in terms of truth tables, it is the case that in order for the adjunctive relation to hold, both x and y must be true. The adjunctive relation is false otherwise. Now this looks suspiciously like the truth functional definition of a conjunctive relation (e.g., x and y). It differs, however, in one important way: Where conjunctive relations are commutative (i.e., "x and y" is equivalent to "y and x"), adjunctive relations are not; hence, "Since x, then y" does not imply "Since y, then x."

The adjunctive formulation seems to capture the sense that laws of nature apply in an inexorable manner to grind out reality. This is expressed simply as the adjunctive proposition that: "Since the law applies, the observed outcome must follow (necessarily)." If the outcome does not follow invariantly upon correct application of the law, we have grounds for falsifying the whole proposition, because in an adjunctive proposition the truth of the conclusion follows necessarily from the truth of the premises. Thus, in this special sense, the falsifiability criterion is preserved.

The verification criterion, however, does not hold for adjunctive propositions at the level of natural law. The observation (y) that some event (x) occurs as predicted by physical law x does not verify that x is a law.

Thus, given y, it is fallacious to affirm x. Although natural laws apply to predict outcomes, no number of observed outcomes can be used logically to verify the law, a fact that is expressed in the noncommutativity of the adjunctive propositional form of natural law.

One might even question the utility of the verification procedure, because natural laws are postulated on more general grounds than observations. The major grounds for accepting or rejecting principles as natural laws is whether or not they fit into the invariance structure of a science, resolving anomalies and relating other principles (cf. Wigner, 1970).

The accuracy with which natural laws predict effects is not so important as the degree to which they contribute to the coherence of explanations for natural phenomena. Because one might predict what one does not understand, prediction alone is an insufficient criterion of the explanatory worth of theories, hypotheses, or laws. Scientific theories or natural laws that help simplify a field will never be abdicated solely on the grounds that they are not predictive. Indeed, they should not be, for the conditional logic of verification does not apply.

Defining Mutual Compatibility in Adjunctive Logic

Let us now return to the notion of mutual compatibility. Compatibility can be defined in the adjunctive propositional form; that is, x is said to be compatible with y if it is the case that since x, then y. Using the symbol "$\succ$" to represent the adjunctive (and, therefore, compatibility) relation, the adjunctive proposition can be written as, $x \succ y$. From this adjunctive schema we define further compatibility relationships through the addition of two symbols: ✧—mutual compatibility—and ⊢ —unidirectional compatibility.

1. *negation:* $x \not\succ y$ (x is not compatible with y).
2. *mutual compatibility:* $(x \succ y) \cdot (y \succ x) \equiv (x ✧ y) \equiv (y ✧ x)$. (Read simply as: when x is compatible with y and y is compatible with x, then x and y are mutually compatible.)
3. *mutual incompatibility:* $(x \barsucc y) \cdot (y \barsucc x) \equiv (x \bar✧ y) \equiv (y \bar✧ x)$.
4. *unidirectional compatibility:* $(x \succ y) \cdot (y \barsucc x) \equiv (x \vdash y) \equiv (y \vdash k)$.

We can now proceed to illustrate Leibniz's argument from the principle of sufficient reason or mutual compatibility, in the sense of the following law, a law that we boldly refer to as the *Law of Existence*.[9]

The *Law of Existence* says that comparatively speaking, that object (or event) exists which has the greatest mutual compatibility with other logically possible objects (or events). To illustrate: Assume a, b, c, d, and e, are all logically possible, (i.e., noncontradictory) objects. (Logically impossible objects are those whose conjunction is false; e.g., the conjunction $x \cdot y$ is false when $y = \bar{x}$, because this entails that x and $\bar{x}$—the contradiction of x—are both true.) Now assume that the following compatibility relations either obtain or do not obtain among the logically possible objects postulated above: (1) $a \bar✧ b$; (2) $a ✧ c$; $a ✧ d$, $a ✧ e$; and (3) $b \bar✧ d$, $b ✧ e$, $b ✧$ c. Then by the Law of Existence, it follows that $\exists a ✧ \exists b$ (read as "the existence of a is mutually compatible with the nonexistence of b"). Thus, the conclusion follows immediately as a necessary fact that a can exist in the same possible world, W_1, as c, d, e whereas b can only exist in a possible world, W_2, containing c and e. This means that by the Law of Existence, the possible world $W_1 = (b \cdot c \cdot d \cdot e \cdot x)$ (where $x \neq b$) exists as an a posteriori fact[10] whereas the possible world $W_2 = (b \cdot c \cdot e \cdot y)$ (where $y \neq a$ or d) does not.

To put the matter differently: The logically possible world that is most likely to exist is that which contains the greatest number of mutually compatible objects. The alternative possible (candidate) worlds contain only a subset of the mutually compatible objects in question. Thus, the Law of

---

[9]Our boldness in this regard is encouraged by the bold charge of this conference—to project an understanding of memory and closely related phenomena (here, perception) in the next half-millennium. The reader's indulgence is requested!

[10]The notion of "a necessary a posteriori fact" is prominent in the remarks that follow. By identifying a fact as necessary, we mean: There is a state of affairs that exists and that could not have been otherwise. A contingent fact, by contrast, is a true fact but one that *could* have been otherwise. Prefacing a fact by "a priori" means a fact that is true independent of existence. Conversely, prefacing a fact by "a posteriori" means that the fact's truth is manifest in existence. A necessary a posteriori fact, therefore, is a fact that is necessarily true by force of existence.

Existence provides a determinate principle of adjunctive (compatibility) logic by which worlds that are merely logically possible (i.e., noncontradictory) may be actualized as a posteriori facts of existence. This law provides a way of imputing the greatest degree of existential import to that logically possible world scheme, commensurate with other equally logically possible world schemes, that possesses the greatest number of mutually compatible objects.

Let us attempt now to apply the Law of Existence to resolve a classical cosmological problem. It is often claimed by the indeterministic reductionist that life is a chance happening in the physical universe, say, resulting from nothing more than the spontaneous mutation of complex molecular forms. By contrast, the determinist wishes to argue that the laws of nature apply in such a strict manner that life was inevitable, in the sense that these laws applied inexorably to grind out life. Unfortunately, neither view seems cogent: The "chance happening" hypothesis obscures the deeper question of what mitigating circumstances necessarily held sway prior to life to allow chance mutations to occur that *could*, in principle, lead to the complex molecular structures underlying life. Even such chance combinations could only occur under mitigating circumstances that constrained certain combinations over others. Unmitigated chance, or truly spontaneous mutation, would logically permit *any* arbitrary combination whatsoever. But the existence of laws of nature, and the selectivity of their initial conditions, logically entailed life as an actuality and not as a mere logical (chance) possibility. This is a clear confusion of the laws of nature with the laws of logic. Laws of nature are not existentially arbitrary, whereas the laws of logical systems may be, because they need only conform to the principle of noncontradiction—a very weak criterion that excludes fewer possible outcomes than do natural laws constrained by precise initial conditions. Whatever is the case in nature is not only logically possible; it is also naturally potential and existentially instantiated (actual). Therefore, the "chance happening" hypothesis fails, not because it is illogical but because it is *only* logical—permitting other possible worlds than the one we actually live in.

But does the determinists' hypothesis fare any better? It seems not, because the view that natural laws have applied inexorably to grind out whatever is the case (e.g., life) must also assume that the initial conditions to which the laws applied to grind out reality were such as to allow whatever happened to happen. Clearly, this is nothing more than a tautology asserting that given the laws, in order for life to be as it is, the initial conditions for it to be as it is must necessarily have prevailed. This is true but trivial; all it asserts is that the necessary (initial) conditions for life must necessarily have been the initial conditions for life.

The question remaining under either hypothesis is how might such regresses be avoided. A third, but scientifically unpopular hypothesis, that attempts to avoid the regress is the teleological argument that asserts that the production of life was the purpose that the laws of nature and initial conditions were designed to accomplish. But this hypothesis leaves unanswered two important questions: First, what is the design of the laws and the initial conditions that permitted life? And second, by what means was this design cosmologically orchestrated? To regress to a "God" hypothesis is to discharge the argument from the purview of science altogether and thus to render it irrelevant to our purposes.

However, there is an argument, unlike any of these, that avoids the regresses they entail by offering a theory of what initial conditions must necessarily exist, not as necessary a priori facts, but as necessary a posteriori facts. This argument might be called the "unique origins" hypothesis. It goes as follows: What now exists is necessarily *uniquely* consistent with that from which it originated. Unique consistency of one thing with another means that neither of the things in question is conceivable without the other (logically, a biadjunctive relation). The argument, implicit in the foregoing, that the science of life and the science of the physical world must be mutually dependent is by no means novel. For instance, Wheeler (1974) suggests that given that the universe is home for man, then the initial conditions for cosmological evolution must have been attuned a priori to the possibility of life tens of billions of years prior to the occurrence of life of any sort (cf. Blum, 1968). Wigner (1970) has argued that the origins of the self-reproducing unit required for life can not be accounted for by quantum mechanics. And in this regard, Pattee (1971) has made the bold suggestion that the biologist might turn the tables on physics by asking, "Can life explain quantum mechanics?"

Consider the following argument of Dicke (1961). All the mechanisms for life that have ever been conceived require elements that are heavier than hydrogen (Wald, 1963). Such elements depend for their production on thermonuclear combustion, which happens to need several billion years of cooking time in the interior of a star. The theory of general relativity tells us that for a universe to provide several billion years of time, it will have to be several billion light years in size. Hence, Dicke's (1961) conclusion that given life, the size of the universe is what it is. Or, as Trimble (1977) remarks more generally: "It seems, in other words, that the Universe must be more or less the way it is just because we are here [p. 85]."

There is a danger in the views of cosmological theorists such as Wheeler and Trimble—that they might be interpreted as merely a resurgance of the perennial, but philosophically discounted, teleological argument. It will serve us well therefore to consider critically what type of logical proposition is entailed by an assertion such as that of Trimble just quoted. For it is our contention that cosmological theorists like Wheeler and Trimble intend to endorse the "unique origins" argument rather than an obtuse version of teleology. Necessarily, the consideration to follow overlaps with and extends the preceding deliberation on the proposed Law of Existence. Indeed, the Law of Existence can be used to demonstrate how one's endorsement of the "unique origins" hypothesis not only avoids the problems of the teleological argument but provides a positive principle by which the actual world (that which is existentially the case) can be individuated from among all logically possible worlds (those which are only logically possible).

We may paraphrase the quote from Trimble in three logically distinct ways:

1. *Because* life is what it is, then the universe is what it is.
2. *If* life is what it is, then the universe is what it is.
3. *Since* life is what it is, then the universe is what it is.

With reference to (1), if it is assumed that life arrived late in the course of cosmological evolution, then the nature of the physical universe would be determined by something that appeared later than it—a clear case of the teleological argument. How some effect can be the cause of something earlier is left unexplained.

The conditional reading of Trimble's quote allows for the possibility that:

1. Life might not have been what it is now, and yet the universe could still be what it is.
2. Neither life nor the universe might have been what they are observed to be; that is, (a) "if F, then T" is valid; and (b) "if F, then F" is also valid. The only reading that is excluded is (c) "if T, then F," which is invalid.

But we would not be happy with the proposition that the nature of life and the nature of the universe are so loosely related.

What we wish to capture is the claim that the nature of living organisms fits with the nature of the universe in a tightly constrained system of mutual compatibility relations. Therefore, the most appropriate propositional form is the adjunctive or, more precisely, the biadjunctive, which captures the sense that the universe and organisms living in that universe are bound together by mutual compatibilities. In other words, since life is what it is, then the universe is what it is—namely an environment for life; conversely, since the universe is what it is (and has been), then life has the character that it does. $(U \succ L) \cdot (L \succ U) \equiv U \diamondsuit L$.

Sensitive to the developing argument, we may say that the biadjunctive expresses the animal–environment synergy whereas the conditional form expresses animal–environment dualism and the causal form expresses a logically opaque teleological hypothesis.

The Law of Existence can be used to argue that among all logically possible worlds, only that world scheme that when elaborated proves to provide a home for the most compatible phenomena is to be ascribed to our actual world. If we assume that reductionism is untenable so that physical (ϕ), biological (β), and psychological (ψ) phenomena are logically distinct objects, then the "unique origins" arguments . . . can be shown to follow from the compatibility logic (i.e., the Law of Existence). Assume the logically possible categories of objects ϕ, β, and ψ. By taking these in all possible schemes, a set of distinct but equally possible worlds are indicated: $W_1 = (\phi)$, a purely physical world without life or mind; $W_2 = (\beta)$, a world where all objects consist of living material governed by biotonic law; $W_3 = (\psi)$, a world of subjective idealism; $W_4 = (\phi, \beta)$, a world without "mind;" $W_5 = (\phi, \psi)$, a world where "mind" resides in inanimate stuff; $W_5 = (\phi, \beta)$, a biotonic world composed solely of living, psychological entities; and, finally, $W_6 = (\phi, \beta, \psi)$. Clearly, by the Law of Existence due to the fact that W_6 consists of a larger set of mutually compatible categories than the other possible worlds, it is more likely to exist than they are.

Let us pursue this rough sketch of a logic of synergistic relations among natural systems through a consideration of two other possible laws.

There are naturally potential objects, events, or worlds that—although not known to exist—could in principle exist under the current conception of natural law if only the initial conditions of cosmological evolution had been otherwise. This suggests the need for a second law of compatibility logic to supplement the Law of Existence; we call it the *Law of Potentiality*. In other words, that object, event, or world that is not mutually incompatible with anything that exists is naturally potential (rather than merely logically possible).

For example, assume b is possible, and let $\exists W$ be the actual world of existing objects; then b is potential ($b!$) if the adjunctive proposition, $(b \succ \exists W) \equiv b!$. On the other hand, given some logically possible object c such that $c \mathbin{\mbox{$\stackrel{\vee}{\diamond}$}} x$ where $x \in \exists W$, then c is not potential (i.e., $\bar{c}!$).

And, finally, there are those naturally potential entities that may exist by virtue of the dependency some existing entity has on them. We call this the *Law of Subordinate Existence:* Given that $a!$, that b, and that $\exists b \in a!$, then it follows that $(\exists b \succ a!) \equiv \exists a$. Intuitively, if a is potential and b, which exists, requires a as a condition of its existence (e.g., an initial condition), then a also must necessarily exist. This means that if $\exists W$ is the actual world scheme embracing b ($b \in \exists W$), then it embraces a as well ($a \in \exists W$), i.e., $(b \in \exists W) \diamond (a \in \exists W)$.

Let us summarize this section by identifying its thrust with respect to the parts that follow. We believe the implications of the mutual compatibility of life and universe to be profound and to bear strongly on the perennial puzzle of perception. Perception is most usefully conceived as an adaptive relation between animal and environment, two terms that are readily recognized as scaled-down versions of "life" and "universe," respectively. In the perspective being developed, animal and environment will be said to be mutually compatible in that a given species adjunctively entails its environment and a given environment adjunctively entails its species. But the understanding of this mutual compatibility and its implications rests with several prefatory considerations.

Environment and Econiche

First among them is the ambiguity of the term *environment*. It has been commonplace in the past 100 years to remark that organisms come to fit the environment by natural selection. But the notion of fit implies complementation, rather like the relation among pieces of a jigsaw puzzle; and insofar as there are many species, there must be at least as many environments for which the species are the apropos complementations. It is terribly evident that the term *environment* is asked to do double duty both as a general animal- or organism-neutral term and as a specific, animal- or organism-related term. Let us reserve *Environment* (with an upper-case initial letter) for the solids, liquids and gases, or the substances and media (interfaced by surfaces) that comprise the planet Earth; this will be the animal-neutral usage. The animal-related usage will be captured by the term *environment* (with a lower-case initial letter) or more advisedly by the term *niche* or *econiche*. The second sentence of this paragraph can then be rewritten partially and more accurately as: Life came to fit the Environment, and organisms came to fit econiches, where Life is used in the general sense commensurate with the usage of Environment.

Fitness of the Environment

It will prove helpful to the developing thesis of animal–environment synergy to reverse the commonly ascribed valences of animal and Environment and take the animal term as the independent variable and the Environment term as the dependent variable. Stripping away a great deal of the variation in the concept of animal, we ask: Given the common properties of living things, what must be the properties of the Environment, so that it might provide a fit to Life? This reiterates Henderson's question of "the fitness of the Environment" (Blum, 1968; Henderson, 1913/1970). If Life and Environment are mutually compatible (just as we have already supposed that Life and Universe are), then it is just as meaningful to ask how Environment came to fit Life as it is to ask how Life came to fit Environment.

An in-depth exploration of the fitness of the Environment is beyond the scope of this paper. It will suffice to limit ourselves to the remarkable thermal properties of water, for they are of great importance to the Life process and they may be taken to illustrate the proposition that Life adjunctively entails Environment.

The properties of water that contribute to its fitness for Life are intimately linked with the properties of the element hydrogen. Examination of the periodic tables indicates the uniqueness of this element: Hydrogen atoms are the lightest and the smallest, permitting hydrogen to enter into more chemical combinations than any other element. Chemical combinations are due in part to the instability of certain electron configurations. In the face of such instability, an atom may host electrons from another atom—in which case we speak of ionic bonding—or two atoms may share a pair of electrons—in which case we speak of covalent bonding. Water is the covalent bonding of three atoms (that is, three nuclei and their attendant electrons), two of hydrogen and one of oxygen. Significantly, the hydrogen atoms are on one side of the water molecule, the oxygen atom on the other. In short, the atoms do not lie in a straight line, and this asymmetry in the structure of the water molecule is of singular importance to the properties of water. The negative charge of the electron clouds opposite the hydrogen atoms attract the hydrogen nucleus of an adjacent water molecule to produce a low-energy, easily formed, easily ruptured bond that is referred to as a *hydrogen bond*. It is the relative ease with which water molecules become hydrogen bonded to form three-dimensional lattices that gives water its special properties. On the average, six water molecules clump together, giving water much higher values for specific heat, latent heat of vaporization, and latent heat of fusion, viscosity, and surface tension than would be the case if the molecules remained separate.

A primary role of water seems to be in preserving a relatively constant temperature for the Earth. Terrestrial and aquatic life as we know it survives in a relatively small range of temperature; water's fitness to Life is manifest in large part by its singularly important contribution to preserving this range.

Consider first water's high specific heat. Compared to other substances, water must gain or lose a large amount of heat before there is an appreciable change in its temperature. This property prevents sharp rises in water temperature that might accompany the night-to-day transition and moderates water temperature extremes that might accompany the seasons. Moreover, with water covering so much of the Earth, its high specific heat prevents sudden shifts in the temperature of the Earth. Equable temperature of the ocean and the moderation of the climate are the principle consequences of water's high specific heat. But there is a third consequence worth noting, and it has to do specifically with the individual organism. Given that water is the principal chemical constituent, a given quantity of heat produces the smallest possible change in the temperature of the body. If some other substance were the principle constituent, the elimination of heat would become considerably more contrived and arduous, and the regulation of temperature during muscular exertion well nigh impossible (Henderson, 1913/1970).

The control of the Earth's temperature is also assisted by water's high latent heat of vaporization. To convert 1 gram of liquid water into water vapor requires approximately 500–600 calories of heat, which of course must be supplied by the adjacent medium, the air. Similarly, to condense 1 gram of water, the same amount of heat must be withdrawn from the water and taken up by the air. The significance of water's high latent heat of vaporization is that the amount of heat required to produce a given amount of vapor in the air is considerably greater for water than for most other substances. It follows, therefore, that water is close to optimal for prohibiting rapid rises in air temperature (as might accompany sunrise).

Consider the related situation of converting water in the liquid state to ice. At the freezing point, 80 calories must be withdrawn from the water to convert 1 gram of water to ice. This conversion warms the air; moreover, water's high *latent heat of fusion* guarantees that large bodies of water will not significantly exceed the freezing point. Below the ice caps of the poles, life finds a haven. But it is due to a curious feature of the water molecule that ice floats on the surface rather than descends—with putatively disastrous results—to the bottom. In the solid state, water molecules do not crowd together, making water one of the few substances that is less dense in the solid state than in the liquid state. Water's greatest density is reached not at the freezing point but at 4°C; liquid at this temperature, the denser water sinks, forcing the warmer water to the surface and thus insuring that freezing proceeds from the top to the bottom and not vice versa.

The foregoing is not exhaustive of the properties of water that fit Life. Ideally, however, it suffices for our purposes. The reader is referred to Henderson (1913/1970) and to Blum (1968) for a fuller account. Let us conclude this piece by recognizing the nonarbitrariness of the relation between water and the earth.

Hydrogen's low atomic weight makes it a good candidate for escaping earth's gravitationaL field. That a hydrogen egress has not occurred to a debilitating degree is due in part to hydrogen's ability to combine with other elements, yielding molecules of sufficient mass to be retained (Blum, 1968). But it is also due in part to the size and temperature of the Earth; a smaller or a hotter Earth and the availability of hydrogen would have been lessened to a degree possibly prohibitive of Life.

Additionally, we may note that in reference to the fitness of water's high latent heat of vaporization, other hydrogen-bonded molecules exhibit a similar fitness. Thus, theoretically, hydrogen fluoride and ammonia could have provided a fluid medium consonant with life. These substances, however, are ruled out, simply because the temperature of the Earth does not permit them to exist in the liquid state. In appreciation of the web of mutual compatibilities, we are reminded that the Earth's temperature is in large part due to its speed of rotation and to its distance from the sun. In short, liquid water and the Earth are compatible, but liquid hydrogen fluoride and the Earth and liquid ammonia and the Earth are incompatible.

Partial and Total Systems

Let us now consider the concept of *system*, for it is of special significance to an understanding of animal–environment synergy. The following description comes from Weiss (1974): A system "...appears as a complex unit in space and time so constituted that its component subunits, by "systemic cooperation," preserve its integral configuration of structures and behavior and tend to restore it after nondestructive disturbances [p. 44]." In reference to system behavior, Mach (1902) observed that when a symmetrical system is deformed in such a way as to destroy the symmetry, the deformation is complemented by an equal and opposite deformation that tends to restore it.

Any entity that we should choose to label a *system* on the basis of the preceding descriptions will have a distinguishable "inside" and "outside." Where a system is contained within another system (as all systems will be, with the exception of the total universe), we may identify the subsumed system as a partial system (cf. Humphrey, 1933). It must necessarily be the case that a partial system cannot, in all practicality, be disengaged (in the sense of observed in isolation) from the system that includes it; it can of course be disengaged in theory. The decomposing of systems is an unavoidable feature of science. It makes the universe of phenomena potentially manageable. Thus, given an isolable collective of entities, the manner of their interrelating can be studied with planned indifference to the fact that the process or structure under observation is sensitive to its surroundings.

But it is a delicate strategy that disengages a partial system from the system that includes it. Considerable caution must be taken to insure that the decomposition does not go so far as to slip by the system (or unit) that is actually exhibiting the phenomena of interest. In particular, the consequences of overdecomposing are twofold. First, the phenomena may appear to be indeterminate and to refer to no underlying law, when in fact at their proper and coarser grain size of analysis, they are determinate and lawful. There is a principle advocated by Weiss (1969) that anticipates this consequence of overdecomposing—namely, that there may well be *determinacy in the gross despite demonstrable indeterminacy in the small* (see also Bohm, 1957). Second, there is a tendency to ascribe erroneous content or function to the partial system. Where a selected system is at the wrong grain size of analysis for the phenomena of interest, that system must take on properties that putatively could secure the phenomena. In what follows we present examples of these two consequences of overdecomposing.

The first example was used, and for very much the same purpose as intended here, by Humphrey (1933). Suppose that the phenomena of interest are the short-period diurnal and semidiurnal tides and the long-period tides whose periodicities range from 14 days to 19 years. And suppose further that these short- and long-period oscillations in sea level were thought to be phenomena of the Earth–Water system. Then it is not difficult to imagine that from the perspective of this system, the phenomena in question would look capricious and that they might be interpreted as the behavior of different systems at different times. But the lawfulness of the tidal phenomena is soon vindicated when the phenomena are understood as indices of a larger system—precisely, the Sun–Moon–Earth–Water system. The later system embodies the laws of which the tides are necessary consequences; in contrast, the partial Earth–Water system does not embody these laws, and so there is no invariant basis in that system for the changes in sea level.

The second example is from Ashby (1963). The example makes the general point that if the total system (from the perspective of the phenomena of interest) is unobservable, the partial system that can be observed may assume "remarkable, even miraculous properties" (Ashby, 1963, p. 114). The magician's trick provides a paradigm case: It looks miraculous, because not all of the significant variables are observable.

Consider a system composed of two interconnected devices A and B and an input I that affects both. Thus A's inputs are both B and I. The device A shows some characteristic behavior R, only when: (1) I is at state y; *and* (2) B is at state z. And it happens to be the case that B is at state z only *subsequent* to I taking the value x.

There are two observers. Observer 1 sees the total system and is able to conclude that R occurs whenever the total system shows a state with B at z and I at y. Observer 2 cannot see B (or does not take it into account). Consequently, knowing the states of A and I is insufficient to reliably predict the occurrence of R. After all, I is sometimes y and sometimes some other state. Nevertheless, Observer 2, by paying attention to earlier states of I, can make reliable predictions about R. If I passes successively through states x and y, then R will occur and not otherwise. It follows, therefore, that Observer 2 can make reliable predictions by taking into account successive values of I that he or she can in fact observe. But suppose that the two observers now argue about the "system." Observer 1 will claim that R is fully accounted for by the *present* state of the system; Observer 2 will claim that R can only be accounted for by considering the *past* states of the system—that is, only when memory is assumed. The point is, however, that the two observers are arguing about different systems (respectively, $A + B + I$ and $A + I$) and that Observer 2 ascribes "memory" to the system as a substitute for failure to observe (or to take into account) B. As the bottom line to this example, we may write that the possession of some property by a system is not wholly an objective property of the system (cf. Ashby, 1963). Rather, the ascription of content or function depends on the relation between the system and the observer. And obviously, properties will be ascribed to the degree that the total system is unobservable (or ignored).

Consider one further example. Weiss (1969) believes that the acription of powers to the gene, such as "controlling" and "organizing," is misguided. Indeed, he argues controversially that it is logically and factually fallacious, for the very reason that the gene (more accurately, the interaction among genes) is an overly decomposed system for the phenomena of interest—say, the growth and development of an organism. The popular reductionist view (e.g., Shaffner, 1967) with which Weiss takes issue fosters the attitude that the gene imparts order to an orderless and logically separate surrounding milieu. This amounts to the claim that the genes have a monopoly on the control of growth and development. The claim is logically weak on two related grounds: One is that it introduces the phenomena of "control," "organization," etc. as first principles—phyenomena *sui generis*; the other is that terms such as "control," "organize," "coordinate" are intentional terms. And as Dennett (1971) remarks, any theorist who uses intentional terms has taken out a loan of intelligence (or rationality) that must eventually be repaid.

The claim is also weak on factual grounds. As Weiss (1969) takes great pains to point out, the milieu in which the genes are enclosed is highly ordered, perhaps as ordered as the genes are themselves. It is therefore more judicious, Weiss argues, to answer the question of "What controls or coordinates?" with "the whole" rather than "the gene." We are reading this argument of Weiss's as saying that control and coordination of organismic development are necessary consequences of the mutual fit among the various biological pieces. Control, coordination, and the like are not phenomena *sui generis*.

This last example is a point of entry into what we take as the most telling feature of natural system dynamics. Given a total system (that is, one for which the phenomena of interest are virtually determinate by its laws), the partial systems of which it is composed must be so structured that for any single partial system, the remainder of the system provides the requisite context of constraint. By a definition we have sketched elsewhere (Turvey, Shaw, & Mace, in press), systems in which an "operational" component and the context of constraint are wedded together into a relatively closed, single unit are designated as *coalitions*. Simplistically conceived, given two systems X and Z that form a coalition, X constrains the degrees of freedom of Z, and Z constrains the degrees of freedom of X. We say that control or coordination or organization in such a system is the product of the fit between, or *dual complementation* of, the two partial systems (Fitch & Turvey, 1978; Turvey et al., in press). It is significant to note that in the coalitional conception, "control," "coordinate," "organize," etc. are not first principles, properties *sui generis*. Nor are they properties to be conceived as properties possessed by one or another partial system, as a gene is said to possess the capacity for controlling and for organizing the encompassing milieu (or as an animal is said to possess the capacity to ascribe meaning to the encompassing Environment). On the contrary, such properties are the properties of the coalition, the minimal system identified relative to the phenomena of interest, which carries its own context.

The Mutual Compatibility of Animal and Environment: Affordances and Effectivities

The animal-neutral conception of Environment, at the very finest grain, is matter and energy understood as particles and the laws governing their motion. At a coarser grain, Environment may be described (as earlier) in terms of solids, liquids and gases. On rewording, this latter description reads as "substances and media interfaced by surfaces."

What we now seek is a partitioning on the coarser grained description of the Environment that yields environments or econiches. That is to say, a partitioning that results in animal-specific (more aptly, species-specific) descriptions. The major criterion for this partitioning is that the descriptions that arise are optimal for understanding how the different species of animal relate to their surroundings as knowing-agents and not simply as biological or physical entities (cf. Shaw & Bransford, 1977).

The partitioning problem has been addressed by Gibson (1977) through the concept of *affordance*. As Gibson (1977) remarks: "Subject to revision, I suggest that the affordance of anything is a specific combination of the properties of its substance and its surfaces taken with reference to an animal [p. 67]." By this conception, an econiche or environment is defined as a set of affordances, or an *affordance structure*.

Examplary of an affordance is a place or surface that supports upright locomotion by a human: a surface that is more nearly solid than liquid, more nearly horizontal than vertical, more smooth than wrinkled, and more near the feet than the head. What is evident, therefore, in the concept of affordance is the notion that properties of substance and surface enter into invariant combinations to comprise an animal-relevant, alternative description of the Environment. The Environment is partitioned relevant to an animal's, or more aptly a species of animal's, capacity for activity.

The principle of mutual compatibility, however, invites a further and complementary partitioning—namely, a partitioning of Life with reference to environments or econiches. The term *effectivity* is offered to complement the term *affordance*, and it is defined subject to revision as follows: The effectivity of any living thing is a specific combination of the functions of its tissues and organs taken with reference to an environment. By this conception, an animal is defined as a set of effectivities, or an *effectivity structure*.

We may collect together the two partitionings in this manner: An econiche is an affordance description of Environment in reference to a particular species; a species is an effectivity description of Life in reference to a particular econiche. And we may schematize the affordance and effectivity conceptions in the following way, in general accordance with the compatibility logic:

An environmental event or situation X affords an activity Y for an animal Z *if and only if* certain mutual compatibility relations between X and Z obtain (i.e., $X \diamond Z$).

An animal Z can effect an activity Y on an environmental event or situation X *if and only if* certain mutual compatibility relations between X and Z obtain (i.e., $X \diamond Z$).

The Concept of an (Epistemic) Ecosystem

The preceding is by way of arriving at a tentative definition of an ecosystem and, hence, animal–environment synergy. Our conception of an ecosystem will differ from more familiar conceptions, for these conceptions forwarded by biologists and ecologists are intended to capture the relation between an animal *as a biological or physical entity* and its habitat. Our conception, on the other hand, is intended to capture the epistemic relation between the animal *as a kowing-agent* and the environment that is known. An ecosystem is a coalition comprising an animal plus a mutually compatible environment (or, equivalently, an environment plus a mutually compatible animal). The animal is a closed (but unbounded) set of effectivities, or goal-directed functions, that identify the potential actions of the animal and that complement the affordances. The environment is a closed (but unbounded) set of affordances, or functionally defined goals, that identify the potential perceptions of the animal and that complement the effectivities. Minimally, an ecosystem is a relational structure with three terms corresponding to the following: an effectivity structure, an affordance structure, and a symmetry operation (to be defined later) that relates the two.

The dualism of animal and environment encourages the view that the animal possesses a model of its environment (e.g., Gregory, 1969); this internal representation is the proposed basis for interpreting the environment's signals and for directing and controlling behavior. In the phrases used earlier, this model or representation is—with reference to perception—the conjunct of a theory of the environment and a theory of how the environment structures energy distributions.

Similarly, the dualism encourages the view that perception *represents* the facts of the environment to the perceiver. A shopworn retort is that if this view were true, would it not require a perceiver, an animal analogue, to perceive the representation? And would this not require another smaller scale representation with its own scaled-down perceiver *ad infinitum*, that is, an unequivocal regress? There is a way to avoid this regress—precisely, by defining perception as the *act of representing* rather than as *a process of using a representation*. But in this usage, it is doubtful that the term *representation* is appropriate.

To represent entails three terms: that which is represented, the representation itself, and that for whom the representation is intended. It seems to us a confusion to treat the act of *using* a representation as being logically independent of the process of *making* a representation. For the concept of representation is user dependent; it must be tailored to fit the user's capabilities.

A representation for one class of users may not be a representation for another class of users; part of the meaning of the term *representation* is the rule or rules required to use it for the purpose it was intended. For instance, a data representation in the programming language of one type of computer may not even be compilable on another type of machine. Similarly, a problem stated in Chinese characters is not a representation of the problem for persons who do not read Chinese. If this argument is valid, then it is not at all clear what it would mean to say that perception is the process of making a representation that is not to be used (perceived) by some agent. Thus, the concept of a "userless" representation is muddled (Shaw & McIntyre, 1974).

In any event, internal representation as the proposed operation that epistemically relates animal and environment is plainly asymmetric. Though it is said that the animal represents (via an internal model) its environment, it is rarely if ever said that the environment represents (via *any* model) its animal; indeed, it would be a very odd thing to say.

In contrast, the synergistic perspective implicates a symmetrical operation binding animal and environment (Shaw, McIntyre, & Mace, 1974; Turvey et al., in press). The mathematical concept of duality (not to be confused with dualism) is offered as a likely candidate for this operation.

A simple interpretation of duality is given by considering a concept defined by means of a diagram consisting of vertices that label sets and arrows, from one vertex to another, that label functions on one set to another (MacLane & Birkhoff, 1967). A "dual" of a diagram can be obtained by reversing the arrows—the dual diagram can then be called the "dual" concept. If in one diagram X is the domain of the function f, in the dual diagram X is the codomain of the function f. Crudely speaking, duality in mathematics is a principle by which one true statement can be obtained from another by merely interchanging two words. Thus, as a further example, in the projective geometry of the plane, the words *point* and *line* can be interchanged, giving the dual statements: "Two points determine a line" and "Two lines determine a point." And in set theory, the relations "contained in" and "contains" can be commuted (with the union becoming the intersection and the intersection becoming the union), leaving the original structure unaltered.

Consider an example of duality in the context of a linear functional (a linear transformation whose codomain is the field of scalars with which we are concerned). The circumstance is that of buying groceries from the perspective of the seller and from the perspective of the buyer.

The customer's shopping list is constructed so as to guarantee a desired balance of carbohydrates, proteins, vitamins, etc. Let the shopping list be (a, b, c,...), and let the price list be [A, B, C,...], so that the cost of the groceries is given by $Aa + Bb + Cc$.... The customer sees the problem as that of choosing a shopping list that meets his or her purposes but that, at the same time, is minimal in cost. In short, with reference to dietary needs, the customer seeks a minimal value of $Aa + Bb + Cc$.... We can identify the customer's vector space as being that in which price lists are functionals and shopping lists are vectors. In contrast, the grocer's vector space identifies the shopping lists as functionals and the price lists as vectors. For the grocer is interested in maximizing profits; so his or her concern is with how the cost of a given shopping list depends on the price list. There is, therefore, a symmetrical relation between the customer's vector space and the grocer's vector space, and the two spaces are referred to as *dual spaces*.

Tentatively, we might regard an animal and its environment (or an environment and its animal) as duals, in which case the relation between the descriptors of the animal and the descriptors of the environment is not one of symbolizing but of complementing. The concepts of affordance and effectivity are dual concepts, and a simple metaphor conveys the gist of this idea: An animal and its environment relate as the two pieces of a two-piece jigsaw puzzle (Fowler & Turvey, 1978).

We can now complete our definition of an (epistemic) ecosystem: It consists of an affordance structure, an effectivity structure, and a duality operation that relates the two.

Perception as an Ecosystem Property

Earlier, attention was brought to the problem of identifying *the* system to which a given phenomenon or set of phenomena corresponded. Recall that "meaning" has been traditionally assigned to the system "animal." Symptomatic of this assignment is the convention of treating sensation as meaningless and perception as meaningful; more generally, it is the distinction drawn between what a thing is and what that thing means—the former being physical and objective, the latter being mental and subjective.

Significantly, the concept of affordance differs from past treatments of meaning in that an affordance is *objective*, defined over the components of an ecosystem. A distinct bonus of a description of the Environment that is animal-related is that it obviates the requirement that the individual animal *add* meaning or value to that which is "merely" physical.

The idea that perceiving is a process that involves a transfer from *meaningless* to *meaningful* is consonant, as noted previously, with animal–environment dualism. But it is an ill-conceived idea, as Gibson (1950) has long maintained. In the perspective of animal–environment synergy, "meaningful perception" is adjunctively entailed by the mutual compatibility of the animal and its environment. Meaning is not a kind of thing that an animal can possess, not a kind of thing by which an animal can impart order to an orderless habitat. Nor is meaning a kind of thing that can be imposed on an animal by the Environment. Meaning is a property of the ecosystem, and individually the animal and the environment constitute *partial* systems with reference to meaning and, in general, to the phenomena of perception. In short, perception and its laws are at the level of description of an ecosystem and not at the level of description of an animal.

The What of Perception Re-examined: The Doctrine of Necessary Specificity

We have acknowledged the traditional complicity between the following two beliefs: One belief holds that the theory of physics has a monopoly on the description of reality; another belief holds that the patterning of energy by an environment (however that patterning is defined) is equivocal and inaccurate —the doctrine of intractable nonspecificity. The complicity lies in the fact that the basic variables of physics constitute a fine-grained description of the energy at the eyes, the ears, etc.—a grain size of description that yields a complicated, chaotic aggregate in contrast to the animal's environment and to the phenomena of perceptual experience (objects, surfaces, events, and the like), which at a considerably coarser grain of description, are coherent, orderly, and systemic. This incompatibility of descriptors, as remarked earlier, is tolerable in the context of animal–environment dualism. In that context there is no reason for surprise at a discontinuity in descriptors; indeed, it is virtually demanded by the received dichotomy of appearance and reality.

In sharp contrast we take the following to be a methodological prescription of animal–environment synergy: With respect to the study of a given phenomenon (such as perception), the animal-related statements and the environment-related statements must be equivalent in grain of analysis, and they must be compatible. If the animal-related statements are that the animal perceives obstacles and apertures as it steers its way through a cluttered terrain, then by this prescription, it would be mistaken to describe the environment-reflected light in terms of photons or in terms of a mosaic of rays of various intensities and wave lengths. Although these descriptions of the light are compatible with a grain of animal-related statements that includes references to individual receptor activity and retinal transduction, respectively, they are not compatible with the grain of description that includes references to the actions of the animal *qua* animal.

It has seemed in the past that only a very fine-grained description of the light is legitimate, because only the basic variables of physics have primary reality status (see Runeson, 1977a, 1977b). But though a very fine-grained description may be exhaustive in terms of the laws of particle physics, there is nothing in that description that *explains* how the light can be information about an animal's environment. If the evolution of vision was the induction of adaptive relations between a fine-grained description of the light and visual systems, then it would be difficult, if not impossible to account for the variety of visual capabilities manifest across species. For what reason should any given type of visual system limit itself to a restricted subset of the possible visual experiences made available by the Environment (von Uexküll, 1957)? At base, the problem arises from the doctrine that physics has a monopoly on describing what light really is. We will have to conclude that there are alternative descriptions of light—no one description more or less real than the other. And this conclusion, it should be noted, is congruent with the ecological approach to the definition of environment; an affordance structure is the reality for a given species.

First steps toward a description of the light at an ecological (as opposed to a cosmological or quantal) scale have been taken (e.g., Gibson, 1961, 1966b; Lee, 1974, 1976; Mace, 1977; Runeson, 1977b). Gibson (1961, 1966b) refers to the enterprise as ecological optics. More generally, when all energy forms are under consideration, the enterprise is referred to as ecological physics. The underlying premise is that at the scale of ecology, an energy medium is not completely free varying; but to the contrary, it is regularly patterned or constrained by the environment so as to be specific to the environment. The environment as a source of constraint on radiant light can be said to condense out environment-specific, complex optical particulars from the environment-neutral, simple optical particulars exhibited at a more molecular level of description. These complex particulars have been referred to by Gibson (e.g., 1966b) as invariants; and Lee (1976) provides an elegant case in point: Rate of magnification of a closed optical contour with internal texture uniquely and invariantly specifies time-to-contact between an animal and an object.

Significantly, the description of radiant light as constrained by an environment is neither redundant nor inconsistent with the most molecular description of the light. This is because a constraint is an *alternative description*, as Pattee (1972) has sought to clarify; and in this respect, an illustration of Medewar (1973) is illuminating. Given the order Euclidean, affine, projective, topology, each successive geometry allows larger equivalence classes than its predecessors and embodies fewer constraints. But what is true about a less constrained geometry, say topology, is not contradicted by a more constrained geometry, say Euclidean. Nevertheless, it is the case that topology cannot explain why two squares that differ only metrically are not equivalent in Euclidean geometry. In short, with respect to the least constrained (and putatively more basic) geometry, the most constrained geometry is not redundant; and neither is it inconsistent.

Importantly, the acceptance of alternative descriptions of the light (or any energy medium, for that matter) weakens the strangle hold of the doctrine of intractable nonspecificity. For in principle, there is a way of describing the light so that proximal stimulation and distal objects are not equivocally or imprecisely related; and this, surely, has been Gibson's (1950, 1961, 1966b) guiding intuition. It is notable that while students of perception in the past five centuries have paid lip service to physics' monopoly on describing light, they have at the same time pursued alternative and generally coarser grained descriptors than those distinguished by physics. This pursuit was inevitable, given the improbability and questioned usefulness of translating from the physicist's fine-grained description of the light to the philosopher's or psychologist's coarse-grained description of visual, phenomenal experience. But herein lies a dilemma. A theorist chooses some grain size of description coarser than the finest grain, presumably because the coarser grain facilitates understanding of the phenomenon in question. The phenomenon is more determinate in reference to the coarser grained description than it is in reference to the finer grained description. At issue for the theorist is the criterion by which to decide on the *proper* grain; ideally, the choice of criterion should not be arbitrary.

On this issue, animal–environment synergy is anything but mute. To begin with, it suggests that that description should be sought which is a partitioning of the ambient light in reference to an animal. An affordance-based partitioning would contrast with a partitioning relative to the transformations of Euclidean geometry. The latter is an animal-neutral partitioning and one that has played a significant role in the past half-millennium of perceptual theory. But partitioning the light relative to Euclidean geometry offers little by way of an understanding of perception as an adaptive relation, and its original usage was perhaps more a matter of convenience than of reason, bolstered by the implicit animal–environment dualism.

It follows (informally) from the compatibility analysis proposed earlier that the logically possible world in which the energy distributions are mutually compatible (that is, invariant or symmetrical) with the facts of the environment is more likely to exist than one in which such compatibilties fail to hold. The upshot is that animal–environment synergy advocates a *doctrine of necessary specificity*, and in so doing it offers a further guideline for choosing the grain of description—namely, that there must be *specificity in the coarse grain despite demonstrable nonspecificity in the fine grain.* That is to say, there *is* a grain of description at which the patterned energy is specific to the environment. The ecological theorist's charge is unequivocal: Pursue ever coarser grain sizes of description until the specificity is realized.

Patently, the doctrine of necessary specificity is the ecological orientation's counter to the traditional doctrine of intractable nonspecificity. Among the accomplices of the latter doctrine was the assumption that the basic variables of physics identify the primary reality and that the registering of these variables constitutes a necessary initial step in perception. In the ecological reformulation a complicity is observed between the doctrine of necessary specificity and the dehypostatizing of the basic variables of physics. The ecological reformulation postulates that complex particulars *qua* invariants, defined over the patterned energy, constitute information about the reality that is specific to the animal—precisely, the affordance structure that is its environment. As a further postulate, the animal's perceptual systems register these invariants directly, without prior registration of the variables basic to physics and without recourse to epistemic mediators (Gibson, 1966b; Mace, 1974, 1977; Shaw & Bransford, 1977; Shaw & McIntyre, 1974; Turvey, 1977). We pursue this latter postulate in the section that follows; but before doing so, let us consider a further implication of the doctrine of necessary specificity.

The doctrine of necessary specificity relaxes the traditional restrictions on the amounts of space and time over which information for a given environmental property might be expressed and to which a given perception might correspond. According to the doctrine, there is no fixed, context-free quantity of the space–time manifold to which can be ascribed the status of "region of perceptual information," in the sense that the information embraced by this region relates to perception whereas the information outside of the region relates to something else such as, for example, memory. Accordingly, it is ill advised, from the ecological point of view, to distinguish perception from memory along the lines that perception is of adjacent order whereas memory is of successive order, or that perception is of the present whereas memory is of the past. Gibson has often spoken of the detection of invariants over time (e.g., Gibson, 1967, 1973) to emphasize that the Newtonian instantaneous moment is not synonymous with the temporal grain of either perception or of the informational support for perception (cf. Turvey, 1977).

In the classical orientation toward events—that is, changes wrought over an object or complex of objects—the registering of form or static pattern was considered basic, and the perception of change was conceptualized as a deduction from sequences of registered static arrangements. As might be expected, a significantly different reading of events is given in the ecological orientation. There are two major components of an event—the nature or style of the change (e.g., rotating, growing, bouncing) and the object properties preserved over the change—and it would follow from the doctrine of necessary specifity that there must be two kinds of invariant information corresponding to these two components. These invariants can be labeled, respectively, *transformational* and *structural* (Shaw & Pittenger, 1977). A transformational invariant is that information, specific to a style of change— that is preserved over different structures "supporting" the change. A structural invariant is that information, specific to an object structure, that is preserved over the styles of change in which the object participates. To perceive an event, therefore, is to detect these invariants.

The Postulates of Direct and Indirect Perception

To say of perception that it is direct, rather than indirect, is to say that it necessarily provides information about how things are (in reference to the effectivities of a given animal) and not merely about how they appear. Traditionally, as noted above, variants of the nonspecificity and independence doctrines such as the argument-from-illusion and the argument-from-incomplete-specification have been used to cast doubt on the claim that perception can in any sense be direct. In order that we might better understand the notion of indirect perception, let us formulate what is meant by the assertion that some observer, O, perceives some state of affairs, S (where S is taken logically as that which is the case). Under the indirect perception idiom, the assertion "O perceives S" means one of several possibilities:

"O perceives S as X."
"S appears as X to O."
"S is perceived as X by O."

The middle term X plays the role of an epistemic mediation for O's perception-knowledge of S. Under the indirect idiom, perception is of some surrogate that *contingently* stands for, or represents, but is not *necessarily* identified with S. To identify the contingent mediary X with what is necessarily true about S, requires an additional inferential step; in other words, O perceives X and then infers that X is to be identified with S, given that sufficient additional evidence to do so is forthcoming (say, from memory of previous occasions on which it *seemed* justified to do so or from application of an a priori logical rule for associating X with S that is deemed useful or correct).

Thus, from this characterization, perception provides only contingent, as opposed to necessary, grounds for identifying that which appears to be (namely, X) with that which actually is (namely, S). Several consequences follow from this that are consonant with the presumed import of the two arguments from illusion and incomplete specification:

1. If what is known (X) through perception about the world (S) is necessarily indirect, then perception-knowledge is at best contingent and must be treated always as potentially suspect.

2. If (indirect) perception-knowledge is merely contingent, then evidence from some source other than perception (e.g., inference or memory) is required to evaluate the worth of perceptual information.

3. Given that perception-knowledge can be shown to be a source of either true or false information about that which is the case, S (e.g., the perceiver's environment), then perception-knowledge, because it involves an inferential step, must be considered a proposition-making activity.

Thus, what might be called the *Postulate of Indirect Perception* can be summarized as follows: *Perception-knowledge consists only of contingent propositions about possible states of affairs that may or may not be demonstrated to be either true or false about the perceiver's actual world (e.g., the animal's environment).*

The Postulate of Indirect Perception has been tacitly adopted by students of perception for the past half-millennium and long before; and it is a logical consequence of the doctrines of intractable nonspecificity and perceptual independence from stimulation. But as we have intimated, this postulate renders the perceptual bases of an animal's knowledge about the dangers and pitfalls of its environment so weak and tenuous, that it is difficult to imagine the successful survival of even one generation of animals, much less the continued evolution of their species over countless generations without a break in the chain. The Postulate of Indirect Perception (or indirect realism) runs counter to the understanding that from the beginning of their association, animals and their environments have enjoyed common causal bases that guarantee their original and continued mutual compatibility.

The argument for a contrary postulate, that of *direct perception* (or direct realism), can be outlined as follows: First what justifies the claim that perception is a valid and reliable source of information for an animal or human about its environment is that perception is necessarily incontrovertible by any other form of knowing the environment (e.g., inference). Second, perception is incontrovertible, because it is necessarily a direct apprehension of that which is true *by force of existence* rather than by force of argument. And third, perception may not be contradicted, because only propositions may be true or false and perception is not a proposition-making activity. *Propositions* are assertions regarding states of affairs that either always obtain or never obtain. *Perception*, by contrast, is not an assertion about states of affairs but is a state of affairs and therefore necessarily obtains (a claim that is explored at length in Shaw et al., in press).

Here is the postulate that summarily captures the sense of the foregoing outline: *If some state of affairs, S is (directly) perceived to be some state of affairs, T, then it is necessarily what it is perceived to be, namely, T.*

This *Postulate of Direct Perception* can be placed in sharp contrast with the Postulate of Indirect Perception by restating the latter in analogous form: *If some state of affairs, S, is (indirectly) perceived by virtue of some other state of affairs, T (e.g., sense data or memories), then it is not necessarily what it is perceived to be namely, T.*

The former postulate can be interpreted as asserting that perceptual information provides direct, unassailable evidence regarding the identity of what is perceived; whereas the latter postulate claims only that perceptual information provides indirect, questionable evidence regarding the identity of what is perceived. (What is perceived is the environment, which—by the definition of environment or econiche given earlier—is species specific. It would be a mistake therefore to read either postulate as naive realism; from the perspective of evolution and ecology, realism is necessarily critical. (See Shaw & Bransford, 1977.)

The Postulate of Direct Perception can be arrived at by virtue of a further consideration of the compatibility analysis, viz., the Law of Existence. It follows (again, informally) that the logically possible world, in which perception is mutually compatible (that is, invariant or symmetrical) with the energy distribution or proximal stimulation as engendered by an environment, is more likely to exist than one in which such compatibiity fails to hold. That is to say, animal–environment synergy advocates a *doctrine of the symmetry of perception and proximal stimulation* as the counterassumption to the traditional doctrine of independence of perception from proximal stimulation. Thus, given an observation in which perception is stable but proximal stimulation appears to be varying, the traditional independence doctrine would foster the acceptance of the observation at face value; the ecological symmetry doctrine, on the other hand, would encourage a search for an alternative description of the proximal stimulation that was as stable as the perception.

The Postulate of Direct Perception is given by the fit between the two aforementioned ecological doctrines. Since a symmetry (law) between the environment (e) and the energy distributions as modulated by the environment (ϕ) holds, and since a symmetry (law) between ϕ and perception (p) holds, then by transitivity a symmetry (law) between e and p holds. That is, $e \diamondsuit \phi$, $\phi \diamondsuit p$, therefore, $e \diamondsuit p$.

On this point we conclude our discussion of the ecological reformulation of perception. It remains for us to do two things: To draw up an inventory of the major contrasts between the legacy of the past five centuries and the ecological reformulation, and to identify some of the implications of the reformulation of perception for the understanding of memory. The inventory

TABLE 9.1

The Legacy of the Last 500 Years	The Ecological Reformulation
Animal–environment dualism	Animal–environment synergy
Conditional or causal logic	Adjunctive logic
Doctrine of intractable nonspecificity	Doctrine of necessary specificity
Doctrine of independence of perception from proximal stimulation	Doctrine of symmetry of perception and proximal stimulation
Experience as constitutive of perception	Experience as preparatory to perception
Postulate of indirect perception (or indirect realism)	Postulate of direct perception (or direct realism)
Events (change) as reconstituted or deduced from static samples	Events as transformational and structural invariants
Operation of representation (a ternary operator or triadic relation)	Operation of specification or duality (a binary operator or dyadic relation)
The theory of perception as independent of the theory of action	Coalitional organization of perceiving (affordance structure) and acting (effectivity structure)
Simple particulars and general-purpose devices	Complex particulars and special-purpose devices

is given in Table 9.1, and the implications for memory are given in the following section.

SOME IMPLICATIONS FOR
THE INTERPRETATION OF MEMORY

How might we view memory, given the ecological reformulation of the problem of perception? If it is admitted that the distinction between the two no longer can be considered to reside in the temporaneity of memory experiences as opposed to the contemporaneity of perceptual experiences, then the basis of their distinction must be sought elsewhere. Especially, we are hard pressed to explain the perception of events that stretch over significant periods of time as "memories" of the cumulative effect of experiences of successive parts of the events. We perceive the concert, the duration of the day from dawn to dusk, the drying up of a puddle over a long, hot afternoon, and so forth (Shaw & Pittenger, 1977). Invoking memory as a process to explain how events are experienced begs the important question of what is experienced, simple or complex particulars, and moreover, stands in contradiction to the Postulate of Direct Perception.

Let us remark on the latter contradiction before pursuing the *what* issue. The Postulate of Direct Perception rules out epistemic mediators. Memories, therefore, cannot be the kinds of things that enter, with sense data, into a recipe whose product is a perception. Put another way, experience cannot be *constitutive* of perception in the sense that experience traces are convention-ally, said to be part and parcel of a perception. Rather, on the ecological reformulation, experience is *preparatory* to perceiving; said succinctly but incompletely, experience attunes or sensitizes perceptual systems to the information that specifies affordances.

Returning to the *what* issue—if memory itself is taken to be the experience of complex particulars (e.g., events), then the concept of memory merges indistinguishably with the concept of perception as reformulated, and no progress is made toward their distinct characterization. The attempt to consider perception of events as merely the stringing together of memory images or representations of successive perceptual experiences runs into perplexing difficulties (besides contradicting the Postulate of Direct Perception).

One such difficulty with the representationalists' (indirect) theory is that the memory images (or repreesntations) of each successive experience must themselves be contemporaneous; they must occur *now*, when we are remembering (Locke, 1971). Thus according to this theory, what we apprehend when we remember is not what has happened (i.e., the successive perceptual experiences) but what is happening now (i.e., the current memory experience). But if that is so, then how can a contemporaneous experience ostensively specify past (noncontemporaneous) experiences? How can a temporal series be rendered manifest in local signs of a spatial series; how can temporaneity be reduced to contemporaneity, or successivities to adjacen-cies?

The so-called trade-off between time and space is well understood, movies and other such recordings being prime examples. But as Pattee (1971) suggests, the puzzle with natural records, such as genes and memories, is not *how* they are made (for there are abundant causal mechanisms to explain their occurrence); rather, the difficulty is to conceptualize *what* is contained in such records. This is the real puzzle of memory. If we understood what constitutes a memory, then we might begin to work out the details of how what is remembered is remembered. Hence it is imperative, if progress is to be made, to hold fast to the distinction between the causal process that supports memory—the physical, chemical, and biological mechanisms—and the epistemic act of remembering as such. To confuse the two is to miss the heart of the puzzle.

The quest for an ecological reformulation of the problem of memory would begin with this distinction: Memory as a causal process that accomplishes record keeping of experience *versus* remembering as an epistemic act supported by such a mechanism but by no means explained by it. An analogy might make this distinction clearer. That the polar planimeter described earlier measures area is no where given as a manifest sign or obvious aspect of its mechanism. One moves the index arm around the perimeter of the closed line-drawing, and the measuring wheel skids and turns until a final value is arrived at for one complete circuit of the index around the figure. A person untutored in the use of the polar planimeter, even if told how to use it, would not immediately grasp what the significance of the act was; there would be no way of knowing what the numeric symbols on the measuring wheel signified. How could there be?—for the causal mechanism provides only support for the epistemic act of measuring area and is in no sense semantically equivalent to the act.

A similar argument can be made with respect to the causal mechanism of memory. Even the most thorough understanding of how it works would bring us no wit closer to understanding what it is that such a mechanism does nor what it signifies. In both cases, the significance of the epistemic act, whether remembering or measuring area, is not obvious but must be discovered. But how might we discover the significances, unless we already have constraining hypotheses regarding *what* it is we believe the devices in question were evolved or designed to perform?

Hence the puzzle of what mechanisms do must be pushed back to the question of why they originated—why they are needed. The desired ecological reformulation of the problem of memory, like that of the problem of perception, requires an insightful attack on the question of origin; for it is here and only here that the secret significance lies of why memory, perception, or other such processes should exist at all.

At least a stab can be made at what may be contained in memory records. Our hunch is that if the ecological reformulation of perception is in the right direction, then the attempt to reformulate the problem of memory should follow suit. First and foremost, memory—like perception—rather than being merely an organismic process, should be a property of an ecosystem. That is to say that memory like perception should be conceptualized in terms of the mutual compatibility of animals (as effectivity structures) with their econiches (as affordance structures).

The following three postulates represent a first effort to address the boundary conditions on learning, generalization of knowledge, and remembering, respectively. (The first postulate is written fully in both affordance and effectivity terms, but the effectivity portion is omitted in the second and third postulates for simplicity of presentation.) *Postulate I (Learning): An environmental event or situation X affords an activity Y for an animal Z, and an animal Z can effect an activity Y on an environmental event or situation X if and only if X and Z are mutually compatible (X ◊ X).*

Where the first postulate states the boundary condition that must be satisfied if learning is to take place in a given situation, the second postulate states the conditions that must be satisfied if knowledge gained in such situations is to be generalized to analogous situations. *Postulate II (Generalization of Knowledge): An environmental situation X affords an activity Y for an animal Z only if another situation W affords the same activity Y for Z where X stands to Y as W stands to Y (i.e., X/Y: W/Y) if and only if X is mutually compatible with Z in the same way that W is mutually compatible with Z [i.e., (X ✧ Z) ≡ (W ✧ Z)].*

This postulate describes the conditions required for the analogical extension of knowledge from one situation to another according to the usual way of analyzing analogies and metaphors (Verbrugge, 1977). Following such an analysis, *X/Y* is the *topic*. *W/Y* is the *vehicle*, and (X ✧ Z) ≡ (W ✧ Z) is the *ground* of the analogy. If the analogy is perceptually defined, then the postulate can be used in principle to capture the notion of perceptual invariants as the ground of the analogy. Finally, we identify the postulate that states the boundary conditions that must be satisfied if remembering is to be an ecologically defined epistemic act and memory a property of an ecosystem.

Postulate III (Memory): An environmental situation X affords an activity Y for an animal Z at some later time t_k only if some situation W affords the same activity Y for Z at some earlier time t_1 where (X/Y: W/Y) if and only if (X ✧ Z) ≡ (W ✧ Z).

This final postulate proposes a view of memory as knowledge that persists by analogical extension (generalization) from earlier to later situations; the second postulate, as already pointed out, can be used *inter alia* to propose a view of generalization by analogical extension over distinct perceptual situations. Hence the second postulate can be said to describe the necessary conditions for perception-knowledge, whereas the third postulate can be said to describe the necessary conditions for memory-knowledge. And in the unpacking and extension of these postulates is defined, in large part, the tack that an ecological orientation would take toward the phenomenon of memory.

REFERENCES

Adler, J. The sensing of chemicals by bacteria. *Scientific American*, 1976, *234*, 40–47.
Anscombe, G. E. M. The intentionality of perception: A grammatical feature. In R. J. Butler (Ed.), *Analytical Philosophy* (2nd series). Oxford: Oxford University Press, 1965.
Ashby, R. *An introduction to cybernetics.* New York: Wiley, 1963.
Ayer, A. J. *The foundations of empirical knowledge.* London: Macmillan, 1940.
Berkeley, G. An essay toward a new theory of vision, 1709. In A. A. Luce & T. E. Jessup (Eds.), *The works of George Berkeley.* London: Thomas Nelson & Sons, 1964.
Bertalanffy, L. von. Chance or law. In A. Koestler & J. R. Smythies (Eds.), *Beyond reductionism.* Boston: Beacon Press, 1969.
Blum, H. F. *Time's arrow and evolution.* Princeton, N.J.: Princeton University Press, 1968.
Bohm, D. *Causality and chance in modern physics.* London: Routledge and Kegan Paul, 1957.
Bolles, R. C. *Learning theory.* New York: Holt, Rinehart & Winston, 1975.
Boynton, R. The visual system: Environmental information. In E. C. Carterette & M. P. Friedman (Eds.), *Handbook of perception* (Vol. III). New York: Academic Press, 1975.
Clark, R. *Einstein: The life and times.* New York: Avon Books, 1971.

Dennett, D. C. *Content and consciousness.* New York: Humanities Press, 1969.

Dennett, D. C. Intentional systems. *The Journal of Phlosophy,* 1971, *118,* 87–106.

Dicke, R. H. Dirac's cosmology and Mach's principle (letter to the editor). *Nature,* 1961, *192,* 440–441.

Epstein, W. The process of "taking-into-account" in visual perception. *Perception,* 1973, *2,* 267–285.

Epstein, W. Historical introduction to the constancies. In W. Epstein (Ed.), *Stability and constancy in visual perception: Mechanisms and processes.* New York: Wiley, 1977.

Fitch, H., & Turvey, M. T. On the control of activity: Some remarks from an ecological point of view. In R. Christina (Ed.), *Psychology of motor behavior and sports.* Urbana, Ill.: Human Kinetics, 1978.

Fodor, J. A. *The language of thought.* New York: Thomas Y. Crowell, 1975.

Fowler, C. A., & Turvey, M. T. Skill acquisition: An event approach with special reference to searching for the optimum of a function of several variables. In G. Stelmach (Ed.), *Information processing in motor control and learning.* New York: Academic Press, 1978.

Gel'fand, I. M., & Tsetlin, M. L. Some methods of control for complex systems. *Russian Mathematical Surveys,* 1962, *17,* 95–116.

Gibson, J. J. *The perception of the visual world.* Boston: Houghton-Mifflin, 1950.

Gibson, J. J. Ecological optics. *Vision Research,* 1961, *1,* 253–262.

Gibson, J. J. The problem of temporal order in stimulation and perception. *Journal of Psychology,* 1966, *62,* 141–149. (a)

Gibson, J. J. *The senses considered as perceptual systems.* Boston: Houghton-Mifflin, 1966. (b)

Gibson, J.J. New reasons for realism. *Synthese,* 1967, *17,* 162–172.

Gibson, J. J. On the concept of "formless invariants" in visual perception. *Leonardo,* 1973, *6,* 43–45.

Gibson, J. J. The theory of affordances. In R. E. Shaw & J. Bransford (Eds.), *Perceiving, acting and knowing: Toward an ecological psychology.* Hillsdale N.J.: Lawrence Erlbaum Associates, 1977.

Gregory, R. L. On how little information controls so much behavior. In C. H. Waddington (Ed.), *Toward a theoretical biology* (Vol. 2). Chicago: Aldine, 1969.

Helmholtz, H. von. (J. P. Southall, Ed. and trans.) [*Treatise on psychological optics*] Rochester, N.Y.: Optical Society of America, 1925. (Originally published in German, 3rd ed., 1909–1911.)

Henderson, L. J. *The fitness of the environment.* Gloucester, Mass.: Peter Smith, 1970. (Originally published by Macmillan Co., New York, 1913.)

Humphrey, G. *The nature of learning.* New York: Harcourt, Brace, 1933.

Hunt, E. *Artificial intelligence.* New York: Academic Press, 1975.

Koffka, K. *Principles of Gestalt psychology.* New York: Harcourt, Brace, 1935.

Lakatos, I. Falsification and the methodology of scientific research programmes. In I. Lakatos & A. Musgrave (Eds.), *Criticism and the growth of knowledge.* Cambridge, England: Cambridge University Press, 1970.

Lee, D. H. Visual information during locomotion. In R. B. MacLeod & H. L. Pick (Eds.), *Perception: Essays in honor of James J. Gibson.* Ithaca, N.Y.: Cornell University Press, 1974.

Lee, D. N. A theory of visual control of braking based on information about time-to-collision. *Perception,* 1976, *5,* 437–459.

Locke, D. *Memory.* Garden City, N.Y.: Doubleday, 1971.

Lombardo, T. *J. J. Gibson's ecological approach to visual perception: Its historical context and development.* Unpublished doctoral dissertation, University of Minnesota, 1973.

Mace, W. M. Ecologically stimulating cognitive psychology: Gibsonian perspectives. In W. Weimer & D. S. Palermo (Eds.), *Cognition and the symbolic processes.* Hillsdale, N.J.: Lawrence Erlbaum Associates, 1974.

Mace, W. M. James Gibson's strategy for perceiving: Ask not what's inside your heat, but what your head's inside of. In R. E. Shaw & J. Bransford (Eds.), *Perceiving, acting and knowing: Toward an ecological psychology.* Hillsdale, N.J.: Lawrence Erlbaum Associates, 1977.

Mach, E. *Science of mechanics: A critical and historical account of its development.* Chicago: Open Court, 1902.

MacLane, S., & Birkhoff, G. *Algebra.* New York: Macmillan, 1967.

Medewar, P. A geometrical model of reduction and emergence. In F. Ayala & T. Dobzhansky (Eds.), *Studies in the philosophy of biology.* Los Angeles: University of California Press, 1973.

Moorhead, P. S., & Kaplan, M. M. (Eds.), *Mathematical challenges to the neo-Darwinian interpretation of evolution.* Symposium Monograph No. 5. Philadelphia, Pa.: Wistar Institute Press, 1967.

Pattee, H. H. The problem of biological hierarchy. In C. H. Waddington (Ed.), *Towards a theoretical biology* (Vol. 3). Chicago: Aldine, 1970.

Pattee, H. H. Can life explain quantum mechanics? In T. Bastin (Ed.), *Quantum theory and beyond.* Cambridge, England: Cambridge University Press, 1971.

Pattee, H. H. Laws and constraints, symbols and languages. In C. H. Waddington (Ed.), *Towards a theoretical biology* (Vol. 4). Chicago: Aldine, 1972.

Popper, K. R. *The logic of scientific discovery.* New York: Harper & Row, 1959.

Rock, I. *An introduction to perception.* New York: Macmillan, 1975.

Runeson, S. On the possibility of "smart" perceptual mechanisms. *Scandinavian Journal of Psychology,* 1977, *18* 172–179. (a)

Runeson, S. *On visual perception of dynamic events.* Doctoral dissertation, University of Uppsala, Sweden, 1977. (b)

Russell, B. *The analysis of matter.* London: George Allen and Unwin, 1927.

Ryle, G. *The concept of mind.* New York: Barnes & Noble, 1949.

Shaffner, K. F. Antireductionism and molecular biology. *Science,* 1967, *157,* 644–647.

Shaw, R. E., & Bransford, J. Introduction: Psychological approaches to the problem of knowledge. In R. E. Shaw & J. Bransford (Eds.), *Perceiving, acting and knowing: Toward an ecological psychology,* Hillsdale, N.J.: Lawrence Erlbaum Associates, 1977.

Shaw, R. E., & McIntyre, M. Algoristic foundations to cognitive psychology. In W. Weimer & D. Palermo (Eds.), *Cognition and the symbolic processes.* Hillsdale, N.J.: Lawrence Erlbaum Associates, 1974.

Shaw, R. E., McIntyre, M., & Mace, W. The role of symmetry in event perception. In R. B. MacLeod & H. L. Pick (Eds.), *Perception: Essays in honor of J. J. Gibson.* Ithaca, N.Y.: Cornell University Press, 1974.

Shaw, R. E., & Pittenger, J. On perceiving change. In H. Pick & E. Saltzman (Eds.), *Modes of perceiving and processing information.* Hillsdale, N.J.: Lawrence Erlbaum Associates, 1977.

Shaw, R. E., Turvey, M. T., & Mace, W. Ecological psychology: The consequence of a commitment to realism. In W. Weimer & D. Palermo (Eds.), *Cognition and the symbolic processes II.* Hillsdale, N.J.: Lawrence Erlbaum Associates, in press.

Skinner, B. R. The experimental analysis of behavior. *American Scientist,* 1957, *45,* 343–371.

Skinner, B. F. *About behaviorism.* New York: Knopf, 1974.

Strong, D. R., & Ray, T. S. Host tree location behavior of a tropical vine (*Monstera Gibantea*) by Skototropism. *Science,* 1975, *190,* 804–806.

Trimble, V. Cosmology: Man's place in the universe. *American Scientist,* 1977, *65,* 76–87.

Turvey, M. T. Contrasting orientations to the theory of visual information processing. *Psychological Review,* 1977, *84,* 67–88.

Turvey, M. T., Shaw, R. E., & Mace, W. Issues in the theory of action: Degrees of freedom, coordinative structures and coalitions. In J. Requin (Ed.), *Attention and performance VII.* Hillsdale, N.J.: Lawrence Erlbaum Associates, in press.

Uexküll, J. von. A stroll through the worlds of animals and men. In C. H. Schiller (Ed.), *Instinctive behavior*. New York: International Universities Press, 1957.

Verbrugge, R. R. Resemblance in language and perception. In R. E. Shaw & J. Bransford (Eds.), *Perceiving, acting and knowing: Toward and ecological psychology*. Hillsdale, N.J.: Lawrence Erlbaum Associates, 1977.

Wald, G. Phylogeny and ontogeny at the molecular level. In A. I. Oparin (Ed.), *Evolutionary biochemistry: Proceedings of the Vth International Congress on Biochemistry*, Moscow, 1961. London: Pergamon, 1963.

Weiss, P. A. The living system: Determinism stratified. In A. Koestler & J. R. Smythies (Ed.), *Beyond reductionism*. Boston: Beacon Press, 1969.

Weiss, P. A. Fundamentals of system causality in nature. In J. Rose (Ed.), *Advances in cybernetics and systems* (Vol. 1). New York: Gordon and Breach Science Publishers, 1974.

Wheeler, J. A. The universe as home for man. *American Scientist*, 1974, *62*, 683–691.

Wigner, E. P. *Symmetrics and reflections*. Cambridge, Mass.: MIT Press, 1970.

Williams, G. C. *Adaptation and natural selection*. Princeton, N.J.: Princeton University Press, 1966.

IV
BIOLOGICAL PERSPECTIVES

10 Learning as Differentiation of Brain Cell Protein

Holger Hydén
Institute of Neurobiology,
University of Göteborg, Sweden

GENERAL CONSIDERATIONS

Most papers of the present conference deal with psychological aspects of memory. Several approaches to memory research have been described within this field. The present chapter deviates considerably from these, because it is working at a molecular, cell biochemistry, and system level. What the other papers take for granted with respect to enduring changes in brain cells during encoding, storage, and retrieval is what the present chapter seeks to understand. There is presently an enormous gap between research at these levels. However, as we are all dealing with the same topic, it seems reasonable that we should be able to meet some time at the end. It may be too early for a merge of these approaches, but it is definitely not too early to formulate common levels for a future integration.

Memory mechanisms should be intimately related to the active genes of brain cells. An important question is whether or not brain mechanisms underlying innate behavior also serve the encoding, storage, and retrieval of information during the life cycle. One thing should be made clear right away: There is no evidence that a molecule can record and store information in its interior like a magnetic tape and later provide the information such that the individual can experience a "psychological memory."

All other organs are by far exceeded by the nervous system in structural complexity. As discussed by von Bertalanffy (1973), the brain is an open hierarchical system, associated with the structures of the brain systems and subsystems. Some of these molecular processes are common for all body cells, and some are highly brain specialized. This specialization in molecular mechanisms is due to the differentiation of the brain cells leaving a certain combination of genes active and other genes silent.

The differentiation of brain cells after birth occurs during critical periods restricted in time. The degree of differentiation obtained through several sources of stimuli (e.g., adequate contact with adults) results in the genetical potentialities of the young adult brain.

It is not surprising that brain protein synthesis has been shown to be important for memory. Proteins have sites for absolute recognition; they can modify function by undergoing conformational changes; and they are constituents of brain cell membranes. An increased demand for protein synthesis of brain cells will be reflected in an increased RNA synthesis and specialized types of RNA. To elucidate meaningful information about specific protein and RNA in brain cells during learning, extremely small samples from defined brain areas have to be analyzed. It is otherwise possible that nonresponding or differently responding areas will prohibit specific changes from very small brain centers from being picked up by analytical procedures Another analytical danger is the fact that the brain consists of two types of cells, neurons and glial cells. The latter even dominate in number, and molecular processes are shown to run in one direction in glial cells and in an opposite direction in nerve cells.

The strategy used in those studies described is to analyze very small, accurately defined areas or nerve cells in the brain during the process of learning a specific task. However, it is also important to trace specific changes through brain systems or in loci and subsystems that may serve main systems.

In the discussion to follow, learning (change of behavior as a result of individual experience) is regarded as a continuous protein differentiation of neurons. The discussion is primarily based on results from experiments in our own laboratory, although results from other studies are referred to as well. In most of the studies described, microchemical techniques have been used for the analyses (for details of this technique, see Hydén, Bjurstam, & McEwen, 1966; Hydén & Lange, 1968).

There are good reasons to believe that learning of a new task first involves *short-lasting* specific changes in the protein pattern in many brain areas. These changes follow a time course and spread through the brain; secondly, they involve a long-lasting and remaining protein differentiation of the nerve cell membrane and synapses. It is assumed that this long-term phenomenon progresses with experience and utilizes a "cooperative" process between a membrane-bound protein called S-100 and an actinlike network associated with synapses and the membrane. Cooperativity means that macro-molecules in a system of ultrastructures act together and switch *from one state to another.*

The key ion in this mechanism is CA^{2+}. S-100 is an acidic, brain-specific protein that is localized both in glia and neurons. Glial cells probably synthesize all of this protein. S-100 has a molecular weight of 21.000 and consists of 3 subunits. The molecule binds avidly calcium.

SOME EXPERIMENTAL CONSIDERATIONS

Many neurobiologists conducting animal learning experiments fall short on a basic aspect of the experimental setup, which is of crucial importance to the interpretation of the data as well as to their generality. In a few cases, monkeys have been used, but mostly rats have been experimental subjects. In its natural environment the rat is active and socially and ecologically well advanced, and an experimental situation should be designed accordingly. The experimental situations typically used in many laboratories (e.g., classical conditioning—having the rat jump to a shelf to escape electric shock or press a bar for food pellets) are discarded as irrelevant. The reason for this is that the hippocampus must function correctly in order for learning to occur. It has been demonstrated that a rat with a damage bilaterally in the hippocampus is unable to learn to solve a task of medium difficulty, whereas it will learn automatized conditioning tasks even better than normal rats. Furthermore, Kimble (1975) has shown that rats with hippocampal lesions cannot cope with novelty situations requiring learning. It may be speculated that the good performance of rats with hippocampal lesions is due to a general inflexibility.

In all experiments in our laboratory we have attempted to create situations that are ecologically more valid than the conditioning experiments used elsewhere. For this purpose we have used a so-called transfer of handedness task. Rats show a preference in handedness; 40% are right-handed, 45% left-handed, and 15% ambidextrous. We used a sharpened-up test originally described by Peterson (1934), Wentworth (1942), and Buresova, Bures, and Beran (1958). The original test arrangement of Peterson was modified in the following way. First, in 23 out of 25 free-choice reachings, the rats showed whether they were left- or right-handed in reaching a narrow, downward-tilted glass tube in order to retrieve, one by one, 4-mm-diameter protein pills with their preferred paw. Half of the glass tube is constantly kept full of protein pills by a special filling arrangement. To induce the rats to reverse the handedness, a glass wall was arranged parallel to the glass tube on the side opposite that of the preferred paw. Space then prohibited the use of the latter, and the rats soon began to use the nonpreferred paw (Fig. 10.1). They were given 2 training periods of 25 minutes each per day for 4 to 5 days. A successful reach is one where the rat quickly grasps a protein pill with the paw and retrieves it. The performance curve is linear up to day 7–8. The three persons handling the training have no knowledge of previous treatment of the rats, and the personnel in the biochemical laboratory received the rats designated only by number. An active control to the experimental rat is an animal that

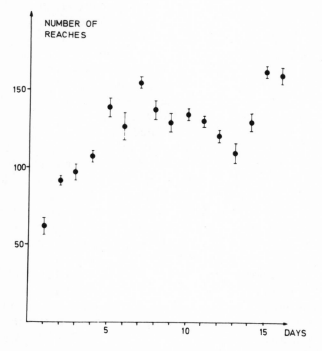

FIG.10.1. Performance curve of a group of 12 rats, given as the average number of reaches as a function of number of training sessions (2 ×25 min per day).

uses its preferred paw to get the same number of food pellets as the experimental rat. The control rat can improve its performance but is not supposed to learn in the sense of organizing a new behavior.

SYNTHESIS OF MESSENGER RNA
AT THE ONSET OF TRAINING

The basic question studied in the experimental situation described is whether learning involves synthesis of mRNA in brain cells. Indirect evidence for this assumption has previously been obtained. Hydén and Egyhazi (1962, 1963, 1964) showed that synthesis of nerve cell RNA with an altered base-composition was observed in rats trained to reverse handedness. Similar results have later been reported by Shashoua (1974) and by Woolf, Willies, Hepburn, and Rosendorft (1974) in brains from goldfish trained in a new swimming skill.

However, the reports of only an increase in amount or synthesis of RNA in brain cells at learning do not seem to be pertinent in the discussion (Kimble, 1975),. Recently, Cupello and Hydén (1976) observed newly synthesized, specific poly-(A)-associated mRNA in hippocampal CA3 pyramidal nerve cells in rats subjected to training to reverse handedness. The animals received $5.6\text{-}^3\text{H}$-uridine intraventricularly before the last training session of 25 minutes, and cell material was taken 1 hour later. RNA was extracted by a phenol-SDS treatment, and the poly-(A)-associated oligo(dT-cellulose binding RNA was quantitated, separated, and counted.

The fractionation pattern showed a clear stimulation in labeling of an RNA component with an S_E value of 25. We found in the same nerve cells from trained rats an increased incorporation into RNA compared to controls. Furthermore, it was a significant stimulation of 8–9 S, 16–17 S RNA in high molecular weight RNA. It is noted that messenger RNA in rat brain has been found to consist of 9S and 16S RNA (Zomzeley–Neurath, Marangos, Hymnowitz, Perl, Ritter, Zayas, Cua, & York, in press).

These data, which show both the stimulation of a specific poly-(A)-associated mRNA (25 S_E) and of 9S and 16S RNA in the CA3 hippocampal nerve cells from trained animals, indicate that gene activation occurs at the establishment of a new behavior in the nerve cells of the main integrating part (CA3) of the hippocampus.

The Question of Specific Localization of Biochemical
Changes in the Brain During Learning

A clear specificity in the localization of both RNA base ratio changes and of protein incorporation has been observed. Rhesus monkeys were subjected to visual discrimination of symbols and delayed alternation training and compared to active controls exposed to the same conditions but at random (Hydén, Lange, Mihailović, & Petrović–Minić, 1974).

After 300 to 500 visual discrimination trials for 10 to 18 days, RNA increase and base-composition changes were detected in nerve cells (5th layer) of the inferior temporal gyrus and in CA3 nerve cells of the hippocampus. The integrity of this cortical area is a prerequisite for the monkey to resolve the task. No changes were observed in the gyrus principalis, which, however, responded at delayed alternation learning. Thus, specific brain regions respond with different RNA changes at the acquisition of different behavioral patterns in monkeys.

Probably, localization of biochemical brain responses differs with species. In the rat, Yanagihara and Hydén (1971) found a consistent stimulation of leucine incorporation into total proteins of CA3 nerve cells in the hippocampus after training. By contrast, incorporation into CA4 cells was increased only during the early period of training. No significant stimulation was detected in CA1 nerve cells after training.

Short-Term Changes of Brain Protein

In a series of learning experiments, we have found that the synthesis of S-100 protein increases in the integrative part of the hippocampus, called the CA3-region. Brain samples from learning rats were compared to those of active controls. The amount of S-100 increases by 15 to 20%, and the incorporation of radioactive valine and leucine by 200 to 300% (Hydén & Lange 1965, 1975). Microchemical separation on capillary gels and immunoelectrophoresis and a very sensitive radioactivity counting technique have been used on samples dissected out from the exposed brain (Hydén et al., 1966; Larsson, 1972). The changes were observed within minutes from the onset of training, which means that the cytoplasmic mechanisms for S-100 synthesis could respond to immediate demands and probably use messenger RNA already present in the cytoplasm (Table 10.1).

In the training procedure the animals show maximal scores of correct responses in 6 to 8 days. Overtraining, on the other hand, does not result in a

TABLE 10.1

	Number of Animals	Number of Gels	Corrected Specific Activity[a]
Half training time	2	5	13.0 ± 0.60
Full training time (through Day 14)	5	10	3.9 ± 0.48
Control	10	24	1.5 ± 0.16

[a]Cpm/μg plus or minus standard error of the mean.

TABLE 10.2

	Number of Animals	Number of Gels	Corrected Specific Activity[a]
Initial training	5	10	3.3 ± 0.40
Training after 14 days	5	10	3.9 ± 0.48
Training after 30 days	14	35	1.8 ± 0.17
Control	10	24	1.5 ± 0.16

[a]Cpm/μg plus or minus standard error of the mean.

maintained high protein synthesis. On the contrary, the protein values decrease to that of control levels (Hydén & Lange, 1970–1971, 1972) (Table 10.2).

An increase in amount and incorporation of labeled precursors in the CA3 region of the hippocampus is also induced in the 14-3-2 protein on reversal of handedness training. The protein 14-3-2 is a neuronal compound. The main part is easily soluble, and a small fraction is localized to the plasma membrane and to the synaptic structure (Grasso, Haglid, Hansson, Persson, & Rönnbäck, 1977; Hydén & Lange 1968, 1969).

A most striking change during training is of the calcium content of the hippocampus, which will modify the molecular structure of the S-100 protein. Ca^{2+} increases in amount from 32 to 48 mEq/g wet weight in the CA3 region. K^+, NA^+, and H_2O do not change. Therefore, the Ca^{2+} increase seems specific, and circulatory effects can be ruled out (Haljamäe & Lange, 1972).

As is well known, Ca^{2+} causes S-100 partly to open up, and hydrophobic groups are exposed (Calissano, 1973). As a consequence of this conformational change, the S-100 protein will be able to interact with membranes. On 20% gel electrophoresis, the S-100 protein appears in two fractions, one of which has a higher mobility (Hydén & Lange, 1970). The samples from the controls that use their preferred paw during retrieval of the objects from the glass tube do not display such a phenomenon. It is highly probable that the newly synthesized S-100 in the hippocampus undergoes conformational changes induced by the increase in Ca^{2+}. S-100 can react with and be incorporated into the nerve cell plasma membrane in the calcium form. This aspect is discussed in more detail later.

Incorporation of labeled amino acids has been followed during training to reverse handedness in various parts of the brain. After training for eight 25-min sessions during 4 days, the incorporation values were high in the hippocampal S-100 and 14-3-2 cell protein and relatively smaller (also lower than values of active controls) in cortical areas. With more training and time, this picture of the hippocampus being the most active area in incorporating amino acids into cell protein reverses (Hydén & Lange, 1972). The values of

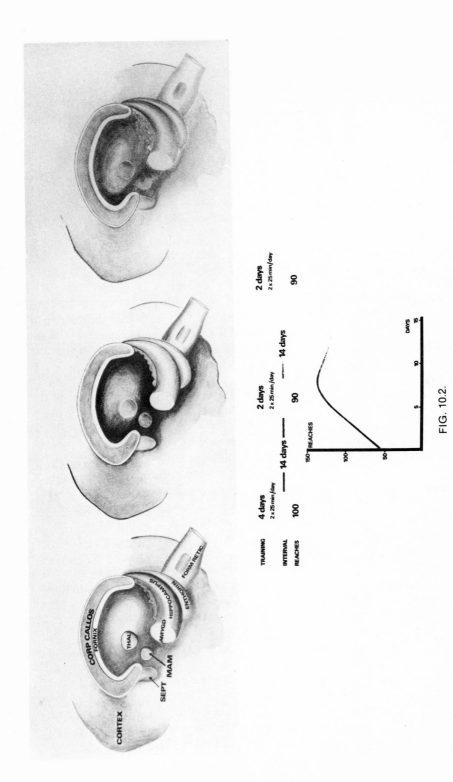

FIG. 10.2.

TABLE 10.3
Relative Specific Activities of 8 Different Brain Areas of Controls and
Days With 14 Days Intermission Between the 3 Training Periods[a]

Brain Area	Training			Control
	4 Days	6 Days	8 Days	
Cortex	0.40 ± .01	0.51 ± .02	0.53 ± .02	1.40 ± .15
Thalamus, nucl. dorso-med.	0.28 ± .01	0.35 ± .02	0.39 ± .03	0.95 ± .15
Entorhinalis	0.25 ± .002	0.32 ± .01	0.46 ± .02	0.84 ± .02
Septum	0.19 ± .004	0.29 ± .01	0.26 ± .01	0.78 ± .12
Corp. mam.	0.39 ± .02	0.48 ± .04	0.43 ± .04	0.87 ± .09
Nucl. dentatus	0.39 ± .02	0.34 ± .01	0.41 ± .03	0.81 ± .03
Hippocampus	0.69 ± .04	0.38 ± .03	0.47 ± .03	0.75 ± .06
Formatio ret.	0.32 ± .01	0.36 ± .03	0.52 ± .03	0.90 ± .03

[a] 9 control rats, 12 trained rats. Control values as averages for the whole training period.

the hippocampus recede to starting levels; and the values of the entorhinal, visual, and sensory–motor cortices increase successively (Fig. 10.2 and Table 10.3). Thus, training to learn seems to induce synthesis of specific protein in the CA3 of the hippocampus and a decrease of precursor incorporation into cells of cortical areas. The reversal in protein activities gives the picture of a wave of protein synthesis that pervades the brain at training and starts in the hippocampus.

In a series of slightly different experiments using reversed handedness and a visual discrimination test, we have also found that proteins other than S-100 and 14-3-2 in the hippocampus respond first among brain areas with a 20 to 25% increase and higher incorporation of precursors. Active controls do not respond in such a fashion (Hydén & Lange, in press). Zomzely–Neurath et al. (in press) have confirmed these findings and observed an increase in S-100 protein and a protein fraction containing 14-3-2 protein in rats during maze learning.

A question raised by the results described, then, is how specifically the S-100 protein is linked to cellular processes that are crucial for learning. One strategy to study this question would be to interfere with the S-100 in the hippocampal area and to observe a possible effect on behavior. Antiserum against S-100 was therefore injected intraventricularly in rats during training to reverse handedness (Hydén & Lange, 1970). A control that the antiserum to S-100 reached the pyramidal nerve cells of the hippocampus was conducted. Controls were injected with the same antiserum from which the antibodies to S-100 had been removed. The results showed that antiserum to S-100 impaired further learning, as demonstrated by the deflected learning curve in Fig. 10.3. Using rats in different behavioral test, Rapport and Karpiak (1976) have confirmed these results.

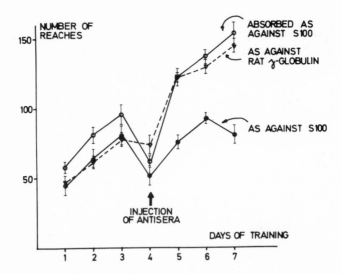

FIG. 10.3. The effect of injection of 60 μl × 2 of antiserum against S=100 intraventricularly in rats trained to reverse handedness. A group of rats was trained for 3 days with 2 sessions of 25 min per day. On the 4th day the antiserum against S=100 absorbed with S=100 was injected intraventricularly. The training was continued for 3 more days. Rats injected with antiserum against S=100 showed a deflection of the learning curve.

Furthermore, it was found that the effect of the antiserum to S-100 injected intraventricularly was an increase in the amount of S-100 protein in the hippocampus and in the thalamus (Hydén & Lange, in press). The observations discussed then suggest that S-100 as a membrane antigen and soluble protein is specifically involved in cellular processes necessary for establishment of a new behavior (Table 10.4).

Any change in the protein pattern of synaptic protein is bound to attract interest. By centrifugating methods, Hydén, Lange, and Perrin (1977) prepared membrane protein of synapses from trained rats and active controls. We found in trained animals a stimulation of certain protein fractions (~30.000 and 80.000 mol. wt.) that was not observed in active controls. This phenomenon was first observed in the hippocampus and later in the

TABLE 10.4

Hippocampus		Thalamus		Training Time
AS S100	AS abs S100	AS S100	AS abs S100	Min
432	368	500	477	0
461	328	487	455	8
419	349	507	457	16
453	368	560	461	25

sensory–motor cortex. Thus the same time-phase shift was observed in the response of the synaptic protein as of the S-100 and 14-3-2 protein (Figs. 10.4 and 10.5).

Comments

Training to learn seems to induce the cells of the hippocampus to respond with a synthesis of specific brain proteins, S-100 and 14-3-2; this response spreads to cortical areas. This activity by the hippocampus ceases to occur when the task has been learned and does not appear on overtraining. Ca^{2+} increases during the stage of specific brain protein synthesis. This seems to be a highly significant phenomenon, as Ca^{2+} induces the S-100 protein to undergo conformational changes. The stability of these changes is demonstrated by the finding that one fraction of S-100 protein gets a higher mobility on electrophoresis. The significance of the Ca^{2+} increase is discussed later. Figure 10.6 summarizes schematically the short-lasting changes discussed.

The short-lasting changes during training also encompass a synthesis of synaptosomal protein, beginning with a transient stimulation in the hippocampal cells of 30.000 and 80.000 mol. wt. synaptic proteins. After a time lapse comes a stimulation in the sensory–motor cortex of 35.000 and 60.000 mol. wt. synaptic proteins.

The time schedule of these events does not indicate a regulation by electrical stimuli. More complicated processes seem to underly the phase-regulated protein stimulation through the brain. It is close at hand to suspect a diffusion of, for example, peptides and Ca^{2+} from the limbic system to the neocortex to initiate cell protein synthesis.

ARE ENDURING MOLECULAR CHANGES A RESULT OF LEARNING MEDIATED BY A TRANSIENT SPECIFIC PROBLEM?

After perception, processing of activities occurs through the brain. Unless interference interrupts, a long-term memory will be established. I would like to raise the question of whether this transitional phase is directly or indirectly mediated by a biochemical mechanism. The background is the following. We subjected rats to reversal of handedness training during 2×25 min/day for 2 days. The animals then had an intermission with no training for 5 days. On the 8th day, the rats got a 25-min training, whereafter different parts of the brain were sampled immediately and after 12, 24, 48, and 72 hrs. In all brain areas studied, we found 24 hrs after training finished an increased incorporation of the labeled precursor (^{14}C-valine) and an increased amount of a particular protein fraction with a molecular weight around 60.000 (Hydén & Lange, in press). Within a further 24 hrs, the stimulation of this protein fraction ceased, and values returned to the low control values (Fig. 10.7).

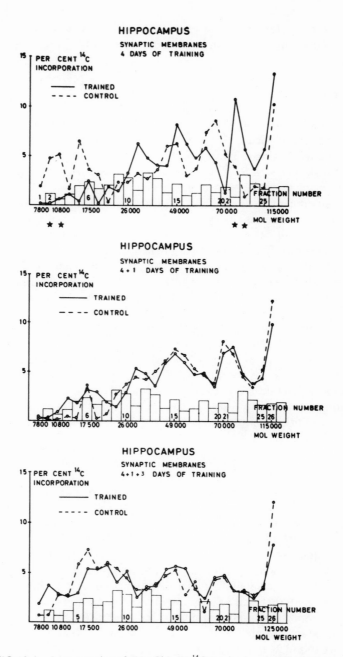

FIG.10.4. Incorporation of 100 μCi L-(U-^{14}C)leucine i.p. Height of columns gives relative amount of the protein fractions. 4 days of training (25 min m2 per day) 4 + 1, 4 + 1 + 3 days. Stars designate significance ($P<0.001$).

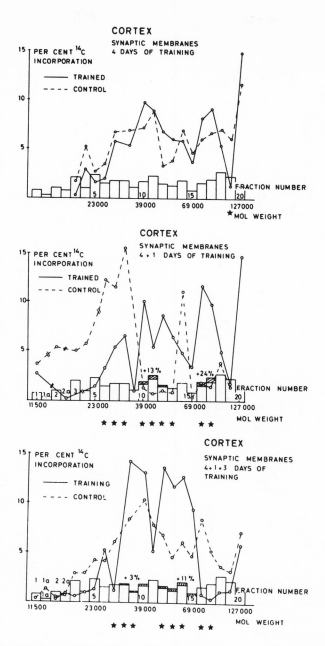

FIG.10.5. Incorporation of L-(U-^{14}C) leucine into protein of the cortical synaptic membrane fraction as a function of training. Note increased incorporation values around mot. wt. 39,000–49,000 and 90,000–110,000. Further training is followed by incorporation increase at 32,000–40,000 and from 48,000 mot. wt. Hatched areas indicate amounts of protein fractions.

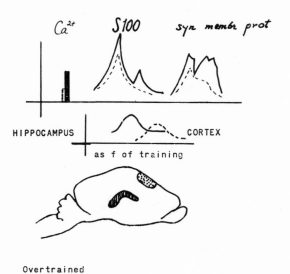

LEARNING

SYSTEM CHANGES in brain cell proteins
increase in
soluble S100 protein
Ca²⁺
synaptic membrane protein

Overtrained
No response

FIG.10.6.

It is interesting that rats that have been subjected to a discrimination test do better when tested 24 hrs after the first training, as if they had increased their score during the intermission without training (Cardo, 1976).

The correlation between the change in behavior and the unexpected increase of a 60.000 mol. wt. protein is thought-provoking. In learning experiments on young people, a similar increase of remembrance was noted 2 to 3 days after finished memory training (Ballard, 1913).

REMAINING PROTEIN DIFFERENTIATION OF NEURONS AS A FUNCTION OF EXPERIENCE AND LEARNING

Membrane-Bound, Brain-Specific Proteins: Key Substances in Learning?

There is a remarkable growth differentiation and change in metabolism during the first postnatal period. Processes grow, nerve fibers become insulated, synapses become structured and enlarged, some of them disappear, and contacts are established with other neurons. Genetically programmed

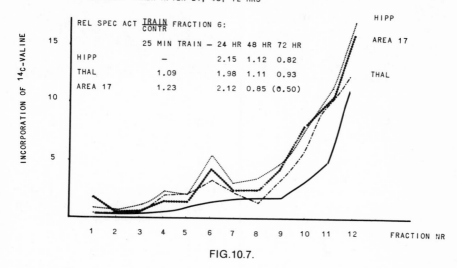

FIG.10.7.

activity starts and is triggered by simple stimuli. Experiential learning begins. For all species this is a period of concentrated learning.

The development of membrane-bound S-100 protein in the plasma membrane and synapses of neurons is a function of time, experience, and learning. This is strikingly demonstrated when nerve cells from postnatally immature animals, such as rat and rabbit, are compared with neonatally well developed animals, such as guinea pigs, with respect to membrane-bound S-100 protein.

For the demonstration of membrane-bound S-100 of nerve cells, a new technique for isolation of fresh nerve cells was developed (Hydén & Rönnbäck, 1975a). The cells to be studied are not touched by instruments or passed through a sieving mesh. A direct reaction was used with fluorescein-conjugated, monospecific antiserum to S-100 with proper controls on isolated nerve cells. The newborn rat (and rabbit) has many embryological characteristics in its structure, metabolism, and behavior during the first 2 weeks. During that time, very little S-100-specific fluorescence can be observed (Hydén & Rönnbäck, 1975b).

During the first postnatal week, the small amount of membrane-bound S-100 (pentanol-extractable) dominates in the rat (Donato, 1976). Quantitatively, this relation rapidly changes, and membrane S-100 will constitute only 10 to 15% of the total S-100. During the first 2 postnatal weeks, a redistribution of the membrane S-100 occurs. In the Purkinje cells of the cerebellum, the membrane S-100 shifts its location from the base of the apical dendrite to the opposite pole of the cell.

a   b

FIG.10.8. Isolated nerve cells incubated with anti-S-100 antiserum conjugated to fluorescein isothiocyanate. (a) Neuron from the Deiters nucleus showing an intense fluorescence over one part of the cell membrane. (b) Vental motor cell from the spinal cord.

When the young rat begins to explore the environment during the 3rd week, the adult membrane S-100 pattern will be established. Typical for several types of nerve cells is a location in the membrane over one cell pole (Fig. 10.8). The large Deiters' nerve cells from the vestibular nucleus are characterized by a heterogeneous distribution of the membrane S-100, mainly around one pole of the cell, differing in pattern when the surface of the cell is scanned circumferentially. The nerve cell membrane seems to be successively differentiated with time and experience in areas rich in S-100 in 30 to 50% of the cell surface. Within this pattern of S-100, the postsynaptic areas also show a high concentration of S-100 (Haglid, Hamberger, Hansson, Hydén, Persson, & Rönnbäck, 1974, 1976; Hansson, Hydén, & Rönnbäck, 1975).

The development of membrane S-100 is different in the guinea pig. At birth, the guinea pig is well developed, eagerly beginning to explore the environment—almost like a miniature of a young adult. The type of nerve cells observed showed already at birth the adult pattern of membrane S-100.

Thus, on one hand, a correlation between the formation of a membrane antigen pattern in the neuronal membrane and the formation of new types of behavior has been established. On the other hand, during the postnatal period when mostly embryonic reflex activity takes place, no formation of S-100 antigen pattern occurs in the plasma membranes.

The acidic protein 14-3-2, which also increased considerably and reversibly during learning, also has a part that is membrane bound. Its location in the neuronal membrane only partly overlaps with that of S-100 protein.

One purpose of neurochemical studies of behavior is to look for a biological principle that is used by the central nervous system in many species for learning per se and that serves memory. It is unsafe to draw firm analogies between results on animals, even monkeys, and the brain mechanisms in man. However, a look at some biochemical data gives at least food for thought. In man, total S-100 develops first in phylogenetically old areas of the brain. A certain S-100 level is reached in most brain areas around the 5th embryonic month. An exception is the frontal cortex, where S-100 cannot be demonstrated until the 7th month. At birth, cortical S-100 concentration has reached that of other regions. At 20 years of age, there has occurred a fourfold increase in S-100 (Zuckerman, Herschman, & Levine, 1970). This indicates a high degree of differentiation in brain-regional S-100, with a graded maturation of cellular S-100 in the frontal cortex to which the high brain functions are localized. Equally interesting is that the levels of S-100 in 22 areas of the human brain show a positive correlation with age from early life to above 60 years (Moore & Perez, 1968). One is tempted to speculate that in man as well as in the rat, the S-100 level in brain develops as a function of individual experience and learning.

An Actinlike Network of Filaments
Attached to Synapses and Membrane

When the pattern of membrane S-100, including synapses, grows as a function of time, learning, and experience, its relation to another membrane-associated protein must be discussed. Below the inner surface of the nerve cell plasma membrane, at a distance of some tens of nanometer, a continuous network extends like an inner skin, closely related to the postsynaptic structure (Hansson & Hydén, 1974). The network is made up of 7-nm diameter microfilaments, each of which consists of two closely coiled unit filaments 2 nm in diameter, with a spacing of 9 nm. There are no loose ends to be seen. The network is closely associated to postsynaptic structures. When synapses are isolated, fragments of the network appear attached to the postsynaptic web. The network, whose density seems to vary with type of nerve cell, can easily be observed by the electron microscope in isolated nerve cell plasma membranes (Fig. 10.9a). Its microfilaments give positive reaction with heavy meromyosin, as does actin; but they do not contain RNA or DNA. Characteristically, the microfilaments are uncoiled at the addition of Ca^{2+} (Fig. 10.9b).

In a discussion of mechanisms that may serve discrimination of stimuli by neurons and change of behavior, it is pertinent to take up the inter-relationship between both membrane-associated proteins, the S-100 protein and the actinlike network. Both proteins can interact via Ca^{2+}.

SYSTEM CHANGES IN LEARNING SERVED BY
CELL MECHANISMS THAT MODULATE
THE CELL MEMBRANE

Any attempt to discuss a hypothesis of mechanisms of learning and memory is hampered by the overwhelming complexity of the problem referred to in the introduction. The following is a working hypothesis, the drawbacks of which

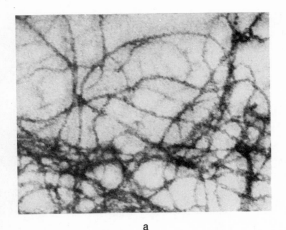

a

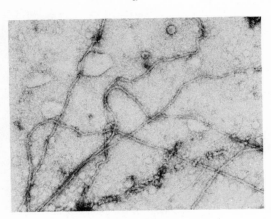

FIG. 10.9 The filaments of the membrane-associated network decoiled by addition of Ca^{2+}. (a) = 60,000; (b)=140,000.

b

are apparent, but whose appeal is that some parts have been tested; other aspects will be tried.

Why do cognitive stimuli and training, which resulted in learning and the establishment of new behavior, induce synthesis of specific protein in brain cells? The same type of training, at random, without learning does not produce such a specific protein synthesis. My view is that cognitive stimuli from the inner and outer environment penetrate into the nucleus of the neuron (and glia) and induce the synthesis of the mRNA. The formation of messenger RNA and its transport from the nucleus to the cytoplasm takes around 15 min (Bennett, Flood, Orme, & Jarvik, 1975). Eventually, the newly synthesized RNA serves as a template for the protein formation and pattern reorganization that occur in synapses, most likely both in pre- and postsynaptic parts and in other parts of the neuronal membranes. The finding of newly synthesized mRNA within less than an hour after started training does not exclude the fact that learning mechanisms also utilize mRNA already existing in the brain cells, as pointed out by Bennett et al. (1975).

I base this argument of a linkage between gene stimulation of brain cells and establishment of new behavior on the recent finding of increased synthesis of poly(A)-associated mRNA of the type S_E 25 and stimulation of 8-9S and 16S RNA in nerve cells of the hippocampus in learning rats. This did not occur in control rats that performed the same task and received the same amount of award. That cognitive stimuli may penetrate into cell nuclei and induce gene activity seems analogous to the effect of sexual stimuli on cells of the reproduction organs or the effect of fright on the suprarenals.

The hippocampus is the dominating active center, leading in time and extent of response. The stimulation of protein synthesis in the CA3 hippocampal cells in the beginning of training surpasses that of other brain areas studied. This short-lasting increase of protein includes the S-100 and 14-3-2 protein and at least two proteins in a higher molecular range belonging to synaptosomal protein. The short-lasting 12- to 24-hour protein changes during learning appear, then, with a delay in cortical areas, including also the entorhinal area. I would like to advance the view that this wave of protein activity going through the brain as the system changes during the linear increase of the learning curve paves the way for the subsequent remaining changes. If this process is interfered with (e.g., by injection of antiserum against S-100 protein), then further acquisition is stopped. What is important is that it has been shown in such experiments that the antiserum injected reaches and interacts with its antigen on the hippocampal cells. According to my view, the short-lasting changes represent a redundancy phenomenon providing the necessary conditions for the next stage.

The remaining changes during learning seem to involve, among other factors, antigen of synapses and nerve cell plasma membranes that modify the neural function. As a function of learning and experience, S-100 is incorporated into a heterogeneous pattern in the nerve cell plasma membrane, including dendrites. The neurons will thus be differentiated in areas of the plasma membrane rich in S-100, which applies also to the postsynaptic areas within this area. The other parts of the membrane, including postsynaptic areas, are poor in S-100 (Fig. 10.10).

FIG. 10.10 Schematic mechanism for modulating synapse and membrane. Membrane contains S= 100 protein, which binds Ca^{2+} and undergoes conformation changes. The actinlike network cannot compete for Ca^{2+}, remains coiled, and exerts tension on the membrane.

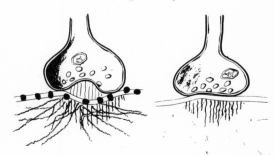

Rose, Hambley, and Haywood (1976) have used imprinting of chickens as learning experiment. Based on biochemical analysis, Rose et al. make the general conclusion that learning implies both transient and enduring biochemical brain changes.

REFERENCES

Ballard, P. B. Obliviscence and reminiscence. *British Journal of Psychology Monographs Supplement*, 19713, *2*, 1–82.

Bennett, E. L., Flood, I., Orme, M. R., & Jarvik, M. Minimum duration and times of protein synthesis needed to establish long-term memory. *5th Congress of International Society of Neurochemistry, Barcelona 1975*.

Bertalanffy, L. V. *General systems theory,* New York: Wiley, 1973.

Buresova, O., Bures, J., & Beran, V. A contribution to the problem of the dominant hemisphere in rats. *Physiologica Bohemoslovenica*, 1958, *7*, 29–37.

Calissano, P. Specific properties of brain-specific protein S100. In D. J. Schneider, R. H. Angeletti, R.. A. Bradshaw, A. Grasso, & B. W. Moore (Eds.), *Proteins of the nervous system*. New York: Raven Press, 1973.

Cardo, B. Memory and the hippocampus. *La Recherche*, 1976, *7*, 742–750.

Cupello, A., & Hydén, H. Pattern of labelling of poly (A)-associated RNA in the CA_3 region of rat hippocampus during training. *Journal of Neuroscience Research*, 1976, *2*, 255–260.

Donato, R. Soluble and membrane-bound S-100 protein in rat cerebral cortex synaptosomes during postnatal development. *Brain Research*, 1976, *109*, 649–655.

Grasso, A., Haglid, K. G., Hansson, H. -A., Persson, L., & Rönnbäck, L. Localization of 14-3-2 protein in the rat brain by immunoelectron microscopy. *Brain Research*, 1977, *122*, 582–585.

Haljamäe, H., & Lange, P. W. Calcium content and conformational changes of S-100 protein in the hippocampus during training. *Brain Research*, 1972, *38*, 131–142.

Haglid, K. G., Hamberger, A., Hansson, H. -A., Hydén, H., Persson, L., & Rönnbäck, L. S-100 protein in synapses of the central nervous system. *Nature*, 1974, *251*, 532–534.

Haglid, K. G., Hamberger, A., Hansson, H. -A., Hydén, H., Persson, L., & Rönnbäck, L. Cellular and subcellular distribution of the S-100 protein in rabbit and rat central nervous system. *Journal of Neuroscience Research*, 1976, *2*, 175–191.

Hansson, H. -A., & Hydën, H. A membrane-associated network of protein filaments in nerve cells. *Neurobiology*, 1974, *4*, 364–375.

Hansson, H. -A., Hydën, H., & Rönnbäck, L. Localization of S-100 protein in isolated nerve cells by immunoelectron microscopy. *Brain Research*, 1975, *93*, 349–352.

Hydén, H., Bjurstam, K., & McEwen, B. Protein separation at the cellular level by micro disc electrophoresis. *Analytical Biochemistry*, 1966, *17*, 1–15.

Hydén, H., & Egyhazi, E. Nuclear RNA changes of nerve cells during a learning experiment in rats. *Proceedings of the National Academy of Sciences*, 1962, *48*, 1366–1373.

Hydén, H., & Egyhazi, E. Glial RNA changes during a learning experiment in rats. *Proceedings of the National Academy of Sciences*, 1963, *49*, 618–624.

Hydén, H., & Egyhazi, E. Changes in RNA content and base composition in cortical neurons of rats in a learning experiment involving transfer of handedness. *Proceedings of the National Academy of Sciences*, 1964, *52*, 1030–1035.

Hydén, H., & Lange, P. W. A differentiation in RNA response in neurons early and late during learning. *Proceedings of the National Academy of Sciences*, 1965, *53*, 946–952.

Hydén, H., & Lange, P. W. Micro-electrophoretic determination of protein and protein synthesis in the 10^{-9} to 10^{-7} gram range. *Journal of Chromatography*, 1968, *35*, 336–351.

Hydén, H., & Lange, P. W. Protein synthesis during learning. *Science*, 1969, *164*, 200–201.

Hydén, H., & Lange, P. W. S100 brain protein: Correlation with behavior. *Proceedings of the National Academy of Sciences*, 1970, *67*, 1959–1966.

Hydén, H., & Lange, P. W. Time sequence analysis of proteins in brain stem limbic system and cortex during training. *Biochimica e Biologia Sperimentale*, 1970–71, *9*, 275–285.

Hydén, H., & Lange, P. W. Protein synthesis in hippocampal nerve cells during re-reversal of handedness in rats. *Brain Research*, 1972, *45*, 314–317.

Hydén, H., & Lange, P. W. Brain proteins in undernourished rats during learning. *Neurobiology*, 1975, *5*, 84–100.

Hydén, H., & Lange, P. W. Increased S100 protein in brain cells induced by antiserum against S100. *Journal of Neurological Sciences*, in press.

Hydén, H., Lange, P. W., Mihailović Lj., & Petrović-Minić, B. Changes of RNA base composition in nerve cells of monkeys subjected to visual discrimination and delayed alternation performance. *Brain Research*, 1974, *65*, 215–230.

Hydén, H., Lange, P. W., & Perrin, C. L. Protein pattern alterations in hippocampal and cortical cells as a function of training in rats. *Brain Research*, 1977, *119*, 427–437.

Hydén, H., & Rönnbäck, L. Membrane-bound S-100 protein on nerve cells and its distribution. *Brain Research*, 1975, *100*, 615–628. (a)

Hydén, H., & Rönnbäck, L. S100 on isolated neurons and glial cells from rat, rabbit and Guinea pig during early postnatal development. *Neurobiology*, 1975, *5*, 291–302. (b)

Kimble, D. P. Choice behavior in rats with hippocampal lesions. In R. L. Isaacson & K. H. Primbram (Eds.), *The hippocampus* (Vol. 2). New York: Plenum Press, 1975.

Larsson, S. Low level tritium and carbon-14 determination. *Analytical Biochemistry*, 1972, *50*, 245–254.

Moore, B. W., & Perez, V. J. Specific acidic proteins of the nervous system. In F. D. Carlson (Ed.), *Physiological and biochemical aspects of nervous integration*. Englewood Cliffs, N.J.: Prentice–Hall, 1968.

Peterson, G. M. Mechanism of handedness in the rat. *Comparative Psychology Monographs*, 1934, *9*, 1–67.

Rapport, M. M., & Karpiak, S. E. Discriminative effects of antisera to brain consitutents on behavior and EEG activity in the rat. *Research Communications of Psychological and Psychiatric Behavior*, 1976, *1*, 115–123.

Rose, S. P. R., Hambley, J., & Haywood, J. Neurochemical approaches to developmental plasticity and learning. In M. R. Rosenzweig & E. L. Bennett (Eds.), *Neural mechanisms of learning and memory*. Cambridge, Mass.: MIT Press, 1976.

Shashoua, V. E. RNA metabolism in the brain. *International Review of Neurobiology*, 1974, *16*, 183–230.

Wentworth, K. L. Some factors determining handedness in the white rat. *Genetic Psychology Monographs*, 1942, *26*, 55–117.

Woolf, C. J., Willies, G. H., Hepburn, H. R., & Rosendorft, C. Time dependence in a neurochemical correlation of a learning task: A non-disruptive approach to memory consolidation. *Experientia*, 1974, *30*, 760–762.

Yanagihara, T., & Hydén, H. Protein synthesis in various regions of rat hippocampus during learning. *Experimental Neurology*, 1971, *31*, 151–164.

Zomzely-Neurath, C., Marangos, Z. N., Hymnowitz, N., Perl, W., Ritter, A., Zayas, V., Cua, W., & York, C. The effect of a behavioral task on neuronal and glial specific proteins. in press.

Zuckerman, J. E., Herschman, H. R., & Levine, L. Appearances of a brain-specific antigen (the S100 protein) during human foetal development. *Journal of Neurochemistry*, 1970, *17*, 247–251.

11 Patterns of Activity in the Cerebral Cortex Related to Memory Functions

David H. Ingvar
University Hospital, Lund, Sweden

INTRODUCTION

During measurements of the blood flow in the brain of conscious patients with neurological and psychiatric disorders, we have over the last years made some observations on memory functions that are summarized here. The measurements were carried out for diagnostic purpose with the informed consent of the patients, often in conjunction with cerebral arteriography. Our findings do not form a systematic study of memory mechanisms, because important limitations beset the cerebral blood flow technique that we are using.

The cerebral blood flow is normally controlled by the activity of the neurons, a mechanism termed the *metabolic control of the cerebral circulation* (Ingvar & Lassen, 1975). Due to this relationship, multiregional blood flow determinations can be used to study the distribution of functions in the brain. A display of the blood flow in various regions of a hemisphere thus gives a picture of the activity distribution in superficial cortical structures mainly. The displays have been termed *cerebral functional landscapes* or "cerebral ideograms" (Ingvar, 1977).

In this paper the distribution of function in the resting brain is described. Apparently, this pattern, which pertains to resting wakefulness (consciousness), is related to some form of memorization and recall. When abnormalities of memory functions are found clinically (e.g., in demented patients), there are deviations from the normal flow distribution. During motor ideation—when a subject tries to conceive of a moment without actually carrying it out—memory mechanisms are also involved, and the

247

cerebral ideogram recorded is highly different from the one pertaining to the actual movement. It is concluded that the isotope technique used in the present studies permits a new type of direct analysis of cerebral mechanisms related to memory.

TECHNICAL CONSIDERATIONS

By means of the intra-arterial 133 Xenon clearance technique, the blood flow in the human brain can be determined in several regions simultaneously in conscious nonanesthetized subjects (Lassen & Ingvar, 1971). The matter requires the injection of a gamma-emitting isotope bolus (3-5 mCi of Xe-133 in 2–4 ml saline) into the internal carotid artery. This procedure can be added to a cerebral angiography without any significant risks. With the aid of batteries of detectors containing up to 254 units placed at the side of the head, regional flow values are then obtained from a similar number of regions. Each detector "sees" the arrival and subsequent clearance of the isotope within its field of vision. The disappearance rate (clearance) is a function of the blood flow in the area observed. The impulses recorded by the detectors are fed to a computer, which automatically calculates the regional flow rates, which in turn can be displayed on a color television screen. Such color charts give a topographical display of the flow/activity distribution in the hemisphere labeled with the isotope (a cerebral ideogram). Each measurement takes about 15 minutes, and the irradiation involved is negligible. Up till now, we have in our laboratory carried out 600 brain flow measurements. In other units, several thousand studies have been made. The complications rate has been extrememly low.

Regarding memory research, one important limitation besets the present Xe-133 technique, which mainly measures the lateral hemisphere surface. Indeed, memory mechanisms include mesial hemisphere structures, especially the hippocampus and the fornix as well as other limbic parts. These structures are only to a limited extent included in the present measurements. Their activity changes in memory tasks and in various states of consciousness can only be studied with three-dimensional methods for measuring the change of the cerebral blood flow and the metabolism (Kuhl, Phelps, Hoffmann, Robinson, & MacDonald, 1977).

Clinically, the above-mentioned method has mainly been used to study cerebral vascular disorders, brain tumors, traumatic brain injuries, brain infections, and organic dementia. Over the last 10 years, several international symposia have dealt with the method described and its theoretical basis, as well as with the clinical results obtained. A review of recent results was presented at the international cerebral blood flow symposium in Copenhagen (Ingvar & Lassen, 1977).

Findings in Normal Brains

The Resting Conscious State. We have recently reported that the resting conscious state is characterized by a typical distribution of activity in the cerebral cortex (Ingvar, 1975; Ingvar & Schwartz, 1974). In subjects resting awake with closed eyes in a silent laboratory, not feeling pain or being purposely exposed to sensory stimulation, not being spoken to deliberately or asked to solve problems, the distribution of flow is not uniform, as might be expected, but shows a typical "hyperfrontal" character. The flow in regions anterior to the Sylvian and Rolandic fissures in premotor and frontal parts is 5 to 25% higher than the hemisphere mean flow. In regions posterior to the same line, the flow is correspondingly lower, especially in temporal and parietal regions. The same distribution appears to prevail at rest in the right (nondominant) hemisphere. Thus at rest the activity (in absolute terms) is about twice as high in frontal regions as in certain temporal structures.

The hyperfrontal resting pattern (see Figure 11.1) is easily changed if general anesthesia is induced by injection of a barbiturate. Physiological sleep also induces an increase of the flow in temporal regions, and the hyperfrontal pattern changes radically, as indicated by a few observations.

The normal resting cerebral ideogram of wakefulness shows that the neuronal activity is higher in precentral frontal parts of the cortex where motor (efferent) functions are located, whereas correspondingly lower activity prevails postcentrally and temporally over afferent-gnostic regions (primary and secondary sensory regions and surrounding association cortex).

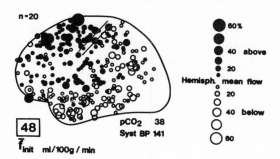

FIG.11.1. *The "hyperfrontal" activity distribution in the normal resting conscious brain.* Superimposed plots of the cerebral blood flow (in ml/100 g/min) distribution in 20 subjects (left hemisphere). In each individual, the hemisphere mean flow (activity) has been used as reference, and regional deviation from this mean has been plotted with symbols denoting percentual values in accordance with the scale to the right. Note marked preponderance of high values (=high activity) in premotor and frontal regions and relatively low flows postcentrally and in temporal parts.

There are no cyto-architechtonic, or angio-architectonic features of the cortex to explain this flow difference. It hence appears to signal a fundamental feature of the normal brain activity pertaining to the undisturbed state of conscious awareness. In this state, there is apparently a functional "structure" of the activity distribution that implies a higher activity in efferent motor parts of the cortex as compared to in afferent-gnostic regions.

In precentral and frontal parts of the cortex, there are centers responsible for the programming of a goal-directed behavior. The resting hyperfrontal cerebral ideogram therefore may signal an anticipatory "simulation of behavior" going on in the brain when one is conscious and when one's thoughts are not directed in any specific direction by an afferent input.

In the present context, the question might be raised as to what extent memory is involved in the process of resting conscious awareness. Indeed, this important and highly complex problem cannot by far be fully elucidated by the present results. However, it is evident that the foregoing presumed programming of future behavior must require access to memories of different kinds, e.g., previously synthesized behavioral programs that more or less completely might have been used and tested earlier. There is fairly solid clinical evidence that such programs are located in premotor and frontal structures.

It is further of interest that resting conscious awareness with its accompanying memory activity is characterized by a relatively low flow (activity) in the temporal cortex, which is generally considered to be of a great importance for memory functions (Penfield & Jasper, 1954).

The interpretation given above of the hyperfrontal resting regional cerebral blood flow (rCBF) pattern is supported by the fact that an increased sensory output, such as cutaneous sensory stimulation which increases the level of awareness (consciousness), makes the hyperfrontal pattern stand out even more clearly; and this effect is even more pronounced during electrical stimulation causing discomfort or slight pain (Ingvar, Rosen, Eriksson, & Elmqvist, 1976).

Motor Ideation.   If one tries to conceive of a certain type of movement without carrying it out—for example, a slow, rhythmic clenching of the right hand—one must use certain memory functions. It is then necessary to try to recall what the moment in question looked like, how it felt, etc. We have recently shown that motor ideation gives rise to a moderate general increase of the hemisphere blood flow, which is most marked in frontal and temporal regions. In temporal parts, a doubling of the flow/activity was recorded in several regions. This provides, for the first time, direct evidence that the ideational recall of a certain simple bodily function, a movement, augments the neuronal activity in the temporal and frontal lobes without any accompanying behavioral changes.

The pattern of motor ideation differed distinctly from the one during an actual movement of the hand (see Fig. 11.2) when the sensory–motor region, especially its middle and postcentral parts, was strongly activated. Automatic movements do not activate temporal structures so much, because apparently during such performance the brain is constantly "reminded" of the movement itself by the afferent sensory in-flow from the moving limb (Ingvar & Philipson, 1977).

Here the results of Roland and Larsen (1976) must be mentioned. They showed with the Xe-133 technique important differences in the cerebral ideograms recorded during serial automatic movements and during movements involving problem solving (tactile discrimination). There are several aspects in the observations that relate to memory mechanisms. At present, however, it is difficult to relate them to classical concepts on the physiology and psychology of memory.

Psychological Testing.   Psychological testing involving memorization, recall, and reasoning also changes the cerebral functional distribution. A digit-span backward test, for example, that requires immediate recall activates frontal lobes, more so during the first time the test is administered than during the second (Risberg & Ingvar, 1973; Risberg, Maximilian, & Prohovnik, 1977). Premotor and frontal regions appear to be of critical importance for the serially organized thinking involved in an immediate recall test of the digit-span backward type.

Tests of reasoning, e.g., Raven's matrices, activated both pre- and postcentral association areas while the activation of temporal structures was limited. This again indicates that temporal structures are especially involved in the visualization of, the imagination of, and the recall of complex abstract situations, whereas the immediate memory, necessary for recall of series of digits, activates premotor structures markedly. Here, it should be recalled that our measurements have mainly included the lateral surfaces of the hemisphere cortex. Hence, important functional changes may take place with different distributions during the tests mentioned.

Findings in Abnormal Brains

In *organic dementia* of primary degenerative type (Alzheimer's disease) or due to cerebrovascular disease (multi-infarct dementia) or brain injury, memory impairment is often a prominent and early symptom. In such patients a significant regional decrease of the blood flow in the temporal region is often recorded. This supports the general notion that temporal structures play a fundamental role for memory functions (Hagberg & Ingvar, 1976).

Recently, Hagberg (1977) has further analyzed the relationship between the resting blood flow pattern in 16 patients suffering from organic dementia. He

A.   RESTING CONDITIONS

B.   Rt HAND MOVEMENTS CONCEIVED

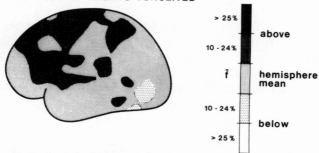

C.   Rt HAND MOVEMENTS PERFORMED

FIG.11.2. *Changes of the cerebral ideogram from resting (A) to motor ideation (B) and motor performance (C).* Superimposed plots from six subjects (cf. Fig. 11.1) of relative distributions of flow/activity in the left hemisphere. Note the marked differences between rest (A) and motor ideation (B) when the subjects were trying only to imagine (recall) clenching movements of the right hand (without any movements). Note also the marked activation of the motor centers when the right hand was actually used (C). Ingvar & Philipson, 1977.

demonstrated that flow reductions outside the temporal region put their inprint also on the defective performance in memory test. Thus a low performance in test of paired associates was accompanied by a temporal *and* parietal flow decrease. Memory for objects was accompanied by a temporal and frontal flow decrease, and so was the test for memory for geometric design. In contrast, tests for vocabulary and memory for design did not show any correlation to localized flow reductions.

Memory functions in *chronic schizophrenia* have been the object of much debate. One important reason for this is that memory functions cannot easily be tested in poorly cooperating, deteriorated schizophrenics. We have found that patients of this type have an abnormal resting distribution of the blood flow of the hypofrontal type and that this pattern is very difficult to change in many cases by means of psychological testing or verbal stimulation (Franzen & Ingvar, 1975). Several patients have shown an abnormally high flow also in temporal regions, and this may be related to the hallucinatory experience that many such patients describe. However, much work has to be done in order to further clarify the relationship of these findings to our present knowledge of memory functions in the brain.

DISCUSSION

A main and principally important finding of the present studies of the activity distribution in the conscious human brain is that various mental states have a functional "structure." Many of the features of the functional landscapes, cerebral ideograms, that we have recorded so far appear to have interesting relationships to memory function. One main finding that should be stretched here and that deviates from current concepts on memory functions in the brain is that the frontal lobes appear to play a functionally dominating role for consciousness and the memory functions involved in this state. The behavioral programming that takes place in the frontal lobes must, it seems, include the organization of several behavioral subprograms into meaningful patterns that are stored to be used when the surroundings of the organisms and the sensory input so demand. It will be interesting in the future to combine studies of the functional distribution in the brain with systematic studies of memory functions in order to further explore how short-term and long-term memory functions influence the cerebral ideogram. In this research, attention should, as it appears, mainly be focused upon not only the frontal lobes but also the temporal region, where memories of ideational type appear to have their seat. A research of this type will undoubtedly clarify fundamental aspects of human memory, and this will have immediate consequences for our understanding of memory deficits in various brain disorders.

SUMMARY

With multiregional measurements of the cerebral blood flow in conscious man, one can obtain a topographical display (a cerebral ideogram) of the distribution of function in a given hemisphere. At rest, during conscious awareness the function is much higher in the frontal lobes than in postcentral and temporal regions. This "hyperfrontal" pattern, which to some extent represents ongoing memory functions, has been interpreted as caused by "simulation of behavior" due to an anticipatory synthesis of behavioral programs in motor efferent parts located in the frontal lobes. An increase of the activity in the temporal cortex has been recorded during attempts of motor ideation. In neurologic and psychiatric disorders, especially in those accompanied by memory deficits, a low flow is often recorded in the temporal region. The studies show that multiregional measurements of the activity distribution in the brain may reveal new and fundamental aspects of the physiology of human memory functions.

ACKNOWLEDGMENTS

The author was aided by the Swedish Medical Research Council (project no. B77-14X-84-13B) and by the Wallenberg and the Thuring Foundations in Stockholm.

REFERENCES

Franzén, G., & Ingvar, D. H. Abnormal distribution of cerebral activity in chronic schizophrenia. *Journal of Psychiatric Research*, 1975, *12*, 199–214.

Hagberg, B. Unpublished manuscript, 1977.

Hagberg, B., & Ingvar, D. H. Cognitive reduction in presenile dementia related to regional abnormalities of the cerebral blood flow. *British Journal of Psychiatry*, 1976, *128*, 209–222.

Ingvar, D. H. L'ideogramme cerebrale. *L'Encephale*, 1977, *III*, 5–33.

Ingvar, D. H. Brain work in presenile dementia and in chronic schizophrenia. In David H. Ingvar & Niels A. Lassen (Eds.) *Brain work*. Copenhagen: Munksgaard, 1975.

Ingvar, D. H., & Lassen, N. A. (Eds.). *Brain work*. Copenhagen: Munksgaard, 1975.

Ingvar, D. H. & Lassen, N. A. (Eds.). *Cerebral function, metabolism and circulation*. Copenhagen: Munksgaard, 1977.

Ingvar, D. H. & Philipson, L. Distribution of cerebral blood flow in the dominant hemisphere during motor performance. *Annals of Neurology*, 1977, *2*, 230–237.

Ingvar, D. H., Rosen, I., Eriksson, M., & Elmqvist, D. Activation patterns induced in the dominant hemisphere by skin stimulation. In Y. Zotterman (Ed.). *Sensory functions of the skin*. London: Pergamon Press, 1976.

Ingvar, D. H., & Schwartz, M. S. Blood flow patterns induced in the dominant hemisphere by speech and reading. *Brain*, 1974, *97*, 273–288.

Kuhl, D. E. Initial clinical experience with 18 F=2=fluro=2=deoxy=d=glucose for determination of local cerebral glucose utilization by emission computed tomography. In David H. Ingvar & Niels

A. Lassen (Eds.). *Cerebral function, metabolism and circulation*. Copenhagen: Munksgaard, 1977.

Lassen, N. A., & Ingvar, D. H. Radioisotopic assessment of regional cerebral blood flow. In J. Potchen et al. (Eds.), *Progress in nuclear medicine* (Vol. 1). New York: Karger, 1971.

Lassen, N.A. Roland, P. E., Lassen, B., Melamed, E., & Soh, K. Mapping of human cerebral functions: A study of the regional cerebral blood flow pattern during rest, its reproducibility and the activation seen during basic sensory and motor functions. In David H. Ingvar & Niels A. Lassen (Eds.), *Cerebral function, metabolism and circulation*. Copenhagen: Munksgaard, 1977.

Penfield, W., & Jasper, H. *Epilepsy and the functional anatomy of the human brain*. Boston: Little, Brown, and Co., 1954.

Risberg, J., & Ingvar, D. H. Patterns of activation in the grey matter of the dominant hemisphere during memorization and reasoning: A study of the regional cerebral blood flow changes during psychological testing. *Brain*, 1973, *96*, 737–756.

Risberg, J., Maximilian, A. V., and Prohovnik, J.

Roland, P., & Larsen, B. Focal increase of cerebral blood flow during stereognostic testing in man. *Archives of Neurology*, 1976, *33*, 551–558.

12 Neuropsychological Research and the Fractionation of Memory Systems

Tim Shallice
National Hospital, London

INTRODUCTION

> Once man achieves the control over erasure and transmission of memory by means of biological and chemical methods, psychologists armed with memory drums, F tables and even on-line computers will have become superfluous in the same sense as philosophers became superfluous with the advancement of modern science [Tulving & Madigan, 1970, p. 437].

This caricature in the finest review article on memory in recent years clearly alludes to one common "fear" about the future total reduction of the psychology of memory to more "basic" sciences. Advances in the neurosciences are often thought to have this implication for the understanding of memory. Its appeal rests on the apparently nonscientific nature of psychology as contrasted with present-day physiology and biochemistry. By contrast, I want to argue that one way in which consideration of brain function assists in our understanding of memory is by helping to make the psychology of memory more scientific in a clearly nonreductionist way, by using neuropsychological evidence to support information-processing theory.

If, in the spirit of this conference, one attempts to assess how far the present practice of a field could be a guide to its future practice, one crucial question would seem to be whether the field has reached what the French historian-of-science, Bachelard (see Gaukroger, 1976), called its "epistemological break" and what Kuhn (1962) would describe as the end of its "pre-paradigm" period. That two such similar concepts have developed within very different philosophical traditions—Anglo-Saxon empiricism and French rationalism—suggests that they correspond to an aspect of reality.

Of these two approaches, the Kuhnian one has the disadvantage of stressing the upheaval in the social practice of a science leading to a new "normality" of practice. We know from the history of behaviorism that this is no guide to the achievement of solid intellectual gains. The French structuralist approach has the advantage of concentrating on the theoretical systems involved. Before the period of the "break," although much empirical information is available, the concepts of a field are not sharply separable from everyday ones. The break occurs with the solution of certain key theoretical questions. Following this period, the set of concepts used have a clear separate identity, a complex and consistent structure, and the problems of the field are articulated in terms of its concepts alone. In my view, this approach overemphasizes internal factors in the history of science and the separateness of each field and so is not really adequate for dealing with the complexity of the interrelation between the different types of concepts necessary in the human sciences. It does, however, provide a criterion for assessing whether it is more probable that a field should develop by improving (or transcending) its present theoretical positions, or instead by rejecting them virtually entirely and starting anew—as has occurred in the transition from behaviorism to cognitive psychology. More concretely, when with the benefit of hindsight one is able to look back on the period 1955–1980 in the area of memory, will the transition from a verbal learning to an information-processing approach have the characteristics of an epistemological break? Alternatively, will the transition be viewed only as an example of a change in scientific fashion prior to an epistemological break, which is to be explained primarily in terms of factors external to the field itself?

In the late 1960s, the information-processing approach to cognition appeared to be becoming the first satisfactory "problematic" (or paradigm) in the area. This conceptual system derived from electrical engineering, computer technology, and increasingly artificial intelligence was reasonably internally consistent, was sharply differentiated from everyday concepts, and was increasingly helpful in explaining a wide variety of empirical phenomena. Standard seminal papers in this approach to memory were those of Waugh and Norman (1965), Sperling (1967), and Atkinson and Shiffrin (1968).

Yet disillusion was soon to set in. The clear theoretical outlines of the late 1960s were to be rapidly blurred by the usual mass of confusing empirical information produced by the data production-lines of modern psychology operating on "functional autonomy of methods" principles (Tulving & Madigan, 1970), a natural consequence of the social organization of psychological research. The most eloquent chroniclers of the new pessimism were Tulving and Madigan, who foresaw the existence of hundreds of different but similar theories, all vying for the attention of possible adherents, but which could only be discriminated by factor analysis. It is noteworthy that the most influential memory theory of the last few years—that of Craik and

Lockhart (1972)—consciously rejected models that separated out discrete processors and stores in favor of a vague continuum of processes. In related fields, even some of the best-known practitioners of the information-processing approach renounced it (Neisser, 1976; Turvey & Shaw, this volume).

In my view, however, the problem lay not with the theoretical framework of the late 1960s but with the empirical methods available for assessing theories. Consider, for instance, the quantitative approach to memory theorizing (e.g., Murdock, 1974; Sternberg, 1969). If one is to test a quantitative model of a particular process, one requires a situation in which the properties of the model are manifested relatively independently of other systems (whose properties are not better understood) and a means of making measurements. Thus the derivation of the inverse square law of gravitation required the existence both of a situation in which its properties were dominant over all other factors—planetary orbits—and a means of making exact measurements of that situation—the history of planetary positions in the night sky.

Even if a memory system were to obey such a simple law, it is unlikely that either the appropriate experimental situation or method of measurement would exist. On an information-processing approach, any experimental procedure inevitably involves the operation of a large number of highly complex systems in addition to the memory system under investigation—systems underlying motivation, strategies, effort, comprehension, and so on. Moreover, all our measurements involve averaging over a large number of trials, which must involve parameters changing due to learning, fatigue, and so on and often involve averaging over properties of stimulus materials such as words with their own source of quantitative complexity. In addition, group designs nearly always involve averaging over the performance of different subjects. It therefore seems unlikely that a quantitative finding obtained in a memory experiment bears any simple relation to a property of an underlying memory system.

Yet the alternative to quantitative data-fitting is the approach of standard experimental psychology, namely the realizing of each competing model on an ever-increasing number of experimental procedures—each necessitating its own extra ad hoc assumptions, which in turn require testing (see Allport, 1975; Newall, 1974). Given the crudeness of the orthodox psychological experiment as a theory tester, it might appear that Tulving and Madigan were right in implicitly suggesting that with an information-processing framework the rate at which plausible alternative theories can be generated will greatly exceed the rate at which they can be refuted.

It is within this context that I would like to discuss the potential contribution of neuropsychology. It provides a complementary and potentially more reliable way of refuting some of the possible information-processing models. I would like to discuss the potential of neuropsychology first for fractionating memory systems and then for providing evidence relevant to the properties of one of them.

I intend to illustrate the power of fractionation by examining the STS/LTS distinction, because in my view it provided the first major advance in the information-processing approach to memory although it is now rather out of favor. Neuropsychological evidence has been frequently cited in support of the distinction (e.g., Atkinson & Shiffrin, 1968). Yet in the latest *Annual Review* article in which the STS/LTS distinction has been discussed at length and that should be authoritative, Postman (1975), in rejecting the distinction, pointedly ignored neuropsychological evidence, merely stating in mandarin fashion; "The existing data [from brain-damaged patients] do not impress us as unequivocal, more important, extrapolations from pathological deficits to the structure of normal memory are of uncertain validity [p. 308]."

It is not entirely clear to which data Postman is referring as being "not unequivocal" but possible to the disagreement in the literature on the performance of amnesic patients on the Brown –Peterson task (e.g., Baddeley & Warrington, 1970; Cermak & Butters, 1972; Cermak, Butters, and Goodglass, 1971), the main empirical, as opposed to theoretical, dispute in the neuropsychology of memory that has occurred to date. In that case, he would appear to have misunderstood the logic of neuropsychological methodology with respect to fractionation of function. It is therefore possibly worth spelling out certain standard neuropsychological points for cognitive psychologists.

Strong neuropsychological evidence for the existence of neurologically distinct functional systems depends on double dissociation of function (e.g., Teuber, 1955; Weiskrantz, 1968). A dissociation of function requires that patients exist whose performance on task A is normal but on task B is much worse than the normal range, a monotonic relation between damage and performance being assumed.

As an example of a dissociation in memory, consider the performance of "pure" amnesics on digit span (as task A) and on an LTS forced-choice word recognition memory test of Warrington (1974) (as task B) (Warrington & Weiskrantz, personal commnunication). Figure 12.1 shows the forced-choice recognition memory scores of 200 normal subjects and 10 amnesic patients. Most of the amnesic patients score well below the normal range. By contrast, their mean digit span was 6.8, range 5–9. The obvious inference from a dissociation is that a system exists that is damaged in these patients and is critically involved in task B but not in task A. However, it is possible to account for such a dissociation without assuming that different systems are critically involved in the two tasks, given that performance/resource functions (Norman & Bobrow, 1975) for task A asymptote well below the level of resource available in normal subjects. Then a damaged system could still produce normal performance on task A, although not on task B. This

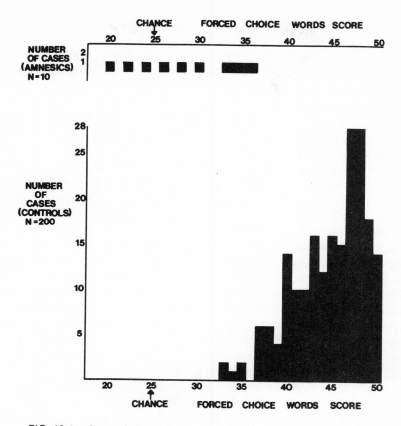

FIG. 12.1. Comparison of the performance of normal subjects (Warrington & Golding, personal communication) and amnesic patients (Warrington & Weiskrantz, personal communication) on one of a number of tests that discriminate amnesic patients from controls quantitatively—forced-choice verbal recognition memory (Warrington, 1974). A score of 25 would be expected by chance.

type of argument becomes plausible if normal performance on a task is at ceiling. However, if another group of patients exists who have normal performance on task *B* but not on task *A*, so providing a double dissociation, then different systems must be critically damaged in the two groups of patients. (Performance/resource arguments cannot handle double dissociation except trivially by assigning one deficit to resource-limited process and the other to data-limited processes.)

It might be claimed that when two groups of patients are selected from all neurological patients according to their showing complementary dissociations, inferences to normal function are liable to a selection artefact. Two types of argument show this to be unlikely. First, from the neurological perspective, most neurological patients have widespread lesions; so associated deficits and not dissociations are to be expected, whether or not tasks are performed by a common underlying system. The existence of a dissociation is therefore a priori unlikely. Moreover, once a dissociation had been obtained, similar lesion sites—where ascertainable—can be predicted in the patients who show it, which should differ from those found in patients with the complementary dissociation. For instance, the syndrome to be interpreted as an STS deficit is found in patients with left parietal lesions (Warrington, Logue, & Pratt, 1971). By contrast, the amnesic syndrome occurs with hippocampal/mamillary body lesions (Brierley, 1966). (It should be noted that the relation between syndrome and lesion site is sufficiently powerful to act as a guide to neurosurgery, for instance, in operation for cerebral tumor.) Second, from the experimental perspective, if two selected subjects—normal or neurological—show a *reliable* double dissociation, then for those two subjects the two tasks are being conducted at least in part by different systems. Since the methodology of typical psychological experimentation ignores individual differences in process, theoretical inferences from neurological evidence are in principle not inferior to that from normal experimentation. More practically, inferences from dissociation in neurological patients should be testable by studies of intertask correlations in normal subjects.

Seemingly "equivocal" data can arise when one set of patients shows a reliable dissociation between their level of performance on two tasks but another set do not. Thus the performance of some amnesic patients on the Brown–Peterson task can be dissociated from their extremely bad performance on most LTS tasks (Baddeley & Warrington, 1970; Cermak, 1976). Other amnesic patients, however, show an association (Cermak & Butters, 1972; Cermak, Butters, and Goodglass, 1971). Both sets of data can be explained, if one assumes that functionally separate systems are involved, in that the former patients have their lesions restricted to one system but for the latter group the lesions affect both systems. Given that the latter patients were Korsakoff patients where widespread lesions are the norm (Victor, Adams, & Collins, 1971), such an account is anatomically plausible. The alternative possibility—that the two types of task differ in the amount of resource required—can be rejected, as patients with deficits to STS (discussed later) show the complementary dissociation. In general, where one group of patients shows a dissociation between performance on two tasks and another group shows an association, one needs extremely strong counter arguments not to base inferences to normal function on the dissociation. The association can be assumed to arise from the existence of multiple deficits.

Finally there are the questions of the relibility of patient data and of its "abnormality." Experiments performed on patients tend to be somewhat different from those conducted on normal subjects. The patient is after all a patient and has to be treated as a sick person, not just as a cooperative robot, and so cannot be placed in a booth in front of a VDU for an hour or so. Thus very tight control over procedure has to be replaced by clinical skills. However, the magnitude of the effects makes this relatively unimportant.

It may be argued that neuropsychological syndromes represent abnormal adaptations of the nervous system, such that these patients are not performing any tasks in the same way as are normal subjects. Yet, in a "pure" example of a particular syndrome, all tests that do not involve a particular neurological system will be performed at the same level as controls. Thus in the "pure" amnesic syndrome, intellectual skills are unimpaired (see Zangwill, 1966). In the "pure" STM syndrome, such as case J. B. (Shallice & Butterworth, 1977; Warrington, Logue, & Pratt, 1971), virtually all cognitive skills are unimpaired. The "abnormal adaptation" argument cannot plausibly explain the preserved abilities of such patients.

THE FRACTIONATION OF LONG- AND SHORT-TERM VERBAL MEMORY

If one considers verbal memory tasks, a double dissociation exists between tasks clearly involving long-term retention and those that can be ascribed critically to the operation of the auditory–verbal STS—for example, span and the recency effect in free recall. It has long been known that amnesic patients perform poorly on the former tasks, as discussed above, and can perform well on the latter (Baddeley & Warrington, 1970; Drachman & Arbit, 1966; Zangwill, 1946). By contrast, patients exist who are generally intellectually unimpaired, whose performance on these latter tasks is extremely poor (digit spans of less than 3.5), but whose performance on LTM tasks is normal (Saffran & Marin, 1975; Shallice & Warrington, 1970; Warrington, Logue, & Pratt, 1971; Warrington & Shallice, 1969, 1972; and, in essence, Tzortzis & Albert, 1974) (see Table 12.1). For instance, if one

TABLE 12.1
Long-Term Memory Tests on STM Patients[a]

Tests	Case 1	Case 2	Case 3	Controls
Wechsler P.A. learning (success score)	11	18	11	14.8
Wechsler Logical Memory (items recalled)	11.5	9.5	10	9.3
Ten-word learning (number of trials)	7	10	9	9.0

[a]Performance on three tests of LTM: paired associates, short story retention, and free-recall learning to criterion. (Adapted from Warrington, Logue, & Pratt, 1971.)

compares the two types of patient on immediate and delayed free recall, then the amnesics are grossly inferior at delayed recall, whereas the STM patients show an abnormally small difference between immediate and delayed recall (see Table 12.2). Similarly, on immediate free recall the amnesics show a normal recency effect, but the earlier part of the curve is grossly abnormal (see Fig. 12.2); the STM patients by contrast have a recency effect limited to the last item (see Shallice & Warrington, 1970; Warrington, Logue, & Pratt, 1971).

The existence of a double dissociation is evidence for the existence of neurologically separable systems. It does not enable one to infer what the systems are that are separately involved in the two sets of tasks and which are differentially impaired in two types of patients. For instance, the above results could logically be interpreted in terms of a dissociation between the ability to retrieve traces rapidly and the ability to retrieve weak traces—that is, between different aspects of the retrieval system in a single store. Although this is not Kinsbourne's (1972) position, it is compatible with his argument that the specific STM deficits arise from retrieval deficits, not storage deficits. His argument, however, cannot account for a number of aspects of the STM patient data, namely Brown–Peterson forgetting with a single item, probe recognition deficits, and the existence of order errors in reduced span (see Shallice & Warrington, 1977). Moreover the inability of amnesics to learn digit strings very slightly longer than their span (e.g., Drachman & Arbit, 1966) makes any interpretation of their deficit in terms of an inability to retrieve weak traces extremely implausible.

The double dissociation, in fact, fits very well with the standard, late-1960s two-store view of auditory–verbal memory (e.g., Atkinson & Shiffrin, 1968; Baddeley, 1976; Waugh & Norman, 1965) with the proviso that the stores be thought of as in parallel rather than in series (Shallice & Warrington, 1970).

TABLE 12.2
Immediate and Delayed Free-Recall Results[a]

	Rate	I	D	STS Cap.
Amnesics	1/3sec	3.07	1.11	2.16
Controls	1/3sec	4.95	3.30	2.45
STM patients	1/2sec	3.53	3.00	0.65

[a]Mean words correct on an immediate (I) and a delayed (D) 10-word test and the capacity in items of STS (STS Cap.) as estimated by Baddeley's (1970) method. The data of the control group and the amnesic group are quoted from Baddeley and Warrington (1970) and that of the STM patient group from Warrington, Logue, and Pratt (1971) (using a different set of words).

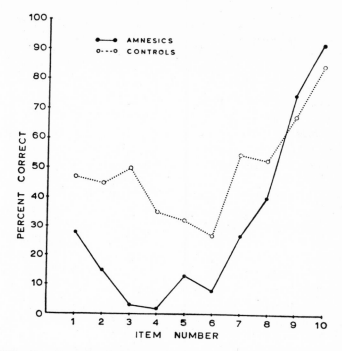

FIG. 12.2. The immediate free recall of amnesic patients and normal controls. Subjects read words aloud at a 3-sec rate. (From Baddeley & Warrington, 1970.)

In my view, no plausible interpretation of the double dissocation exists that does not assume that separate memory stores are involved. The view that attributes STS and LTS results to different types of activation of the same store (e.g., Atkinson, Herrmann, & Wescourt, 1974; Norman, 1968) would seem to predict incorrectly that patients with severe STM deficits should have LTM deficits—and probably also intellectual ones (see Shallice & Warrington, 1970). It is unclear how the levels-of-processing view, in which memory is a mere "by-product" of perceptual activity (Craik & Lockhart, 1972), would cope. There are no gross defects in the ability of STM patients to process perceptually material on which they show gross memory deficits. They can, for instance, make accurate semantic judgments about words presented at the rate at which their very low span is measured (Warrington, Logue, & Pratt, 1971; Warrington & Shallice, 1969). One could argue that the dissociation is that between the retention of phonological and semantic traces, which also have different temporal characteristics. However, traces must presumably exist somewhere. This would therefore appear to be no more than a reformulation of a parallel stores view (e.g., Shallice & Warrington, 1970), being less satisfactory, as it does not enable one to discuss the specific characteristics of particular stores such as in the case of STS—its use of temporal order. The inadequacy of competing theories of the syndrome is not the only reason for assuming that the deficit is one of an auditory–verbal STS. The neuropsychology results are in fact compatible with more specific properties of STS; but since these are now much more disputed than they were in 1970, the discussion will be postponed until after the neuropsychological evidence has been presented concerning the function of STS.

Other Types of Fractionation

I have concentrated on the amnesic/STM patient fractionation, because it is the best documented example available in the neuropsychology of memory literature and because it speaks to a very central issue in the information-processing view of memory. Various other examples exist in the literature. The most widely quoted is the dissociation between LTM for verbally and nonverbally processed material (e.g., Milner, 1971; Signoret & Lhermitte, 1976; Starr & Phillips, 1970). An analogous dissociation exists for STM between visual and auditory–verbal material, the existence of a separate visual STS being clearly supported by the superior, short-term visual retention of the STM patients (see Shallice & Warrington, 1977; Warrington & Shallice, 1972). Clinically apparent though not yet experimentally demonstrated is the dissociation between control processes and storage (e.g., Luria, 1966; Signoret & Lhermitte, 1976).

One dissociation of especial interest is that between semantic and episodic memory suggested by Tulving (1972) mainly on the basis of phenomenological considerations but for which it is hard to supply orthodox experimental psychological support (see Baddeley, 1976). Although the picture is not yet clear, clinical evidence appears to provide a fractionation supporting Tulving's position. Amnesic patients can have not only preserved vocabulary but also good general knowledge. Thus a patient of Lhermitte and Signoret (1972) with no evident intellectual impairment did not appear to remember a single event which had happened since the beginning of his illness and also had a severe retrograde amnesia. Yet he was described as being "extremely exact" in his scholastic knowledge as regards historical dates, the geographical position of towns and countries, and of works of literature. In contrast, Warrington (1975) has recently described patients who are not clinically amnesic—they are well-orientated in time and place and are able to refer backwards and forwards to events in their lives, both near and far—and yet have a gross defect in semantic memory, their knowledge of the meaning of words and of the significance of objects being abysmal; lower level perceptual skills are, however, preserved.

NEUROPSYCHOLOGY AND THE PROPERTIES OF THE AUDITORY-VERBAL, SHORT-TERM STORE

In the previous section my aim was to briefly indicate the potential breadth of the neuropsychological approach, given that its methodology is accepted. In this section I want to reinforce the earlier methodological arguments by showing that one can also make inferences about the function of a system that has been isolated using neuropsychological evidence. In addition, my aim is to illustrate the reliability of this approach by showing that such inferences can fit with ones that could be made from the normal experimental literature. To do this, I will take one system—auditory-verbal STS—and examine three aspects of its function: whether it is speech-based, and whether it is part of the speech input system, and/or of the speech output system.

Throughout this discussion I presuppose that only a single store (auditory-verbal STS) is *mainly* responsible for the retaining of the information used in span, although other stores such as peripheral auditory stores, visual STS, and LTS may well contribute when retention in auditory-verbal STS is specifically impaired. More complex theories that postulate two or more stores as jointly undertaking this, such as that of Baddeley and Hitch (1974), are therefore not directly confronted. However, any multiple-store theory has to explain how, why, and which parts of a span string are in any one store and not in the others; from a simple trace-strength notion, traces in one store would tend to dominate.

On isolating the STM defect, we argued that it resulted from damage to a store specific to speech (Shallice & Warrington, 1970), and others have also assumed that the store or stores contributing to span performance are speech specific (e.g., Morton, 1970). We have since obtained more solid evidence. If one compares the short-term retention by the STM patients of three nonverbal sounds (meaningful noises) with three verbal sounds, when verbal mediation is suppressed by concurrent counting, then a pattern of performance very different from normal subjects' is obtained (Shallice & Warrington, 1974) (see Fig. 12.3). As expected, verbal material is retained much more poorly by STM patients than by controls, but this is not so for nonverbal sounds. The significant interaction cannot be attributed to a ceiling effect, as normal subjects find the meaningful noises significantly the more difficult to retain. [The apparently different results obtained by Tzortzis and Albert (1974) are simply explained by their failure to employ a suppression task and so prevent verbal mediation; this benefits the controls more than the STM patients.] The anatomical location of the lesion that results in a deficit of auditory-verbal STM is also compatible with a speech-specific function, because the lesion is within the speech regions of the cortex (Warrington, Logue, & Pratt, 1971).

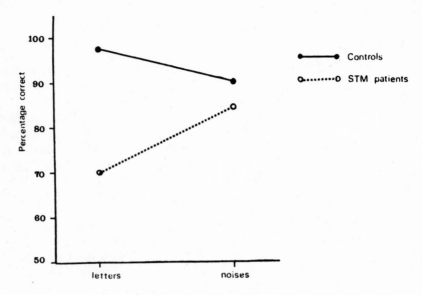

FIG. 12.3.   Performance of STM patients on retention of three letters and three meaningful sounds when concurrently counting. (From Shallice & Warrington, 1974.)

In the normal experimental literature, one finding that strongly suggests that a store exists specific to speech input is the result of Morton and Chambers (1976) that a stimulus suffix only has a deleterious effect on final item recall in auditory–verbal span if the suffix is a speech sound and not if it is a physically very similar nonspeech sound. Morton and Chambers, in fact, interpret this effect in terms of the speech-specific nature of a store that only contributes to a small part of span performance—the precategorical acoustic store (Crowder & Morton, 1969). However, Frankish (1973) has found that the auditory superiority effects, which this concept was invented to explain, are not limited to final span positions if very small but consistent pauses are introduced in the input string so that it is perceived as being grouped. This is more compatible with the view derived from Morton (1978) that the stimulus suffix interferes with a marking or anchoring process introduced by the speech perception system, which provides a suitable retrieval cue to the final item within the auditory–verbal STS. The nature of the interference produced by the stimulus suffix—phonological not acoustic—would indicate that the store involved in span was speech based.

However, even if one accepts the concept of the precategorical acoustic store, a similar conclusion holds. The main store for span retention would appear not to utilize acoustic coding. As it receives input from the speech-based, precategorical acoustic store, it would presumably have at least as abstract a level of coding. As the acoustic/phonological similarity effect operates for all items in the span string (Baddeley, 1968), that level of coding is presumably phonological.

If the store primarily responsible for span performance is specific to speech, the question naturally arises as to whether it is part of the speech output system—corresponding to, say, Morton's (1970) response buffer—or whether it is part of the input system as in Sperling and Speelman's (1970) theory, or part of a central system as in Baddeley and Hitch's (1974) working memory. The evidence of the STM patients bears directly on this issue. A very central locus, for instance, seems implausible given the dissociation between their span performance and their preserved intellectual skills (see also Shallice, 1975).

Output systems that maintain verbal information in some form prior to articulation must exist. It would seem very plausible that they play a role in span. Damage to an output buffer of the sort postulated by MacKay (1970) or Fromkin (1971) to explain certain types of speech errors would, however, be expected to lead to impairment of spontaneous speech. Working with one of the STM patients, JB, we have recently shown that a dissociation can be obtained between speech production and span (Shallice & Butterworth, 1977). Thus, in this particular patient, a detailed analysis of her speech with respect to rate, pausing, and number and types of errors found it to be entirely normal except for a very slight—and not relevant—increase in function word errors, even though her span was only 3.4 digits (more than two standard deviations below the mean). This therefore suggests that the locus of poor span performance is not the output buffer, for this appears to be quite intact.

The inference that the main auditory–verbal store is not part of the speech output system, in fact, fits with experimental findings on normal subjects. Thus Levy (1971) showed that articulatory suppression, which would be expected to interfere grossly with the use of a speech output buffer, has virtually no effect on the retention of rapidly presented items, provided there is auditory input, but has a massive effect if the input is only visual. The deficit with visual presentation is to be expected if articulatory suppression hinders the recoding of visual information either into an output store or into a nonperipheral input store by means of inner speech (Sperling, 1967). The lack of any effect of suppression with auditory presentation, however, only fits with the view that the auditory–verbal STS is an input speech store. At the fast rate of presentation used, maintenance rehearsal—prevented by articulatory suppression—would not be expected to be of use for auditory input, both from introspection (Sperling & Speelman, 1970) and from the comparison of active and passive strategies in short-term retention (Hockey, 1973). Similarly, articulatory suppression eliminates effects attributable to auditory–verbal STS when visual input is used but not when auditory input is used as one would expect on the input-store view. This applies both to acoustic confusion effects (Murray, 1968; Peterson & Johnson, 1971) and to the word-length effect (Baddeley, Thomson, & Buchanan, 1975). To assume that just because covert articulation is used in the normal, short-term retention of visual input, that articulatory traces are necessarily involved is fallacious, as Sperling and Speelman (1970) have shown. This is even valid for deaf children who, as Dodd and Hermelin (1977) have shown, can utilize a phonological code derived from lip reading. Thus the evidence from nonneurological subjects also seems to support an input-store view.

Finally it seems unlikely for functional reasons that an output buffer would be of use in span situations. It must store sufficient material to allow continuous speech that is presumably of the order of a phrase (Fromkin, 1971). This amount is well below the temporal and capacity limits necessary for retention of a string of unconneted, unrelated items—ordinary span—and well below sentence span. Moreover, there are problems in assuming that the output buffer even complements another store, because under many assumptions it would merely duplicate storage of stronger traces in the other store. Its role in memory experiments would therefore be merely that of being part of the maintenance rehearsal system operating on one item at a time.

By contrast, there are good functional reasons for postulating that a sizable store should exist to retain the surface structure of speech in case the initial parsing falls behind input in realtime or even initially fails completely as in Lashley's (1951) well-known writing/righting example, so that backtracking becomes necessary (as assumed by some artificial intelligence programs for speech comprehension; see Wanner & Maratsos, 1975). That surface structure (in contrast to gist) is retained in a short-term store is a well-known finding (Johnson–Laird & Stevenson, 1970; Sachs, 1967). That such a store would play a major role in span performance has been suggested many times (e.g., Baddeley, 1976; Green, 1973; Jarvella, 1971; Saffran & Marin, 1975; Shallice, 1975; Shallice & Warrington, 1970).

The problem with attempting to test this theory by neuropsychological means is that it predicts an association between performance on different tasks and not a dissociation, so that one is faced by the danger of a spurious correlation arising from damage to anatomically but not functionally related systems. The evidence can, however, be suggestive. At a gross clinical level, the STM patients appear to comprehend normally. However, subtle speech-comprehension deficits exist for all STM patients so far studied in this respect. Thus our STM patients had a deficit on the Token test of De Renzi and Vignolo (1962) in which patients have to obey instructions containing much nonredundant information such as, "Put the red circle between the yellow triangle and the green triangle" (Warrington et al., 1971). More impressively, Saffran and Marin (1975) showed that in many cases, their patient, IL, who had a span of less than three items, was able to provide a semantically acceptable paraphrase of a sentence that he could not repeat; but if there was a clause at the beginning of the sentence or particularly if the subject and object were reversible, paraphrase performance deteriorated. Our comprehension studies remain incomplete, but they appear to show very similar characteristics.

There is a very interesting parallel in the normal literature. Levy (1977) has shown that concurrent counting (i.e., articulatory suppression) affects short-term retention of certain aspects of sentences when they are visually presented but not when they are auditorily presented. The visual deficit was found for tasks involving both so-called lexical difference detection and so-called semantic difference detection. A lexical difference detection involves a synonym being substituted for one of the nouns in a sentence, leaving meaning unaltered. Semantic difference detection involves the switching of subject and object names. If, following Kleiman (1975), one assumes that the main short-term store involved in reading is the auditory–verbal STS, then articulatory suppression will hinder access to it. The deficits produced by articulatory suppression in the reading of normal subjects, especially as they do not occur with auditory input, might then be expected to mirror the *auditory* comprehension deficits of STM patients. In both cases, little use can be made of the auditory–verbal STS in comprehension. Direct semantic decoding of individual words is, however, possible. For STM patients this is known not to depend on STS (Warrington & Shallice, 1969). For normal subjects, direct semantic decoding of individual words in reading does not depend on a phonological transformation (e.g., Baron, 1973; Bower, 1970; Green & Shallice, 1976; Kleiman, 1975).

The inability of STM patients to produce the lexically correct word in sentence retention, even though gist is preserved (Saffran & Marin, 1975; Shallice & Butterworth, 1977), in fact, corresponds to the deficit that Levy (1977) found on lexical difference detection. The tendency that STM patients have of reversing subject and object (Saffran & Marin, 1975) corresponds to Levy's (1977) semantic difference detection deficit. These correspondences are made more striking when contrasted with those on the preserved retention of gist. In a more complex experiment, Levy (1978) used paraphrase detection, where the negative test sentences are semantically quite different from the stimuli. In this situation, articulatory suppression of visually presented sentences produces no significant deficit. This corresponds to the ability of STM patients to grasp the gist of syntactically simple sentences. Levy's experimental situations are complex, and the possibility of subjects using different strategies in different situations undoubtedly exists; so the parallels with the STM patient's performance must be tentative, especially given the danger involved in assuming associations between neurological deficits to be causal. Yet the parallels remain very suggestive.

The findings with STM patients then support the view that auditory–verbal STS is a store that retains phonologically processed information for use in certain types of the more complex syntactic and semantic comprehension processes; but that given relatively simple syntactic structure, comprehension often does not require the use of this store. Yet the existence of STS has frequently been rejected, just because its properties appeared not to fit with this function (e.g., Craik & Lockhart, 1972; Murdock, 1974; Postman, 1975). Most of these arguments have already been answered (Shallice, 1975). In particular, the objection has been raised by Shulman (1970) and Raser (1972) that the evidence of the differential contribution of phonological and semantic information in short- and long-term retention (e.g., Baddeley, 1966; Kintsch & Buschke, 1969) does not preclude the existence of a short-term semantic trace, which would suggest that short-term stores were general rather than specific in content. However, these authors base their argument on the results of synonym recognition experiments. Yet detailed consideration of their results indicates that the rapidly decaying trace in that situation is more likely to be a phonological one (Shallice, 1975). (Of course, this does not mean that a semantic trace does not exist in STM experiments, only that its decay rate is at least an order of magnitude slower.)

One major problem remains for the present approach, namely that of the very different measures of the "capacity" of the store (e.g., Craik & Lockhart, 1972; Murdock, 1974). (The question of decay rates [Craik & Lockhart, 1972; Murdock, 1974] is basically the same problem, given most assumptions about the operation of the store.) A capacity of two to three items for STS, as derived from the recency effect, clearly would not be appropriate for a store with the function of retaining surface structure. It has been argued (Shallice, 1975) that free recall is much inferior to span as a paradigm for estimating STS capacity. In free recall, the input strategy of the subject is biased toward semantic encoding, and the output strategy—as far as STS is concerned—has to mimic running memory span. As amnesics have normal span (Baddeley & Warrington, 1970; Drachman & Arbit, 1966) and as the acoustic confusion effect occurs at all serial positions in span performance (Baddeley, 1968), the assumption that span has a large LTS component (Craik, 1971) is very implausible. It presumably then depends mainly on STS.

However, even word span provides a lower estimate of STS capacity than does sentence span (Craik & Masani, 1969; Jarvella, 1971). One possible explanation of the discrepancy can be derived from the accessibility/availability distinction (Tulving & Pearlstone, 1966). If accessing the decaying traces in auditory–verbal STS requires retrieval cues, these will presumably be connected to its function and relate to speech-relevant characteristics such as word order, pause patterns, end effects, and intonation. It is therefore not surprising that these four factors all have a considerable effect on measures of "capacity" [e.g., Ingleby (see Broadbent, 1971); Frankish, 1973; Crowder & Morton, 1969; Glanzer, 1976 respectively]. Thus lower measures of capacity would be expected to be derived from the monotonous staccato presentation of syntactically unrelated words—that is, the typical short-term memory experiment—than from actual speech. In addition, interactive models of speech comprehension (e.g., Allport, this volume) would predict that even if surface structure is retained in a short-term store, its retrieval can be facilitated by semantic and syntactic information retained separately. Thus the low measures of STS capacity derived from STM experiments do not rule out a speech comprehension function.

GENERAL DISCUSSION

The aim of the previous section has not been to provide a complete review of the normal literature as it relates to the function of the auditory–verbal STS. Problems remain, particularly concerning the recency effect in free recall (see Baddeley & Hitch, 1977). Rather the aim has been to show that a hypothesis about the existence and function of a particular memory system, derived from the study of a small number of carefully selected neurological patients, fits with one interpretation of the experimental literature on normal subjects. If this argument is correct, then it would strengthen the general case for the use of neuropsychological evidence as a means of rejecting alternative hypotheses. By assisting in maintaining the number of plausible models within reasonable bounds, it would support the position taken earlier—that information-processing theory is capable of real advances.

At a more general level, the relation presented here between information-processing psychology and neuropsychology is not one of reduction. In the present paper, neuropsychological evidence has been interpreted by using information-processing theory; so it might appear to involve a reduction of neuropsychology to information-processing psychology! However, the more purely neuropsychological aspects of the syndromes have been ignored. Neuropsychology has its own mode of data collection, a craft process different from that of experimental psychology. It has a partially independent theoretical structure determined in part by neurological considerations and its own theoretical disputes at times orthogonal to ones in cognitive psychology. For instance, the issue of the relation between conduction aphasia and STM is a complex one that has not been discussed here (see, e.g., Kinsbourne, 1972; Shallice & Warrington, 1977).

The nature of the relation between information-processing theory and neuropsychology is, in my opinion, a precursor of the type of relation between knowledge systems that must be developed in the human sciences. A real mediating link has been developed between fields of knowledge that will remain partially autonomous. Were a large number of fields related in such a manner, then any theory developed in one field could be mapped into a number of other fields. In the case of memory, for instance, artificial intelligence would be another obvious candidate for the development of mediating links with information-processing psychology, and phenomenology might be a further possibility (see Shallice, 1978). The weakness of any individual empirical test—due to the lack of precise data—could be compensated by breadth, as in early Darwinian theory in biology. The strength of the whole would be much greater than that of the sum of its parts. The development of theory in the physical sciences, at least as philosophers of science and psychologists have conceived it, would, then, not be an appropriate model for the development of theory in the human sciences, contrary to the dominant opinion for much of psychology's history.

ACKNOWLEDGMENTS

I should like to thank Graham Hitch, John Morton, and Elizabeth Warrington for their very helpful comments on an earlier draft of this paper.

REFERENCES

Allport, D. A. The state of cognitive psychology. *Quarterly Journal of Experimental Psychology,* 1975, *27,* 141–152.

Atkinson, R. C., Hermann, S. J., & Wescourt, K. T. Search processes in recognition memory. In R. L. Solso (Ed.), *Theories in cognitive psychology: The Loyola Symposium.* Hillsdale, N.J.: Lawrence Erlbaum Associates, 1974.

Atkinson, R. C., & Shiffrin, R. M. Human memory: A proposed system and its control processes. In K. W. Spence & J. T. Spence (Eds.), *The psychology of learning and motivation.* New York: Academic Press, 1968.

Baddeley, A. D. Short-term memory for word sequences as a function of acoustic, semantic and formal similarity. *Quarterly Journal of Experimental Psychology,* 1966, *18,* 362–368.

Baddeley, A. D. How does acoustic similarity influence short-term memory? *Quarterly Journal of Experimental Psychology,* 1968, *20,* 249–264.

Baddeley, A. D. Estimating the short-term component in free recall. *British Journal of Psychology,* 1970, *61,* 13–15.

Baddeley, A. D. *The psychology of memory.* New York: Basic Books, 1976.

Baddeley, A. D., & Hitch, G. Working memory. In G. H. Bower (ed.), *The psychology of learning and motivation* (Vol. 8). New York: Academic Press, 1974.

Baddeley, A. D., & Hitch, G. Recency re-examined. In S. Dornic (Ed.), *Attention and performance* (Vol. 6). New York: Academic Press, 1977.

Baddeley, A. D., Thomson, N., & Buchanan, M. Word length and the structure of short-term memory. *Journal of Verbal Learning and Verbal Behaviour,* 1975, *14,* 575–489.

Baddeley, A. D., & Warrington, E. K. Amnesia and the distinction between long- and short-term memory. *Journal of Verbal Learning and Verbal Behaviour,* 1970, *9,* 176–189.

Baron, J. Phonemic stage not necessary for reading. *Quarterly Journal of Experimental Psychology,* 1973, *25,* 241–246.

Bower, T. G. R. Reading by eye. In H. Levin & J. Williams (Eds.), *Basic studies in reading.* New York: Basic Books, 1970.

Brierley, J. B. The neuropathology of amnesic states. In C. W. M. Whitty & O. L. Zangwill (Eds.), *Amnesia.* London: Butterworth, 1966.

Broadbent, D. E. *Decision and stress.* London: Academic Press, 1971.

Cermak, L. S. The encoding capacity of a patient with amnesia due to encephalitis. *Neuropsychologia,* 1976, *14,* 311–326.

Cermak, L. S., & Butters, N. The role of interference and encoding in the short-term memory deficits of Korsakoff patients. *Neuropsychologia,* 1972, *10,* 89–96.

Cermak, L. S., Butters, N., & Goodglass, H. The extent of memory loss in Korsakoff patients. *Neuropsychologia,* 1971, *9,* 307–315.

Craik, F. I. M. Primary memory. *British Medical Bulletin,* 1971, *27,* 232–236.

Craik, F. I. M., & Lockhart, R. S. Levels of processing: A framework for memory research. *Journal of Verbal Learning and Verbal Behaviour,* 1972, *12,* 599–607.

Craik, F. I. M., & Masani, P. A. Age and intelligence differences in coding and retrieval of word lists. *British Journal of Psychology,* 1969, *60,* 315–319.

Crowder, R. G., & Morton, J. Precategorical acoustic storage (PAS). *Perception & Psychophysics,* 1969, *5,* 365–373.

De Renzi, E., & Vignolo, L. A. The token test: A sensitive test to detect receptive disturbances in aphasics. *Brain,* 1962, *85,* 665–678.

Dodd, B., & Hermelin, B. Phonological coding by the deaf. *Perception & Psychophysics,* 1977, *21,* 413–417.

Drachman, D. A., & Arbit, J. Memory and the hippocampal complex II. *Archives of neurology,* 1966, *15,* 52–61.

Frankish, C. *Grouping, pauses and rehearsal.* Paper presented to the Experimental Psychology Society, Cambridge, England, 1973.

Fromkin, V. A. The non-anomalous nature of anomalous utterances. *Language,* 1971, *47,* 27–52.

Gaukroger, S. W. Bachelard and the problem of epistemological analysis. *Studies in History and Philosophy of Science,* 1976, *7,* 189–244.

Glanzer, M. Intonation grouping and related words in free recall. *Journal of Verbal Learning and Verbal Behaviour,* 1976, *15,* 85–92.

Green, D. W. *A psychological investigation into the memory and comprehension of sentences.* Unpublished Ph.D. thesis, University of London, 1973.

Green, D. W., & Shallice, T. Direct visual access in reading for meaning. *Memory & Cognition,* 1976, *4,* 753–758.

Hockey, G. R. J. Rate of presentation in running memory and direct manipulation of input-processing strategies. *Quarterly Journal of Experimental Psychology,* 1973, *25,* 104–111.

Jarvella, R. J. Syntactic processing of connected speech. *Journal of Verbal Learning and Verbal Behaviour,* 1971, *10,* 409–416.

Johnson-Laird, P. N., & Stevenson, R. Memory for syntax. *Nature,* 1970, *227,* 412.

Kinsbourne, M. Behavioural analysis of the repetition deficit in conduction aphasia. *Neurology,* 1972, *22,* 1126–1132.

Kintsch, W., & Buschke, H. Homophones and synonyms in short-term memory. *Journal of Experimental Psychology,* 1969, *80,* 403–407.

Kleiman, G. M. Speech recoding in reading. *Journal of Verbal Learning and Verbal Behaviour,* 1975, *14,* 323–338.

Kuhn, T. S. *The structure of scientific revolutions.* Chicago: University of Chicago Press, 1962.

Lashley, K. S. The problem of serial order in behaviour. In L. A. Jeffress (Ed.), *Cerebral mechanisms in behaviour.* New York: Wiley, 1951.

Levy, B. A. Role of articulation in auditory and visual short-term memory. *Journal of Verbal Learning and Verbal Behaviour,* 1971, *10,* 123–132.

Levy, B. A. Reading: Speech and meaning processes. *Journal of Verbal Learning and Verbal Behaviour,* 1977, *16,* 623–638.

Levy, B. A. *Speech analysis during sentence processing: Reading versus listening.* Manuscript submitted for publication, 1978.

Lhermitte, F., & Signoret, J. L. Analyse neuropsychologique et differenciation des syndromes amnésiques. *Revue Neurologique,* 1972, *129,* 161–178.

Luria, A. R. *Higher cortical functions in man.* London: Tavistock, 1966.

MacKay, D. G. Spoonerisms: The structure of errors in the serial order of speech. *Neuropsychologia,* 1970, *8,* 323–350.

Milner, B. Interhemispheric differences in the localization of psychological processes in man. *British Medical Bulletin,* 1971, *27,* 272–277.

Morton, J. A functional model of memory. In D. A. Norman (Ed.), *Models of human memory.* New York: Academic Press, 1970.

Morton, J. Perception and memory. In *Cognitive psychology, Course No. D303.* Milton Keynes: Open University Press, 1978.

Morton, J., & Chambers, S. M. Some evidence for "speech" as an acoustic feature. *British Journal of Psychology,* 1976, *67,* 31–45.

Murdock, B. B., Jr. *Human memory: Theory and data.* Potomac Md. Erlbaum Associates, 1974.

Murray, D. J. Articulation and acoustic confusability in short-term memory. *Journal of Experimental Psychology,* 1968, *78,* 679–684.

Neisser, U. *Cognition and reality.* San Francisco: Freeman, 1976.

Newall, A. You can't play 20 questions with nature and win. In W. G. Chase (Ed.), *Visual information processing.* New York: Academic Press, 1974.

Norman, D. A. Toward a theory of memory and attention. *Psychological Review,* 1968, *75,* 522–536.

Norman, D. A., & Bobrow, D. G. On data-limited and resource-limited processes. *Cognitive Psychology,* 1975, *7,* 44–64.

Peterson, L. R., & Johnson, S. T. Some effects of minimizing articulation on short-term retention. *Journal of Verbal Learning and Verbal Behaviour,* 1971, *10,* 345–354.

Postman, L. Verbal learning and memory. *Annual Review of Psychology,* 1975, *26,* 291–335.

Raser, G. A. Recoding of semantic and acoustic information in short-term memory. *Journal of Verbal Learning and Verbal Behaviour,* 1972, *11,* 692–697.

Sachs, J. S. Recognition memory for syntactic and semantic aspects of connected discourse. *Perception & Psychophysics,* 1967, *2,* 437–442.

Saffran, E., & Marin, O. S. M. Immediate memory for word lists and sentences in a patient with deficient auditory short-term memory. *Brain and Language,* 1975, *2,* 420–433.

Shallice, T. On the contents of primary memory. In P. M. A. Rabbitt & S. Dornic (Eds.), *Attention and performance* (Vol. 5). London: Academic Press, 1975.

Shallice, T. The dominant action-system: An information-processing approach to consciousness. In K. S. Pope & J. L. Singer (Eds.), *The stream of consciousness: Psychological investigations into the flow of private experience.* New York: Plenum Press, 1978.

Shallice, T., & Butterworth, B. B. Short-term memry impairment and spontaneous speech. *Neuropsychologia,* 1977, *15,* 729–735.

Shallice, T., & Warrington, E. K. Independent functioning of the verbal memory stores: A neuropsychological study. *Quarterly Journal of Experimental Psychology,* 1970, *22,* 261–273.

Shallice, T., & Warrington, E. K. The dissocation between short-term retention of meaningful sounds and verbal material. *Neuropsychologia,* 1974, *12,* 553–555.

Shallice, T., & Warrington, E. K. Auditory-verbal short-term memory and conduction aphasia. *Brain and Language,* 1977, *4,* 479–491.

Shulman, H. G. Encoding and retention of semantic and phonemic information in short-term memory. *Journal of Verbal Learning and Verbal Behaviour,* 1970, *9,* 499–508.

Signoret, J.-L., & Lhermitte, F. The amnesic syndromes and the encoding process. *In Neural mechanisms of learning and memory.* Cambridge, Mass.: MIT Press, 1976.

Sperling, G. Successive approximations to a model for short-term memory. *Acta Psychologia,* 1967, *27,* 285–292.

Sperling, G., & Speelman, R. G. Acoustic similarity and auditory short-term memory: Experiments and a model. In D. A. Norman (Ed.), *Models of human memory.* New York: Academic Press, 1970.

Starr, A., & Phillips, L. Verbal and motor memory in the amnesic syndrome. *Neuropsychologia,* 1970, *8,* 75–88.

Sternberg, S. Memory-scanning: Mental processes revealed by reaction-time experiments. *American Scientist,* 1969, *57,* 421–457.

Teuber, H.-L., Physiological psychology. *Annual Review of Psychology,* 1955, *9,* 267–296.

Tulving, E. Episodic and semantic memory. In E. Tulving & W. Donaldson (Eds.), *Organization of memory.* New York: Academic Press, 1972.

Tulving, E., & Madigan, S. A. Memory and verbal learning. *Annual Review of Psychology,* 1970, *21,* 437–484.

Tulving, E., & Pearlstone, Z. Availability versus accessibility of information in memory for words. *Journal of Verbal Learning and Verbal Behaviour,* 1966, *5,* 381–391.

Tzortzis, C., & Albert, M. L. Impairment of memory for sequences in conduction aphasia. *Neuropsychologia,* 1974, *12,* 355–366.

Victor, M., Adams, R. D., & Collins, G. H. *The Wernicke-Korsakoff syndrome: A clinical and pathological study of 245 patients, 82 with postmortem examination.* Oxford: Blackwell, 1971.

Wanner, E., & Maratsos, M. *An augmented transition network model of relative clause comprehension.* Cambridge, Mass.: Harvard University, 1975. Mimeograph.

Warrington, E. K. Deficient recognition memory in organic amnesia. *Cortex,* 1974, *10,* 289–291.

Warrington, E. K. The selective impairment of semantic memory. *Quarterly Journal of Experimental Psychology,* 1975, *27,* 635–657.

Warrington, E. K., Logue, V., & Pratt, R. C. T. The anatomical localisation of selective impairment of auditory–verbal short-term memory. *Neuropsychologia,* 1971, *9,* 377–387.

Warrington, E. K., & Shallice, T. The selective impairment of auditory–verbal short-term memory. *Brain,* 1969, *92,* 885–896.

Warrington, E. K., & Shallice, T. Neuropsychological evidence of visual storage in short-term memory tasks. *Quarterly Journal of Expeimental Psychology,* 1972, *24,* 30–40.

Waugh, N. C., & Norman, D. A. Primary memory. *Psychological Review,* 1965, *72,* 89–104.

Weiskrantz, L. Some traps and pontifications. In L. Weiskrantz (Ed.), *Analysis of behavioural change.* New York: Harper & Row, 1968.

Zangwill, O. L. Some qualitative observations on verbal memory in cases of cerebral lesion. *British Journal of Psychology,* 1946, *37,* 8–19.

Zangwill, O. L. The amnesic syndrome. In C. W. M. Whitty & O. L. Zangwill (Eds.), *Amnesia.* London: Butterworth, 1966.

13 Neuropsychology of Complex Forms of Human Memory

Alexander R. Luria[1]
University of Moscow, U.S.S.R

INTRODUCTION

Experimental studies of memory during the last century marked a major advance in the history of the science of psychology. In 1885, H. Ebbinghaus began publishing his results in the field of memory. His main aim throughout his investigations was based on the following goal: to separate memorizing from every influence of sense or meaning and to analyze how the "senseless items" are retained, preserved, and retrieved. Starting with this as his major goal, Ebbinghaus piloted a long series of psychological investigations by doing a careful, detailed analysis of the basic problems relating to learning, retention, and retrieval. He avoided the aspect of the "senseful" organization of these processes. In a similar vein, even in behavioristic science involving "conditioning" and "learning" principles, this basic trend of studying the mechanisms of "memory traces" was pursued with great interest.

A significant turn of events occurred in memory work when Sir Frederic Bartlett broke the above tradition. He showed in his classical work entitled *Remembering* (1932) that both memorizing and remembering contain complex structures comparable to a "reconstruction" of the material that has to be preserved or retrieved. Both L. S. Vygotski and A. N. Leontiev attempted to show in similar fashion that memorizing and retrieval are complex systems of "mnestic activity" (or "mnestic behavior") in which the subject: (1) initiates the goal, e.g., to retain information given in the *present* in

---

[1]The text of the present chapter was originally written by Professor Luria. The editor of the book is responsible for the proofreading of the text.

order to retrieve it in the *future* ; (2) upon retaining the information given, attempts to turn to the *past* and retrieve the material already given; and finally, (3) selects only those items that were presented earlier.

It was H. Bergson who in 1896 first offered a description of the structure of "voluntary memory" or "mnestic activity." He characterized this form of conscious human activity as a "memory of the soul" in contra-distinction to "memory of the body." These skills were observed in animals and were viewed as basically different in their origin and psychological structure. The notion of preserving an event for the future and retrieving this specific form of data from the past remained up till the present a characteristic feature of the highest forms of human "mnestic activities." The psychological structure of mnestic activity can be described, psychologically, in the following manner.

When considering human conscious activity (the German word *Tätigkeit* expresses this process more precisely than the general English term *activity*), one first sets out with a *motive*—e.g., to satisfy the experimenter, to demonstrate the subject's performance ability, etc. Secondly, it takes on a lucid character in the form of a concrete *goal* [e.g., first to preserve and then to retrieve a certain item (group of words, phrases, or text)]. Finally, retrieval is made by paying attention to preserving the *coherence* of the item given while at the same time blocking out all extraneous associations. The subject at this point either can: (1) store and retrieve the material presented immediately; or (2) use some coding process. The essence of this entire process lies in the fact that the subject compares the results of the material retrieved with that presented. The focus of attention is on preserving its coherence while screening out all the extraneous features. The single most important factor to this entire process is attempting to make the data presented and retrieved a "closed system" (i.e., closed to all extraneous and confounding influences except the actual material preserved and coded). Corollary to this objective is avoiding any possibility of converting it over to an "open system" (i.e., a system that allows one's immediate impressions and/or associations to confound the preservation of coherence and coding of the material memorized).

NEUROPSYCHOLOGICAL METHOD

The above account given of conscious, active mnestic processes and especially of verbal memory (i.e., the memorizing and retrieval of series of words, phrases, and even whole texts) was presented as a psychological description. But now we come to the main task of this presentation by asking ourselves the following question: Can we regard the components of the whole mnestic activity as *independent units,* or are they included in the process as an indivisible whole entity that resists any attempts at separation? A strictly psychological approach dealing only with normal subjects can hardly give a complete answer to this question. Therefore, an approach using a different method has been applied to the study of this problem to obtain additional answers. One such approach is the use of the *neuropsychological method*. The origin and development of neuropsychology—a new branch of psychological science—makes use of recent advances in the fields of neurology and neurosurgery that can be applied to the study of brain–behavior relationships.

Early and precise topical diagnosis of local brain lesions (i.e., tumors, hemorrhages, traumas, etc.) became necessary in light of the insufficiency of early methods used in classical neurology. When carefully applied in diagnosis, such methods were suitable for studying sensory, motor, reflex, and muscle tone actvity, covering approximately one-third of the hemispheres of the human brain. The remaining two-thirds having to do with the organization of the highest forms of mental processs remained muted.

In a series of earlier publications, it was shown (Luria, 1966; 1970, 1973, 1976a, b) that parts of the human cortex that were closely associated with the special form of mental activity suffered in local brain lesions. Of further importance was the observation in several patients studied that they suffered in different ways when nonsimilar parts of the brain were injured. This then led to a study of higher cortical functions in man using the neuropsychological method for analysis. It was discovered that higher mental processes could be characterized as "functional systems" in which each part of the brain plays its own highly specific role. When used as a method for making a detailed analysis of psychological processes, neuropsychology can single out the basic underlying factors. This method has been used successfully during the last several decades in the analysis of functions of perception, motor activity, speech, writing, reading, calculation and problem solving, cognition, and memory. A careful study of *how* these processes are distributed in patients with local brain lesions has shown reliable results in support of our main goal—breaking down the complex processes just discussed into their component parts and singling out the main factors involved in their structure. At his point, the neuropsychological method is applied to a study of mnestic action, especially verbal memory, in an attempt to see the power and utility of this approach in yielding a detailed description and analysis of a complex structure and its process involved in psychological activity.

There is a surfeit of data in the literature to suggest that separate words have a complex semantic structure with a complex denotative and connotative meaning, and that their memorization probably includes a process that blocks the connotative meanings. It also can include approaches of choice as to the general meaning to be memorized and retrieved. The same suggestions can be applied in considering a phrase or a complex test.

The memorization task includes a selection of focus with regard to the phrase or text's "Thema" and "Rhema." At the same time, all extraneous associations (i.e., outside of the coherent or "closed" system) must be blocked.

The reconstruction of a phrase of text, as Bartlett has pointed out, includes this process of selectivity of the basic meaning, strictly adhering to the requirements of this "closed system."

The coherent verbal system, which in the case of a text includes "communication of events" and "communication of relations" described in Uppsala, Sweden, by C. Svedelilus 80 years ago (Svedelius, 1897), includes separate lexical, paradigmatic, syntagmatic, and semantic elements. All of these components are organized integrally, into this coherent system. In considering the *manner* in which the verbal communication components are organized:

1. Are all the components of a verbal communication system mentioned based on independent units?

2. Or do they become constructed from indivisible coherent wholes?

These queries directly lead to the more important, general one of "what is the psychological structure of the retention and the retrieval of the text like?" For example, can one suppose that the general meaning or sense of the text is simply the mere product of association of its separate parts, or, in the vein of the Wurzburger School, that the semantics of the whole text as to its meaning and deep emotional overtones are to a certain extent independent from separate components and should be thought of as special, psychological wholes?

A purely psychological investigative approach cannot be adequately applied to the above question. The experiments of the Wurzburger School and observation of Sir Fredric Bartlett were only able to point out that the remembering of a complex text is simply a "reconstruction" where the basic semantic meaning remains intact and is reproduced by quite different words and phrases. It is necessary to use a different approach, the neuropsychological method of investigation, to make a more detailed study of the relationship between the special components of the text (lexical, grammatical, syntactical) and its entire semantic organization for better clarity and understanding.

It is well established that the human brain can be viewed as being organized neuropsychologically into at least three basic functional blocks. The first of these blocks includes formations of: (1) the highest brain stem (thalamus, hypothalamus); (2) the limbic zone; and (3) the ascending reticular activating formation. It is responsible for the modulation of the cortical tone, which is of decisive value for the more highly specialized functional activities of the brain.

The second block includes the posterior parts of the brain, which act as an apparatus for reception, elaboration, and retention of highly specialized information. Its parts are of a modality-specific character. Whereas the temporal cortex provides the elaboration of acoustic structures (phonemes included), the parieto-occipital parts of this block are closely associated with the elaboration of the visuospatial information and with the transition from successively given stimuli to simultaneous inner cerebral schemes.

The third block includes formation of the anterior parts of the hemispheres—motor, premotor, and prefrontal parts included. Whereas the premotor parts play a decisive role in elaboration of skilled movements, kinetic melodies, and the lower parts of premotor zones of the major hemisphere (usually involving fluent speech), the prefrontal parts of this block are responsible for: (1) preservation of stable motives, plans, and programs of complex forms of behavior; and (2) the control of the realization of these plans (cf. Luria, 1966, 1973).

With all this serving as a working framework for our discussion, we can now turn to our basic question: What kind of a disorganization of complex speech processes and especially of verbal memory is seen after local lesions of one particular, circumscribed part in one of these blocks? It is highly probable that in attempting to observe principal forms of verbal (and verbal memory) disturbances in these cases, we can come closer to shedding some light on the basic question of this discussion.

As to the material of this study, we chose the analysis of retention and retrieval of comprehensible texts. These included *fables* [i.e., short texts that have both a coherent superficial meaning (for example, an event of an animal's life) as well as a coherent inner subtext or sense expressing, as a rule, some general moral or motive underlying the superficial event of the text]. Two short fables by Leo Tolstoi, which we used, serve as examples of a selected text. The first is "The Hen With the Golden Eggs." It reads as follows:

A peasant had a hen who laid golden eggs. He wanted to become rich at once and killed the hen; but he found nothing. The hen was as all hens are.

The second is "The Jackdaw and the Doves." It reads as follows:

A jackdaw heard the doves were well fed and painted itself white and came to the doves. They didn't recognize him and accepted the jackdaw. But suddenly the jackdaw yelled as he did formerly. The doves recognized him and turned him out. He returned home, but the jackdaws did not recognize him and didn't accept him.

We chose this type of verbal information, because its retention and retrieval yielded extraordinarily rich data for our analysis.

During repetition of this text, several components can be lost:

1. The subject could easily lose separate lexical items (e.g., nouns or verbs).
2. One could lose paradigmatic relations expressed by complex grammatical forms.

3. One could lose the fluency of the retrieval of the text.
4. One could lose the text as a coherent "closed system" (replacing it with a system open to all extraneous influences, impressions, or associations).

Let us now look at what kinds of disorganization were observed in patients with different local brain lesions. A normal, intact subject who either listened to or read the text was instructed to first memorize and then retrieve it. This was accomplished with hardly any difficulty. Often he used words different from the text (e.g., *blackbird* instead of *jackdaw, pushed him out* instead of *turned him out*). However, the serial position of separate elements remained intact, and the general meaning as well as the subtext (or sense) of the fable were easily retained.

A very different set of data was obtained in patients with local brain injuries, especially with lesions of the left temporal lobe. It is well known that in left temporal lobe cases, phonemic structures of words can be highly disturbed. The word loses its constancy and is often an effect of "alienation of word meaning." The word is no longer recognized, and a set of spontaneously evoked alternatives (partially equivalent in sound, morphological structure, and semantics) can be observed. These patients, instead of saying *jackdaw*, give such responses as *cornflakes* (morphologically similar, double-rooted word) or *blackbird* (semantically similar). Thus, the nominal phrases of communication become severely disturbed.

What was totally unexpected was the following observation: Patients exhibiting these kinds of defects could easily grasp the whole meaning. Even the subtext (sense) of the whole story, paradoxical dissociation of destroyed lexical elements, and preserved coherence of the whole text were observed as well. The following is one such example illustrating this observation. The patient X with a tumor in the left temporal lobe retrieved the story "The Jackdaw and the Doves" as follows:

> One... old... old spinster... met a nice young lady... and the young girls asked her: "please remain!" But then they looked at the old... spinster... and she cried "Kral! Kral!"... and they recognized she was not nice and turned her away... what was she to do?... She went... to him... No.!... to her house... and she was told, "No, you are not one of ours... go away". What is the moral of the story? You must not change; you must remain as you are!

Although all lexical components of nominal phrases are heavily disturbed, the coherency of the whole fable as to its general meaning and sense is preserved. The inner mechanisms of this kind of retrieval of the text are unknown. Partially preserved are the lexical generalizations and perhaps the prosodic components that seem to play an important role. But the *dissociation of destroyed lexical components and the coherence of the whole text that remain well preserved as a "closed system," as well as its goal-linked reconstruction, are seen to be relatively preserved, too.*

A similar picture can be observed in cases of *pure amnestic* or *semantic* aphasia associated with lesions of the infraparietal or temporo-parieto-occipital lesions of the major hemisphere. In these cases, words lose their relations to the hierarchical, paradigmatically organized systems, and the subject begins to experience difficulties in remembering separate words. The same anomalies appear in retrieval of family names, which as a rule have only a poor association with paradigmatically organized codes. In these instances, the patient tries to find the word needed and block the necessary association, which produces a situation close to the "tip-of-the-tongue" phenomenon. These patients are unable to grasp immediately the logical relations of words included in the "communication of relations" observed by Svedelius (1897). Gramatically structured phrases such as *brother's father, father's brother, a circle under a triangle,* and *the triangle under the circle* are hardly distinguishable.

The most remarkable fact in all of these cases is the patients dissociation of the highly disturbed lexical and logico-grammatical codes, while at the same time having a fully preserved grasp of the general meaning and sense of the text presented to them. Although unable to grasp immediately the logical relation between two noun components, they nevertheless try to overcome this difficulty by converting simultaneous schemes into long chains of successively organized operations. These phenomena have been described thoroughly in a special book entitled *The Man With a Shattered World* (Luria, 1972).

We followed up the cases where paradigmatically organized phonemic, lexical, or logico-grammatical components were disturbed (fluent speech and grasping the meaning and sense of the whole text were preserved). At this point, we can turn our attention to the different forms of defects where *nominal* phrases remain intact but *verbal* phrases undergo a breakdown. This form of a breakdown in verbal communication and marked defects in the retrieval of the text is associated with lesions of the lower portion of the premotor area of the major hemisphere and connections within the anterior temporal zones. The syndrome most commonly seen in these cases is strongly associated with a breakdown of "inner speech" and its predicative functions. The "telegraph style" of the reproduction of the text is the fundamental symptom observed. Patients falling into this group preserve only nominal phrases whereas verbal phrases are fractured. In trying to reproduce the whole text of the fable, "The Jackdaw and the Doves," the patient might say something like: "Oh... the jackdaw... the doves... good food... the white color... deception... a cry... " etc.

The most distinguishable feature in these patients is that only the verbal operations suffer markedly whereas the text as a coherent, "closed system" remains intact. In this group we never observed cases in which patients extended their responses beyond the limits of coherent whole meaning of the text (i.e., the text as a "closed system" is preserved). All extraneous impressions or associations are blocked, and the same dissociation described previously is seen. A breakdown of single components of speech associated with a fully preserved text as a coherent system is typically in all forms of defects described.

The second basic group of verbal memory defects in contrast to the subgroups already described presents a very different picture. This is particulary true in cases closely associated with lesions of the higher brainstem and the walls of the third ventricles, along with accompanying massive lesions of the *frontal lobes*. All components of the verbal memory (phonetic and lexical, syntactic and semantic) remain intact, but the coherent meaning of the whole text is highly disturbed. The "closed system" referred to earlier becomes a system open to extraneous influences (e.g., impressions, associations, and perseveration). The patient is unable to retrieve the whole meaning of the coherent system, losing the ability to block influences lying outside of this "closed system." These disturbances of mnestic action can be seen in "dreamy states" associated with lesions of the thalamic–hypothalamic system. It can be further observed that in patients with lesions of the frontal lobes, when stable motives and goals are broken down, neither the realization of plans and programs nor their stable control is possible.

The retrieval of the text in these cases can be disturbed in other ways as well. Sometimes, the coherent text given is replaced by the patient's immediate impressions and at other times by extraneous associations that one is unable to block. Sometimes, an inert perseveration that replaces the program of the reproduction of the text given appears. The following excerpts are presented to illustrate kinds of breakdown of the goal-linked process in the retrieval of the text.

We begin with a case in which the goal-linked mnestic activity is partly preserved but where collateral associations either become unblocked or retard blocking. Patient *A* . a scientist with a cranio-pharyngeoma involving the basal parts of the frontal lobes, tries to retrieve the fable, "The Hen with the Golden Eggs."

> A peasant. . . a small bourgeois, who liked money. . . had a hen. . . it's very nice to have poultry. . . who laid golden eggs. . . you know how precious gold is in our time of inflation. . .

It can be clearly seen that each component of the story retrieved results in a series of peripheral associations that are posteriorly blocked, giving the patient the possibility of returning to the story's coherent meaning.

In more expressed cases, this coherence is totally broken down, and the patient, beginning retrieval of the text, comes under the influence of immediately present impressions, unblocked collateral associations, or inert perseverations. Here is one such example. Patient *B*, a man of 46, was analyzed by a lady-physician who is the author's assistant. He was asked to retrieve the fable, "The Jackdaw and the Doves," and begins his story as follows:

A jackdaw...jackdaw,...jacky...the girl Jacky came to the Neurosurgical Institute...and the surgeon fell in love with her...and proposed to her...

It is evident that the "closed system" of the fable has broken down due to immediate impressions on the part of the patient. The "jackdaw" becomes "Jacky" (in Russian, "Galka" has two meanings: a kind of bird and a girl's name). Instead of retrieving the story, the patient slides into a series of irrelevant impressions: "the girl Jacky," "the Neurosurgical Institute," "the surgeon," etc.

Other patients in this group tend towards sliding into extraneous associations, and the coherent "closed system" becomes disrupted but in a different manner. Patient *C*, age 40, is a teacher with a massive tumor of the frontal lobes who was asked to retrieve the fable, "The Jackdaw and the Doves." He starts to tell the story in the following way:

The jackdaw learned that the doves were well fed and came to their family...they didn't accept the jackdaw...he flew to the forest, and began to fly around, asking "where is the banquet?"

When asked what is the sense of this story, he replied:

It is difficult to say. Perhaps they led the jackdaw with plenty of knowledge...which had no basic significance...and they let him fly around... the jackdaw went to the primary school...

It can be seen that the coherent "closed system" has broken down but in instances due to the influences of collateral associations of the patient's former experience.

Perhaps the most remarkable case was where all the factors resulting in the breakdown of the coherent system mentioned were accompanied by an inert repetition of some sections of the story. Patient *K*, a student with a severe trauma of both frontal lobes, was asked to retrieve and tell the story, "The Jackdaw and the Doves." He began this task as follows:

The jackdaw learned that the doves were well fed. He came to the doves...there he had his nest...He flew from his nest...and circled around...and came back to the nest...and flew again...and he became exhausted [a reflection of the patient's own exhaustion]...and he came back to his nest...and he recovered...and he flew again...and he became exhausted...and came back to the nest...

All these factors [i.e., immediate impressions ("he became exhausted"), unblocked collateral associations, and, last but not least, repetitions of single elements that became inert stereotypes] resulted in a breakdown of the text's coherent system entering into the retrieval process.

CONCLUSION

The description presented above provides a clear example of how the neuropsychological method can be used as a tool in the study and analysis of retrieving the meaning and sense of a coherent text involving verbal memory. As has been shown, lesions of different parts of the human brain can result in the breakdown of different "links" of mnestic activity and the retrieval of verbal content based on a text's meaning.

A most fundamental conclusion we were able to draw from the data presented is that different components of mnestic processes and memorization of a coherent text can suffer independently to a significant degree.

In lesions of the posterior parts of the brain (including the inferior region of the premotor area of the major hemipshere), certain components and *operations* of verbal memory (e.g., phonemic, lexical, morphological, syntactic, and semantic) can all be affected while the whole text as a coherently "closed system" remains intact. On the contrary, regarding lesions of the deep structures of the brain associated with "dreamy states" as well as in massive lesions of the frontal lobes, the situation is just the reverse. Single components and operations of verbal memory remain intact while the goal-linked mnestic activity resulting in the retrieval of the coherent text suffers. The "closed system" thus gives way to one that is open to all extraneous influences.

All that has been said can be applied to the opening of new vistas for studies concerning the process of active verbal memory and analysis of the various factors involved in this complex psychological proces. It is hoped that these initial efforts will stimulate a series of further experiments that will continue to show the richness, diversity, and complexity of the process just studied.

ACKNOWLEDGMENTS

The author wishes to express his thanks to Dr. Lawrence Majorski for editing the English version of this manuscript.

REFERENCES

Bartlett, F. C. *Remembering: A study in experimental and social psychology.* Cambridge, England: Cambridge University Press, 1932.

Bergson, H. L. *Matiere et memoire*. Paris: Presses Universitaires de France, 1896.

Leontiev, A. N. *Development of memory*. Moscow: Krupskaya Academy of Communist Education Press, 1930.

Luria, A. R. *Higher cortical functions in man*. New York: Basic Books, 1966.

Luria, A. R. *Traumatic aphasia*. The Hague: Mouton, 1970.

Luria, A. R. *The man with a shattered world*. New York: Basic Books, 1972.

Luria, A. R. *The working brain*. Middlesex: Penguin, 1973.

Luria, A. R. *The neuropsychology of memory*. Washington, D. C.: Winston, 1976. (a)

Luria, A. R. *Basic problems of neurolinguistics*. The Hague: Mouton, 1976. (b)

Svedelius, C. *L'analyse du language*. Doctoral dissertation, University of Uppsala, 1897.

V REALITY PERSPECTIVES

14

Organization and Repetition: Organizational Principles With Special Reference to Rote Learning

George Mandler
University of California, San Diego

THEORY AND DATA

The Background of Organization

One of the motivating sources of modern cognitive psychology of memory is the concept of organization. Organization theory does not as yet have well-defined postulates, but it has an honorable history. In modern times it is anchored in the contributions of the Gestalt theorists, who taught us that organizations (the structures relating constituent elements to each other) have characteristics that are different from the sum of the characteristics of the constituent elements; or, to put it correctly, that the whole is *different* from the sum of its parts. Köhler, Wertheimer, and Koffka showed us that structure may not only be perceived in the environment but also imposed on it and particularly that productive thinking is the result of the discovery and use of these organizations or structures. Katona (1940) produced a sense of closure with his book on organization and memory, though the closure was also enforced by the predominant behaviorist and stimulus–response thinking that surrounded his work 40 years ago.

Whereas there are a number of psychologists who could be given full credit for bringing organizational constructs into the more recent history of experimental psychology, my favorite candidate is W. R. Garner, who reminded us that structure is definable, measurable, and useful and—even more important—avoided neobehaviorist hairsplitting about meanings and little hidden stimuli and responses by reasserting one of the main gestaltist postulates that *structure is meaning*.

My initial interest in writing this paper concerned what organization theory might have to say in a practical sense and particularly how it might address problems of so-called rote learning and teaching. But as I returned to primarily structural considerations of memory, I discovered that these general principles are helpful in putting order into a variety of different areas of current memory theory and research.

In what follows I shall first briefly allude to the various phenomena that seem to be subsumed under general organizational principles. I present some principles of memorization that are relevant first to the continuum of structures that process, elaborate, and store memorial materials and second to the processes whereby these structures are effectively integrated. I then return to the experimental literature and show how these principles apply to problems of repetition. Given this hopefully reasonable integration of the field, I then address the problem of rote learning in particular, first to find proponents and influences of rote learning concepts, then to reject the concept as such, and finally to make some suggestions for the application of repetition and elaboration to problems of learning and teaching.

I begin by describing two dimensions of organization that I have found useful in interpreting a variety of different, often disparate appearing, phenomena. The first dimension, which I call the *integration dimension*, refers to the degree to which the to-be-remembered items form functional *units* of thought and/or action; a highly integrated item is one in which the constituent elements of the response or action form a highly coherent unit. The second dimension of organization, which I call the *elaborative dimension*, refers to the degree of interrelatedness of the to-be-remembered item with other units in memory. Thus, integration measures the *within-unit organization*, whereas elaboration measures the *between-unit organization*.

The integrative dimension corresponds to what in another time and another language was called "response integration" (cf. Hovland & Kurtz, 1952; Mandler, 1954; Underwood & Schulz, 1960).

Following these earlier attempts, I will assume that the degree of integration is primarily a function of the frequency of repetition. The more frequently a memory unit is accessed, the more integrated that unit will become. This is in contrast to the elaborative dimension in which frequency of repetition appears *not* to be a factor. I have elsewhere suggested that free recall is primarily a function of the number of stable structures that can be imposed on the material, either in sorting experiments (Mandler, 1967b, 1977) or in list learning where lists are structured around certain focal concepts (Mandler & Graesser, 1976; Mandler, Worden, & Graesser, 1974). In these experiments, degree of elaboration rather than number of repetitions seem to be the operative factor.

Perhaps the most influencial recent step in focusing on the elaborative aspect of organization is that taken by Craik and his associates in their emphasis on "depth of processing." In its most elegant form, the notion of "depth" has been identified rather directly with our notion of the elaborative dimension. I shall return to this topic later. For now we can assume that the depth of processing principle (i.e., that the deeper the processing, the easier the recall) can be restated to mean that the more elaborate the encoding of a unit, the better its eventual retrieval.

Perhaps the experimental evidence that best illustrates the distinction I am making here grows out of the work contrasting the effects of maintenance and elaboration rehearsal by Bjork and by Craik and his colleagues. Woodward, Bjork, and Jongeward (1973), for example, showed that merely maintaining an item without the need or intention to store it for future retrieval produces no gain for future recall but does show regular increments in recognition as a function of rehearsal time. On the other hand, elaborated material shows effects both on recall and recognition. It is this kind of demonstration that lies at the heart of the distinctions to be made between these two kinds of organization. In the following section, I develop the characterization of these two dimensions more completely and show how this view can organize a wide variety of results in the experimental literature.

Before proceeding, a comment is necessary on the unit of analysis that is to be addressed. In the dimensional analyses to follow, the unit is always defined by the target material. What is "to-be-remembered" determines the amount of elaboration and integration that will be necessary for retrieval; thus the unit may be a word, a sentence, or a story. In fact, under some circumstances the target unit will change in the course of acquisition, as in the case of the learning of a series where the target changes from some small constituent of the series to ever larger sections or chunks. Or, in a list of words, the individual items may be integrated by repetition and elaborated by the relations among words; at *the same time* as the relations among the words constitute the integration of the *list*, a discovery of the categorical structure of the list represents its elaboration.

Two Dimensions of Organization

The organization of to-be-remembered material varies independently on two dimensions. One of these is the *integrative dimension*, which refers to intrastructural integration; the other is the *elaborative dimension*, which refers to the degree of interstructural organization.[1]

Figure 14.1 shows these two orthogonal dimensions of organization, with one dimension describing the increasing elaboration of structures and the

---

[1]Shortly after the completion of this chapter, Barbara Hayes–Roth published her paper (1977) on knowledge-assembly theory. The similarities between her approach and mine are highly gratifying.

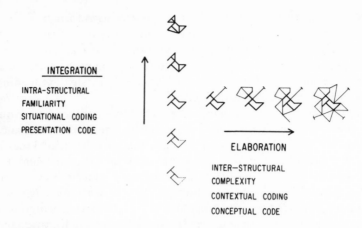

FIG. 14.1.   The two dimensions of organization shown in a graphic analogy. For the elaboration dimension, a single structure is related increasingly to other external structures and becomes part of a more extended structural system. For the integration dimension, the nine nodes are at first weakly connected and become more strongly connected. The verbal descriptions for the two dimensions show four sets of previously used distinctions that map into integration and elaboration.

other showing the increasing integration or compactness of these structures. As an *aide memoire*, I have also shown some other concepts that could be applied to these two organizational dimensions. I now turn to a more detailed discussion of these dimensions, with the understanding that I cannot, nor do I intend to, present anything that could be called a theory of organization. Our knowledge of structural relationships is relatively virginal, though we have all used the concept fairly successfully for some years. The major stumbling block towards a predictive theory is that we have no adequate metric or algebra of structures. Primarily for these reasons my discussions will be more allusive than precise and more programmatic than theoretical.

Integration.   Increasing integration of a mental structure is in part related to the increasing invariance of its relational components. For example, when we first learn a word (either as a child or some foreign word as an adult), neither the action component of speaking that word nor the representational component of mentally manipulating that item is invariant from the start. I refer in this case specifically not to any change in the class of components that are used in building up a specific structure but rather to changes in the relations among the components of the unit. Motor skills are a nice example of how this internal integration proceeds. One could argue that we often know the types of movements necessary for some complex skill (such as bicycle riding or playing tennis) but that the specific tokens used in execution of these skills may vary from time to time and that the relation among them has not yet become predictable. Thus, structural integration refers to such phenomena as structural invariance and structural compactness. It is seen frequently in such phenomena as the acquisition of new or foreign words, motor skill learning, and serial learning. It also occurs, however, in the integration of very complex mental structures such as language or the grammar of action, the structure of a novel or a play that becomes better and better "known."

If one asks what kind of variables contribute to the integration of cognitive or action structures, two old friends become immmediately useful. I refer here to *repetition* and *reinforcement*. The successful repetition of a particular structure contributes to its increasing integration and compactness. "Successful repetition" of course refers to the fact that not only is a particular structure repeated but that it produces certain predictable outcomes internally or in the external world (what our associative friends have called "reinforcement").

If the internal integration of a particular target unit is the primary index of the integrative dimension, a secondary integrative effect is probably more important for an understanding of memorial processes. Sheer repetition (or maintenance rehearsal) of previously well integrated items also produces integrative effects. Both in the laboratory and in everyday experience, the target material to be remembered consists of words, sentences, phrases, visual configuration, etc.—all of which have either been previously integrated into functional units (as in the case of words) or at least present very few, if any, novel structural configurations to the rememberer (as in phrases or sentences).

Repetition of these well-integrated units apparently has the same kind of consequence as the integration of the unit itself. Repetition is the major functional variable in such integration and "recognition" its most visible product. As a first step in understanding such second-order integrative processes, it is useful to remember that structural development is a hierarchical recursive process. Once a particular unit has been integrated and functions as a single chunk, then it can become a node in another, higher order unit. A phoneme becomes part of a word, a word part of a phrase, a phrase becomes the unit of a sentence or a paragraph. Similarly, structural rules that order phonemes or those that order words in sentences are transferable and applicable to new words and new sentences.

What are these integrations that result from the repetition of words, phrases, and sentences? Various attempts to describe the process are implicit in the labels that have been used for it. "Occurrence information" indicates some recent encounter; "familiarity" probably best describes the phenomenal result of recent and frequent encounters; "presentation code" summarizes a host of possible local and highly specific encodings; and "situational coding" refers to some structural integration between the to-be-remembered unit and the physical situation in which it was encountered (cf. Fig. 14.1).

There have been few theoretical attempts to explain these effects. A notable one is by Atkinson and Wescourt (1975), who ascribe the familiarity effect to the access of the conceptual store by the purely perceptual code. Every time a conceptual store node of a particular unit is accessed, its "activity" is raised and its "strength" incremented. Although this is an appealing notion and explains many of the repetition effects, it fails to explain why temporary, brief, experimental effects can overrride the repetition effects of the natural language that must be several orders of magnitude larger.

Although I do not believe that such descriptive "strength" notions are adequate, there are several possible mechanisms, any one or all of which may be useful explanatory devices. One such mechanism involves the distinction between the target material behaving in a unitary fashion (as a node) and the character of its internal structure. When accessing a word, only its "chunked" representation (the "conceptual node") is necessary in order to store it, elaborate it, or to produce it. Repeated presentations make possible attention to its internal structure and even may restore internal aspects that have been "lost" or misconstructed over time. Concretely, repeating a word, for example, draws attention to its spelling, its phonemic constitution, pronunciation, etc. Repetition of such well-integrated items might increment the original integration or emphasize some specific structural characteristics internal to the unit.[2] To the extent that we "know more" about an item as a result of such processes, it will appear more "familiar" on a subsequent encounter with its copy. Similarly, to the extent that such an encounter requires a pattern-matching procedure, such a match will be more successful, the more detailed information about the internal structure of the item has been recently stored. And finally, one of the more likely intrastructural candidates for identification and storage by repetition is the temporal–spatial ordering of the constituent elements. Spatial orderings are likely to demand priority attention. Thus, in the *short term*, presentation and repetition of sequences of to-be-remembered units will enhance serial order information. Such a process could account for the apparent independent storage of serial order information in short-term memory experiments (e.g., Baddeley & Hitch, 1974; Estes, 1972; Murdock, 1974).

Another process that can account for the effects of repetition of previously integrated units involves the structural integration of the target and its immediate situational (physical) context (cf. Woodward, Bjork, & Jonge-

---

[2]There exists additional evidence that sheer repetition focuses on the internal structure of verbal material. Research on semantic satiation has shown that extensive "rote" repetition of words not only changes the perceptual character of the words but also changes the extrastructural (meaning) characteristics immediately following the repetition task. These findings indicate that under these artificial conditions, the enhancement of integration takes place at the cost of some elaborative features.

ward, 1973). Such a temporary integration between the unit and some situational cue has the advantage of being independent of frequency effects in the natural languages as well as being situation specific. The difficulty with the concept is that it is difficult to distinguish from contextual effects that are clearly elaborative. I appeal to a process that makes the target unit a part of the physical, perceptual situation, just as a letter is a part of a word or a handle part of a door. It is different from the process that identifies a word as a member of category or a door as something made by a carpenter. To use another analogy, the item "belongs" to the situation and is identified as familiar, but it is not elaborated in that context. The integration of an item and a situation is the same process that integrates phonemes into a new word, but it is different from the elaborative process that relates the word to a sentence. For such situational integration to occur, we need make no reference to the "meaning" (interstructural elaboration) of either the word or the situation.

These two processes permit the extension of the integration concept to already integrated units. They also permit a distinction between familiarity and frequency effects in the integrative sense and the derivative effects that are found in the phenomena of frequency *judgments* and list differentiation (cf. Hintzman, 1976).

Structural Elaboration.   Structures vary in the degree to which they are part of another more general structural system or, specifically, in the degree to which at the time of encoding (or at the later time of retrieval) they are part of a structural network connecting them to other structures that may be coordinate, subordinate, or superordinate. Thus, a particular motor skill practiced in a variety of different contexts, but essentially context independent, may have relatively little interstructural complexity. Knowing what a particular word (structure) rhymes with represents a little more interstructural complexity, in that it is related to some rhyming rule or even specifically to some other words with which it rhymes. High levels of interstructual complexity are shown in what we know about our friend Joe, things that have to do with contextual relations under which we have known him, his relationships to other people in the world as a whole, his jobs, likes, dislikes, and so forth. From the point of view of memory research and theory, we may sometimes encode many things only for purposes of a particular situational use and therefore only in terms of some intrastructural relation (such as the question of how a word is spelled). But we need to encode most to-be-remembered material in terms of more complex relations such as what particular category the word is a member of, or what sentences it plays a part in, or how it fits into the structure of a particular story.

We shall have occasion to return to the different kinds of procedures that produce organizational development in the integrative dimension. As a start, we can say that the integrative dimension will be entered and incremented as a function of the current state of the particular structure, repetitions of that structure, and attention to internal characteristics of that structure (such as spelling or simple serial ordering). When we enter the elaborative dimension, individuals will be instructed (or contextually constrained) to process and elaborate the to-be-remembered unit in terms of varying degrees of interstructural relations—when we are instructed to find a rhyme, or a category for a particular word, to remember a sentence, or to parse a story.

The graphical illustration in Fig. 14.1 shows how a particular structure may be related to other units and/or to other systems of organization. The more embedding of the target unit in other structures and the more relations exist to other structures, the more complex and elaborate is the organizational encoding of the unit.

For purposes of illustration, the structures on the elaborative dimension in Fig. 14.1 are all shown at a relative high degree of integration. I shall discuss shortly the relation between the integrative and the elaborative dimensions and the retrieval space defined by them. For the time being, it is important to note that complex structures, just as simple structures, may be well integrated or not. Clearly, for example, some complex motor skills may at first consist of many related constituents but eventually end up as a well-integrated whole. As a corollary, these integrated structures may end up as single accessible and functional nodes on some other complex structure. In other words, we shall often find a complex coaction of the two dimensions.

Relations Between Integration and Elaboration.   An appealing example of the interaction between the two dimensions can be found in the 1 + 1 method of serial learning (Mandler & Dean, 1969). Figure 14.2 shows the results of an experiment where the participants were given a 50-word list, 1 word at a time. Thus on Trial 1, Word 1 was presented and recalled; on Trial 2, Word 2 was presented, and Words 1 and 2 were recalled; and on Trial n, Word n was presented, and the recall of all words from 1 to n was required. Of particular interest are the data in panel B, which show that new words (beyond the immediate memory span) occur at first in variable output positions but eventually settle down to invariant positions as they become integrated into the series. Panel A shows that performance becomes stable at or near the time when the integration of a particular subset has been achieved.

These experimentss also demonstrate the constant interplay of the two dimensions. Whereas from one point of view the ongoing process can be seen as the integration of larger and larger serial structures, the addition of new items also elaborates the existing ones and provides new interstructural connections. Similarly, the experiment shows the changing definition of the to-be-remembered unit from a single word to a serial structure (cf. also Rumelhart, 1977). The particular task employed here apperars to create an almost optimal learning situation. As integration and elaboration are both

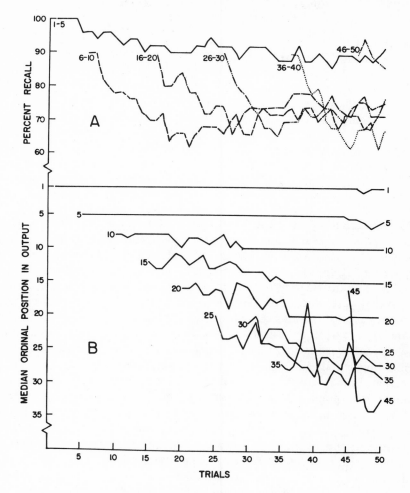

FIG. 14.2.   Recall and output position of new items added in an incremental serial learning task (1 + 1). A total of 50 words was presented, one item on each trial with the requirement to recall that item and all previous ones. Panel A shows percent correct performance on successive trials for selected sets of five words added to the list. Panel B shows the output position of every fifth word added to the list for all trials subsequent to its input. The graph shows the median position in the output of all subjects of the *n*th word for trials *n* to 50.

used in an interactive process in this task, acquisition is rapid and produces unusually high levels of memory performance. I argue later that the analysis of tasks in terms of optimal integration and elaboration can promote more effective performance in general as well as improved learning situations.

Figure 14.3 shows the retrieval space generated by the two dimensions. At the time of encoding, original acquisition, learning, or first encounter with the particular event, the operations performed by the remembering individual

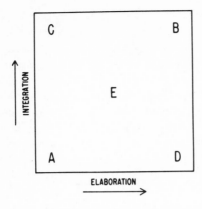

FIG. 14.3. The two-dimensional retrieval space with selected instances A to E. See text for discussion.

determine the location of the target item for future retrieval. It is useful to remind psychologists who hope to develop theories of memory applicable to people in the real world that the design preferred by nature is often called "incidental" learning. Most of people's lives are not conducted under conditions of instructions to memorize a particular event; rather, we retrieve events that were experienced under a variety of different conditions, typically without such instructions. As it has already been shown experimentally (cf. Mandler, 1967b) that instructions to organize material are equivalent to instructions to memorize, it might help if we stopped considering memory as being "incidental" and instead started talking about the organization of experience and its effect on retrieval. In terms of experimental and theoretical analyses, this point is important because where and how a particular event will be located in the memory space will be determined by the conditions under which it is experienced and the implicit and explicit instructions that nature (and experimenters) give to the experiencing individual. However, contrary to the encoding specificity principle, we need to know not only how a particular event was encoded at the time of its encounter but also what possible retrieval cues are available (over and beyond the encoding cues) at the time of recall or recognition. For example, I may be given some important new data by a colleague at a meeting, and I may code it as "Ebbinghaus told me that repetition did not affect learning." The structure of that particular information is importantly encoded with respect to Ebbinghaus, because it was surprising that he would: (a) report that kind of an observation, or (b) report anything at all in 1977. When telling a student about those findings sometime later, it would be easy for me to tell her that it was Ebbinghaus who gave me that information. Now consider the same data heard at a very busy and crowded scientific meeting in the course of an extensive paper session. In attempting to preserve all the valuable information to be gleaned from the meeting, I might simply code the information without paying any particular attention to the author of the paper (assuming, of course, that it is not Ebbinghaus). At some later time, I again report the data to a student, and he asks for more information so that he can obtain further details from the author. My first response is, "I don't remember who the author was." But I then might go through an extensive search process generating candidates, authors, eliminating some because I remember some other paper that they in fact delivered, focusing on others because it is highly likely that they would generate these kinds of data; and I might eventually come up with one or two possible names. These examples illustrate that at the time of retrieval we may have more information available than was coded at the time of presentation and that the whole armamentarium of long-term memory may be brought into play in order to retrieve a particular target event.

It is important to note that both dimensions require retrieval of sorts. Neither elaborative nor integrative/situational information is "contained in the stimulus." Even in the classical "recognition" experiment, we need to retrieve both kinds of information about a particular target item. There is, however, one major distinction between these two retrievals, specifically with respect to their automaticity. Posner and his associates have been very successful in making the distinction between processes that are performed in the "automatic" or in the "conscious" mode. Processes in the automatic mode occur without intention or awareness and do not interfere with ongoing mental activity (cf. Posner & Snyder, 1975; also, LaBerge & Samuels, 1974). It appears that integrative information (the processing of a word, for example) is automatically available as soon as a target item has been registered and the appropriate address for that particular structual configuration has been found in long-term storage. Automaticity implies: First, the retrieval and decoding occur automatically in the sense that the mere presentation of the item (and attention to it, of course) generates the integrated code, and such generation is essentially impervious to either positive or negative instructions on the issue (we cannot tell a subject to notice or not to notice the familiarity of some event). Second, the retrieval of *this* kind of information requires very little from a limited capacity system. Apart from the amount of conscious effort or capacity required in paying attention to the item as such, this "retrieval" process itself requires no conscious capacity. In contrast, elaborative structural information requires increased conscious capacity and effort, probably increasing with the elaborateness of the structural information in which the target item is involved (cf. Atkinson & Wescourt, 1975; Mandler, 1975b). To the extent that there might be gradients of capacity needs on the two dimensions, it is likely that capacity requirements decrease as the integrative dimension increases, whereas capacity requirements increase as the elaborative dimension increases.

As far as the two-dimensional retrieval space is concerned, we can now consider the various structural manipulations and their expected effect on retrieval. I elaborate later what is assumed here—namely, that in the "recognition" paradigm the first access is by way of integrative (familiarity) information. If that information is insufficient, a second access to "recognition" is provided by retrieval processes. Figure 14.3 shows some specific cases:

1. The two most obvious cases are A and B. An item located at A would have a very low degree of structure on both dimensions, whereas an item located at B would have a high degree of structure on both dimensions. Clearly we would expect practically no retrieval for A items, and this should hold true both for recognition and recall tests. On the other hand, B items will be easily recalled, because they have a high degree of structural elaboration and presumably many different access routes to their retrieval; they are also highly integrated items and therefore would be "recognized" without any subsequent retrieval attempts.

2. C items are interesting, because they are highly integrated but have relatively little elaboration. We return to these cases in particular in our discussion of repetition, but for the time being we can note that typically these items have undergone extensive maintenance rehearsal; but there has been no attempt to elaborate the coding or to relate them to other kinds of structures.

3. D items, on the other hand, have received relatively little integration but extensive elaboration. Assuming they are not rejected immediately because of the invocation of a low criterion on the familiarity–integration dimension, it should be possible to retrieve units in this category. These are, for example, items in a free-recall test that are generated on the basis of conceptual search processes but that are essentially indistinguishable from conceptually related distractors. In the real-world situation, one might imagine a student being able to recall a class of chemical formulas but being unable to distinguish which of that class was the correct one that was presented in a lecture. These kinds of codings presumably give rise to many of the errors in multiple-choice tests. There is evidence that items like this, in a recognition test, would receive very long reaction time as against the short reaction times produced by B or C items (cf. Mandler & Boeck, 1974).

4. Items designated as E are interesting, because they show an interplay between the two dimensions. In recall, these items may not be immediately retrieved but may well become candidate items following generation based on some conceptual rule; and they are then, in most cases, correctly checked on the basis of their integrative value. In a recognition test, these items would not immediately be called "old" on the basis of their evaluative dimension but might be recognized as "old" following some retrieval check.

The Organization of Memory

It is commonplace that the probability that some particular piece of information can be retrieved is a function of the organization of the item at the time of presentation (encoding) and the codes or cues presented at the time of retrieval. The most extreme form of this position is Tulving's encoding specificity principle, which says that there exists a perfect symmetry between the two (Tulving & Thomson, 1973). Only those cues or codes used at the time of presentation will be effective at the time of retrieval. However, because the principle quite properly defines these codes and cues in terms of the remembering person's mental organization, it is questionable whether the principle is testable. Given that a particular cue is not "presented" at the time of encoding, it can be argued that its effectiveness at the time of retrieval may be due to the fact that the individual performed the encoding covertly without being told to do so. Conversely, not presenting an effective cue (that had been encoded) at the time of retrieval seems not to prevent retrieval if the individual remember covertly produces the cue and recalls the target item. Because there is some evidence that a definition of encoding and cueing in terms of presentation by the experimenter is inadequate, we must abandon the promised land of simple principles and return to the complexities of the human mind.

I believe that we must accept a multiaccess and multichecking mode of memory retrieval. To put it simply, there is a variety of ways in which material can be coded at the time of presentation; there is an equally large number of ways in which material can be retrieved. Furthermore, if the retrieval produced units or items with uncertain status (e.g., low confidence of prior presentation), then checking processes must be available to examine these candidate units (cf. Miller, 1962, for an earlier advocacy of this view).

Storage, retrieval, and checking mechanisms can draw on all possible dimensions of memory organization. The presentation and conceptual codes that we have advocated in the past are one such example. Items presented for recognition are automatically checked for familiarity; if they fail to reach some criterial value, retrieval mechanisms are invoked to determine that item's retrievability. If successful, the item is called "old." In the discussion to follow, I restrict myself to a double access model based on integrative and elaborative information only.

Memory phenomena in the real world abound with examples of double and even multiple access retrievals. For example, consider the "recognition" of somebody's face as "familiar" but not knowing who the person is until one has gone through elaborate contextual and generative retrieval processes. Conversely, trying to remember the name of the hotel one stayed in the last time one visited a particular town may be aided by consulting a list of the town's motels (generating candidate items) until one finds a "familiar" name. Other dimensions that may be used to provide informational access include problem solving and inferential and deductive processes. For example, I know that I cannot give somebody directions in the streets of Uppsala within five minutes of my first arrival in the city. Similarly, I do not start a search for my telephone number in Toronto during 1959 until I can determine whether I lived there during that year.

Recall and Recognition.   Most memory tasks require both integration and elaboration. In fact, most tasks are best described in terms of some vector in the memory space shown in Fig. 14.3. The recognition–recall distinction illustrates this interaction. The notion that "recognition" tests involve at least two processes, and specifically that they require some kind of retrieval, goes back at least to Muller (1913). When we discovered that categorical structures not only determined recall (Mandler, 1967b) but also recognition, we suggested a dual access process whereby recognition depends either on occurrence information (cf. Bower, Lesgold, & Tieman, 1969) or on retrieval processes when the occurrence access is inadequate (Mandler, 1972; Pearlstone, Mandler, & Koopmans, 1969). A more elegant version of this process was advanced by Atkinson and Juola (1974).

In general, the distinction between recall and recognition is a remnant of vague, common-language usage, and it is difficult to find a useful and serviceable *psychological* distinction that can survive the challenge of boundary exemplars (cf. Linton, 1975; Mandler, 1976; Tulving, 1976). One can rescue the terminology by using the terms to describe experimental conditions such that a presentation of a physical copy of the to-be-remembered items is a necessary and sufficient condition for calling a task a "recognition test." However, we must then remind ourselves that both recall and recognition tests involve retrieval processes that have been variously considered to be recognition and recall processes. I now illustrate the complexity of the processes involved in the two kinds of tests with respect to two traditional experimental paradigms, word list and paired-associate acquisition.

Following the presentation of a *list* of words, a *recall test* involves at least the following series of tests:

1. Retrieval of focal semantic items that organize the list (cf. Mandler & Graesser, 1976) or category concepts in the case of categorized lists.
2. Retrieval of items using the cues generated in Step 1; this step depends on the degree of structural elaboration performed during input.
3. Generation of additional candidate items based either on the organization of the list in terms of subject-imposed focal nodes or in terms of the organizing categories. This step appears to be optional but will be carried out if appropriate instructions are supplied (cf. Rabinowitz, Mandler, & Patterson, 1977).
4. A check of the candidate items for familiarity (integrative dimension); output then depends on some criterial test.

On the other hand, a "recognition" test for *list* items involves the presentation to the subject of copies of the original items as well as related or unrelated distractors. The test sequence becomes:

1. A test for situational "strength" based on integrative factors. If the item exceeds some critical value, it is called "old." There may be another low criterion such that if the item falls below that level, it is called "new" (Atkinson & Juola, 1974).

2. Items that fail the tests in Step 1 are subjected to a retrieval check; are they retrievable given the mechanisms used for free recall? Steps 1 and 2 from the "recall" test are initiated; and if the item is retrieved, it is called "old."

One interesting consequence of this sequence is to observe "recognition" tests when the integrative dimension is essentially uninformative. Given the rather low level of integration usually produced in laboratory experiments, we would expect these values (the familiarity) to decay fairly rapidly and "recognition" to depend primarily on the two processes in Step 2 of the "recognition" test. In fact, elaborative organizational variables are more effective in recognition 1 week after presentation than they are in an immediate test (cf. Mandler, Pearlstone, & Koopmans, 1969, for verbal material; Mandler & Ritchey, 1977, for visual material). Similarly, in the delayed "recognition" of categorized lists, the hit rate for old items drops slightly; but the false-alarm rate for categorically related distractors increases dramatically (Rabinowitz, Mandler & Patterson, 1977).

In the *paired-associate* paradigm, we require *recall* of the complete pair, given presentation of one member of the pair. The structural representation that we assume here involves the holistic storage of the pair, i.e., the pair is stored as a unit structured by the relational coding of the two words (cf. Mandler, 1970). Recall involves:

1. Registration of the retrieval cue, provided by the experimenter.

2. A search process for a unit (a pair) of which the presented item is a member. Given the typical instructions given to the experimental participants, this retrieval process is often strongly directional. We know that semantic generational strategies are not usually invoked (Tulving & Thomson, 1973). On the other hand, there is evidence for some structural organization of left-hand vs. right-hand members of pairs (Segal & Mandler, 1976), and some search strategies might involve these organizations.

In the case of "*recognition*" there is a number of possible tests that could be invoked—specifically, of the pairs or of either one of the members of the pair. The one that has attracted most attention recently involves "recognition" of the B member of the A–B pair. Such a test involves:

1. A test of the presented items in terms of integrative familiarity, invoking one or two criteria.

2. For those B items that fail to be "recognized" on the basis of the integrative dimension, a search process will be initiated. As should be obvious

from the above, this search process will invoke an attempt to find a "pair" of which B is a part. Failure to find such a structure results in failure to recognize that item.

It follows from the above that the recall of B (given A) involves a different access problem than the recognition of B, requiring the accessibility of A. We have shown extensively that the so-called phenomenon of recognition failure (Watkins & Tulving, 1975)—where B can be recalled but not recognized—is essentially a function of the failure to retrieve the A–B pair, given B (Rabinowitz, Mandler & Barsalou, 1977).

It should be obvious from the foregoing examples that there is no simple theoretical distinction between recognition and recall; that one cannot either accept or reject encoding specificity as a simple principle on this evidence; nor can one accept a generation–recognition hypothesis as a basic retrieval principle (Kintsch, 1970) or reject it out of hand (Tulving, 1976). In summary, recognition and recall tasks involve information from both organizational dimensions. For any particular task, the balance between the two will favor one or the other dimension. Thus recognition tasks frequently but by no means always draw heavily on the integrative dimension. The analysis presented here avoids the error of identifying a particular class of *tasks* with specific psychological *processes*.

Depth of Processing and Structural Elaboration. The organizational view of memory was significantly strengthened with the advent of the depth of processing research initiated by Craik and his collaborators (e.g., Craik & Lockhart, 1972). Both points of view, organizational and depth, have stressed the mechanisms and processes that are responsible for memory phenomena; and both have been essentially orthogonal to the multistore view of human memory. In fact, the depth of processing research has undermined our hopes for the multistore view.

Some of the proponents of depth of processing have not been quite as ready as I have been to see the parallel between these two points of view. We have always maintained with Craik and Tulving (1975) that "the operations carried out on the material, not the intention to learn, as such, detemine retention [p. 269]." But there is a contrast when Craik and Tulving note that it is "now possible to entertain the hypothesis that optimal processing of individual words, *qua* individual words, is sufficient to support good recall [p. 270]." That is in an inadequate and misleading analysis. Whereas a single word is *presented* to the subject, subjects are told what organizational processes they are to use in terms of the structures to which the word is to be *related*.

On the other hand, it was exactly an extension of the depth of processing view, such as presented by Craik and Tulving (1975), that made it possible to see the obvious connection to organizational concepts. Craik and Tulving modified the original depth of processing notions and the implication that processing must proceed serially from "shallow" to "deep" processing by suggesting instead the concept of elaboration or spread of processing. They note that although the verbal stimulus may be identified as a particular word, the encoding of that word is elaborated by the context of additional contextual and semantic encodings. They conclude that memory performance "depends on the elaborateness of the final encoding [p. 291]." Consistent with the necessity for "good" structures, they note that their experimental results insist that a more elaborate structure will only increase retrievability of a target item if the "target stimulus is compatible with the context and can thus form an integrated encoded unit with it [p.291]." This rephrasing of the structural point of view says that only when an item can be embedded in the relationships required by a particular structure will that embedding improve accessibility.

If we look at the memory space in Fig. 14.3, the elaborative dimension (the abscissa) is equivalent to the elaboration or spread of processing advocated by Craik. It is the elaborateness of the structure in which a target unit is embedded that will determine it accessibility. It is not what the subject *does* with the material that is remembered (cf. Craik & Tulving, 1975), but rather it is the product of such manipulations that is remembered.

At the same time we can answer questions about the second dimension and its effect on the elaboration or depth of processing notion. Whereas Craik and Lockhart originally suggested that repeating the same operation of processing code should not significantly affect subsequent retrieval, there are now data available that suggest that repeated encodings (at the same depth) do improve subsequent retrieval (Craik & Tulving, 1975, Experiments 3 and 4; Nelson, 1977). There are two ways in which such repeated encodings may improve retrieval; first, having performed a particular encoding operation on a particular target item once, subjects may have "extra time" to perform some *other* elaboration of the item; second, and more important, sheer repetition of the target word may increase integrative aspects of the target word and thus move the target item up the ordinate of our space. The most likely increase in accessibility is probably some vector that increases the value on both dimensions.

The double access model presented here also makes some specific predictions about the use of different kinds of retrieval cues. For example, the effect of repetition depends on what is done at each repetition of the item and usually and primarily is seen in "recognition" tests, whereas providing subject with additional retrieval cues should improve recall performance. Similarly, providing retrieval cues that are relevant for more elaborate structures than were used at the time of encoding is likely to be less effective than providing retrieval cues that are coordinate with the elaborateness of the structure that was encoded at presentation.

Nelson (1977) presents some data in his Experiment 3 that are relevant. He shows that encoding repetitions increase both recall and recognition but that cued recall is effective only for semantic encodings and not for phonemic encodings.

It is not my purpose here to review the extensive data on depth of processing, except to note that the organizational approach may lead to more extensive and vigorous analyses of elaborated structures, which might provide us with a theoretical continuum on which the depth or elaboration of processing notions can be based.

With these general considerations, I now turn to a recent realm of research that has related repetitions to organization and address the question of different kinds of rehearsal.

Organization and Repetition.   Our insights into the effects of rehearsal have developed cumulatively and rapidly over the past decade. Starting with the multistore models (e.g., Atkinson & Shiffrin, 1968; Waugh & Norman, 1965), we moved to an analysis of externalized rehearsal processes (Rundus, 1971) and by 1973 to the distinction between at least two different rehearsal processes (Craik & Watkins, 1973; Woodward, Bjork, & Jongeward, 1973). Craik and Watkins (1973) used an incidental learning task that required subjects only to maintain information to make it accessible in some short time later. There were no effects in final free recall. Woodward et al. (1973) and Bjork and his associates (cf. Bjork, 1975), using "forget" instructions, showed that they had no effect on final recall; whereas "remember" instructions produced increasing recall as a function of increasing delay during which subjects tried to "remember."

The general position at the current time seems to be that we can distinguish between maintenance and elaborative encoding. The former maintains the material through repetition in the current focus of consciousness; whereas the latter, elaborative encoding, uses the repetitions for elaboration of the presented items. In terms of the language used here, we would assume that the maintenance rehearsal produces primarily integrative results, whereas elaborative rehearsal produces structural elaboration. Wodward et al. (1973) had already shown that maintenance rehearsal, although having no effect on recall, does affect recognition in the final test. In fact, their position is the forerunner of my use of the concept of integrative/situational encoding, because they assumed that maintenance rehearsal increases the associative links between the target items and the situation in which it occurs.

As a final reminder of the short-term differential effect of maintenance and elaborative rehearsal on recall and "recognition," I would like to present some data taken from a paper by the late Wayne Bartz (1976). In one experiment, Bartz presented subjects with 8-word lists in which 4 words were cued for remembering and 4 for forgetting. There was a total of 36 consecutive lists,

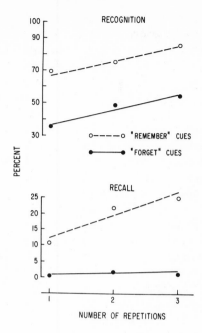

FIG. 14.4. Recognition and recall of items that were presented one, two, or three times, either with "remember" or "forget" cues. (From Bartz, 1976.)

and each word was presented 3 times: once in the first 12, once in the second 12, and once in the last 12 lists. In addition, each word was cued either for remembering or forgetting at each presentation, which resulted in 8 patterns of cueing. The main results were that a final recall test showed that recall was a function of the relative recency of a remember cue, whereas a final recognition test was independent of the patterning of the cues but was a direct function of the number of times a word had been presented. In a second experiment, Bartz presented individual words one to four times across lists. In Fig. 14.4 I present some selected data from this experiment. By looking only at the final recall and the final recognition of words that had been presented one, two, or three times with either "remember" or "forget" cues we obtain two functions. Figure 14.4 shows that recognition is a linear function of the number of prior repetitions with identical slopes for both remember cues and forget cues. Obviously, as we would expect, remember cues are more effective; but all these cues do is to raise the general level of the function, not the slope. Final recall, however, is a function of the number of remember cues that have been presented with a particular word. The number of repetitions with a forget cue does not increase final recall, nor does there seem to be any significant amount of recall for items that have been given "forget" instructions.

As far as the short-term testing situation is concerned, we can conclude that any kind of contextual or instructional set that does not require elaborative encoding, but that does require the subject to rehearse (repeat) a target item, will produce increased recognition; that is, on the presentation of a physical copy of the target item, its integrative/familiarity value can be accessed and will produce increased recognition performance. However, such repetitions have essentially no effect on final recall, presumably because the instruction and the context do not produce any elaboration or structural complexity relative to the target item.

What are the longer term effects of repetition on recall? We have already noted that situational integrative codes generated in the laboratory produce relatively little in the way of lasting retrieval codes for "recognition" tests. But more important for an understanding of so-called rote learning is the effect of repetitions on long-term recall. Our general position is, and has been since Mandler (1967b), that it is not the number of repetitions or rehearsals of an item that produce long-term retrievability but rather the elaboration and accessibility of the organization of which the item is a part. We have demonstrated at length (Mandler, 1967b, 1977) that inthe sorting task, in which subjects organize "unrelated" sets of words, it is not the number of times the word has been seen or sorted but rather the stability of the organization of which the word is a part that determines final recall. Similarly, in fairly long-term situations, Tulving (1967) has shown that sheer repetition is not a particularly effective method for producing long-term retrieval. In a research report addressed primarily to a somewhat tangential issue, we have presented evidence that prior repetitions are essentially ineffective in producing final recall whereas prior recalls are extremely effective (Mandler, Worden, & Graesser, 1974). In Experiment 2 it was possible to look at the number of times an item had been presented to the subject and, independently, at the number of times the item had been recalled prior to the final recall. Figure 14.5 shows those data. The number of presentations does not affect recall, but there is a very dramatic effect of prior recall on final recall. Except for the ceiling effect, which suggests that no real increases are possible beyond three prior recalls, the data imply that prior activations of the elaborated structures used for retrieval make these structures more effective in subsequent recall.

These were the conclusions that we presented at the time. However, subsequent analyses of the data from Experiment 1 of that study suggest a somewhat different view. In particular, I want to address two groups in that experiment. One group of subjects was given 6 trials of 16 words each. After the presentation of each list on the trial, some of the words that were recalled on that trial were replaced by new items. This again makes possible an analysis of a final recall (after the conclusion of the 6th trial and its recall) in terms of both prior number of presentation of items and prior recall of these words. I should note that the analysis of these two factors was essentially

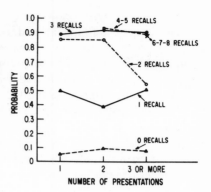

FIG. 14.5. Probability of final recall as a function of number of prior recalls and prior presentations (from Mandler, Worden, & Graesser, 1974). Subjects were given a total of five trials. After each trial, a recall test was given, and some items were dropped and others added for presentation on the next trial.

identical with the one presented in Fig. 14.5 for Experiment 2. However, we had another group who was given 16 new words (from the common pool) on each of the 6 trials. These 6 different lists were also followed by a final recall test. In Fig. 14.6 we have presented the probability of a final recall of all the items as a function of the list on which the items appeared. The data in Fig. 14.6 (for 6 separate independent lists) show that the probability of final recall of previously recalled items is a linear function of the list on which the item was previously recalled. These data are of course consistent with Bartz's data in a quite different context, with the most recent retrievals being the most effective in the final recall. On the other hand, final recall of previously presented items that have not been previously recalled is very slow and shows only a very slight increase in terms of recency. In terms of the magnitude of the effects, prior presentation without adequate storage (as indexed by failure of recall) has little or no effect on final retrievability.

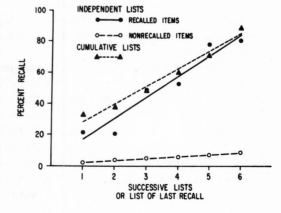

FIG. 14.6. Percent final recall as a function of trial (list) of previous recall. Subjects in the "independent" list group were given successively six different lists and a recall of each list. In the "cumulative" group, subjects were also given six lists, but the list on trial $n + 1$ contained some of the old items from trial n and some new items. The "cumulative" function plots the last list (trial) on which an item was recalled. The final recall followed the sixth list for both groups.

Given these items that were recalled only once, we realized that the data shown in Fig. 14.5 confound frequency and recency of prior recalls. The more frequently an item has been previously recalled, the more likely it was that it had also been recalled recently. We therefore reanalyzed the comparable experiment from Experiment 1 (which used the same items as the independent experiment just presented) and have plotted in Fig. 14.5 the probability of final recall for this group, in which items were dropped out and replaced and therefore had differential frequencies of recall. The data in Fig. 14.5 for these "cumulative" lists show that here, too, the probability of final recall is a linear function of the list on which an item was last recalled. Additional analyses indicated that in fact it is not the number of prior recalls but the recency of a prior recall that most directly affects final recall and accessibility. For example, for items where the last recall was on Trial 6, the probability of prior recall was constant whether they previously had shown five, four, three, or two recalls. A correlational analysis indicated that the recency of a prior recall accounts for about 82% of final recall variance, whereas the frequency of previous recall accounts for only 12% of that variance.

We can conclude from these data that sheer repetition (and incidentally repetition of the presented words by the subjects) has little effect on long-term retention. However, prior successful encoding (and recall) does affect such retention. In terms of organizational and structural factors, it is highly likely that the recency effect that we and Bartz have demonstrated is probably related to the loss of retrieval cues over time. It is also possible that the recency effect may be inextricably tied up with situational encoding and that over time, situation, perceptual, and physical cues become less effective in providing access to these complex structures.

Another possibility is that this laboratory situation is atypical. Each prior recall occurs in a different context, and the elaboration that is used for one list or context may be inappropriate for the next. In that case prior elaborations are discarded as new ones are adopted, and it is only the most recent one that is effective for final recall. Under other conditions successive retrievals in identical or similar contexts may produce better cumulative elaboration and long-term retrieval effects.

We can now turn to the more general question of "rote" learning and teaching. I do so with some degree of assurance that sheer repetition of the item by a learner is likely to have an effect of increasing integration and familiarity of the target event; but whether or not that repetition has any effect on the acquisition of lasting knowledge depends on the particular situation in which the learner is placed. If the situation encourages, in fact demands, elaboration of the target event in terms of other long-term processes or the relational encoding to other events within the particular situation, then we will find long-term retrieval effects. However, if the instruction or context simply requires repetition without any demand on structural elaboration, we should find no beneficial effects on long-term memory or retrieval.

THE APPLICATION OF ORGANIZATIONAL PRINCIPLES

I move now from the area of theory and data to the more vague, but also more useful, area of the application of the two major organizational principles. I restrict this application to the general notion of rote learning (in part to destroy it and in part to revive it in a different form), to the misuse of the concept of rote learning as a specifiable human ability, and finally to the implication of the two principles for limited capacity consciousness and for a definition of the learnable.

Rote Learning Revisited

The notion that sheer repetition of to-be-remembered material—"learning by rote"—can lead to the acquisition of knowledge in the broad sense is clearly wrong. There are beneficial uses of repetition, however; and some repetitions may be necessary for the eventual acquisition of knowledge. A psychology of education must carefully analyze the conditions and tasks of learning in order to determine the uses of repetition. By reviving the uses of repetition, I do not want to revive discarded notions of "rote learning." I want to advocate judicious task analyses that will tell us when repetition might be useful and when not.

A Short History of Rote Learning. The *Oxford English Dictionary* lists one of the definitions of the verb *rote* as: "To learn or fix by rote," followed by the observation: "*obsolete, rare.*" It is one of my purposes to contribute to the obsolescence of the term in general and also to decry the fact that it is not as rare as it should be. Conversely, as should be obvious from the preceding, I want to rescue certain repetition effects as being useful in the complex steps that make it possible for us to store knowledge and retrieve it at some later point. But even in that rescue attempt, I want to avoid the term *rote* simply because of the excess baggage it carries with it and the rather disastrous implication its advocacy and use have had in the past.

I first want to introduce some historical material, and I am indebted to a Norwegian colleague who published a book in 1964 entitled *A Re-evaluation of Rote Learning* (Bjorgen, 1964). Some of the material to follow is drawn from his illuminating review of the literature.

In contrast to the *Oxford English Dictionary*, some of the specialized, professional dictionaries are more instructive for our purposes. English and English (1958), for example, define rote learning as a process of memorizing that requires no understanding but merely the reproduction of words in the exact form in which they are presented. Interestingly enough, they add that this kind of learning does not *preclude* the unintentional understanding of the relationships involved. Drever (1952) defines rote learning as involving mere repetition and also adds that it is done "without any attempt at organization."

I think we can all agree that rote learning is a form of acquisition of material that involves no learning, no organization, and is typically achieved by mere repetition. It should be obvious that the individual who has "learned" something by rote cannot relate it to anything else but can recite it. Apart from performing parlor tricks, the learner has not achieved very much in the way of understanding or knowledge of the world.

What is puzzling about the foregoing is that there is a continuing tradition, most pronounced from 1880 to 1950, that implies that certain kinds of knowledge and information acquisition are in fact accomplished by rote, that the learner is not thereby limited to mere recitation, and that a significant basis for so-called higher mental processes can be found in the laws governing rote learning (cf. Hull, Hovland, Ross, Hall, Perkins, & Fitch, 1940). English and English, for example, note that "conditioning" is equated by some authors with rote learning. As Bjorgen pointed out nearly 15 years ago, what is puzzling is that the sort of thing that psychologist use in the laboratory and call rote learning seems to have very little relationship with the definition of the term. We have known now for many years that the so-called rote learning task we used in the "verbal learning" laboratories involves much meaning, much learning of relationships, and very little sheer repetition.

However, there is no simple escape from this paradox. The obvious route would be to say that there was simply a confusion in the common language, that a particular word used in a particular context meant something different in another context, and we can avoid the whole dilemma by issuing a general apology for our misuse of the word *rote* and forget it. As I show shortly, there is at least one influential line of research that not only uses the term in both senses but implies that in fact the typical verbal learning experiments involve exactly the kind of rote learning that the average English speaker of the word, however obsolete or rare it is, still understands.

Why are those of us who have moved from verbal learning to memory experiments (however identical the actual experiments may be) still saddled with the notion of rote learning? With the advent of behaviorism, the general hope was expressed that we could do the same kinds of experiments with humans in the verbal learning laboratory that we were doing with animals in the conditioning laboratory. Conditioning and animal learning were known then (though not known anymore) to be primarily a function of the number of repetitions of a particular behavior or the number of reinforcements or the number of cs–us pairings. The next step simply described learning in the tradition of behaviorism and in the older tradition of Ebbinghaus as the growth of strengths or behaviors or associations as a function of prior repetitions. The fact that there was another tradition that concluded no such thing had very little effect on the avalanche of behaviorist dogma that swept over all of us. Too few of us read G. E. Müller (1913) or Selz (1924) or paid any attention to the Gestalt psychologists (cf. Katona, 1940).

The second tradition, arm in arm with behaviorism, was the American functionalist movement, which avoided any kind of complex theoretical enterprise and instituted the tradition of describing results in terms of conditions under which they were obtained (a belief in salvation that united functionalists and behaviorists). (See also Mandler, 1967a.)

You may argue that we have come a long way from those prejudices and that nobody talks about "rote" learning anymore; why bring it up again? My reply is that it is true we have given up the old meaning of rote learning, and even such a stalwart defender of the functionalist tradition as Underwood was able to describe the verbal learning tradition in a very "meaningful" way, even though he used the title of "rote learning" in 1964. But my purpose is twofold: first to remind you that there are those among us who still feel that repetition has some explanatory effect, that rote learning is alive and well; and second to revive the notion that some kinds of repetition (though not rote learning) may be useful mechanisms for facilitating the acquisition of knowledge.

Who still believes that mere repetition is an interesting explanatory factor? Probably nobody does seriously. What is missing is the realization that repetition per se is useful when it provides an opportunity for the active learner for organizational activities and, independently, for the integration of material. Pining for our lost youth, when independent variables were defined by strict manipulations by the experimenter, some writers are still unhappy that rehearsal and/or repetition cannot be defined in mere presentation trials but rather are defined in terms of what it is that the learning subject in fact does in our laboratory (cf. Dark & Loftus, 1976; Nelson, 1977). More serious, however, is the claim made during the past 5 years that mere "rote" procedures can achieve some knowledge of the world or are, in fact, central to human abilities as well as to the acquisition of simple laboratory memory tasks.

Rote Learning as a Human Ability. Consider the following kinds of statements: The "ability consists of rote learning and primary memory; it is the capacity to register and retrieve information with fidelity and is characterized essentially by a relative lack of transformation, conceptual coding, or other mental manipulation intervening between information input and output. " These "abilities are best measured by rote-learning tasks: serial learning, repeated trials of free recall of a number of successively presented familiar uncategorized objects, pictures, or nouns, and tests of short term memory such as digit span." This is not a citation of the ilterature of the 1900s, the 1920s, or even the 1950s. It is from an article published in 1974 by Jensen. I am not surprised if people who might not know better still equate memory experiments with rote learning, but somebody who has worked as recently as the 1960s on memory research cannot seriously suggest that short-term memory and the free recall of uncategorized lists represent equivalent tasks. Was he serious? Unfortunately, he was. Jensen published a two-level theory of mental ability in 1970, and the quotes I have given you are a later definition of "Level One ability." Level Two, "in contrast, is characterized by mental manipulation of input, conceptualization, reasoning, and problem solving."

As some of you might, I ascribed these definitions to a momentary lapse, until I found a 1973 paper that deals specifically with the free recall of categorized and uncategorized lists. In brief, Jensen and Frederiksen (1973) postulated that there would be no difference between a black and white population in Level One ability but that there would be large diffferences in Level Two ability between black and white children, particularly at later ages. The reader may guess which population was predicted to be superior in conceptual ability. Leaving aside for a moment the implied notions as to the processes that are involved in the free recall of unrelated and of categorized words, it is possible to look at these data in terms of the organizational processes advanced here.

Assuming that the children have a basic understanding of the words that made up the various lists, past research as well as current theory suggests that the two tasks involve two classes of processes. In the free recall of "unrelated" lists of words, the individual is required to impose some sort of structure on the items in the list. Tulving (1962) has referred to the process as "subjective organization." There is nothing in the list as such that provides a ready-made structure that is discoverable and usable by the learner. More important, perhaps, in light of the data that I am addressing here, is the fact that the individual learner's conceptual ability is given free rein. In the case of categorized lists, however, the situation is more complex. If subjects are not informed about the categorical structure of the list, then the individuals may or may not discover such a structure. Lack of adequate information either at the time of input or at the time of output (cuing) presents an unanalyzable experimental problem, as we do not know, in absence of other information, whether the individuals did or did not discover the categorical structure and whether they in fact used such categorical structure if discovered (cf. the discussion of discovery and use in Mandler, 1967a). In any case, some subjects will discover and use the categorical structure and some subjects may not.

The question then is whether differential discovery and use would be expected for a low socioeconomic-class, black group of children as compared with a high socioeconomic class, white group of children. The answer, in light of extensive comparative evidence (cf. Scribner & Cole, 1976) is affirmative. Both semantically and syntactically, the linguistic structure used by black, lower-class children (black English) is significantly different from the standard, white, middle-class reference group. None of the children in the Jensen and Frederiksen study were given any instructions as to the categorized material, nor cued for recall; in fact, the material used for presentation were common objects, and recall was tested for the names of the objects without any instructions as to categories. There is direct evidence in the Jensen and Frederiksen study that the discovery and use of semantic categories is central to this kind of categorized free-recall task. Whereas there is a very slight difference in recall in categorized lists for second-grade, black and white children, there is a very large difference at the fourth grade. In part this is due to the fact that white, middle-class fourth graders do much better on categorized lists than do the second graders on the *identical* lists. Thus, even members of the white, middle-class reference group have to know more about the categorical semantic structure of the language before they can discover and use the structure embedded in the categorized list.

Given these considerations, a rather curious conclusion emerges if one is to consider free-recall scores as measures of mental ability. When the memorial task is dependent entirely on the children's active manipulation of the material, the imposition of conceptual categories, and complex thought processes applied to otherwise "unrelated" materials [relatively uncontaminated by the requirements of cultural and social (semantic) learning], we find that black and white children do equally well. The data say that in a task less affected by educational and cultural factors but involving complex mental processes, black, lower-class children do as well as white, middle-class children. If one were in the uncertain business of determining racial abilities, one could say that black children, on the basis of the Jensen and Frederiksen studies, are not only as able as white children but are able to overcome the additional handicaps of lower economic and social status. I do not want to make any such claim, because I believe that complex, human mental activity cannot be subjected to simple-minded analyses.

What I do want to do is return to the kind of reasoning behind Jensen's theory of mental abilities. In the original presentation in 1970, we are told, for example, that "the registration of the items' meaningfulness is mainly a level Two process, involving the arousal of the subjects' network of verbal associations [p. 85]." Or again on the free recall of unrelated lists we are told that the free recall of uncategorized lists "requires noting more than ... the reproduction of the input [p. 91]." Or, "a noncategorized list is made up of unrelated or remotely associated items which cannot be readily grouped according to supra-ordinate categories. Subjective organization of the items in the list is likely to consist of pairs of items related on the basis of primary generalization, clang association, or functional relationship [pp. 95–96]."

The impression is strong that all of this is a case of studied ignorance (and there is very little indication of any awareness of the literature of the past 20 years). Since much of the audience for these empirical and theoretical confusions are in the educational establishment, one despairs of the amount of cleaning up the rest of us will have to do in order to help our nonpsychologist colleagues become aware of the 20 years of literature that contradict such simple-minded and misleading generalizations. Unfortunately, this is a task all of us will have to face. All I can do at the present time is to suggest some general principles based on what we do know about organizational processes that might be helpful in the educational enterprise as such.

Organization and Learning

If we are to address the question of learning in the wider sense, I assume that, as with all useful knowledge, we are concerned with information that is readily available in the appropriate situation and also relatable to other kinds of knowledge. By defining the availability of knowledge in terms of "appropriate" context, we can avoid nit-picking about the relevance of one kind of knowledge or another or about a priority system within knowledge inventories. All we need to know is that some knowledge acquired by the learner will be useful in some context in which it is appropriate or required. Knowledge, structured by itself, must be placed within a larger structure that provides retrievability given the appropriate conditions, situations, or instructions. The other requirement, that it be relatable to other knowledge, insists that things that we know should make sense in a larger context. We rarely need to know something that is not related to something else known or appreciated. A problem-solving strategy must be applicable to different kinds of problems and must be relatable to certain goals. The requirement insists that the structure of some acquired knowledge be related to other knowledge systems. In brief, these requirements say that acquired knowledge is and must be meaningful, both locally and generally (see also Ausubel, 1969). In these terms, all knowledge that we acquire is acquired as a function of structural elaboration. However, the language that I have chosen to describe these phenomena suggests that permanence of new structures is a function of their integration, whereas their accessibility is a function of extensive complexities and elaborations.

There is some advantage in considering the mental structures that produce thought and action parallel to the structures that produce skills; in fact, in adopting Bartlett's (1958) suggestion of considering thinking as an instance of a skill. The parallel also has the advantage of bringing cognitive psychology in closer contact with the problems of the organization of action and may extend organizational and cognitive theories to an acting as well as a thinking organism (cf. Mandler, 1975c).

Just as in the acquisition of a complex motor skill, the acquisition of new cognitive skills requires a command of the constituents as well as the construction of new structures from these constituents. The mastery of constituents requires integration. Elaboration—the construction of new systems, structures, or organizations—follows requirements of the task and instructions. With these two basic steps, we can then see the dialectic of structural development as new structures are developed, become integrated, and become the constituents or the components of new structures—structures that are in turn elaborated, integrated, and so forth. One of the obvious reasons why the constituent component structures of a larger system must be integrated is that, as I have noted before, unintegrated and structurally "loose" systems require a great deal of attention or—as I would call it—conscious capacity. With too much conscious capacity required for the constituents, the construction of a new structural system is apt to be difficult if not impossible. I return to the question of teaching and capacity limitations later.

There is no doubt that integration of structures can take place without, or at least with minimal, structural elaboration. Children often learn poems without knowing their "meaning," and they may also learn the alphabet as an integrated system, frequently before using it for elaborative learning. Similarly, medical school students learn something about the internal structure of bone and organ systems in essentially integrative ways before relating these integrated components to other, larger systems.

These anecdotal examples suggest that component systems and component structures very often need purely integrative organization before they can be used in complex systems. Presumably, such complex systems cannot "use" unintegrated or badly integrated components because of capacity problems; in any case, there is evidence that both mental structural readiness and prior structural integration are needed for the acquisition of new complex structures. For example, Welch (1940), in one of the more courageous attempts to test the rote learning tradition, gave some of his participating children hundreds and even thousands of trials in the acquisition of concepts without achieving any success. Following Piaget (1953), the conclusion would be that unless the mental structures are such that they can assimilate new information, no amount of repetition will produce a receptive mental structural system. Similarly, in the comprehension of language, Newport and Gleitman (in preparation) have shown that comprehension of a request or command to a child is independent of its sheer repetition. Comprehension or request following will occur independent of the number of opportunities to comprehend that have occurred prior to the successful event. Of immediate interest are some conclusions by Gelman and Gallistel (1978), which show that young children need to have acquired a "rote" command of counting skills before they can apply counting transformations.

These various observations suggest a resurrection of the concept of rote learning but in an entirely different guise. Specifically, integration by repetition of component skills may not only be useful but also necessary for the construction of complex mental structures and the acquisition of knowledge. However, the important lesson is that repetition has no consequences in terms of the acquisition of knowledge or useful information as such. Rather, it is a necessary prolegomenon to elaborative, meaningful structure development. Certainly, in terms of its past usage, the conclusion is that there is no such thing as "rote" learning but there are repetition effects that apparently must precede some kinds of useful learning.

Consciousness and Learning. I have previously insisted that any respectable cognitive psychology of the 1970s should concern itself with problems of conscious processing and conscious capacity (Mandler, 1975a, 1975c). In brief, I have argued that some of the so-called short-term memory effects, most of the limited processing effects described by Miller (1956) in both unidimensional judgment and short-term memory, and most of the problems of central and focal attention and its limitations can be subsumed under the concept of a limited conscious capacity system. I said then that the term *consciousness* apparently produces a great degree of unease in traditional experimental psychologists. Luckily, that situation seems to have improved somewhat. Bjork (1975) is willing to talk about consciousness, and others are edging closer. For example, Shiffrin (1976) talks about "automatic search" that bypassses the necessity for extended comparison processes (one of the characteristics of consciousness) and talks about memory capacity often coexistensively with attentional capacity. Craik and Levy (1976) abandon the concept of primary memory by appealing to the *allocation of attention,* a term also close to notions of limited apprehension and conscious capacity.

The limited capacity of the conscious (attentional) process proscribes certain kinds of acquisitions. If a particular task requires all available conscious capacity, then in the process of the performance of such a task very little new structural development can take place; very little new information can be developed. It is only when the task that currently occupies an individual has become well integrated, compacted into chunks that require less capacity (and therefore become more or less automatic), that new knowledge can be attained. Knapp (1978) has investigated this particular problem with respect to language acquisition in children and suggests that the acquisition of new syntactic structures depends on the automatization of previous and currently-being-integrated syntactic structures.

I suggested earlier that the amount of capacity required for elaboration increases as elaboration becomes more complex, and the amount of capacity required for integration decreases as a particular structure becomes better integrated. In Fig. 14.7, I have applied these notions to the memory space. I have assumed that the capacity requirement for elaboration is a negatively

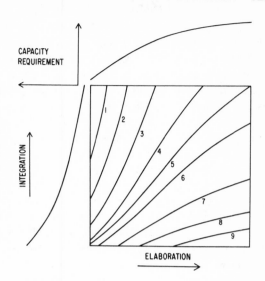

FIG. 14.7. Iso-capacity curves in the two-dimensional memory space. The functions adjacent to the abscissa and ordinate show the capacity requirement as a function of increasing elaboration (capacity requirement increases) and increasing integration (requirement decreases). The iso-capacity curves connect points in the memory space that require the same amount of conscious capacity, going from 1 (minimal requirement) to 9 (maximal requirement).

accelerating growth function, whereas the capacity requirement for integration is a decreasing function, as shown in Fig. 14.7. Given these requirements, we can then construct iso-capacity curves. These curves connect points requiring a constant amount of capacity as a function of the level of integration and elaboration of a particular to-be-remembered structure or unit. The arbitrary numbering assigned to these curves, going from 1 to 9, shows increasing amount of capacity needed for these particular tasks. The tasks described in our discussion of Fig. 14.3 (A to D) can be related to capacity limitations. Automatic motor skills are found close to capacity function 1, whereas complex unintegrated tasks are found near 9. More important, it is now possible to describe certain tasks that may be difficult if not impossible to acquire. If, for example, iso-capacity curve 8 describes some upper limit of available capacity, then all those cases falling below and to the right of it will be opaque to acquisition. Teaching children tasks for which they do not have the requisite skills or trying to comprehend the meaning of a complex paragraph without having any integrative grasp of any of its constituents would fall into this general area.

Reprise. From the identification of two dimensions of mental organization, I have moved to an analysis of recent work on depth of processing and on rehearsal, to a re-evaluation of the recognition–recall distinction, and to a review of the effects of repetition on memory. These analyses suggested the possibility of describing optimal conditions of storage and *pari passu* optimal conditions of retrieval. Similarly, an appropriate analysis of educational tasks should eventually permit the identification of optimal conditions of learning in the classroom. Both psychologists and teachers need to know when the integration of constituents is a prior condition for efficient elaboration or when elaborative plans and structures are useful guides to eventual integration. Sometimes the learner will need to know the building blocks first and sometimes the general organization of the material to be acquired. Or there may exist conditions in the real world where we can effectively apply optimal conditions discovered in the laboratory. For example, I was delighted when Sylvia Scribner recently described an encounter with a local teacher in Liberia who was using the incremental (1 + 1) serial method very effectively.

As a corollary to these insights, we may not only develop appropriate methods in the laboratory for the effective use of this two-dimensional model but also relieve the real dilemma of deciding when repeated practice of skills and knowledge may be useful and when a waste of time. The trend in the past few decades away from "rote" learning has not been replaced by an informed use of either repetition or elaboration. The former is merely known to be bad, the latter good. An appropriate psychological analysis of educational tasks should move us away from superficial value judgments.

ACKNOWLEDGMENTS

Preparation of this paper was supported in part by National Science Foundation Grant No. BNS 76-15154 and Grant No. MH-15828 from the National Institute of Mental Health to the Center for Human Information Processing. I am deeply indebted to Jean Mandler and David Rumelhart, who diligently read and commented on two previous drafts and, with varying success, tried to convince me to remove or repair inconsistencies, errors, ambiguities, and unjustified claims. All of my work, at least when successful, has been influenced by my student–collaborators and, particularly in recent years, by Arthur Graesser, Jan Rabinowitz, and Patricia Worden.

REFERENCES

Atkinson, R. C., & Juola, J. F. Search and decision processes in recognition memory. In D. H. Krantz, R. C. Atkinson, P. Suppes (Eds.), *Contemporary developments in mathematical psychology.* San Francisco: Freeman, 1974.

Atkinson, R. C., & Shiffrin, R. M. Human memory: A proposed system and its control processes. In K. W. Spence & J. T. Spence (Eds.), *The psychology of learning and motivation* (Vol. II). New York: Academic Press, 1968.

Atkinson, R. C., & Wescourt, K. T. Some remarks on a theory of memory. In P. M. A. Rabbitt & S. Dornic (Eds.), *Attention and performance V.* New York: Academic Press, 1975.

Ausubel, D. P. A cognitive theory of school learning. *Psychology in the Schools,* 1969, *6,* 331–335.

Baddeley, A. D., & Hitch, G. Working memory. In G. H. Bower (Ed.), *The psychology of learning and motivation* (Vol. 8). New York: Academic Press, 1974.

Bartlett, F. *Thinking: An experimental and social study.* New York: Basic Books, 1958.
Bartz, W. H. Rehearsal and retrieval processes in recall and recognition. *Bulletin of the Psychonomic Society,* 1976, *8,* 258.
Björgen, I. A. *A re-evaluation of rote learning.* Oslo: Universitetsforlagets, 1964.
Bjork, R. A. Short term storage: The ordered output of a central processor. In F. Restle, R. M. Shiffrin, N. J. Castellan, H. R. Lindman, & D. B. Pisoni (Eds), *Cognitive theory* (Vol. 1). Hillsdale, N.J.: Lawrence Erlbaum Associates, 1975.
Bower, G. H., Lesgold, A. M., & Tieman, D. Grouping operations in free recall. *Journal of Verbal Learning and Verbal Behavior,* 1969, *8,* 481–493.
Craik, F. I. M., & Levy, B. A. The concept of primary memory. In W. K. Estes (Ed.), *Handbook of learning and cognitive processes* (Vol. 4). Hillsdale, N.J.: Lawrence Erlbaum Associates, 1976.
Craik, F. I. M., & Lockhart, R. S. Levels of processing: A framework for memory research. *Journal of Verbal Learning and Verbal Behavior,* 1972, *11,* 671–684.
Craik, F. I. M., & Tulving, E. Depth of processing and the retention of words in episodic memory. *Journal of Experimental Psychology: General,* 1975, *104,* 268–294.
Craik, F. I. M., & Watkins, M. J. The role of rehearsal in short-term memory. *Journal of Verbal Learning and Verbal Behavior,* 1972, *12,* 599–607.
Dark, V. J., & Loftus, G. R. The role of rehearsal in long-term memory performance. *Journal of Verbal Learning and Verbal Behavior,* 1976, *15,* 479–490.
Drever, J. *A dictionary of psychology.* Baltimore: Penguin Books, 1952.
English, H. B., & English, A. C. *A comprehensive dictionary of psychological and psychoanalytic terms.* New York: Longman, 1958.
Estes, W. K. An associative basis for coding and organization in memory. In A. W. Melton & E. Martin (Eds.), *Coding processes in human memory.* Washington, D. C.: Winston, 1972.
Gelman, R., & Gallistel, C. R. *The young child's understanding of number.* Cambridge Mass.: Harvard University Press, 1978.
Hayes–Roth, B. Evolution of cognitive structures and processes. *Psychological Review,* 1977, *84,* 260–278.
Hintzman, D. L. Repetition and memory. In G. H. Bower (Ed.), *The psychology of learning and motivation* (Vol. 10). New York: Academic Press, 1976.
Hovland, C. I., & Kurtz, K. N. Experimental studies in rote learning theory. X. Pre-learning syllable familiarization and the length–difficulty relationship. *Journal of Experimental Psychology,* 1952, *44,* 31–39.
Hull, C. L., Hovland, C. I., Ross, R. T., Hall, M., Perkins, D. T., & Fitch, F. B. *Mathematico-deductive theory of rote learning.* New Haven, Conn.: Yale University Press, 1940.
Jensen, A. R. A theory of primary and secondary familial mental retardation. In N. R. Ellis (Ed.), *International review of mental retardation* (Vol. 4). New York: Academic Press, 1970.
Jensen, A. R. Interaction of level I and level II abilities with race and socioeconomic status. *Journal of Educational Psychology,* 1974, *66,* 99–111.
Jensen, A. R., & Frederiksen, J. Free recall of categorized and uncategorized lists: A test of the Jensen hypothesis. *Journal of Educational Psychology,* 1973, *65,* 304–312.
Katona, G. *Organizing and memorizing.* New York: Columbia University Press, 1940.
Kintsch, W. Models for free recall and recognition. In D. A. Norman (Ed.), *Models of human memory.* New York: Academic Press, 1970.
Knapp, D. *Automatization and language acquisition.* Unpublished doctoral dissertation, University of California, San Diego, 1978.
LaBerge, D., & Samuels, S. J. Toward a theory of automatic information processing in reading. *Cognitive Psychology,* 1974, *6,* 293–323.
Linton, M. Memory for real-world events. In D. A. Norman, D. E. Rumelhart, and the LNR Research Group, *Explorations in cognition.* San Francisco: Freeman, 1975.
Mandler, G. Response factors in human learning, *Psychological Review,* 1954, *61,* 235–244.

Mandler, G. Verbal learning. In Mandler, G., Mussen, P., Kogan, N., & Wallach, M. A. *New directions in psychology: III.* New York: Holt, Rinehart & Winston, 1967. (a)

Mandler, G. Organization and memory. In K. W. Spence & J. T. Spence (Eds.), *The psychology of learning and motivation* (Vol. I.) New York: Academic Press, 1967. (b)

Mandler, G. Words, lists, and categories: An experimental view of organized memory. In J. L. Cowan (Ed.), *Studies in thought and language.* Tucson: University of Arizona Press, 1970.

Mandler, G. Organization and recognition. In E. Tulving & W. Donaldson (Eds.), *Organization of memory.* New York: Academic Press, 1972.

Mandler, G. Consciousness: Respectable, useful, and probably necessary. In R. Solso (Ed.), *Information processing and cognition: The Loyola Symposium.* Hillsdale, N.J.: Lawrence Erlbaum Associates, Inc. 1975. (a)

Mandler, G. Memory storage and retrieval: Some limits on the reach of attention and consciousness. In P. M. A. Rabbitt & S. Dornic (Eds.), *Attention and performance V.* London: Academic Press, 1975. (b)

Mandler, G. *Mind and emotion.* New York: Wiley, 1975. (c)

Mandler, G. *Memory research reconsidered: A critical view of some traditional methods and distinctions.* Paper presented at the 21st International Congress of Psychology, Paris, July 1976. (Tech. Rep. No. 64, Center for Human Information Processing, University of California, San Diego, September 1976.)

Mandler, G. Commentary on "Organization and Memory." In G. H. Bower (Ed.), *Human memory: Basic processes.* New York: Academic Press, 1977.

Mandler, G., & Boeck, W. Retrieval processes in recognition. *Memory & Cognition,* 1974, *2,* 613–615.

Mandler, G., & Dean, P. J. Seriation: Development of serial order in free recall. *Journal of Experimental Psychology,* 1969, *81,* 207–215.

Mandler, G., & Graesser, A. C., II Analyse dimensionelle et le "locus" de l'organisation. In S. Ehrlich & E. Tulving (Eds.), *La memoire semantique.* Paris: Bulletin de Psychologie, 1976. (english version: Tech. Rep. No. 48, Center for human Information Processing, University of California, San Diego, January 1976.)

Mandler, G., Pearlstone, Z., & Koopmans, H. J. Effects of organization and semantic similarity on recall and recognition. *Journal of Verbal Learning and Verbal Behaivor,* 1969, *8,* 410–423.

Mandler, G., Worden, P. E., & Graesser, A. C., II. Subjective disorganization: Search for the locus of list organization. *Journal of Verbal Learning and Verbal Behavior,* 1974, *13,* 220–235.

Mandler, J. M., & Ritchey, G. H. Long-term memory for pictures. *Journal of Experimental Psychology: Human Learning and Memory,* 1977, *3,* 386–396.

Miller, G. A. The magical number seven, plus or minus two: Some limits on our capacity for processing information. *Psychological Review,* 1956, *63,* 81–97.

Müller, G. E. Zur Analyse der Gedächtnistätigkeit und des Vorstellungsverlaufes. *Zeitschrift für Psychologie,* 1913. Ergänzungsband 8.

Murdock, B. B., Jr. *Human memory: Theory and data.* Hillsdale, N.J.: Lawrence Erlbaum Associates, 1974.

Nelson, T. O. Repetition and depth of processing. *Journal of Verbal Learning and Verbal Behavior,* 1977, *16,* 151–171.

Newport, E. L., & Gleitman, H. Maternal self-repetition and the child's acquisition of language. *Papers and Reports on Child Language Development,* 1977, *13,* 46–55.

Piaget, J. *The origin of intelligence in the child.* London: Routledge and Kegan Paul, 1953.

Posner, M. I., & Snyder, C. R. R. Attention and cognitive control. In R. L. Solso (Ed.), *Information processing and cognition: The Loyola Symposium.* Hillsdale, N.J.: Lawrence Erlbaum Associates, 1975.

Rabinowitz, J. C., Mandler, G., & Barsalou, L. Recognition failure: Another case of retrieval failure. *Journal of Verbal Learning and Verbal Behavior,* 1977, *16,* 639–663.

Rumelhart, D. E. *Introduction to human information processing.* New York: Wiley, 1977.

Rundus, D. Analysis of rehearsal processes in free recall. *Journal of Experimental Psychology,* 1971, *89,* 63–77.

Scribner, S., & Cole, M. Etudes des variations sub-culturelles de la memoire semantique: Les implications de la reserch inter-culturelle. In S. Ehrlich & E. Tulving (Eds.), *La memoire semantique.* Paris: Bulletin de Psychologie, 1976.

Segal, M. A., & Mandler, G. Directionality and organizational processes in paired-associate learning. *Journal of Experimental Psychology,* 1967, *74,* 305–312.

Selz, O. *Die Gesetze der produktiven und reproduktiven Geistestätigkeit.* Bonn: Cohen, 1924.

Shiffrin, R. M. Capacity limitation in information processing, attention, and memory. In W. K. Estes (Ed.), *Handbook of learning and cognitive processes* (Vol. 4). Hillsdale, N.J.: Lawrence Erlbaum Associates, 1976.

Tulving, E. Subjective organization in free recall of "unrelated" words. *Psychological Review,* 1962, *69,* 344–354.

Tulving, E. The effects of presentation and recall of material in free-recall learning. *Journal of Verbal Learning and Verbal Behavior,* 1967, *6,* 175–184.

Tulving, E. Ecphoric processes in recall and recognition. In J. Brown (Ed.), *Recall and recognition.* London: Wiley, 1976.

Tulving, E., & Thomson, D. M. Encoding specificity and retrieval processes in episodic memory. *Psychological Review,* 1973, *80,* 352–373.

Underwood, B. J. The representativeness of rote verbal learning. In A. W. Melton (Ed.), *Categories of human learning.* New York: Academic Press, 1964.

Underwood, B. J., & Schulz, R. W. *Meaningfulness and verbal learning.* Philadelphia, Pa.: Lippincott, 1960.

Watkins, M. J., & Tulving, E. Episodic memory: When recognition fails. *Journal of Experimental Psychology: General,* 1975, *104,* 5–29.

Waugh, N. C., & Norman, D. A. Primary memory. *Psychological Review,* 1965, *72,* 89–93.

Welch, L. A preliminary investigation of some aspects of the hierarchical development of concepts. *Journal of General Psychology,* 1940, *22,* 359–378.

Woodward, A. E., Bjork, R. A., & Jongeward, R. H., Jr. Recall and recognition as a function of primary rehearsal. *Journal of Verbal Learning and Verbal Behavior,* 1973, *12,* 608–617.

15

Reading Comprehension and Readability in Educational Practice and Psychological Theory

Walter Kintsch
Douglas Vipond
University of Colorado, Boulder

INTRODUCTION

One would think, naively, that the relationship between psychology and education should be analogous to that between, say, physics and engineering. Even a cursory look reveals that this is not at all the case. The theoretical and scientific underpinnings of education are for the most part homegrown and surprisingly independent of mainstream psychological research. For their part, psychologists rarely waste a thought on educational problems. Indeed, at least in the United States, of the two most significant fields of application—clinical psychology and education—we seem to have quite abandoned any claims on the latter. Although clinical psychology exists as a large and active subarea in almost every psychology department in the country, educational psychology is practiced in departments of education—not in psychology departments at all.

Why do psychologists have such a love affair with clinical practice and show such little interest in what appears prima facie at least a promising and significant a field of application? We can't answer this question, but we propose that historically the schism between psychology and education is a fairly recent one (coinciding with the rise of clinical psychology, incidentally) and that there are signs that a more balanced relationship between psychology and education might be restored in the next few years. Educational psycholgists are beginning to realize the limitations of approaches not based upon a thorough understanding of human information-processing characteristics, and academic psychologists are becoming intrigued by the idea that some of their playthings might actually have some good uses in the real world.

On Psychology and Education

If we take a look at the history of psychology and education, we find a very different picture 100 years ago from that prevailing today. Psychology once functioned as a basic science for education. Nowhere is this clearer than in the work of Herbart (1776–1841), whose ideas had an enormous and long-lasting influence on education. For Herbart, education took its aims from ethics, whereas psychology was there to show it the means and hindrances to these aims. Central to Herbart's psychology was what one could call a theory of organized thinking. Thinking implied organization and structure, discrimination between what is important and unimportant, a conscious, deliberate association of what belongs together. A chaotic, undifferentiated jumble of ideas in which "there is no settled top or bottom, nor even an ordered series; everything is mixed up together" is not thought (Herbart, 1893, p. 138). The goal of instruction was thus not a mere accumulation of knowledge. Instead, instruction was seen as the complement of experience: It arranges and connects the formless and dispersed fragments collected by experience. In order to achieve this, learning must proceed from the known to the unknown—the doctrine of apperception. Apperception means to combine a number of sensory bits into a unity. But how does this unification occur? Kant had proposed an innate unifying power, but according to Herbart it was what the learner already knows—a well-organized background of experience—that makes possible the assimilation of a new idea. Children can interpret and respond to a new situation only if they have a stock of recalled, related ideas. Herbart called this stock of ideas the "apperceptive mass." His doctrine had a strong impact upon education. It led to the idea of the curriculum: subject matter organized so that the pupil passes from familiar to closely related but unfamiliar content.

Today, these ideas sound both common-sense and very modern. Indeed, one could characterize the efforts of some contemporary cognitive psychologists as an attempt to reformulate Herbart's theories and to re-establish them as guidelines for education. This does not mean that psychologists should or could ever tell educators what to do. Herbart and many others after him maintained that psychology's job was to state the laws that education then must use to achieve its own ends. For instance, James Sully (1886) distinguished between theoretic and practical science, noting, however, the close connection between them: "Education," he said, "needs continually to revert to psychology [p. 17]." In the same vein, John Dewey suggested that the knowledge of structure and function of the human being can help rescue education from its "purely empirical and rule-of-the-thumb stage." The knowledge of psychology can transform the school from a "mere workshop into an effective instrument in the building of character" (Dewey, 1964, p. 198).

Hugo Münsterberg was another psychologist who gave careful consideration to the question of the relation between psychology and education.
Münsterberg (1898) maintained that although psychology could not be of any
direct use to the teacher, it could be indirectly useful through the medium of a
scientific educational theory. A science of education should crystallize
educational principles out of psychological substance. But who is going to
develop this scientific educational theory? It cannot be the individual teacher,
nor can it be the traditional psychologist. Münsterberg recommends that it be
done by "psycho-educational scholars," who thereby will establish a "linking
science" between psychological theory on the one hand and educational
practice on the other. Of course psychology is only one of the sources of
scientific education—Münsterberg stresses that the causal analysis of
psychical elements (i.e., psychology) must be combined with teleological
considerations provided by history, religion, and literature. Also, the interests
of psychologists and educational scientists are bound to differ; the science of
education must find its own answers to the questions it considers important,
because it is quite likely that these would not be important from the
psychologist's viewpoint: "In spite of seductive titles. . . we [psychologists]
have too seldom problems which belong to his field" [p. 131].

Münsterberg favors establishing "psycho-educational laboratories" as "the
most natural step forward" (p. 131). In these labs, problems would be worked
on that had educational interest. The methods of experimental psychology
may be adopted, but not necessarily the content.

> When in the quiet experimental working place of the psycho-educational
> scholar, through the steady co-operation of specialists, a real system of
> acknowledged facts is secured, then the practical attempts of the consulting
> school psychologist and of the leader of experimental classrooms have a safer
> basis, and their work will help again the theoretical scholar till the co-operation
> of all these agents produces a practical education which the teacher will accept
> without his own experimenting [pp. 131–132].

Probably the most influential psychoeducational scholar of this century
was Edward L. Thorndike. Thorndike believed that there were two main ways
that psychology could help education become more efficient. First, particular
teaching methods could be rigorously evaluated by using the results of
teaching (e.g., test scores, examples of handwriting). Second, teaching
methods could be consistent with the child's nature and the laws of learning.
Education and psychology are closely related, because these laws of learning
are supplied to education by psychology. According to Thorndike (1906): "To
change what is into what ought to be, we need to know the laws by which the
changes occur [p, 60]."

But what "ought to be?" According to Joncich (1962), in his earliest
writings Thorndike accepted the conventional view that the aims of education

are determined elsewhere; psychology's role is merely to show the most efficient ways of attaining them. Later, Thorndike saw a greater place for psychology in educational goal setting. There were two aspects to this. First, psychology could help clarify existing goals. For example, the goal that "children in school should learn to write legibly" could be operationally defined as: "At the end of the second grade the average child will have reached level X on standard handwriting scale Y." Second, psychology could enlarge or change society's goals. Psychology could reveal new facts about human behavior that could change what society considers worth doing. Jonçich (1962) points out a nice example of this from Thorndike's own work. His research on the learning potential of adults helped stimulate adult educational programs. Until then, most people had thought that only children were worth educating.

From Münsterberg to Thorndike there has thus existed a well-articulated program for the cooperation between psychology and education. This program has not yet borne the fruit its originators had hoped for. Educational research, instead of being based in psychology, has become empirical, data rich and theory poor, in danger of becoming stuck in that "rule of thumb stage" Dewey warned against, and distrustful of academic psychology. The reasons for this distrust are perfectly valid, of course: Too many grandiose promises have been made that couldn't be kept, à la Watson's "guarantee" to take any normal infant and "train him to become any type of specialist I might select—doctor, lawyer, artist, merchant–chief" (Watson, 1924–25, pp. 82–85). Perhaps the main reason for the present state of affairs was that psychology simply was not ready to deliver the goods. Our theories were, and to some extent still are, too crude to be of much use to the educational researchers, especially in those areas of complex information processing that are of greatest interest to them.

Today there is a resurgence of interest on the part of both educators and psychologists in the cooperation between the two disciplines. An excellent example of this trend is represented by the contributions in Klahr's 1976 book, *Cognition and Instruction*. A new breed of psychologists—cognitive psychologists—claim that they have something that will be of use to education. The jaundiced spectator will be forgiven for regarding this merely as another boom to be followed by the inevitable bust. Our own bet is that cognitive psychology has a good chance of becoming that solid scientific underpinning of an educational technology that educational psychologists from Herbart to Dewey have been calling for.

As an illustration of a line of research potentially useful for solving a long-standing practical educational problem, we describe here some work on readability. This work grew out of a model of text comprehension that has been the major focus of our research for a number of years now. What we report here is purely speculative. The work on the model itself is in an unfinished, fluid state; and we shall not attempt here to present a serious test of its implications for readability. but we do outline a program for such a test and show how modern psychological theory might provide us with some interesting insights into this long-standing, important, and recalcitrant applied problem.

Readability is of considerable practical significance to educators and publishers of educational materials. We briefly discuss the traditional approach with its successes and limitations. It is an empirical, atheoretical approach that deals well with certain aspects of the problem but entirely neglects others. Our model, which enables us to deal with some of these neglected aspects, appears to have some powerful implications for a redefinition of the problem of readability.

The Puzzle of Readability

Who cares about readability? Psychologists don't—not any more. Figure 15.1 shows that, as indexed by number of references in *Psychological Abstracts,* interest in readability peaked in the 1950s but has been at zero for nearly a decade now. Educators do still care, however. The *Education Index* shows strong interest through the 1960s, and it seems to be holding through the 1970s. Unfortunately, number of studies is not a sure measure of progress. Research on readability has been thoroughly practical and unanalytical, so that we now have techniques for measuring readability but little under-

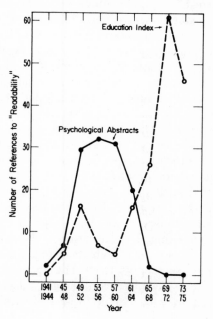

FIG. 15.1. Readability in psychology and education.

standing of what we are measuring. However, by taking a more complex approach to text structure and text processing, cognitive science may make contact with the art of education and may even prevent readability from going the way of all Flesch.

Later, we touch on some of these new directions in readability research. First, we want to consider the traditional work. But before doing either, we need to ask: How has readability been defined, and why is it important?

A dictionary definition subclassifies readability into: (a) the legibility, (b) the reading ease, and (c) the interest value of a text. Klare (1963, p. 1) agrees and adds: (d) comprehension ease. Chall (1958) also supports this definition but then says: "The idea underlying readability measurement is the appropriate matching of reader and printed material [p. 9]." This notion of matching reader and text implies a more complicated, interactive view of readability. It is the gist of Gilliland's (1972) definition, also. As we shall see, actual practice has not kept up with this sophisticated definition, largely because it is based upon an impoverished psychology of reading.

Is readability important? Again quoting Chall (1958): "Readability is now the concern of all those who depend upon communication through the printed word [p. 154]." Bormuth (1975) makes the more intriguing point that literacy, a basic human right, can be functionally increased *either* by improving literacy skills *or* by improving the readability of written language.

Formulas. For those "who depend upon communication through the printed word," a pertinent question is whether the material will be read and, if read, understood by those it was intended for. Thus an educational publisher might be interested to know that a book said to be suitable for eight-graders would be more appropriate for twelfth-graders instead. Similarly, teachers, broadcasters, and journalists want to know in advance whether a particular text is likely to be read with understanding, or read at all.

Formulas were invented to meet this need. A large number of prose passages were available (the McCall–Crabbs Standard Test Lessons in Reading, 1925, 1950, 1961). It was known for each selection how many questions could be correctly answered by children of various ages. There was, however, no theory that would relate in any way the nature of the questions that could or could not be answered from a text to either the structure or content of the text, or to the information-processing capacities and strategies of the reader. In fact, the questions were constructed intuitively and haphazardly, thus frustrating any hopes for a more analytic approach from the very beginning. The other side of the formula was handled in similarly inadequate ways. In the absence of a theory of text structure and text processing, researchers selected a number of fairly obvious surface features of the text (e.g., average word length). Then, by linear regression, they determined to what extent these variables predicted question-answering scores. The formulas differ from one another in the number, weights, and types of variables used. Once several formulas had become popular, later formulas used the earlier ones as their criterion.

There are now about 50 readability formulas. They aren't going out of fashion, either. Klare (1974/75) summarized 24 new formulas that appeared between 1960 and 1974, as well as 6 recalculations of the 30 or so that existed up to then. (The earliest formulas appeared during the 1920s.) Some of them are esoteric (e.g., intended only for chemistry and physics textbooks, or for shorthand dictation materials). Many are automated. Some are incredibly detailed (e.g., Bormuth, 1969; he used the cloze comprehension test as criterion and developed 24 formulas with up to 20 different variables each).

Almost every formula proposed has a word variable and a sentence variable. Klare (1974/75) noted that the word factor has consistently higher predictive value than the sentence factor; this is true for other languages as well as for English.

It is important to keep in mind that formulas have predictive validity only. If long words and long sentences *caused* comprehension difficulty, shortening them would remove the difficulty, which is obviously not so. It is amazing, but apparently true, that for predictive purposes simple word and sentence counts are satisfactory at all. Klare (1974/75) says the evidence on this is "now quite conclusive."

Limitations.   The problem is not with the formulas but with our theories. Given these technological riches, we have failed to dig deeper, to reach a true understanding of text comprehension. Formulas do a job, but they leave a lot unexplained. For example, it is said that an abstract, complex discussion is accompanied by many conjunctions. Clearly, the conjunctions do not cause the difficulty—they are merely an index of it. What, then, is at the root of the trouble? A formula that includes conjunctions as one of its factors is still at the "symptom" level.

Formulas sometimes give perplexing results. Lockman (1956) computed the Flesch Reading Ease scores of nine sets of instructions for psychological tests. He then had 171 naval cadets rate the instructions on "understandability." However, the rank-order correlation between the two sets of measurements was −0.65 ($p < 0.05$). With true military reserve, Lockman concluded: "It would appear that reading ease scores and understandability ratings were not measuring the same thing [p. 196]." One wonders why not.

Another distressing result was Stevens and Stones's (1947) readability analysis of several standard psychology books. The distress was due to Kurt Koffka's being found more readable than, of all people, William James. Partly this was an artifact: Stevens and Stone used the early Flesch formula in which "personal references" were a factor. Koffka happened to use them frequently, although not usually in a personal sense. But even so, readability formulas fail to tap the real differences between Koffka and James. Hebb and Bindra (1952) identified one of these as what we might today call "processing instructions:" those little tips and cues that allow the reader to organize and integrate sequential material. James typically says, "I am now talking about B, not A," whereas with Koffka, you just don't know where you are.

Indeed, these higher-level features of text organization are probably the most serious omission from readability fomulas. Chall (1958, p. 55) pointed out that the McCall–Crabbs Test Lessons, the prototypic criterion, were too short to reveal such factors even if they had been there. In this sense there was from the beginning a bias against including higher-level features in the formulas. Readability formulas cannot even discriminate between scrambled and well-ordered words; much less can they detect scrambled sentences or paragraphs. Even the cloze test, used as a measure of readability, would be unable to distinguish a well-ordered passage from one with its paragraphs rearranged.

Klare (1963) noted four more limitations of formulas. They measure only style, not content. They measure only one aspect of style—difficulty— ignoring dramatic effectiveness, appropriateness, and so on They are not perfect indicators even of style difficulty, and they are certainly not measures of *good* style.

Our own criticisms of readability formulas are more modest. We do not attempt anything as ambitious as measuring good style. Nor are we able to identify all the factors that contribute to reading difficulties; we do not even try to construct the perfect formula. Instead, we outline some considerations based on a model of reading comprehension that suggest a number of additional text and reader characteristics that determine reading ease. Note that we propose to add to the existing formulas: We do not doubt that long sentences, unfamiliar words, and abstractness produce reading difficulties. It is just that this is not the whole story. And note that we do not provide the whole story, either. Our model is young and blemished. It points to a few new things, but a deeper understanding of reading processes will undoubtedly identify other important variables. First, however, we want to specify somewhat more precisely our misgivings about existing readability formulas and the whole traditional approach to this problem.

NEW DIRECTIONS

Although readability formulas are by no means useless for practical purposes, they are far from adequate. We shall illustrate this point by means of some sample texts, where differences in readability scores and differences in a number of criterion measures are uncorrelated. Furthermore, the existing work on readability is close to useless from a theoretical perspective. It tells us very little about what makes a text easy or hard to read, and it is totally severed from research in cognitive psychology concerned with the process of reading comprehension. Instead, the traditional approach is an atheoretical one and relies on correlating plausible predictor variables (i.e., text properties) with plausible behavioral criteria of readability. The trouble is that typically neither set of variables is adequate. We have mentioned the problems with the predictor variables used in current readability formulas. They are concerned with word and sentence properties at a superficial level; at best, they are correlated with whatever makes a text easy or hard, but they are not the causes themselves. The problem is that the predictors commonly used do not directly reflect either the content or the organization of a text. Reading comprehension is ultimately a process of acquiring information. The nature and structure of that information—that is, the characteristics of the meaning of a text, as well as the processes involved in deriving this meaning from the written text—are, we assume, the real determinants of readability. That is where we must look for predictor variables—not to replace current ones, but to supplement them. This of course requires a theory of reading comprehension, or at least the rudiments of such a theory.

The problem of criterial variables is a different one and quite analogous to that encountered with intelligence tests. We know (in our hearts) what we mean by readability, but there appears to be no one behavioral index that we could consider as adequate. Traditional practice has been quite unsatisfactory. Using a previous formula to validate a new one is certainly the worst of the commonly used procedures. Having subjects rate readability is not much better. People's intuitions are usually good, but too much reliance upon them is risky; and more direct procedures should be preferred if they are available. The cloze procedure, on the other hand, is probably actually misleading. It measures the statistical redundancy of a text, which is a far cry from its comprehensibility. By that score, a high-order statistical approximation to English that nevertheless constitutes incomprehensible gibberish would be preferred to a well-organized text with less predictable local patterns. That leaves as more adequate indicators of comprehension difficulty such measures as reading time, amount recalled, number of questions answered correctly, the ease with which a text can be typed or translated, and various eye movement statistics. The last three of these are quite atheoretical. They may be useful as practical indicators of comprehensibility, but they reflect comprehension only indirectly and are therefore not very useful for analytic work. (Things might change, however, as our sophistication in the use of eye-movement techniques increases or if we would look at the actual pattern of translation or typing, not merely at some global statistic.)

At this point, reading time, recall, and question answering are probably the most useful measures available. Note, however, that the use of these measures is theory dependent or rather should be theory dependent. It makes no sense to simply ask questions—any kind of question that occurs to the researcher—about a text. Much misuse has occurred in this way (e.g., when comprehension of a story is indexed by asking for some irrelevant detail). Asking questions is meaningful only if we have a fairly precise theory of text structure and text processing and if we know the role of the information tapped by our questions in terms of the total structure and process. Without such a theoretical understanding of a text, question answering is of dubious value. Indeed, being able to answer some irrelevancy correctly may sometimes be a sign of not understanding rather than a point to be scored for comprehension.

Recall of a text (or summarizing, if the text is long) has not been used as much as it should be as a criterion variable in readability studies. The reason lies in the impossibility of scoring recall protocols without some theoretical foundation. Scoring for words won't do; and scoring for meaning—if it is not to be arbitrary—presupposes some model for the representation of meaning. A number of such models are now available, and we can expect a wider use of recall and summarization techniques. However, if one is interested in comprehensibility, recall scores can never be considered in isolation, because they depend crucially on reading times. There is an obvious trade-off between reading times and recall. We have found, for instance, that if subjects control their own reading times, they recall about the same amount of information from a paragraph, regardless of its difficulty. Readers compensate for a hard text by increasing their processing time. On the other hand, if the time allowed for reading is fixed, differences in recall appear; the hard paragraphs are now recalled less well than the easy ones (Kintsch, Kozminsky, Streby, McKoon, & Keenan, 1975). Thus, neither reading time nor amount of recall alone provides a satisfactory index of processing difficulty, but only their combination.

In Table 15.1 four texts are shown that come from a set of paragraphs kindly made available to us by Ernst Rothkopf. According to their Flesch scores, paragraphs *Jimmy* and *Rocket* should be easy to read, whereas paragraphs *Animal* and *Law* should be moderately hard ones. In Table 15.2 we have summarized some of the behavioral data that Rothkopf has collected on these paragraphs. Recall data are not available, but in any case a fairly clear picture emerges. First of all, note that the cloze data do not correspond well with all the other behavioral data; the *Rocket* paragraph—which achieves the highest cloze score—takes longest to read, requires the largest number of regressions, fixations and saccades; and is the second worst in terms of the typing strokes per reading time and strokes per chain measures. These measures however, correlate almost perfectly among themselves; the average rank order of the four paragraphs on these measures is *Jimmy* > *Animals* > *Law* > *Rocket,* with the differences between the first and second as well as between the second and third paragraphs being more pronounced than that between the last pair. We propose to regard this rank order, based upon six rather different measures, as a behavioral index of the readability of the four paragraphs. Our goal is to match this rank order, based upon considerations about text structure and comprehension processes that are described in the next section of this paper.

Note that the Flesch scores of the four paragraphs, also listed in Table 15.2, do not predict the behavioral data. According to the Flesch scores, *Rocket—*

TABLE 15.1
Four Sample Texts[a]

(Rocket)

A great black and yellow V-2 rocket forty-six feet long stood in a New Mexico desert. Empty, it weighed five tons. For fuel it carried eight tons of alcohol and liquid oxygen.

Everything was ready. Scientists and generals withdrew to some distance and crouched behind earth mounds. Two red flares rose as a signal to fire the rocket.

With a great roar and burst of flame the giant rocket rose slowly and then faster and faster. Behind it trailed sixty feet of yellow flame. Soon the flame looked like a yellow star. In a few seconds it was too high to be seen, but radar tracked it as it sped upward to 3,000 miles per hour.

A few minutes after it was fired, the pilot of a watching plane saw it return at a speed of 2,400 miles per hour and plunge into earth forty miles from the starting point.

(Jimmie Cod)

A long time ago the little fishes of the sea were at school down under the water, safe from dangerous animals. One pupil, Jimmie Cod, was not studying. He was looking at something dangling in front of him. He could not take his eyes off this shiny object. When the teacher of history asked him what he thought of the whale that swallowed Jonah, he replied, "It looks good enough to eat." Everyone was amused at Jimmie's strange answer and all turned to look at him. He was not thinking of school or history lessons, but he was getting hungrier every minute. Suddenly, while teacher and pupils were looking it happened. Jimmie took a quick bite and swallowed that shiny something which had been hanging just before his nose. Then like a flash he went up, up, out of sight. And no one in the class saw Jimmie Cod again.

(Animal Defenses)

Although a very large number of animals rely upon concealment, and another multitude upon agility in flight—by swimming, running, or flying—a sizeable group show willingness to stand and defend themselves. Usually these animals have either armor in the form of scales, bony plates, or various types of exoskeletons, or definite weapons of some sort. Antlers, horns, and defensive use of teeth have been mentioned. More specialized weapons include the quills of the porcupine, which are modified hairs set among the fur.

(Poor Law)

The working of the poor law had not only tended to keep wages down and to perpetuate local inequalities by immobilizing some of the population. After the wars the burden of rates, in certain areas and on certain shoulders, became intolerable. There is no need to treat as representative those extreme cases, often quoted in contemporary controversy, in which the rates equalled or exceeded the annual value of the land; but it is certain that everywhere the burden hung heavy about the neck of the small holder or proprietor. The system helped to depress the "yeomanry".

---

[a]From Ernst Rothkopf (personal communication).

TABLE 15.2
Test Statistics for the Four Paragraphs Shown in Table 15.1[a]

	Jimmy	Rocket	Animals	Law
Cloze score	.69	.72	.57	.50
Reading time per line in seconds	2.04	2.49	2.18	2.39
Typing strokes per reading time	14.00	10.97	12.05	10.09
Typing strokes per chain	49.05	38.81	35.76	33.26
Eye movement data:				
Number of regressions	1.69	2.09	1.85	2.01
Number of fixations	7.59	8.69	7.86	8.51
Number of saccades	4.90	5.60	5.01	5.50
Flesch R.E. score[b]	81	75	46	46

[a] All data and scores are from Ernst Z. Rothkopf (personal communication).
[b] These are our Flesch scores, based on Flesch's (1948) own formula; EZR used a simplified (computer-aided) formula, and so his numbers are slightly different: 78, 84, 40, 41.

which is in fact the hardest paragraph—should be almost as easy as *Jimmy;* and *Animals* should be no different from *Law.* This is clearly not the case for most of Rothkopf's data, except for the cloze scores. These are in fact predicted quite well by the Flesch scores; but because the cloze scores contradict the other measures considered here, this predictive success is pointless. We have not picked the four paragraphs at random. Instead, they were selected to show that texts equated for readability scores may still vary considerably in behavioral measures of reading ease and that the theory described in the next section permits us to understand some of the reasons for this variability. That is, we want to illustrate our theory with this material— not test it in any serious way.

Toward a Psychology of Text Comprehension

If readability is not simply a question of long words and long sentences, then what is it? Recent research on text comprehension gives us at least a partial answer to this question. We review first the theoretical base of this research, citing relevant experimental results in support of our contentions wherever they are available. In the next section, we discuss the implications of this work for the concept of readability.

Our main point is that because we are mainly interested in how much and how easily a reader comprehends what he or she reads, the readability of a text can only be evaluated if one has an explicit model of the processes involved in text comprehension. We offer only a crude, first approximation to such a model, but even that will turn out to be a fairly powerful tool.

The Representation of Meaning

Our approach is based upon the model for the representation of meaning in memory developed in Kintsch (1974). Comprehension is assumed to involve the construction of the meaning of a passage from written text (or, for that matter, from speech; we talk about reading here simply because the eventual applications are to reading). The meaning of a text is represented by its *text base,* which is a structured list of *propositions.* A proposition consists of a predicate with one or more *arguments;* arguments are *concepts* or propositions themselves. A concept is realized in the language by a word (or by more than one word if there are synonyms) or sometimes by a phrase. For convenience, we denote concepts by their corresponding English word; but it is important to remember that we are not dealing with words at all, but with abstract concepts. We have adopted the convention of writing the names of word concepts in capital letters (to distinguish them from words) and of writing the predicate of a proposition first. For example, in (TRACK, ROCKET, RADAR) the predicate is TRACK; the first argument is ROCKET, which functions in the semantic role of an Object; and the second argument is RADAR, in the semantic role of Instrument. In English the proposition could be expressed as *Radar tracked the rocket* or *The rocket was tracked by radar* or—in the right context, say in answer to an appropriate question—just as *Radar.* Furthermore, it is often convenient to number propositions so that if one proposition serves as the argument of another, we can simply refer to it by number and need not write it out again. Thus, the minitext base.

1. (GREAT, ROCKET)
2. (STAND, ROCKET)
3. (LOCATION: IN, 2, DESERT),

could be expressed as *The rocket was great. It stood in the desert;* or preferably, *The great rocket stood in the desert.*

The first step in all of our analyses is to convert a given text into its propositional text base. This procedure has been justified in Kintsch (1974) and is explained in more detail by Turner and Greene (1977). In the present paper we simply accept it as it is and use it. It is not a very elegant procedure, and it certainly would not be suitable if our concern were with the finer points of logic or semantic analysis. But it is simple and relatively robust. We find that with some experience any researcher gets to use it quite easily and, more important, arrives at substantially the same result as other users. Exactly how we proceed has been described in detail in the manual prepared by Turner and Greene mentioned above. However, if others find some of our practices objectionable (e.g., our high-handed approach to quantifiers), modifications and improvements will not destroy the system. That is, the same pattern of results should be obtained with a somewhat modified system, though actual numerical values would of course be changed. This robustness, as well as its simplicity, we take to be highly desirable characteristics of our system of analysis.

Table 15.3 shows the text base for the first two paragraphs of the *Rocket* text that was discussed previously (Table 15.1). The 31 propositions are ordered in the same way as they are expressed in the text (i.e., a proposition "occurs" when its predicate or one of its arguments first occurs). In interpreting the text base, it is important to note that once a concept is introduced, repetitions of it are assumed to have the same referent unless otherwise indicated. Thus, wherever ROCKET appears, it refers to the same physical object introduced in the first proposition. References to another

TABLE 15.3
The Text Base for the First Two Paragraphs of *Rocket*

1	(GREAT, ROCKET)
2	(BLACK, ROCKET)
3	(YELLOW, ROCKET)
4	(V-2, ROCKET)
5	(LONG, ROCKET)
6	(FORTY-SIX FEET, 5)
7	(STAND, ROCKET)
8	(IN, 7, DESERT)
9	(NEW MEXICO, DESERT)
10	(EMPTY, ROCKET)
11	(WEIGH, 10)
12	(FIVE TON, 11)
13	(FOR, 14, FUEL)
14	(CARRY, ROCKET, 17)
15	(EIGHT TON, 16)
16	(WEIGH, 17)
17	(AND, ALCOHOL, OXYGEN)
18	(LIQUID, OXYGEN)
19	(READY, EVERYTHING)
20	(AND, SCIENTIST, GENERAL)
21	(WITHDRAW, 20, DISTANCE)
22	(SOME, DISTANCE)
23	(CROUCH, 20)
24	(BEHIND, 23, MOUND)
25	(EARTH, MOUND)
26	(TWO, FLARE)
27	(RED, FLARE)
28	(RISE, FLARE)
29	(REFERENCE, FLARE, SIGNAL)
30	(PURPOSE, 28, 31)
31	(FIRE, $, ROCKET)

rocket or to rockets in general (e.g., *Rockets are expensive*) would require the introduction of a new concept ROCKET, to be distinguished by an index number. Hence, we need no further notation to indicate that *great, black, yellow,* etc., are all predicated of the same object.

What have we gained by analyzing paragraphs in this way? What is the use of translating a perfectly transparent text into this slightly obscure and rather clumsy conceptualese? We did it because we hoped that the relationship between meaning—as represented here—and behavioral indices would be a more clear-cut one than that between words and behavior or at the very least, that doing so would help us understand some phenomena that cannot be accounted for if we are concerned merely with words and not with meanings. More specifically, it is clear that the time it takes to read a text depends on the number of words involved. However, we know that two texts of equal length are not always equally easy or hard to read, in part of course due to the characteristics of the words and word sequences used. But even when such variables are controlled (e.g., when two texts have comparable Flesch scores), differences in the ease with which they are comprehended remain, as we have shown previously. Looking at text bases, we can begin to see why.

First, texts may be comparable in word length, but they may differ in the number of propositions expressed by these words. Kintsch and Keenan (1973) have systematically varied the number of propositions in a text base while keeping constant the number of words in the text. They observed that reading time increased regularly as a function of the number of propositions in the text base. Reading time depends not so much on the number of propositions that are expressed in a text but rather on the number of propositions that a reader actually derives from the text. Indeed, for the range explored by Kintsch and Keenan, each proposition processed sufficiently so that it could be produced on an immediate recall test added about 1.5 seconds to the reading time. The longer the texts were, the more time was required for the processing of each additional proposition. Furthermore, scientific prose required more processing time per proposition than simple narratives. Obviously, the number of propositions in a text base is not the only determinant of processing difficulty, but it is an important one.

Another one was identified by Kintsch et al. (1975). It is the number of different arguments that are used in a text base. We constructed texts that were equal in the number of words as well as in the number of propositions; they differed, however, in that in some paragraphs the same concepts were used over and over again as propositional arguments whereas in others, new concepts were continuously introduced. Thus, the first kind of text says much about a few things, whereas the latter says little about many things. It is not intuitively obvious which of the two types of texts should be harder to process, because the few-arguments paragraphs are necessarily complex structurally with many embeddings both at the propositional and syntactic level, which might have been expected to offset the disadvantage of having to deal with many different concepts in the many-arguments paragraphs. Interestingly, it did not; the more different arguments were used in a text base, the longer it took subjects to read the paragraph for each proposition recalled. Thus, a basic difficulty encountered in comprehension appears to be the establishment of new concepts, whereas repeating an established concept appears to involve simpler operations.

The texts that we have discussed so far were all rather short ones. For instance, in the study just mentioned we worked with 70-word paragraphs, each of which was based upon a 25-proposition text base. For the paragraphs with few different arguments, there were 0.29 different arguments per proposition, whereas for the paragraphs with many different arguments, this ratio increased to 0.64 on the average. For the moment we shall restrict our attention to texts of these lengths (say, up to 150 words or so), for if we work with much longer texts a whole set of new considerations arises that can be safely neglected with the kind of materials used here. Comprehending a long text, we argue later, involves not only the construction of a propositional text base but also its organization in terms of a macrostructure. For short paragraphs, the macrostructure (intuitively, the gist) and microstructure (i.e., the text base as discussed earlier) need not be distinguished. Hence our problem is simplified, and we show below that our results can be extended from this oversimplified situation to longer texts without modification of the principles invovled.

Coherence

We have now identified two text base statistics that appear to affect readability: the propositional density of a text and the number of new concepts per proposition. If comprehension really involves the construction of a text base as we hypothesize, it is easy to see why the number of propositions should play a role. Our second finding is not as obvious, but it has some far-reaching implications: Introducing a new argument is harder than repeating an old one. This suggests that argument repetition might serve an important function in the formation of a text base. Indeed, we have so far talked about text bases as if they were a list of unrelated propositions. Clearly, this is not the case: Texts must be coherent. In terms of our model, a text base must have some kind of property that distinguishes it from an arbitrary list of propositions. The problem of text cohesion is of course an old one to which a good deal of effort has been devoted by linguists and logicians. We do not propose to solve it here. Instead, we opt for a crude but effective solution: We suggest that a text base is cohesive if it is connected by argument repetition. Thus, two propositions are connected if they share a common argument. (For instance, in the previous example, propositions 1 and 2 are connected because they share the argument ROCKET; and Propositions 2 and 3 are connected because 2 itself is an argument of 3.) A text base is connected if there exists at least one path from every proposition to every other one. For example, 1–2–3 is connected because 1 is connected to 2 and 2 is connected to 3. Defining cohesion in terms of argument repetition is not very satisfactory linguistically, but it is quite sufficient for present purposes. It is very simple, completely objective, and seems to account for a major portion of the variance in cohesiveness of texts. Thus, a more sophisticated theory might not be very much better for practical purposes than our crude one, though it would constitute a desirable gain in elegance.

Armed with this definition of coherence, we can now begin to formulate a simple processing model of comprehension or, to. be more precise, the component of the total process having to do with the establishment of coherence. This model will give us some further insights into what makes a text easy or hard to comprehend.

The emphasis on coherence is by no means new in psycholinguistics. Clark (1976) talks about the importance of "bridging" in text comprehension, and Haviland and Clark (1974) have provided some experimental results that are directly relevant to our point. Subjects can comprehend a sentence more rapidly when it is connected directly via argument repetition to a preceding sentence than when it is not. This result suggests that when a new argument is introduced, the reader must establish in episodic memory a concept node for that argument but that if an argument is repeated, the reader merely connects it with an already established node. Thus, the formation of a text base is formally equivalent to the construction of a graph in which propositions that share an argument are connected to the proposition that first introduced that argument.

Table 15.4 shows how the first 31 propositions of the *Rocket* paragraph are organized into a text base. We have chosen the proposition underlying the main clause of the first sentence (P7) to head the network and to introduce the concept ROCKET (had there been a title, it would have provided us with the superordinate proposition). From P7 there are connections to all propositions that repeat the argument ROCKET. P6 is connected to P5, because P5 is embedded in P6 as one of its arguments; P9 shares an argument with P8 (but not with any more higher level propositions) and is therefore connected to it. P19 and P20 start new subgraphs, because they do not share an argument with any of the propositions in the main graph. Hence the text base is not coherent by our definition, and coherence must be established via inference. Presumably, in this case, *Everything was ready* would be expanded to *Everything was ready (to fire the rocket)*, and *Scientists and generals* would be connected to the text base by something like *who were directing the firing of the rocket.* In previous work (Keenan & Kintsch, McKoon & Keenan, both in Kintsch, 1974; as well as Baggett, 1975), evidence has been obtained that

TABLE 15.4
The Coherence Graph for the Text Base of *Rocket*

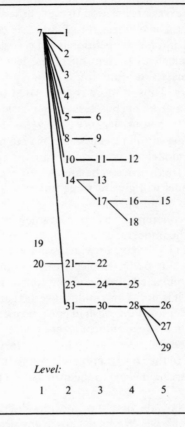

readers indeed make such inferences during the process of reading. These inferences then become a part of the memory representation of the text just as any other proposition in the text base. Here, we are not really concerned with the process of inference making as such, but only with its repercussions with respect to readability. We postulate that whenever such inferences are required by a text, this will add significantly to the reader's processing load during comprehension and hence affect the readability of the text. Thus, a paragraph that can be analyzed into a connected graph should be easier to process than a paragraph that does not form a coherent text base.

A Processing Model

In constructing the graph in Table 15.4 we have simply arranged all 31 propositions according to their pattern of argument repetition. Suppose we had worked with the whole *Rocket* paragraph of 150 words, which amounts to 74 underlying propositions. We could easily arrange all 74 propositions in the way we have done the 31 in Table 15.4—but clearly this can hardly be what a reader does during comprehension! One of the central facts about cognitive processes is that the human capacity to hold information in short-term memory or working memory is severely limited. A reader can't juggle around 74 propositions at a time or even 31 for that matter! At any one time, a real processor must somehow work with a portion of the text base, annexing it to the growing graph, and then proceed to the next section, carrying along in one's working memory not the whole graph but only a selected subset of it to which the new, incoming part of the text base can be connected. In order to work with such a model, one has to make some rather specific assumptions about the details of this process. Many of these assumptions are at this point no more than educated guesses. Nevertheless, it is useful to work out the consequences of such a processing model for text comprehension, even though we can put no stock in some of the details.

First, we must set some limits on the number of propositions that can be worked on in parallel. Clearly, this should be a free parameter of the model, but just to be able to do some calculations we shall assume for the moment that readers chunk the text base into groups containing 6 to 10 propositions. As shown in Table 15.3, the propositions are ordered in terms of the surface structure from which they are derived. We also assume that the surface structure guides the chunking: Groups of propositions of the desired size are formed on the basis of sentence or phrase boundaries. There is good psychological evidence for an initial segmentation of texts on the basis of sentence and phrase boundaries (e.g., from the work of Jarvella, 1971, or Aaronson and Scarborough, 1977). Thus, although the chunking size we selected is clearly abitrary, the general principle involved is psychologically plausible.

Given a group of input propositions, these are ordered on the basis of argument repetition in the same way as we constructed Table 15.4. From the resulting graph, a subgraph is selected to be retained in short-term memory in order to provide some interconnections for the next processing unit. The main graph itself is stored in long-term memory (in some probabilistic way), from which it can be retrieved if it becomes necessary to do so. The to-be-retained subgraph must be limited in size. Just for the sake of concreteness, we work all our examples with short-tem memory limits varying between 4 and 7. Clearly, an efficient processor would not select the to-be-retained propositions at random. Intuitively, there are two considerations that should play a role: Important propositions, high up in the graph, should be favored, as well as recent propositions. These two principles do not, however, specify a unique selection strategy. Of the many possible, reasonable strategies we have chosen what we call the "leading-edge rule." It seems to give a nice balance of our two goals—to favor superordination and recency. We describe the strategy in detail later. Here it is important to realize that a different selection strategy, as long as it somehow achieves the desired bias of superordination and recency, would alter the actual numbers presented later but hardly the pattern of results.

Next, we must specify what happens when no connections exist between the set of input propositions and the subgraph retained in short-term memory for that purpose. In such a case we assume that a search of long-term memory is made to determine whether there is a proposition already stored by means of which the new set of propositions could be connected with the existing network. If so, this proposition is reinstated in working memory. Such reinstatement searches, whether or not they actually result in a reinstatement, must be expected to contribute greatly to comprehension difficulty.

Finally, if a text base is interconnected in parts, as described here, the resulting graph will often differ from the ideal one (that is, from the one that would be constructed if there were no memory limitations as in Table 15.4). Therefore, reorganizations of the text base might be required after the original network has been established. For instance, some proposition (and with it the whole subgraph subordinated to it) might be annexed to a proposition far down in the graph during the part-by-part processing of the input. But as the whole graph becomes available, a connection to a higher-order proposition might be noticed, thus requiring a reorganization of the network.

Thus, we have three plausible sources of reading difficulty arising from the process of text-base construction: reinstatement searches (successful ones as well as unsuccessful ones), reorganizations, and the number of unconnected graphs. Parenthetically, we should also mention here that the model predicts not only how hard a particular text should be but also what part of the text will be recalled. Each time a particular proposition is selected and retained in the short-term memory set, it receives further processing (e.g., it may be interconnected with other propositions). Each processing must be expected to increase the chances that the proposition will be successfully stored in long-term memory and hence be recallable. In fact, we have here a version of the Atkinson–Shiffrin (1968) buffer model, applied to reading comprehension. Because the selection strategy proposed here is biased in favor of superordinate propositions, it follows that such propositions should on the average be better recalled. This is of course precisely what has been reproted previously on several occasions (Kintsch & Keenan, 1973; Kintsch et al., 1975): The probability of recalling a proposition depends very much on the level of that proposition in the text-base hierarchy.

An Example.   An example will clarify the essential features of the proposed model. In Table 15.3 the first 31 propositions of the text base of the *Rocket* paragraph are shown; the text itself is reprinted in Table 15.1. The first sentence contains nine propositions. It is, therefore, the first processing unit that we have to deal with. Its organization is shown in Table 15.5 (a). The

TABLE 15.5
The Construction of the Text Base for *Rocket*,
With $6 \leqslant I \leqslant 10$ and Two Values of s

$s = 4$:	$s = 7$:

(a) CYCLE A: Input P1–P9

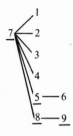

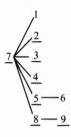

(b) CYCLE B: Input P10–P18

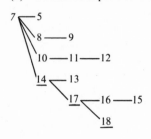

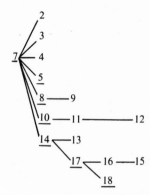

(c) CYCLE C: Input P19–P25

(d) CYCLE D: Input P26–P31

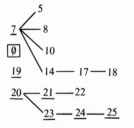

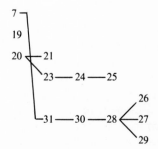

simplest graph structure is obtained by making P7 the superordinate node, as in Table 15.4. Assume now a short-term memory limit $s = 4$. The leading-edge strategy selects the four underlined propositions for retention in short-term, memory. Informally, the strategy specifies the following selection order: First, pick the leading edge of the graph [i.e., the most recent (highest-numbered) proposition at each level; for clarity, we have placed the propositions at each level in a separate column]. Start at the top node and continue until the required number of propositions is selected. Next return to the highest level that still contains nonselected propositions, and pick them in the order of recency until the limit is reached. In Table 15.5 (a), there are three levels, and we first select the most recent proposition at each level—that is, P7, P8, and P9. Because there are no further propositions at Level 1, we go to Level 2 and pick the most recent propositions from that level (i.e., P5). With a short-term memory capacity of $s = 7$ propositions, 4, 3, and 2 would also be selected from Level 2 with this strategy.

With the four (or seven, depending on s) propositions thus selected and held in short-term memory, we now enter Cycle B. The input set now contains the propositions underlying the next two sentences, because the next sentence by itself is too short, containing only two propositions. Therefore, it is combined with the following sentence, which produces an input set of nine propositions altogether. Because P10 and P14 contain the argument ROCKET and the other propositions are connected to them, the whole set can be annexed to the main network. Again the leading edge of the graph is selected (plus some other propositions if $s = 7$) and carried over into Cycle C. The input now contains seven propositions from two sentences. However, two separate graphs are constructed from these propositions; one contains the single proposition P19, and the other graph is headed by P20. In both cases reinstatement searches must be initiated, which remain unsuccessful because there are no propositions in long-term memory to which any of the new materials could be connected. Finally, a new short-term memory set is selected according to the leading-edge strategy, and we enter Cycle D where the input consists of the six propositions of the next sentence. Because none of these connect to any of the propositions in the short-term memory set when $s = 4$, another long-term memory search is required. This time the search is successful, returning P7, to which the present input propositions can be annexed. The result is the graph structure shown in Table 15.5 (d). Note however, that for $s = 7$, no reinstatement search occurs in Cycle D; P7 is still in the short-term memory set, and the input is simply connected to it. In either case, we are left with a text base that consists of three separate graphs. Furthermore, in just four cycles, two long-term searches were required when $s = 4$ and one when $s = 7$. We might expect, then, that this text would be quite hard to read, especially for readers with a small short-term memory capacity. Note also a further effect of the larger short-term memory capacity; many more propositions are underlined in Table 15.5 when $s = 7$ than when $s = 4$, which means that these propositions receive an additional rehearsal. Hence a higher and somewhat modified pattern of recall is predicted.

In Table 15.6 we show some computations for the same text base with the size of the input chunks varied. Again, note that the large input size requires one less reinstatement search and also fewer reorganizations. The only

TABLE 15.6
The Construction of the Text Base for *Rocket*,
With $s = 5$, and Two Values of I

$2 \leqslant I \leqslant 5$	$11 \leqslant I \leqslant 16$

(a) CYCLE A: Input P1–4   CYCLE A: Input P1–12

(b) CYCLE B: Input P5–9

(c) CYCLE C: Input P10–12

(continued)

TABLE 15.6 *(continued)*
The Construction of the Text Base for *Rocket*,
With *s* = 5, and Two Values of *I*

$2 \leqslant I \leqslant 5$	$11 \leqslant I \leqslant 16$

(d) CYCLE D: Input P13–14   CYCLE B: Input P13–28

```
1     7                                         8
  \   10 — 11 — 12              7 <  10 — 11 — 12
   \  14 — 13                        14 — 13
```

(e)   CYCLE E: Input P15–18 $\boxed{\emptyset}$

```
1     7                          19
  \   10                         20  — 21 — 22
   \  14     13                    \ 23 — 24 — 25
          17     16 — 15
              18                 28  — 26
                                    27
```

(f)   CYCLE F: Input P19–22

```
1  — 10
  \ 14 — 17 — 18
```

$\boxed{\emptyset}$

```
19
20 — 21 — 22
```

(g)   CYCLE G: Input P23–25

```
1

19
20  — 21 — 22
  \ 23 — 24 — 25
```

(continued)

TABLE 15.6 *(continued)*
The Construction of the Text Base for *Rocket*,
With $s = 5$, and Two Values of I

$2 \leqslant I \leqslant 5$	$11 \leqslant I \leqslant 16$

(h) CYCLE H: Input P26–28

$\underline{19}$

$\underline{20}$ —— 23 —— 24 ——25

$\boxed{\emptyset}$

$\underline{28} \diagup^{\underline{26}}_{\underline{27}}$

(i) CYCLE I: Input P27–31

19

20   26
28 ⟵ 27
      ＼29
       30 —— 31

CYCLE C: Input P29–45
(Shown only to P31)

7
19
20
31 —— 30 —— (28) —— 27
                    ＼29

reorganization occurs in Cycle C, where P28 (circled) is annexed to P30, thereby connecting a separate subgraph formed in Cycle B to the main graph. If the input size is restricted to less than five propositions, on the other hand, this reorganization—if it occurs at all—would have to occur during a "check" of the entire graph following the construction of the whole text base; there is no motivation for a long-term memory search in Cycle I! Thus, small input chunks may result either in unconnected graphs (and ensuing retrieval problems) or in costly reprocessing.

Control Processes

So far, we have discussed the comprehension process in somewhat of a vacuum, namely without considering the goals and control processes that govern it. These, however, are crucial components of the total process, and their function must be made explicit in a model. There seem to be two distinct aspects to this problem: (1) questions having to do with the reader's purpose and set; and (2) the use of the reader's knowledge base in acquiring new information. The two interact—purpose and set are certainly not independent of the general knowledge a person has—but the distinction is a useful one nevertheless. Sets can be readily manipulated—by instructions, a title, or implicit task demands. The reader's knowledge, on the other hand, specifically his or her familiarity with the subject matter of the text being read, must be regarded as a constant for present purposes.

There are abundant empirical demonstrations of the crucial role of purpose or set in comprehension. Rothkopf (1977) has reviewed a large body of research that shows that consideration of purpose can often override text structure effects. Anderson and Pichert (1978) demonstrated that subjects remember quite different things from a passage when they read it with different perspectives (e.g., the description of a house read from the viewpoint of a potential buyer or burglar). In a more analytic vein, Kozminsky (1977) has shown how the pattern of recall changes predictably as a function of which of two possible titles has been assigned to it. A title identifies a superordinate proposition, so that the reader will start his or her graph with the title proposition as the top node. So if the same text is given two different titles, it will be organized into different graphs. As we have already shown, however, this organization determines the pattern of rehearsal for the various text propositions and hence the pattern of recall. Thus, a priori predictions are possible as to which propositions will be recalled best with which title. These predictions are borne out in Kozminsky's data.

How are purpose and set effects to be understood within the present model? Manipulations of set by means of title (or prequestions, or assigned perspectives) present no problems, because they specify the nature of the propositional network to be constructed. Indeed, rather the opposite is true: It is the neutral case, where there are no direct indications about the topic of a paragraph, that is troublesome, because it is not always obvious how topic propositions should be identified in these cases.

The model also suggests, however, some less obvious ways in which the reader's goals may influence the comprehension processes, ways that might become fruitful objects of empirical investigation. For instance, suppose someone reads a text not with the general goal of comprehending all of it as well as possible, but with some special purpose in mind. (In some recent experiments in our laboratory, we had subjects read stories with instructions to find out what they could about the role of women in the society from which the story originated.) The model would suggest that now a special-purpose text base is constructed in which the propositions related to the reader's goal are emphasized. Specifically, the strategy for selecting propositions to be retained in short-term memory during successive input cycles would be changed. Instead of the leading-edge strategy we have discussed, a strategy of picking purpose-related propositions could be employed. Clearly this could result in an incoherent text base, but the propositions that would remain unrelated to the main network would be those irrelevant to the reader's purposes, and hence it would not matter if these were irretrievable.

Consider a different case. Suppose a reader's goal is general comprehension, but he or she just wants to skim the text rather than to process it more deeply. The present model might be able to mimic such behavior by increasing the number of input propositions beyond the point where a reader could process all of them. For example, the input set might be increased to the propositions underlying a whole paragraph (rather than a phrase or sentence, as we assumed earlier); but only a random fraction of them—say a total of 6 to 10—are in fact derived from the text, so that all further processing is based upon this fraction of the actual text.

With respect to the question of how the reader's knowledge base affects the comprehension process, we have, unfortunately, very little to say here. That this effect is of paramount importance has been believed and asserted for a very long time, as discussed previously. Serious empirical and theoretical investigations are, however, barely beginning. Voss (1977, personal communication) has reported one of the few sets of experimental data that is relevant and supportive of the old claim that knowing much about a topic (baseball, in Voss' experiments) helps you to learn new things about it more easily. Similarly, Greeno (1976) and a handful of other researchers have laid an empirical and theoretical foundation for further work in this area. The present model is not directly concerned with these questions, but the facilitative effect of knowledge may be represented in several ways. Part of the effect may be outside of the specific domain of the model; we have nothing to say here about how propositions are derived from a text in the first place (instead, we are merely concerned with their coherence). It appears likely that this initial process of extracting the meaning from a text would be greatly facilitated by relevant knowledge. If so, less processing capacity would have to be devoted to this component of the comprehension process, leaving more available for the operations discussed here. In consequence, either the number of propositions in the input set could be increased (without loss of propositions, as in skimming) or the number of propositions carried over in short-term memory. Either way would provide substantial processing advantages.

Another way in which knowledge would be beneficial—in fact crucial—in comprehension is in the inference processes that are required whenever an incoherent text base is constructed. We have suggested that these inferences constitute a major source of reading difficulty. For high-knowledge readers this difficulty should be greatly reduced, whereas for readers without the necessary knowledge it would be insurmountable and lead to the formation of disjointed, impossible-to-retrieve text bases.

We cannot elaborate these suggestions in any serious way here. We simply raise them to show that the model proposed here is flexible and complex enough to allow for the incredibly wide variety of comprehension strategies that people use. Thus armed, we return to our main concern with readability.

Readability Reconsidered

What are the implications of the model that we have outlined here for readability? Some of the ways that we have used to analyze texts have already been shown to be important for readability in earlier work: The density of propositions in a text has been identified as one such factor by Kintsch and Keenan (1973), and the number of different arguments has been investigated by Kintsch et al. (1975). The processing model proposed here suggests a few other factors that might be important.

One of them is the number of separate graphs for each text that result when a coherent network is constructed. There are two ways this could influence readability. A text base that breaks down into several incoherent parts should be harder to recall than an otherwise equivalent but coherent one; the lack of coherence should produce retrieval difficulties. Specifically, we would predict that subjects will forget whole subgraphs at a time, somewhat in the way that whole conceptual categories are omitted in the recall of categorized word lists. This is, however, not a necessary outcome, because a reader would normally connect such a text base by inferring appropriate connecting propositions. If such an inference occurs, we would not expect retrieval problems, but on the other hand the very fact that an inference was required during comprehension should add to the difficulty of the comprehension process. Thus, according to the model, incoherence has two effects that stand in a trade-off relationship: It either produces recall difficulties (one of our indices of readability), or it produces problems during comprehension itself (which would be reflected in such comprehension indices as reading time or perhaps the pattern of eye movements). Therefore, we suggest that the number of inferences required to connect a text base (which is one less than the number of subgraphs produced) might be one important factor in determining the readability of a text.

Another one must certainly be the number of long-term memory searches and reinstatements of propositions into short-term memory, if our model has any psychological validity at all. Again, we have no way of knowing whether a particular reader will actually go through this reinstatement process or not. If not, he or she should encounter retrieval problems at the time of recall, because the reader will have constructed a disconnected text base. If the reader does go through the reinstatement process, the time and effort required to search long-term memory and reinstate a proposition in short-term memory should be reflected in various processing difficulty indices.

Finally, we suggest that the number of reorganizations required to arrive at the best-organized text base might also be a predictor of reading difficulty. It is even less obvious than in the two cases just discussed that a reader will actually perform these reorganizations during comprehension. But, once more, failure to reorganize will leave the reader with a poorly structured text base—which should show up in such tasks as recall or question answering. Perhaps our expectation is not unreasonable, then, that a text that requires several reorganizations before its propositions are put into their proper relationships should be harder to read than one that doesn't. Let us take an example from the *Law* paragraph to see what is involved. In Cycle C (for the medium input length) the following sentence fragment is processed. *There is no need to treat as representative those extreme cases, often quoted in contemporary controversy;* this sentence fragment is decoded into P18-25. Because no connections exist to the propositions carried over in short-term memory, a long-term memory search is initiated that is, however, unsuccessful. Hence a new subgraph is constructed; the simplest graph (i.e., the graph with the fewest levels) involving P18–25 is obtained by using P21 as the superordinate node. In Cycle E, however, a connection occurs between the rest of the text base and the detached subgraph established in Cycle C; the connective *but* indicates the relationship between the sentences. A reader may disregard this relationship but in this case has not really understood the text fully and might answer questions wrongly, or with a long latency, or make errors in recalling or summarizing. On the other hand, if the relationship is properly incorporated into the text base, then a reorganization is required; the detached subtree with P21 as its head must be annexed in its proper place to the main graph; and to do so, the arrangement of the propositions in the subgraph must be altered in some cases.

There may be other factors important for readability that our model helps to identify. For instance, there is a rather substantial difference in the depth of the trees constructed: The text base for the *Law* paragraph has 16 levels, whereas that for *Jimmy* has only 4.

We don't know at this point whether level is in fact significant in this respect, just as we don't know whether inferences, reinstatements, and reorganizations will turn out to be important. But we think that such variables are worth investigating and that some of the variance not accounted for by present-day readability formulas might have its source in just these factors.

Analysis of the Sample Paragraphs

For the four paragraphs of Table 15.1, we can do a surprisingly good job in predicting their readability in this way. It will be remembered (Table 15.2) that the paragraphs can be ordered in terms of reading ease in the following way: *Jimmy* > *Animals* > *Law* > *Rocket*, with the difference between the last pair being relatively minor. Table 15.7 shows the statistics discussed earlier for these four texts. Because the texts differ in length, values per 100 words

TABLE 15.7
Readability Statistics for Four Sample Paragraphs

	Jimmy	Animals	Law	Rocket
Proposition density (per 100 words)	36	48	42	45
Different arguments (per proposition)	0.27	0.32	0.40	0.55
Required inferences (per 100 words)	0	0	2.08	2.00
Reinstatements (average) (per 100 words)	0.55	1.60	3.12	1.44
Reorganizations (average) (per 100 words)	1.00	2.20	5.21	5.88

rather than the actual numbers are reported to facilitate comparison among paragraphs. The number of reinstatements and inferences depends, of course, rather crucially upon the short-term memory and chunk-size parameters of the model (Tables 15.5 and 15.6). We do not know the true values of these parameters; therefore, we have presented here averages over a few reasonable parameter values. Specifically the short-term memory size s was varied from 4 to 7 while restricting the input chunk to between 6 and 10 propositions; in addition, input chunk sizes of 2–5, 6–10, and 11–16 were selected for fixed s = 5. The numbers shown in Table 15.7 are the averages of these six conditions.

Although Table 15.7 is merely guesswork, the model statistics discriminate nicely between the four texts and in just about the right way. *Jimmy* is easiest on all counts. *Animals,* like *Jimmy,* requires no inferences and has relatively few different arguments and reorganizations; however, the average number of reinstatements is rather high, and its proposition density is the highest of the four paragraphs. *Law* is difficult on all counts. *Rocket* presents a more unbalanced picture; it is worst on two measures but requires relatively few reinstatements. Thus, the rank order of difficulty as it emerges from the data shown in Table 15.2 is matched successfully.

A closer look suggests that our model can do much better than predict average data. It implies some interactions between text characteristics and reader characteristics that may be very important for the whole concept of readability. In Table 15.8 we have plotted the number of reinstatements and reorganizations as a function of short-term memory capacity. There are some interesting trends here. In terms of reinstatements, *Jimmy* is always quite easy and *Law* the hardest; *Animals,* however is quite hard for small s but becomes the easiest one for s = 7! Similarly, *Rocket* is sensitive to short-term memory capacity; it is very hard for readers with a small short-term memory capacity (note the 7.33 reorganizations per 100 words); but for a reader with a good short-term memory, these difficulties largely disappear.

TABLE 15.8

Number of Reinstatements Per 100 Words and Reorganizations Per
100 Words as a Function of Short-Term Memory Capacity (s),
With Input Chunk Size Fixed ($2 \leqslant I \leqslant 5$)

	Paragraphs			
	Jimmy	Animals	Law	Rocket
$s = 4$ Reinstatements	0.67	2.41	3.12	1.33
Reorganizations	4.00	2.41	4.17	7.33
$s = 5$ Reinstatements	0.67	2.41	3.12	1.33
Reorganizations	0.67	2.41	4.17	7.33
$s = 6$ Reinstatements	0.67	1.20	3.12	0.67
Reorganizations	0	2.41	4.17	7.33
$s = 7$ Reinstatements	0.67	0	3.12	0.67
Reorganizations	0	2.41	4.17	0.67

The picture is a similar one when the size of the input chunks is varied, as
shown in Table 15.9. For the reader who processes only small chunks, *Rocket*
and also *Animals* present serious obstacles, whereas a good reader (that is,
one who processes large chunks) has little difficulty with them.

In Fig. 15.2 we have combined the data from Tables 15.7 to 15.9 into a
single value for each text and processing-parameter combination. This was
done simply by transforming all numbers to z scores and computing the
average z-score over all predictor variables. This is certainly not a proposal
for a new readability formula. We merely wanted to illustrate in a simple way
the text-by-capacity interactions discussed earlier. Note that in general the
predicted order of reading difficulty corresponds quite well to the Table 15.2

TABLE 15.9

Number of Reinstatements and Reorganizations Per 100 Words
as a Function of the Size of Input Chunks (I),
With Short-Term Memory Capacity Fixed ($s = 5$)

		Paragraphs			
		Jimmy	Animals	Law	Rocket
$2 \leqslant I \leqslant 5$	Reinstatements	0.67	3.61	4.17	2.67
	Reorganizations	1.33	2.41	7.29	12.00
$6 \leqslant I \leqslant 10$	Reinstatements	0.67	2.41	3.12	1.33
	Reorganizations	0.67	2.41	4.17	7.33
$11 \leqslant I \leqslant 16$	Reinstatements	0	0	2.08	2.00
	Reorganizations	0	1.20	7.29	0.67

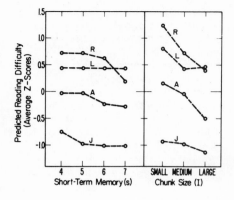

FIG. 15.2. Reading difficulty as a function of the capacity of working memory (the parameters s and l).

data; however, for good readers (good in terms of our model parameters) *Rocket* becomes easier than *Law*. Figure 15.2 was constructed by weighting all predictor variables equally; obviously, through differential weighting much more dramatic interactions could be generated.

Macrostructures

Suppose we are dealing not with a brief paragraph out of context but with a chapter in a book, a newspaper or journal article, or with a lecture—that is, with the kind of long texts that people actually encounter. How could one use these methods of analysis for assessing the readability of such texts? We propose to do so without any change in these methods whatever, except that we no longer concern ourselves with the local problem of coherence but with the coherence of the overall organization of the text. Technically speaking, we propose to apply the methods of coherence analysis to the macrostructure of the text. The concept of macrostructure has been discussed elsewhere (e.g., Kintsch & van Dijk, 1975; van Dijk & Kintsch, 1977). Basically, the idea is that the meaning of a text is represented not merely by the proposition list that directly underlies the verbal expressions but also by a set of macropropositions that organize the text into subunits and that serve as labels for these subunits. Coordinated with each text base, we have therefore a list of macropropositions that correspond, intuitively, to the gist of the text. These macropropositions must be organized into a coherent whole, just as the original list of micropropositions was organized. Thus, we can ask the same kinds of questions about the macropropositions of a text as we did before: How many networks do the macropropositions form? For given processing parameters, what is the expected number of reinstatements and reorganizations that are required in the processing of the macropropositions? Again, we assume that reorganizations, long-term memory searches, and required inferences add significantly to the difficulty of texts. The following example suggests that this might indeed be the case.

Eisenhower and Stevenson. During the 1952 presidential campaign, some observers maintained that Stevenson's speeches were too difficult to understand and too formal and scholarly in comparison with Eisenhower's. In order to gain some insights into the legitimacy of these arguments, Siegel and Siegel (1953) analyzed six speeches from both candidates, given on the same days, by means of the Flesch Reading Ease formula (Flesch, 1948). Their results in no way confirmed popular beliefs. There was only a minuscule 1.5 difference in the reading scores for Eisenhower and Stevenson, with both scores at the borderline between "standard" and "fairly difficult"; Eisenhower came off slightly worse with a score of 58.8 compared to Stevenson's 60.3. Siegel and Siegel suggested, therefore, that the complaints that Stevenson talked over the heads of his audience were not justified.

We have analyzed two of these speeches. Eisenhower does somewhat worse (Reading Ease = 55) than Stevenson (Reading Ease = 61), which means that he uses slightly longer words and sentences. But the formula is misleading; just reading these two speeches, one gains a fairly strong impression that Eisenhower's is the more comprehensible speech. What underlies that intuition?

We set out to analyze the macrostructure of these two speeches. Although van Dijk and Kintsch (1977) have described macro-operators that permit us to derive the macrostructure of a given text in a semialgorithmic way, we have used here a more empirical procedure for the determination of the macrostructure. First we asked raters to divide each speech into macro-units. We told them to draw a line through the text wherever they thought a new text segment started. Whenever half or more of the raters agreed on a segmentation, we located a unit boundary. The first differences between the two texts appeared at this point: People agreed much better about where new text units started in the Eisenhower speech than in the Stevenson speech [χ^2 (3) = 16.08, P = .001]. By some fortunate accident, however, the two speeches, which did not differ much in length, were divided into about the same number of units by this procedure (18 for Eisenhower and 19 for Stevenson). We then gave the speeches, divided into these 18 or 19 units, back to the raters and asked them to write a brief label for each unit—a sentence that would represent the gist of the unit. Next we threw away all statements mentioned by only one judge and from the remaining ones obtained a list of macropropositions for each text unit. A total of 31 macropropositions, varying between 1 and 4 per unit, were thus obtained for the Eisenhower speech; and 32, varying between 0 and 3 per unit, were obtained for the Stevenson speech.

Then we put these macropropositions through the processing model. The size of each input cycle is of course determined here, because each text unit must be treated as a separate cycle. The size of short-term memory was first put at s = 4. The macrostructure of the Eisenhower speech turns out to be a single, coherent network; in its construction, two reinstatement searches are required and three reorganizations. On the other hand, the Stevenson speech falls apart into three separate networks, thus necessitating two inferences to establish connectivity. Furthermore, three reinstatement searches are required for the Stevenson speech, plus a total of 11 reorganizations. When the short-term memory capacity is increased to 7, the Stevenson speech becomes somewhat easier, whereas the Eisenhower speech does not change at all, though it still remains easier to comprehend in terms of number of inferences and reorganizations required.

Thus, our model computations do what the Reading Ease scores couldn't; they discriminate between the two speeches and identify the Eisenhower speech as the more comprehensible. In addition, they suggest why the Stevenson speech is so hard: It is poorly organized, requiring the comprehender to infer connections between parts of the speech that are not stated explicitly. Furthermore, Stevenson's speech is written in such a way that the organization that the comprehender arrives at must be restructured extensively before he or she can become aware of existing interrelationships among the various text elements. Interestingly, these problems interact with the short-term memory capacity of the reader and are most serious for poor readers. Compared with Stevenson's, Eisenhower's speech is much better organized in the sense that our model has fewer problems in constructing a coherent macrostructure for it.

CONCLUSION

We realize that by analyzing a few examples, we have proven nothing yet. But these analyses suggest that a research program to investigate readability within the framework developed here would be promising. It is quite probable that the outcome of such a program might be the decision that the concept of readability is beyond salvation. If our model tells us anything, it is that readability is not somehow an inherent property of texts but is the result of the interaction between a particular text (with its text characteristics) and particular readers (with their information-processing characteristics). Thus, the *Rocket* paragraph is easy for someone who processes large chunks and has a large short-term memory carry-over capacity. For a poor reader, however, this text is the hardest of the ones we have investigated here. Readability must be defined for specific texts and specific readers. The single readability score must be replaced by a readability profile that shows how a particular text would be responded to by different readers.

The situation here is somewhat analogous to that with respect to IQ scores. At best the IQ is a rough-and-ready index, useful for certain practical purposes. Theoretically, however, the concept of a single, context-free intelligence is not only wrong but may be outright harmful (e.g., Medawar, 1977) and must be replaced by a thorough analysis of the information-processing demands of particular tasks and the capacities of particular individuals (Estes, 1976).

We hope that we have stressed sufficiently that we make no claim of having identified all the factors that make a text easy or hard for someone to read. But number of propositions, number of different arguments, the inferences required to connect a text base, as well as the long-term memory searches and reorganizations that are necessary in its construction appear to be important factors. Not that they could not be elaborated. For instance, we simply counted how many inferences a text requires. Surely not all inferences are equally difficult, some being simple and obvious, whereas in other instances complex inferential chains might be required (e.g., Clark & Haviland, 1977). We have avoided specifying the nature of the inferences in our model, but clearly a theory of inferences would not only remove a deficiency in the model but further improve its predictive power.

The two model parameters—input size I and short-term memory carry-over capacity s—both depend on how many propositions a reader can work with at a time. That is, the capacity of short-term or working memory in a general sense is reflected in the values of both parameters. We are assuming that the parameter I depends primarily on how familiar a reader is with the text being read. If one reads familiar material—in Herbart's term, material that fits into and is easily connected with the reader's apperceptive mass—the process of decoding the text into propositions is presumably easier than for unfamiliar material; and hence more propositions can be processed in parallel. Thus, I should be large for familiar material. At present, this is nothing but a speculation; but experimental tests appear feasible (e.g., using a procedure like Jarvella's, 1971, to measure the immediate memory span for familiar and unfamiliar materials).

Whether the second parameter of the model also depends on familiarity is an open question at this point. There are indications that the short-term memory capacity is not simply a constant number of chunks but varies with the internal complexity of these chunks (for a discussion, see Kintsch, 1977, chap. 4.2.2), but further research is clearly necessary to clarify the present situation.

Certainly, individual differences in short-term memory capacity, and especially individual differences in the speed with which short-term memory can be accessed and reorganized (see Hunt, Lunneborg, & Lewis, 1975), should affect the value of s in the model. Thus, quite specific predictions could be made for the readability of a text for different populations of readers.

If the ideas we have outlined work out, they will be one more small contribution toward a normalization of the disturbed relationship between education and psychology. Cognitive theory might enable us to improve educational technology, in the spirit of Münsterberg's proposals. Whether this goal can now be achieved depends, above all, on one thing—psychology's success in constructing reasonably comprehensive and adequate theories of human cognitive functions.

ACKNOWLEDGMENTS

We are deeply indebted to Dr. Ernst Z. Rothkopf for the use of his materials and data. This research was supported by Grant No. MH15872 from the National Institute of Mental Health.

REFERENCES

Aaronson, D., & Scarborough, H. S. Performance theories for sentence coding: Some quantitative models. *Journal of Verbal Learning and Verbal Behavior,* 1977, *16,* 277–303.

Anderson, R. C., & Pichert, J. W. Recall of previously unrecallable information following a shift in perspective. *Journal of Verbal Learning and Verbal Behavior,* 1978, *17,* 1–12.

Atkinson, R. C., & Shiffrin, R. M. Human Memory: A proposed system and its control processes. In K. W. Spence & J. T. Spence (Eds.), *The psychology of learning and motivation: Advances in research and theory* (Vol. 2). New York: Academic Press, 1968.

Baggett, P. Memory for explicit and implicit information in picture stories. *Journal of Verbal Learning and Verbal Behavior,* 1975, *14,* 538–548.

Bormuth, J. R. *Development of readability analyses.* Washington, D.C.: U.S. Office of Education, 1969. (ERIC Document #ED029-166)

Bormuth, J. R. Reading literacy: Its definition and assessment. In J. B. Carroll & J. S. Chall (Eds.), *Toward a literate society.* New York: McGraw-Hill, 1975.

Chall, J. S. *Readability: An appraisal of research and application.* Columbus: Ohio State University, 1958.

Clark, H. H. Inferences in comprehension. In D. LaBerge & S. J. Samuels (Eds.), *Basic processes in reading: Perception and comprehension.* Hillsdale, N.J.: Lawrence Erlbaum Associates, 1976.

Clark, H. H., & Haviland, S. E. Comprehension and the given-new contract. In R. Freedle (Ed.), *Discourse production and comprehension.* Norwood, N.J.: Ablex, 1977.

Dewey, J. What psychology can do for the teacher. In R. D. Archambault (Ed.), *John Dewey on education: Selected writings.* New York: Random House, 1964. (Originally published, 1895.)

Estes, W. K. Intelligence and cognitive psychology. In L. B. Resnick (Ed.), *The nature of intelligence.* Hillsdale, N.J.: Lawrence Erlbaum Associates, 1976.

Flesch, R. A new readability yardstick. *The Journal of Applied Psychology,* 1948, *32,* 221–233.

Gilliland, J. *Readability.* London: University of London Press, 1972.

Greeno, J. J. Cognitive objectives of instruction: Theory of knowledge for solving problems and answering questions. In D. Klahr (Ed.) *Cognition and instruction.* Hillsdale, N.J.: Lawrence Erlbaum Associates, 1976.

Haviland, S. E., & Clark, H. H. What's new? Acquiring new information as a process in comprehension. *Journal of Verbal Learning and Verbal Behavior,* 1974, *13,* 515–521.

Hebb, D. O., & Bindra, D. Scientific writing and the general problem of communication. *American Psychologist,* 1952, *7,* 569–573.

Herbart, J. F. *The science of education* (H. M. Felkin & E. Felkin, trans.). Boston: Heath, 1893.

Hunt, E., Lunneborg, C., & Lewis, J. What does it mean to be high verbal? *Cognitive Psychology,* 1975, *7,* 194–227.

Jarvella, R. J. Syntactic processing of connected speech. *Journal of Verbal Learning and Verbal Behavior,* 1971, *10,* 409–416.

Joncich, G. M. Science: Touchstone for a new age in education. In G. M. Joncich (Ed.), *Psychology and the science of education: Selected writings of Edward L. Thorndike.* New York: Teachers College, Columbia University, 1962.

Kintsch, W., & van Dijk, T. A. Comment on se rapelle et on résume des histoires. *Langages,* 1975, *40,* 98–116.

Kintsch, W., & van Dijk, T. A. Comment on se rapelle et on résume des histoires. *Languages,* 1975, *40,* 98–116.

Kintsch, W., & Keenan, J. M. Reading rate and retention as a function of the number of propositions in the base structure of sentences. *Cognitive Psychology,* 1973, *5,* 257–274.

Kintsch, W., Kozminsky, E., Streby, W. J., McKoon, G., & Keenan, J. M. Comprehension and recall of text as a function of content variables. *Journal of Verbal Learning and Verbal Behavior,* 1975, *14,* 196–214.

Klahr, D. *Cognition and instruction.* Hillsdale, N.J.: Lawrence Erlbaum Associates, 1976.

Klare, G. R. *The measurement of readability.* Ames: Iowa State University Press, 1963.

Klare, G. R. Assessing readability. *Reading Research Quarterly,* 1974/75, *10,* 62–102.

Kozminsky, E. Altering comprehension: The effect of biasing titles on text comprehension. *Memory & Cognition,* 1977, *5,* 482–490.

Lockman, R. F. A note on measuring "understandability." *Journal of Applied Psychology,* 1956, *40,* 195–196.

McCall, W. A., & Crabbs, L. M. *Standard lessons in reading.* New York: Teachers College Press, 1925, 1950, 1961.

Münsterberg, H. Psychology and education. *Educational Review,* 1898, *16,* 105–132.

Rothkopf, E. *Ten years of prose learning research.* Invited Address, Division C, American Educational Research Association, New York, April 15, 1977.

Siegel, A. I., & Siegel, E. Flesch readability analysis of the major pre-election speeches of Eishenhower and Stevenson. *The Journal of Applied Psychology,* 1953, *37,* 105–107.

Stevens, S. S., & Stone, G. Psychological writing, easy and hard. *American Psychologist,* 1947, *2,* 230–235.

Sully, J. *Outlines of psychology.* New York: Appleton, 1886.

Thorndike, E. L. The principles of teaching. In G. M. Jonçich (Ed.), *Psychology and the science of education: Selected writings of Edward L. Thorndike.* New York: Teachers College, Columbia University, 1962. (Originally published, 1906.)

Turner, A., & Greene, E. *The construction of a propositional text base.* Technical report, University of Colorado, April 1977.

van Dijk, T. A., & Kintsch, W. Cognitive psychology and discourse. In W. Dressler (Ed.), *Current trends in text linguistics.* Berlin: de Gruyter, 1977.

Watson, J. B. *Behaviorism.* New York: People's Institute Publ. Col, 1924–25.

16

Applied Cognitive and Cognitive Applied Psychology: The Case of Face Recognition

Alan Baddeley
MRC Applied Psychology Unit,
Cambridge, England

INTRODUCTION

Times are changing. the invitation to talk about applied problems in a symposium on memory is something that would have seemed extremely odd only a few years ago. For many years applied psychology seems to have been regarded either as an occupational net, providing work for those who were not good enough to reach the ethereal heights of "pure" psychology, or at best as a pardonable perversion practiced among a few eccentric groups of experimental psychologists such as my own in Cambridge. Applied experimental psychology appears to be in danger of achieving respectability, perhaps even popularity. As someone who kicked the applied habit some 10 years ago and then relapsed. I would like to take this chance of talking about some of the attractions of applied work, together with its snags and frustrations. As I tend to have a rather concrete mind, I base my paper on a problem of some practical importance that has been concerning my own and other laboratories during recent years, namely that of remembering and recognizing faces.

APPLIED RESEARCH

But first, a few words about applied research and its growing popularity. Why should this be? First there has been a basic change in attitudes away from the ivory-tower view of the 1960s that the pursuit of knowledge—any knowledge—for its own sake was sufficient end in itself. Most of us like to feel that what we are doing is at least potentially useful. The argument that an understanding of man will inevitably be of great value is a powerful one but only if you are convinced that what you are doing is making a significant advance in our understanding. And few of us are as confident on that score as we were 10 years ago. These doubts are shared by those who hold the purse strings, which provides another very practical reason for an interest in applied research. When money is scarce, research yielding practical benefits will inevitably seem attractive to governments who must ultimately justify their expenditure to the taxpayer.

There are, however, others, less tangible advantages to be gained from applied work. It is often technically both more demanding and more satisfying than straightforward laboratory research. For example, my own most long-standing applied interest is in the performance of divers in the open sea. Although I believe that such work can be of value at a practical (Baddeley & Flemming, 1967), theoretical (Godden & Baddeley, 1975), and methodological level (Baddeley, 1966), I must confess that its main attraction is the satisfaction I derive from the challenge of obtaining good, replicable, and meaningful data under very hostile conditions.

Although such methodological masochism may not be to everyone's taste, applied work does have other, less perverse attractions. It often involves collaboration with nonpsychologists—engineers, physiologists, or educators, for example—an experience I certainly find both stimulating and rewarding. It also provides a reminder that we really do have a set of valuable skills that other professions do not acquire. There is nothing like watching a good medic or engineer try to design an experiment on people for improving one's confidence in the usefulness of experimental psychology.

Finally, I would like to suggest that real-world problems enhance our pursuit of "pure psychology," both by drawing attention to interesting and important questions and by ensuring that our theories and concepts do not become too laboratory or paradigm bound—in short, in ensuring their ecological validity. Research areas of theoretical importance that entered the laboratory from real-world problems are numerous. They include current approaches to selective attention (from air-traffic-control problems), vigilance (from watch keeping), signal detection theory (sonar), short-term memory (telephony), and—for Mike Turvey and Bob Shaw—ecological optics (from landing planes). Note that many of these stem from the wartime years—when applied work was respectable—or from Britain—where we make our class distinctions on other grounds than the pure–applied dichotomy—at least in psychology!

However, good applied work is hard to do, and it is easy to end up with results that are at least as trivial and frustrating as those from routine laboratory research. It is important first to distinguish between cognitive applied psychology and applied cognitive psychology. Cognitive applied psychology (with the emphasis on the "applied"— is first and foremost concerned to provide a usable, practical answer to a practical problem. As such its aims are quire different from applied cognitive psychology (with the emphasis on "cognitive"), which is concerned with understanding "real-life" problems in a theoretically satisfying way. It could perhaps be better termed "ecologically valid," or "relevant" cognitive psychology, if these terms did not already sound so pompous.

There are of course pitfalls in applied work. The "find me a cure for cancer" problem is one. It would of course be very nice to discover a cure for schizophrenia, or to revolutionize the educational system, or even to speed up the rate of learning to read, or to reduce the number of dyslexic children. However, the chance that a single research project will make very substantial progress toward any of these goals is surely very low, and to pretend otherwise is likely to lead to a rapid loss of credibiity. Another temptation is the "high-speed serial exhaustive scanning in female black homosexual drug addicts" problem. This involves taking a laboratory technique in which one happens to be interested at the time and applying it to a group of subjects who present a social problem that is sufficiently pressing and fashionable to yield large amounts of research funds. That is not of course to say that one should not tackle socially important questions or that one should not use the full armory of concepts and techniques that have been devised in the laboratory. However, simply combining the two rarely seems to work.

By this point, I feel that I have uttered enough pompous platitudes to justify even a 500th birthday and so would like to attempt to illustrate some of these points using research on face recognition, a problem of considerable applied importance that happens to have been concerning my own unit over the last 2 or 3 years.

FACE RECOGNITION

Lineup Studies

There has in recent years been a good deal of concern on both sides of the Atlantic over the role of person recognition in the judicial process. Buckhout (1974) cites a case of two innocent men, George Morales who was arrested for robbery and Lawrence Berson who was arrested for rape. Both were convicted, primarily on recognition evidence. Subsequently, a third person, Richard Carkone, was arrested for a further crime and admitted having committed both the other offenses. In this case all three men were physically very similar, but the evidence cited by Buckout and others suggests that this need not be the case, given the unreliabiity of eye-witness identification. There has in Britian been a whole series of cases of conviction on highly controversial eye-witness evidence; and following a particularly implausible prosecution based on the recognition evidence of a schoolboy, the legal guidelines have been changed so that eye-witness evidence is not of itself sufficient for a conviction.

What can psychologists contribute to this particular rpoblem? We have of course known for many years that eye witnesses are highly unreliable (see Hunter, 1957, for a review of the earlier work). Apart from this, we know remarkably little about perceiving and remembering people or faces. We know that processing of faces tends to rely particularly on the right hemisphere of the brain and that faces are hard to recognize upside-down. Some would say it relies on a special face-processing system, although the evidence for this is far from compelling (see Ellis, 1975, for a good review). We know that people remember faces better than pictures of snowflakes but worse than pictures from magazines, but apart from this the great body of information on faces has told us remarkably little.

Considering this as a cognitive applied problem, what can we tell the world that might conceivably be useful? The most obvious role, and one that has perhaps been developed most, is that of warning of the dangers of false identification. Buckhout's work is a good example of this (Buckhout, 1974). One can of course avoid the problem of false identification altogether by simply not using eye-witness evidence, but this is almost certainly unacceptable in a society with an increasing rate of violent crime.

A more satisfactory solution is to attempt to make the process of identification fairer and more reliable. A good example of this type of work comes from Helen Dent (1977) of the University of Nottingham. She is particularly concerned with children as witnesses and has compared the ability of children to identify a man involved in a classroom incident under various lineup conditions. In one condition, the children were required to select the man from a line of "suspects," using the standard procedure of walking up and down and pointing out the man in question. She observed that the children found this a rather frightening experience and tended to shy away and not look adequately at the men. She compared this procedure with one in which pictures of the various men were shown on slides. The results are shown in Table 16.1. It is clear that despite the presumed loss of visual information involved in using slides rather than a real person, the detection rate is improved by this procedure, which the children also appeared to find much less stressful.

Reproducing Remembered Faces

The lineup procedure is essentially one for collecting or evaluating evidence against an arrested suspect. Very frequently, however, the difficulty is in catching the criminal rather than in convicting him or her. Consider a recent

TABLE 16.1
Identification Performance (%) for Children Tested by
Color Slides or Live Identity Parade[a]

	Color Slides	Live Parade
Correct identifications	29.03	12.2
Incorrect identifications	31.45	32.1
No identification made	39.52	55.59

[a]From Dent (1977).

example from my own city, Cambridge, which began to hit the national news headlines due to the activities of a rapist. He was clearly a local resident who knew the area well, and given the size of population one might think it should not take too long to apprehend him. Although he worked mainly at night, there were descriptions from his victims that were used by the police to create a representation based on the Photo-fit technique, a system devised by Jacques Penry (1971a). He had the idea of providing an extensive set of facial features based on photographs including sets of noses, chins, hairlines, eyes, etc. These could be fitted together by the witness to produce any of five billion permutations. The Photo-fit of the Cambridge rapist, which was featured regularly in the local newspaper, is shown in Fig. 16.1. Nonetheless, the rapes continued, a state of affairs that caused great concern in Cambridge, although no doubt by New York standards it was very small beer. Groups of undergraduates banded together and volunteered to sleep in girls' bedrooms, and, not to be outdone, Oxford developed its own rapist, The end to the rapist's career came in a nurses' hostel with an attempted rape that was heard by nearby eel fishermen, who apparently operate at night and who sounded the alarm. He was subsequently caught escaping from the scene of the crime on a bicycle, dressed as a woman. His picture is shown in Fig. 16.2. Note that though there are similarities between individual features of the Photo-fit and the face, the overall impression is very different. His victims tended to perceive him as younger and larger than he turned out to be. However, one can hardly blame the Photo-fit system for this, as he typically would wear a wig and on occasion a mask with the word "Rapist" written across the forehead!

Even when a face has been perceived and indeed remembered clearly, the problem of enabling the witness to communicate this information is clearly a very difficult one. Techniques such as the Photo-fit procedure just described, Identikit (a line-drawing equivalent of Photo-fit), and the use of sketch artists all represent attempts to tackle this problem. There typically, however, tends to be little in the way of validation of such procedures, and the British Home Office recently commissioned work on the Photo-fit procedure from a group at the University of Aberdeen. In one study, Ellis, Shepherd, and Davies

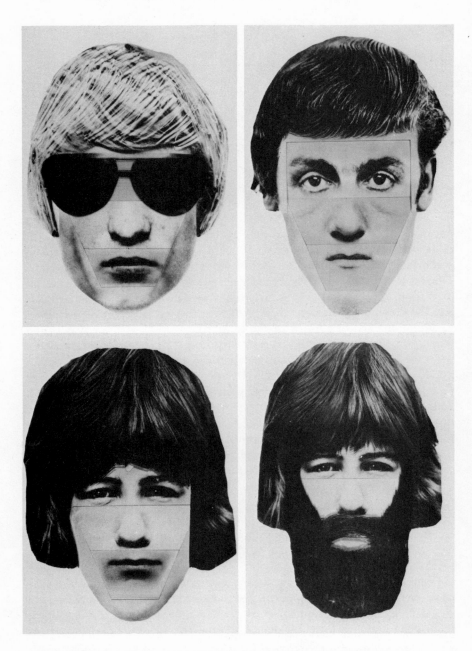

FIG. 16.1. Four Phot-fit representations produced by witnesses of the Cambridge rapist. The lack of consistency is clearly in part due to his use of disguise, which included wigs, a beard, dark glasses, and on occasion a mask.

FIG. 16.2. A photograph of the Cambridge rapist after capture. Note that although individual features were often accurately reproduced, the overall appearance is very different from the Photo-fit representations. Although inaccurate representation may be actively misleading, its publication probably does play an important role in maintaining the alertness of the general public.

(1975) required their subjects simply to copy a photograph of a face using the Photo-fit technique. Some of their subjects' attempts are shown in Fig. 16.3, where the photograph to be copied is on the left and the best and the worst six examples are shown on the right. Their results showed very clearly that even when no problem of initial perception or subsequent retention is involved, their subjects' ability to use the procedure to create a likeness was extremely variable. There are no doubt cases when either the face is very distinctive or the witness is very able, in which Photo-fit is useful; but it is hard to avoid the suspicion that there may be many cases in which the Photo-fit representation is actively misleading.

Why should people find this task so difficult? One possibility is that the Photo-fit technique is based on inappropriate assumptions about the way in which we perceive faces. The system operates in terms of independent facial features. It may well be the case that we perceive faces as a gestalt that is not readily decomposed into its constituent features. Evidence relevant to this point comes from a series of studies carried out at the Applied Psychology Unit in connection with the evaluation of a course intended to improve the

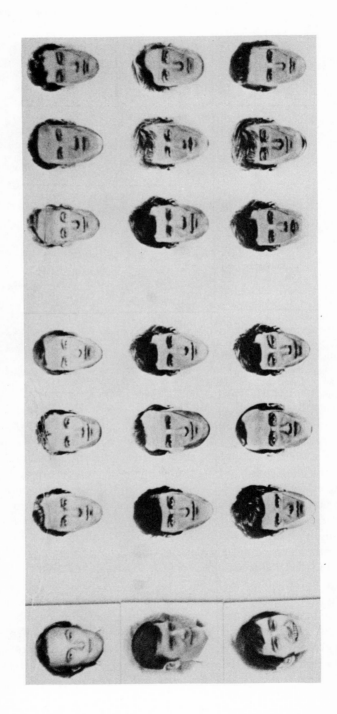

374

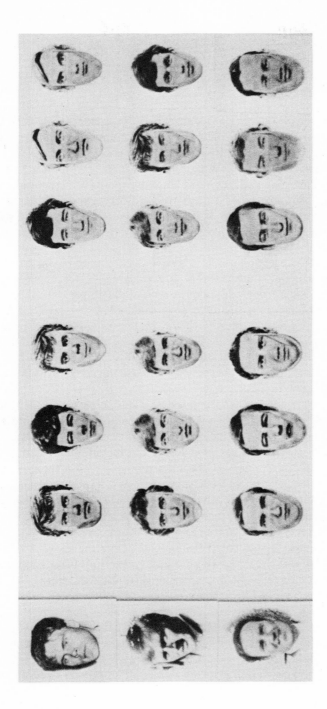

FIG. 16.3.   Results of the Photo-fit study by Ellis, Shepherd, and Davis (1975). The six stimulus faces used are shown in the left-hand column. The six attempts at reconstructing them are shown alongside each one. The first three reconstructions, columns 2, 3, and 4 from the left, are those made by good encoders; the three right-hand ones were made by subjects rated as poor encoders.

participants' capacity for remembering and recognizing faces (Woodhead, Baddeley, & Simmons, in press).

Training Face Recognition

There are a number of occupations such as that of policeman, store detective, or airport passport officer in which an ability to remember and recognize faces would be extremely useful. In addition to devising Photo-fit, Penry has applied his system to the problem of training for the recognition of faces (Penry, 1971b). The Applied Psychology Unit was invited to evaluate a course on person recognition that relied quite heavily on an approach similar to that advocated by Penry, and after some thought we agreed. It is perhaps worth digressing to discuss why we felt the need to think hard before undertaking this project. An applied project is presumed to have some practical consequence—in the present case, to improve the ability to train a person to recognize faces. It could be argued that such research is likely to strengthen society's control over the individual for either legitimate *or* repressive purposes. This is certainly a factor to be considered. We ourselves decided that on balance this danger is outweighed by the potential gain from the legitimate use of such information for controlling crime and minimizing miscarriage of justice due to false recognition. Others might well disagree on this point and would presumably therefore choose not to work in this area. However, I return to this point later.

The course covered 3 days in which lectures, discussions, practical work, and field exercises were used with considerable imagination and enthusiasm. The teaching involved three components: observation, memory, and description. Observation was concerned with age, height, build, walk, dress, habits, mannerisms, and faces. The teaching of memory was primarily based on feature selection. A typical instruction was to exaggerate a feature or aspect of the person in the mind, rather as a cartoonist might. It was suggested that this would act as a screening process so that if, for example, the wanted individual was known to have wide-set eyes and thin lips, then people who did not have these characteristics could be eliminated from the search. The main aid in this teaching was the Photo-fit kit. Finally, description was encouraged by discussion of appropriate labels for "visible distinguishing marks." Typical examples were the labeling of eyebrows as *low, elevated, curved,* or *slanting.* The verbal descriptions were frequently derived from the work of Penry (1971b). For further details, see Woodhead et al. (in press).

Our first attempt at validation of the course involved testing the participants' memory for faces before and after training. We then compared their performance with that of a group of similar subjects who received no training between the first and the second tests. Subjects were shown 24 successive slides, each of a male face and each visible for 10 seconds. Although

TABLE 16.2
Effect of a Training Scheme on
Recognition Memory for Faces

| | Mean Performance (d′) | |
	Trainees	Controls
Day 1	1.05	1.20
(s.d.)	(0.38)	(0.46)
Day 4	1.12	1.12
(s.d.)	(0.44)	(0.44)

24 faces might seem to be a large number, the course did aim to train for recognition of many people, not just one or two. Subjects were advised to memorize the faces as people who, when next seen, might appear differently. After a 15-minute interval, a sequence of 72 faces was presented. This comprised the 24 target faces together with 48 distractors. Each item was visible for 10 seconds, and during this time the subject was required to decide whether he had seen the face before or whether it was a new face. Three days later the procedure was repeated, using a different but equivalent set of faces. During the interval, the experimental group, which comprised 26 young men, attended the training course while the 22 control subjects performed their normal work. The results are shown in Table 16.2, from which it is clear that the training course had no reliable inluence on performance. Although there is a very slight tendency for discrimination, measured by $d′$, to improve in the trained men and deteriorate in the untrained, this interaction is far from significant ($F = 1.33$, $d.f.$ 1, 44, $p > .10$).

We were very surprised at the complete absence of an effect, but it could be argued that the task we had used was very different from that for which subjects were being trained and that a more appropriate test would be to use face matching. This would be analogous, for example, to the task of a passport official who was looking for a limited number of suspected hijackers and who had their photographs available. For this test, each subject was given four target faces, each one a 6.5 × 5.0 cm photograph of a young man. Subjects were first allowed 4 minutes for pretest study of the target photographs, which they were allowed to retain while comparing them with a series of 240 test slides, each present for a 10-second exposure. The test series comprised 240 faces that contained four examples of each of the four target faces. Once again, subjects performed the task twice with two equivalent sets of material, separated by an interval of 3 days during which half of the subjects participated in the training course while the other half continued with their normal work. The results of this study are shown in Table 16.3. As in the previous study, there is a slight but nonsignificant suggestion that the training

TABLE 16.3
Effect of a Training Scheme on
a Matching Task with Four Faces

	Mean Performance (d')	
	Trainees	*Controls*
Day 1	3.75	3.87
(s.d.)	(1.42)	(1.14)
Day 4	4.03	3.95
(s.d.)	(1.24)	(1.30)

course might improve performance. One certainly could not conclude from these results that the course was effective; but as performance was relatively high, it is conceivable that any improvement might have been masked by a ceiling effect. We therefore decided to perform a third experiment in which a task is made more difficult by requiring the subjects to look out for 16 different target faces.

The procedure was equivalent to that used in the previous experiment with the exception that each subject had a board containing 16 rather than four faces and was allowed 8 minutes prior study. Again, 240 slides of faces were shown for 10 seconds each, but in this case each of the 16 faces occurred only once. A total of 28 trainees and 20 control subjects were tested. The results of this and the previous study are shown graphically in Fig. 16.4. From this, it is clear first of all that we have succeeded in making the task more difficult. Second, in this case we *have* obtained a significant effect of the course on performance, but it is in the opposite direction to that predicted. Although the

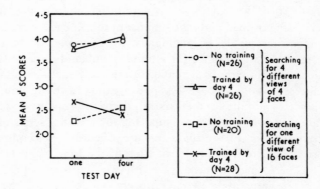

FIG. 16.4. Results of two studies evaluating a training course in face recognition. The course had no effect on the task of searching for 4 faces; it actuallly impaired performance in a task involving searching for 16 faces. (Data from Woodhead et al., in press.)

trainees started off at a slightly higher level than the controls, they showed significant *deterioration* following the course (t = 2.02, *d.f.* = 44, p = 0.05), whereas the controls showed a nonsignificant trend in the direction of improvement.

Of our three experiments, only one has produced a reliable effect and that in the direction of suggesting that the training course actually *impairs* recognition. The course was carried out with apparent efficiency and enthusiasm and reflects an extensively used approach to face recognition, so its complete failure is both unexpected and worrying. Taken together with the results of Ellis, Shepherd, and Davies (1975), it suggests that the individual-feature-based approach to face recognition underlying Penry's work may be mistaken. This in turn suggested that we should move from the cognitive applied problem of evaluating a specific course to the applied cognitive issue of what factors influence memory for faces.

Encoding Faces

There is some evidence to suggest that inducing a subject to process a face as a person leads to better retention than suggesting that he or she concentrate on physical characteristics (Bower & Karlin, 1974; Warrington & Ackroyd, 1975). The Bower and Karlin study attempted to apply Craik and Lockhart's levels of processing view to the retention of faces, arguing that shallow processing based on physical features should lead to poorer subsequent recognition than deeper processing based on judgments of the personality characteristics of the person portrayed. They duly found that photographs that had been judged on the basis of the honesty or likeableness of the person represented were subsequently better recognized than photographs that had been categorized as male or female. However, although it is plausible to assume that the primary difference between these two categorizations is one that involves processing depth, one cannot rule out the possibility that categorization according to sex leads to poor retention not because it is a "shallower" judgment but simply because it involves either less processing or involves the processing of physical dimensions that are inappropriate for making distinctions among persons of the same sex. Karalyn Patterson and I therefore decided to perform an experiment more directly concerned with the distinction between physical features and personaity, utilizing some of the physical features that are advocated in the Penry system.

We therefore presented our subjects with sets of either six or 24 faces, which half the subjects were required to categorize on the basis of physical features and about which the other half were required to make personality judgments. Each target face was presented for 28 seconds, and during this time the subjects were required to rate four characteristics of the face on a 5-point scale. In the physical features condition, the rating scales involved: (1) small-nose–large-nose; (2) thin-lips–full-lips; (3) eyes-close-together–eyes-far-apart; and (4) round-face–long-face. In the personality condition, subjects rated the people represented as: (1) nice–nasty; (2) reliable–unreliable; (3) intelligent–dull; and (4) lively–stolid. Subjects were told that they would subsequently have to remember the faces and that the categorization might help them to do so. After a 4-minute break, they went on to the test series (including all targets plus twice as many distractors), during which each slide was presented for 10 seconds and subjects were required to decide whether the face was new or old. For further details, see Patterson and Baddeley (1977).

The effect of encoding instructions, with discrimination performance expressed in terms of d' for the features condition = 1.50, for the personality group = 1.94. This is a significant but far from dramatic effect, suggesting that categorizing faces in terms of personality is only somewhat better than judging physical features. The magnitude of this effect is much smaller than that observed by Bower and Karlin, reinforcing the suspicion that judgments of sex represent a particularly limited processing dimension and cannot be regarded as a characteristic of physical judgments in general. We had suspected that judgments based on physical features might conceivably be better for our short list of items; but although there was a highly significant tendency for performance to be better with shorter lists, this effect did not interact with either instructions or the other variables in the experiment. The other major variable involved two kinds of changes in appearance of the target photographs between presentation and test. Some targets were changed from full-face, unsmiling view at presentation to three-quarter, smiling view at test. Recognition performance under these conditions was as good as that for identical pictures at presentation and test, which suggests that subjects were indeed remembering the face as a person, or at least a three-dimensional surface, rather than in terms of a specific, two-dimensional pattern. The second kind of appearance change involved disguises or substantial changes in pose, hair style, dress, etc., and this manipulation reduced recognition performance almost to the level of chance.

Disguises

To summarize, our experiment seems to have shown that categorization on the basis of personality characteristics does indeed lead to enhanced performance compared to purely physical judgments, but the size of the effect is relatively small and does not suggest a very strong basis for recommending techniques on how to recognize faces. By far the largest effects to emerge were those based on disguise, and these were explored further in the second experiment of Patterson and Baddeley (1977). The material for this experiment was based on pictures of 10 men, each of whom was photographed from three different views (full-face, three-quarter-face, and profile) in each of eight versions of appearance. (1) natural; (2) with glasses; (3) with a wig; (4) with glasses and a wig; (5) with a beard; (6) with beard and glasses; (7) with wig and beard; and (8) with glasses, wig, and beard. One of these eight versions was selected at random for each of the 10 target men. For each subject tested, five of the 10 were presented as targets, all in full-face view, whereas the other five served as distractors.

In the first phase of the experiment, subjects learned names for their five targets; and when they had learned to respond with the appropriate name, the second stage of the experiment began. In this the subject was presented with a series of 80 slides comprising all five targets and all five distractors, each in all of the various versions of appearance. The results are shown in Fig. 16.5, from which it is clear that disguise has a marked and systematic effect, with performance ranging between almost 90%—when an unchanged three-quarter view is presented—to a level of 30% detection—when wig and beard are changed and the test photograph is in profile view. More specifically, there is a consistent tendency for profiles to be more difficult than three-quarter view and for the presence or absence of a wig or beard to have a clear and marked effect on performance. The only deviation from this simple pattern of results comes from glasses, where a change does produce an overall decrement but one that depends on its combination with other factors. For instance, a change in glasses alone produced no reliable effect in the case of three-quarter view but did substantially impair recognition in profile. In conclusion, the study clearly corroborates the previous experiment in emphasizing the potency of disguise and extends its findings in showing that even relatively small modifications in appearance will produce clear and systematic decrements in recognition of faces.

Although I have argued for a distinction between cognitive applied and applied cognitive psychology, the last two experiments show that in any specific instance the boundary between the two may be far from clear. The experiments began with the intention of testing general principles of face

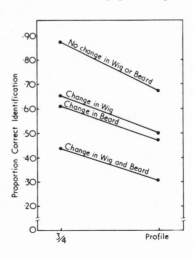

FIG. 16.5. Proportion of correct identifications as a function of changes in pose, wig, and beard. (From Patterson & Baddeley, 1977.)

memory and in particular whether levels of processing provided a useful framework. Although the results do show some effects of processing level, they are discouragingly small, particularly in contrast to the massive effects of disguise on subsequent recognition. In exploring this, the second experiment might be regarded as a piece of cognitive applied research, research that is in principle much more helpful to the fugitive than to the police. So much for our moral scruples about the risk of helping society rather than the individual! However, I suspect that our findings on the effectiveness of disguises would be unlikely to surprise criminals, terrorists, or for that matter the Cambridge rapist.

Semantic Memory for Faces

The final set of experiments I would like to describe also reach across the boundary between pure and applied research, being carried out as a piece of ecologically valid cognitive psychology having interesting implications for the applied experiments described previously. It concerns part of the PhD thesis of a Cambridge research student, Vicki Bruce. Although it was carried out at the Appied Psychology Unit and supervised by myself, it is quite independent of the applied project just described and stemmed from ideas that preceded contact with either myself or the group doing applied research on faces. All the work we have described, and indeed most of the work on faces in the literature, has been concerned with the presentation and subsequent recognition of unfamiliar faces. Bruce (1977) points out that we know virtually nothing of the processes underlying the much more frequent task of recognizing the faces of our friends and acquaintances at work, shopping, or in photographs. It is this problem, which might be termed *semantic memory for faces,* that she tackles. She begins by using a visual search task that one might term the *face-in-the-crowd technique* in which subjects are required to search for one, two, four, or eight familiar politicians within blocks of 15 faces. This is compared with a similar search using names of politicians. The results show a negatively accelerated function, with subjects being consistently more rapid searching for one face or one name than for two or more, but with the function flattening between two and four. The negative acceleration remains even when plotted on a logarithmic scale and seems to suggest that subjects may be using a different strategy when searching for one or possibly two items in contrast to four or eight. We return to this point later. Although subjects were initially faster at scanning names than faces, this difference disappeared with practice, leaving very comparable functions for the two types of material. Bruce went on to manipulate systematically the similarities between targets and distractors. The "face-in-the-crowd" technique proved unwieldy for this, so she moved to a slightly different task.

The new technique was somewhat analogous to the task of meeting a friend off a train. One would stand at the ticket barrier and observe each person passing through. Of major theoretical interest is the time taken to decide that a given face is *not* one's friend. Presumably, someone who resembles the friend physically would be rejected relatively slowly, but what about semantic factors? Would a close associate of one's friend take longer to reject? Perhaps indeed anyone familiar might tend to delay the decision. This was tested in an experiment requiring subjects to detect pictures of the last four British Prime Ministers—Callaghan, Wilson, Heath, and Home. These are all familiar faces to the British public; they form a clear semantic category but do not have any obvious physical characteristics that set them apart from other people of a similar age. Several different examples of each target face were randomly intermixed with nontarget, distractor faces, which were of eight types. These were derived from all possible combinations of the two levels of three factors: visual appearance, semantic category, and familiarity. Half of the groups were visually similar to one or more of the targets, as based on ratings by other subjects, whereas the other half were rated as dissimilar. Both similar and dissimilar categories were split equally between politicians and actors or TV personalities; and in both cases, half were rated as familiar by the subjects, who almost invariably correctly named them, whereas the remainder were judged as quite unfamiliar. The slides were then presented in random order to housewives, who decided as quickly as possible whether each face was or was not that of one of the targets.

The negative response times (*non*targets) are shown in Fig. 16.6. (These times include a constant of about 0.7 secs, due to lag in the operation of the projector.) The following results were all significant whether measured across subjects or across slides. First, there is a clear effect of visual similarity, regardless of whether the face is familiar or unfamiliar. This is reasonable and

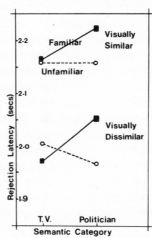

FIG. 16.6. Time taken to decide that a photograph was not one of four target politicians as a function of semantic category, familiarity, and visual similarity to the target politicians. (From Bruce, 1977.)

expected, suggesting simply that the subjects do use physical features in making their decisions. There is no main effect of semantic category but a clear and significant category × familiarity interaction; no other factors or interactions approached significance. How should the familiarity × category interaction be interpreted? First of all, the absence of a category effect for unfamiliar faces is of course unsurprising; it simply indicates that there were no particular stylistic characteristics of politicians' photographs as opposed to people from television. In the case of familiar faces, however, the semantic category of a distractor does affect performance whether the distractor is visually similar to the target faces or not. The reason why this is crucial becomes obvious if we attempt to apply some simple models.

Let us assume a model in which the recognition process is based on a sequence of decisions of which the first is whether or not a face is visually similar to one of the targets. If it is visually dissimilar, the subject responds "no" and need proceed no further; whereas if it is visually similar, the subject goes on to check the semantic characteristics. Such a model would produce a category effect only for faces that are visually similar to the target, because dissimilar faces should never reach the category judgment stage. The presence in Fig. 16.6 of a reliable category effect for *dissimilar* items allows one to reject this model.

An alternative model might be to assume that the subject first of all makes a semantic decision and then proceeds to decide whether the face is visually appropriate for one of the targets. This, however, would produce a visual similarity effect only for semantically appropriate items, and clearly this is not the case. We therefore seem to be forced to some model of the type shown in Fig. 16.7, which allows for the simultaneous influence of both semantic and visual information.

In the experiment just described, subjects were required to search for four targets. It may very commonly be the case, however, that we are looking for only one person, as in our railway station example. The earlier visual scanning experiments carried out by Bruce indicated that searching for one single item may possibly be qualitatively different from searching for four or more. It is possible, for example, that the subject may be able to hold some form of representation of a single face that will allow the performance of a very rapid physical match; Tversky (1969) has shown something analogous to this, at least with schematic faces. Bruce therefore went on to repeat her experiment but now requiring subjects to search for only one face, that of Harold Wilson. The results differed from the previous study in one major respect—namely, the semantic category was important only for the visual similar items, and even on these items the effect was not as reliable as before. In short, subjects appear to be behaving according to the first model described, which implies that they make an initial decision on the basis of broad physical characteristics, and that only if the item is physically similar to

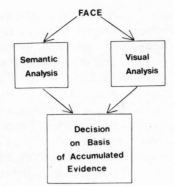

FIG. 16.7.   Schematic model suggested by Bruce's first experiment;
subjects appear to be analyzing the
faces presented both semantically
and visually before reaching a decision.

Harold Wilson do they go on to perform a more detailed analysis that may
include semantics.

The results of this last experiment are rather less robust than the previous
study, and Bruce suggests it should be replicated before drawing any strong
theoretical conclusions from it. It does, however, tentatively suggest that
subjects are able to hold the physical characteristics one, but not four, faces in
a form that allows a rapid matching decision to be made.

CONCLUSIONS

At this point, it might be worth returning to our more applied questions. It
will be recalled that both our training course evaluation and our levels of
processing experiment required subjects to deal with a minimum of four
target faces. We found little evidence for the value of inducing the subjects to
analyze faces into their constituent physical features; on the contrary, this
procedure appeared to be less conducive to the recognition of faces than a
strategy of processing faces in terms of the assumed personality characteristics of the person portrayed. This is consistent with Bruce's first experiment,
which suggests that the semantic characteristics of faces are an important
determinant of recognition. Note, however, that her second experiment
implies that this may perhaps not be the case when one is searching for only a
single face and opens up the possibiity that physical features may be a useful
point of emphasis when searching for a single person.

Even if this were the case, it would not of course necessarily imply that the
concern with individual features advocated by Penry would necessarily be
helpful. Subjects very probably treat faces in a gestalt way, with the whole
being different from the sum of its parts. It would nonetheless be interesting to
rerun the Woodhead et al. experiments (in press) using detection of a single
face; unfortunately (or perhaps fortunately), this is no longer possible, as the

course has now been modified. As the course was aimed at training people to search for several potential targets at the same time, even if we were to find that the Penry approach worked for single targets, it would not be particularly helpful. However, as Laughery and his colleagues have pointed out (Laughery, Alexander, & Lane, 1971; Laughery, Fessler, Lenorovitz, & Yoblick, 1974), the problem is often one in which a witness is attempting to recognize a single face from a set of mug shots or a lineup; and under these circumstances, it is at least *possible* that a Penry approach might be helpful. It is clearly worth further exploration.

The experiments just discussed primarily represent the work of our own laboratory on one applied memory problem that happens to have concerned us over the last 2 or 3 years. It is offered, not as an example of how things should be done, but simply because it provides a convenient illustration of a number of characteristics of applied research. What are they? Consider first of all our evaluation of the training course. The aim was a very practical one and was achieved; we discovered that the course failed to fulfill its function. In order to obtain this information, it took us nearly 2 years; and had the course not already been running, it would have taken even longer. This is always likely to be a problem with evaluation of training and suggests that an experimental psychologist can be most useful if he or she works in collaboration with an occupational psychologist who is creating and developing the course for practical purposes. It could be argued that the amount of information gained from our study is minimal; and although I believe that our result is of theoretical interest when fitted into the general context of face recognition, one would not recommend this as the best way to determine how one perceives or remembers faces. The great advantage of such experiments is that although they are limited in their aim, they do come up with a clear empirical answer that can be used for coming to a practical decision.

Robert Pirsig makes a similar point rather nicely in his book, *Zen and the Art of Motorcycle Maintenance.* When discussing the problem of diagnosing a mechanical fault on a motorcycle, he suggests for really difficult problems that if all else fails, something approaching scientific method can be used. "When I think of formal scientific method an image sometimes comes to mind of an enormous juggernaut, a huge bulldozer—slow, tedious, lumbering, laborious, but invincible. It takes twice as long, five times as long, maybe a dozen times as long as informal mechanics' techniques, but you know in the end you're going to *get* it" (Pirsig, 1977, p. 100). The limitation of such an approach is that although it can evaluate existing ideas, it is unlikely to create new ones. It is important not to underestimate the value of people like Penry who have what they consider to be a good idea and who have enough drive and persuasion to turn their ideas into practical terms. Equally, however, it is important that we do not adopt a system simply because it is persuasively sold; we must be prepared to check that the procedures adopted by society are not only plausible but are in fact valid. In making this type of assessment, the skills of the applied experimental psychologist are very valuable.

So much for cognitive applied psychology, what about applied cognitive? Here our aim is not simply to apply our techniques to practical problems but to attempt to understand the phenomena of the natural world. This is likely to be more attractive to the "pure experimental" psychologist and also a more viable route into applied work. It is less dependent on outside contacts and likely to interface more obviously with current theoretical concerns. It basically demands a willingness to step back from the paradigms with which we all tend to become preoccupied and to use our theoretical concepts and techniques to examine the problems outside the laboratory. In some cases, as in our own use of the concept of levels of processing, they may prove to be of somewhat limited value; but in others, as in the case of Bruce's utilization of techniques developed for the study of visual search, I am sure they will reveal new insights into basic cognitive processes.

REFERENCES

Baddeley, A. D. Influence of depth on the manual dexterity of free divers. A comparison between open sea and pressure chamber testing. *Journal of Applied Psychology*, 1966, *50*, 81–85.

Baddeley, A. D., & Flemming, N. C. The efficiency of divers breathing oxyhelium. *Ergonomics*, 1967, *10*, 311–319.

Bower, G. H., & Karlin, M. B. Depth of processing pictures of faces and recognition memory. *Journal of Experimental Psychology*, 1974, *103*, 751–757.

Bruce, V. *Searching for politicians: An information-processing approach to face recognition.* Paper presented to the Experimental Psychology Society, Sheffield, March 23 1977.

Buckhout, R. Eye-witness testimony. *Scientific American*, 1974, *231*, 23–31.

Dent, H. *Person recognition and juvenile testimony.* Paper presented at the Symposium on Person Recognition, British Psychological Society Annual Conference, Exeter, April 3 1977.

Ellis, H. D. Recognising faces. *British Journal of Psychology*, 1975, *66*, 409–426.

Ellis, H. D., Shepherd, J., & Davies, G. M. An investigation of the use of the Photo-fit technique for recalling faces. *British Journal of Psychology*, 1975, *66*, 29–37.

Godden, D. R., & Baddeley, A. D. Context-dependent memory in two natural environments: On land and underwater. *British Journal of Psychology*, 1975, *66*, 325–331.

Hunter, I. M. L. *Memory: Facts and fallacies.* Baltimore: Penguin, 1957.

Laughery, K. R., Alexander, J. F., & Lane, A. B. Recognition of human faces: Effects of target exposure time, target position, pose position, and type of photograph. *Journal of Applied Psychology*, 1971, *55*, 477–483.

Laughery, K. R., Fessler, P. K., Lenorovitz, D. R., & Yoblick, D. A. Time delay and similarity effects in facial recognition. *Journal of Applied Psychology*, 1974, *59*, 490–496.

Patterson, K. E., & Baddeley, A. D. When face recognition fails. *Journal of Experimental Psychology: Human Learning and Memory*, 1977, *3*, 406–417.

Penry, J. *Photo-fit kit.* Leeds, England: John Waddington of Kirkstall Ltd., 1971. (a)

Penry, J. *Looking at faces and remembering them: A guide to facial identification.* London: Elek Books, 1971, (b)

Pirsig, R. M. *Zen and the art of motorcycle maintenance.* London: Corgi Books, 1977.

Tversky, B. Pictorial and verbal encoding in a memory search task. *Perception & Psychophysics,* 1969, *4,* 225–233.

Warrington, E. K., & Ackroyd, C. The effect of orienting tasks on recognition memory. *Memory & Cognition,* 1975, *3,* 140–142.

Woodhead, M. M., Baddeley, A. D., & Simmonds, D. C. V. On training people to recognize faces. *Ergonomics,* in press.

ACKNOWLEDGMENTS

I am grateful to Vicki Bruce, Karalyn Patterson, and Muriel Woodhead for their valuable discussion and comments. I am grateful to the *Cambridge Evening News* and the Cambridge Constabulary for permission to use Figs. 16.1 and 16.2, to Drs. Ellis, Shepherd, and Davies for permission to use Fig. 16.3; and to Jacques Penry for permission to reproduce those figures based on the Photo-fit technique (Figs. 16.1, 16.2, and 16.3).

Author Index

Numbers in italic indicate the pages on which complete references appear.

A

Aaronson, D., 347, *364*
Abelson, R. P., 64, 67, *84, 88*
Ackroyd, C., 379, *388*
Adams, R. D., 262, *277*
Adler, J., 187, *219*
Albert, M. L., 263, 267, *277*
Alexander, J. F., 386, *388*
Allport, D. A., 64, 66, 78, 79, 81, 83, *85, 89,* 259, *274*
Anderson, J. A., 45, 53, *58*, 111, 113, 115, *118*
Anderson, J. R., 23, 24, 30, *33*, 44, 51, *58*, 150, 151, 159, 164
Anderson, K., 78, *89*
Anderson, R. C., 354, *364*
Anscombe, G. E. M., 181, *219*
Antonis, B., 78, 83, *85*
Arbit, J., 263, 264, 272, *275*
Ashby, R., 203, *219*
Atkinson, R. C., 23, *33*, 39, 47, *58,* 258, 260, 264, 265, *274*, 298, 303, 306, 307, 310, *324*, 348, *364*
Ausubel, D. P., 320, *324*
Ayer, A. J., 180, *219*

B

Baddeley, A. D., 51, *58*, 260, 262, 264, 265, 266, 267, 269, 270, 272, 273, *274*, 298, *324*, 368, 376, 378, 380, 381, *387, 388*

Baggett, P., 345, *365*
Ballard, P. B., 238, *244*
Barbour, I. G., 65, *85*
Baron, J., 271, *274*
Baron, R., 110, *119*
Barraco, R. A., 21, *33*
Barsalou, L., 306, 307, 308, *327*
Bartlett, F. C., 4, *15*, 279, *288*, 320, *325*
Bartz, W. H., 150, 151, *165*, 310, 311, *325*
Baylor, G. W., 68, *85*
Becker, C. A., 79, *85*
Becker, J. D., 67, 68, *85*
Bennett, E. L., 242, 243, *244*
Beran, V., 227, *244*
Bergson, H. L., 4, *15*, 280, *289*
Berkeley, G., 173, 180, *219*
Bertalanffy, L. von, 184, *219*, 225, *244*
Bindra, D., 336, *364*
Birkhoff, G., 207, *221*
Birnbaum, I. M., 20, *33*
Bishop, P., 67, *86*
Björgen, I. A., 315, *325*
Bjork, R. A., 36, 40, 50, *59, 60*, 149, *166*, 295, 298, 310, 322, *325, 327*
Bjurstam, K., 226, 230, *244*
Black, M., 65, *85*
Blakemore, C., 66, *85*
Blum, H. F., 196, 199, 201, *219*
Bobrow, D. G., 67, *85*, 123, 125, 130, 131, 132, 134, 138, *143*, 152, *166*, 260, *276*
Boeck, W., 304, *326*
Bohm, D., 202, *219*
Bolles, R. C., 76, *85*, 170, *219*
Booth, D., 68, *85*

Bormuth, J. R., 334, 335, *364*
Borsellino, A., 106, 108, 114, *118*
Bower, G. H., 24, *33*, 39, 45, 51, *58, 59*, 152, *164*, 306, *325*, 379, *387*
Bower, T. G. R., 271, *274*
Boynton, R., 173, *219*
Bracewell, R., 106, 108, 112, *118*
Bradshaw, J. L, 78, *85*
Bransford, J. D., 25, *33*, 75, *85*, 159, 161, 162, *164*, 171, 205, 212, 215, *221*
Bregman, A. S., 126, *143*
Brierley, J. B., 262, *274*
Broadbent, D. E., 4, *15*, 24, *33*, 69, 80, *85*, 133, *143*, 146, 147, *164*, 272, *275*
Brooks, L., 68, *85*
Brown, J., 5, *15,* 47, *59*
Brown, J. S., 123, *143*
Bruce, V., 382, 383, *387*
Bryden, M. P., 78, *85*
Buchanan, B. G., 69, 75, 84, *86, 89*
Buchanan, M., 270, *274*
Buckhout, R., 369, 370, *387*
Bures, J., 227, *244*
Buresova, O., 227, *244*
Burns, B. D., 61, *85*
Burton, R. R., 123, *143*
Buschke, H., 21, *33*, 272, *275*
Butters, N., 260, 262, *275*
Butterworth, B. B., 263, 269, 271, *276*

C

Calissano, P., 231, *244*
Cardo, B., 238, *244*
Cavanagh, P., 45, *59*, 110, *118*
Cermak, L. S., 260, 262, *275*
Chabot, R. J., 150, *164*
Chall, J. S., 334, 336, *364*
Chambers, S. M., 268, *276*
Chance, J. E., 152, *165*
Charniak, E., 63, 65, 67, 73, 74, *85*
Cheatham, T. E., Jr., 65, *85*
Chestek, R. A., 84, *89*
Chomsky, N., 42, *59*
Clark, H. H., 345, 363, *364*
Clark, R., 191, *219*
Clowes, M. B., 76, *86*
Cole, M., 318, *327*
Collins, A. M., 51, 52, 56, *59*, 81, 84, *86*
Collins, G. H., 262, *277*

Conrad, C., 78, *86*
Cornsweet, T. N., 110, *118*
Corteen, R. S., 78, *86*
Cowen, G. N., 78, *86*
Crabbs, L. M., 334, *365*
Craik, F. I. M., 24, 25, *33*, 47, 50, *59*, 118, *118*, 145, 146, 148, 149, 150, 151, 152, 153, 154, 155, 157, 158, 160, 163, *164, 165*, 258, 265, 272, *275*, 308, 310, 322, *325*
Crothers, E. J., 39, *58*
Crowder, R. G., 21, *33*, 268, 272, *275*
Cua, W., 229, 233, *245*
Cupello, A., 229, *244*

D

Dark, V. J., 150, *164*, 317, *325*
Darley, C. F., 150, *164*
Davies, G. M., 371, 375, 379, *387*
Davis, R., 68, 69, 71, 75, *86*
Dawson, R. G., 21, *33*
Day, C. M., 108, *119*
Dean, P. J., 300, *326*
De Groot, A. D., 160, *164*
Dennett, D. C., 185, 204, *220*
Dent, H., 370, 371, *387*
DeRenzi, E., 270, *275*
Deutsch, D., 81, *86*, 147, *164*
Deutsch, J. A., 81, *86*, 147, *164*
Dewey, J., 330, *364*
Dicke, R. H., 196, *220*
Dodd, B., 270, *275*
Dodwell, P. C., 109, *118*
Donato, R., 239, *244*
Drachman, D. A., 263, 264, 272, *275*
Drever, J., 316, *325*
Dunn, D., 78, *86*

E

Ebbinghaus, H., 3, *15*, 44, *59*
Egeth, H., 80, *86*
Egyhazi, E., 229, *244*
Ellis, H. D., 370, 371, 375, 379, *387*
Elmqvist, D., 250, *254*
English, A. C., 316, *325*
English, H. B., 316, *325*

Epstein, W., 175, 183, *220*
Erdelyi, M., 21, *33*, 147, *165*
Eriksson, M., 250, *254*
Erman, L. D., 69, 71, *87*
Estes, W. K., 25, 30, *33*, 46, 49, 50, 51, 55, *59*, 298, *324*, 363, *364*
Evans, J. D., 150, 151, *165*
Eysenck, M. W., 152, *165*

F

Falkenberg, P. R., 49, 51, *59*
Feigenbaum, E. A., 44, *59*, 67, 69, 76, 84, *86, 88*
Fennell, L. D., 69, 71, *87*
Fennell, R. D., 71, *86*
Fessler, P. K., 386, *388*
Finkelstein, S., 21, *33*
Fiorentini, A., 66, *87*
Fisher, R. P., 160, *165*
Fitch, F. B., 316, *325*
Fitch, H., 168, 204, *220*
Flemming, N. C., 368, *387*
Flesch, R., 340, 361, *364*
Flood, I., 242, 243, *244*
Fodor, J. A., 173, 178, *220*
Fowler, C. A., 188, 208, *220*
Fox, J., 126, 134, *143*
Frankish, C., 268, 272, *275*
Franks, J. J., 25, *33*, 159, 161, 162, *164*
Franzen, G., 253, *254*
Frederiksen, J., 318, *325*
Freud, S., 3, *15*
Frobes, J., 96, *102*
Fromkin, V. A., 269, 270, *275*

G

Gabor, D., 110, *118*
Galanter, E., 4, *15*
Gallistel, C. R., 321, *325*
Garner, W. R., 66, *86*
Gascon, J., 68, *85*
Gaukroger, S. W., 257, *275*
Gelade, G., 79, 82, *89*
Gel'fand, I. M., 188, *220*
Gelman, R., 321, *325*
Geschwind, N., 66, *86*
Gibson, E. J., 152, 160, 162, 163, *165*

Gibson, J. J., 152, 160, 162, 163, *165*, 187, 205, 209, 210, 211, 212, *220*
Gilliland, J., 334, *364*
Glanzer, M., 272, *275*
Glass, A. L., 150, *164*
Gleitman, H., 80, *86*, 321, *326*
Glenberg, A., 149, *165*
Glucksberg, S., 78, *86*
Godden, D. R., 368, *388*
Goldstein, A. G., 152, *165*
Goodglass, H., 260, 262', *275*
Graesser, A. C., II, 294, 306, 312, 313, *326*
Grasso, A., 231, *244*
Green, C., 149, *165*
Green, D. M., 110, *118*
Green, D. W., 270, 271, *275*
Green, J., 78, *89*
Greene, E.,341, *365*
Greeno, J. J., 355, *364*
Gregg, V. H., 160, *165*
Gregory, R. L., 174, 206, *220*

H

Haber, R. N., 109, *118*
Hagberg, B., 251, *254*
Haglid, K. G., 231, 240, *244*
Haljamäe, H., 231, *244*
Hall, M., 316, *325*
Halper, F., 84, *88*
Hamberger, A., 240, *244*
Hambley, J., 244, *245*
Hansson, H.-A., 231, 240, 241, *244*
Haviland, S. E., 345, 363, *364*
Hawkins, H. L., 66, *86*
Hayes-Roth, B., 295, *325*
Hayes-Roth, F., 69, *86*
Haywood, J., 244, *245*
Healy, A. F., 49, 51, *59*
Hebb, D. O., 336, *364*
Heinz, S. P., 147, 148, 152, 153, *165*
Helmholtz, H. von, 174, *220*
Hempel, C. G., 42, *59*
Henderson, L., 82, *86*
Henderson, L. J., 199, 200, 201, *220*
Hepburn, H. R., 229, *245*
Herbart, J. F., 330, *364*
Hermelin, B., 270, *275*
Herrmann, S. J., 265, *274*
Herschman, H. R., 241, *245*

Hewitt, C., 67, 70, *86*
Hilgard, E. R., 43, *59*
Hintzman, D. L., 151, *165*, 299, *325*
Hirst, W., 78, 83, *89*
Hitch, G., 267, 269, 273, *274*, 298, *324*
Hockey, G. R. J., 269, *275*
Hoffman, E. J., 248, *254*
Hovland, C. I., 294, 316, *325*
Huffman, D. A., 63, 76, *86*
Hull, C. L., 316, *325*
Humphrey, G., 187, 202, *220*
Hunt, E., 174, *220*, 363, *364*
Hunter, I. M. L., 370, *388*
Hydén, H., 226, 229, 230, 231, 233, 234,
    235, 239, 240, 241, *244, 245*
Hymnowitz, N., 229, 233, *245*

I

Ingvar, D. H., 247, 249, 250, 251, 252, 253,
    254, 255
Irion, A. L., 21, 22, 23, 24, 26, *33*

J

Jacoby, L. L., 145, 149, 150, 151, 152, 154,
    155, 157, 158, 160, 161, *165*
James, W., 4, *15*
Jarvella, R. J., 270, 272, *275*, 347, 363, *365*
Jarvik, M., 242, 243, *244*
Jasper, H., 250, *255*
Jensen, A. R., 318, *325*
Johansson, G., 94, 95, 99, 100, *102*, 129,
    130, *143*
Johnson, M. K., 75, *85*
Johnson, S. T., 269, *276*
Johnson-Laird, P. N., 270, *275*
Johnston, W. A., 147, 148, 152, 153, *165*
Joncich, G. M., 331, 332, *365*
Jones, R. S., 111, *118*
Jongeward, J., 50, *60*
Jongeward, R. H., Jr. 149, *166*, 295, 298,
    310, *327*
Jonides, J., 80, *86*
Jorpes, J. E., 32, *33*
Juola, J. F., 150, *164,* 306, 307, *324*

K

Kabrisky, M., 108, *119*
Kaplan, M. M., 184, *221*
Karlin, M. B., 379, *387*
Karpiak, S. E., 233, *245*
Katona, G., 4, *15*, 293, 317, *324*
Keenan, J. M., 160, *165*, 338, 343, 348, 356,
    365
Keren, G., 147, *165*
Killion, T. H., 79, *85*
Kimble, D. P., 227, 229, *245*
King, J. 68, 71, *86*
Kinsbourne, M., 264, *275*
Kintsch, W. 75, *86*, 118, *119*, 272, *275,*
    308, *325*, 338, 341, 343, 345, 348, 356,
    360, 361, 363, *365*
Kirker, W. S., 160, *166*
Klahr, D., 332, *365*
Klare, G. R., 334, 335, 336,*365*
Kleiman, G. M., 271, *275*
Klein, K., 152, *165*
Knapp, D., 322, *325*
Koffka, K., 44, *59*, 171, *220*
Kohler, W., 44, *59*
Kohonen, T. 111, *119*
Kolers, P. A., 149, 152, 153, 154, 157, 162,
    165
Konorski, J., 49, *59*
Koopmans, H. J., 306, 307, *326*
Kotovsky, K., 38, *60*
Kozminsky, E., 338, 343, 348, 354, 356, *365*
Kroll, N. E. A., 78, *89*
Kuhl, D. E., 248, *254*
Kuhn, T. S., 6, *15*, 28, *33*, 257, *275*
Kuiper, N. A., 160, *166*
Kurtz, K. N., 294, *325*

L

Laberge, D., 55, *59*, 303, *325*
Lakatos, I., 191, *220*
Lane, A. B., 386, *388*
Lange, P. W., 226, 230, 231, 233, 234, 235,
    244, 245
Larsen, B., 251, *255*
Larsson, S. 230, *245*
Lashley, K. S., 44, *59*, 270, *275*
Lassen, N. A., 248, *255*

Laughery, K. R., 386, *388*
Lawrence, D. H., 80, *87*
Lederberg, J., 69, *86*
Lee, C. L., 49, 50, 51, *59*
Lee, D. H., 210, *220*
Lenat, D. B., 75. *87*
Lenorovitz, D. R., 386, *388*
Leontiev, A. N., 279, *289*
Lesgold, A. M., 306, *325*
Lesser, V. R., 69, 71, *86, 87*
Levine, L., 241, *245*
Levy, B. A., 25, *33*, 146, *164*, 269, 271, *275*, 322, *325*
Lewis, J. L., 78, *87*, 363, *364*
Lhermitte, F., 266, *276*
Liepa, P., 111, *119*
Lindsay, P. H., 128, *143*
Linton, M., 306, *325*
Locke, D., 217, *220*
Lockhart, R. S., 24, *33*, 47, *59*, 145, 148, 149, 150, 151, 152, 157, 163, *164*, 258, 265, 272, *275*, 308, *325*
Lockman, R. F., 335, *365*
Loftus, E. F., 81, *86*
Loftus, G. R., 150, *164*, 317, *325*
Logan, G. D., 80, *87*
Logue, V., 262, 263, 264, 265, 267, 270, *277*
Lombardo, T., 168, *220*
Lunneborg, C., 363, *364*
Luria, A. R., 66, *87*, 266, *276*, 281, 283, 285, *289*

M

Maas, J., 98, 99, *103*
MacDonald, V. S., 248, *254*
Mace, W. M., 174, 182, 186, 204, 207, 210, 212, 214, *220, 221*
Mach, E., 202, *221*
Mackay, D. G., 76, 78, *87*, 269, *276*
MacKinnon, G. E., 78, *89*
Mackintosh, N. J., 76, *87*
MacLane, S., 207, *221*
MacWhinney, B., 160, *165*
Madigan, S. A., 21, *33*, 257, 258, *277*
Maffei, L., 66, *87*
Mandler, G., 24, *33*, 294, 300, 302, 303, 304, 306, 307, 308, 312, 313, 317, 318, 320, 322, *325, 326, 327*

Marangos, Z. N., 229, 233, *245*
Maratos, M., 270, *277*
Marcel, A. J., 66, 78, *87*
Marin, O. S. M., 66, *87*, 263, 270, 271, *276*
Marr, D., 68, 72, *87*, 134, *144*
Masani, P. A., 272, *275*
Mayhew, D., 160, *165*
McCall, W. A., 334, *365*
McCarrell, N. S., 25, *33*, 159, 161, 162, *164*
McEwen, B., 226, 230, *244*
McGauch, J. L., 21, *33*
McGeoch, J. A., 21, 22, 23, 24, 26, *33*
McGill, J., 81,*88*
McGill, W. J., 106, *119*
McIntyre, M., 190, 192, 207, 212, *221*
McKoon, G., 338, 343, 348, 356, *365*
McLeod, P., 83, *87*
Medawar, P. B., 211, *221*, 362, *365*
Meyer, D. E., 44, *59*, 78, *87*
Michotte, A., 130, *143*
Mihailović, L., 230, *245*
Millar, D. B., 130, *143*
Miller, G. A., 4, *15*, 305, 322, *326*
Miller, T. J., 150, *164*
Milner, B., 266, *276*
Minsky, M., 63, 67, 82, *87*
Mitchell, T. M., 84, *89*
Moore, B. W., 241, *245*
Moore, J., 63, 84, *87*, 132, *143*
Moorhead, P. S., 184, *221*
Morris, C. D., 161, *164*
Morton, J., 81, *88*, 267, 268, 269, 272, *275, 276*
Moscovitch, M., 152, *165*
Mowbray, G. H., 78, *88*
Müller, G. E., 306, 317, *326*
Muncey, J. P. J., 66, *85*
Münsterberg, H., 331, *365*
Murdock, B. B., Jr., 21, 25, *34*, 41, *59*, 107, 112, 113, 116, *119*, 259, 272, *276*, 298, *326*
Murray, D. J., 269, *276*

N

Navon, D., 126, 133, 134, 139, *143*
Neisser, U., 25, *34*, 67, 78, 83, *88, 89*, 94, 96, *103*, 109, *119*, 259, *276*

Nelson, T. O., 48, *59*, 150, 152, *165*, 309, 310, 317, *326*
Newell, A., 25, *34*, 63, 64, 69, 70, 71, 84, *87*, *88*, 125, 132, *144*, 146, *165*, 259, *276*
Newport, E. L., 321, *326*
Nii, H. P., 67, 76, 84, *88*
Nitsch, K., 25, *33*, 159, 161, 162, *164*
Norman, D. A., 24, 25, *34*, 44, *60*, 67, 81, *85, 88*, 113, *119*, 122, 125, 128, 130, 131, 132, *143*, 147, 152, *165*, 258, 260, 264, 265, *276, 277*, 310, *327*
Nuwer, M., 110, *119*

O

Orme, M. R., 242, 243, *244*
Ortony, A., 67, *88*

P

Palmer, S. E., 123, 142, *144*
Papert, S., 82, *87*
Parker, E. S., 20, *33*
Pattee, H. H., 172, 196, 210, 217, *221*
Patterson, K. E., 78, *87*, 306, 307, *327*, 380, 381, *388*
Pearlstone, Z., 272, *277*, 306, 307, *326*
Penfield, W., 250, *255*
Penry, J., 371, 376, *388*
Perez, V. J., 241, *245*
Perkins, D. T., 316, *325*
Perl, W., 229, 233, *245*
Perrin, C. L., 234, *245*
Persson, L., 231, 240, *244*
Peterson, G. M., 227, *245*
Peterson, L. R., 5, *15*, 47, *60*, 269, *276*
Peterson, M. J., 5, *15*, 47, *60*
Petrović–Minić, B., 230, *245*
Phelps, M. E., 248, *254*
Philipson, L., 251, 252, *254*
Phillips, L., 266, *277*
Piaget, J., 321, *326*
Pichert, J. W., 354, *364*
Pirsig, R. M., 386, *388*
Pittenger, J., 187, 213, 216, *221*
Platt, J. R., 30, 31, *34*
Poggio, T., 106, 108, 114, *118*
Popper, K. R., 191, *221*

Posner, M. I., 44, *60*, 302, *326*
Postman, L., 24, 30, *34*, 260, 272, *276*
Potter, M. C., 148, 152, *166*
Pratt, R. C. T., 262, 263, 264, 265, 267, 270, *277*
Pribram, K. H., 4, *15*, 45, *60*, 110, *119*

Q

Quillian, M. R., 51, 52, 56, *59*

R

Rabbitt, M. G., 44, *59*, 78, *87*
Rabinowitz, J. C., 306, 307, 308, *327*
Radoy, C. M., 108, *119*
Raphael, 125, 134, 138, *143*
Rapport, M. M., 233, *245*
Rasner, G. A., 272, *276*
Ratcliff, R., 107, 113, *119*
Ray, T. S., 185, 186, *221*
Reddy, D. R., 69, 71, *87*
Reddy, R., 71, *88*, 125, *144*
Reder, L. M., 150, 151, *164*
Reichardt, W., 108, *119*
Restle, F., 157, 162, *166*
Reynolds, P., 78, 83, *85*
Ridley, R. M., 66, *85*
Rieger, C. J., 64, 73, 74, *88*
Riesbeck, C. K., 64, 73, 77, *88*
Rips, L. J., 52, 56, *60*
Risberg, J., 251, *255*
Ritchey, G. H., 307, *326*
Ritter, A., 229, 233, *245*
Ritz, S. A., 111, *118*
Robinson, E. S., 44, *60*
Robinson, Jr., G. D., 248, *254*
Rock, I., 84, *88*, 175, *221*
Rogers, T. B., 160, *166*
Roland, P., 251, *255*
Rönnbäck, L., 231, 239, 240, *244, 245*
Rosch, E. H., 123, *144*
Rosen, I., 250, *254*
Rose, S. P. R., 244, *245*
Rosendorft, C., 229, *245*
Rosenfeld, A., 109, *119*
Ross, R. T., 316, *325*
Rothkopf, E., 354, *365*

Rumelhart, D. E., 67, *88*, 125, *144*, 145, *166*, 300, *327*
Rundus, D., 310, *327*
Runesom, S., 187, 188, 210, *221*
Russell, B., 169, *221*
Russell, S., 64, *88*
Ryle, G., 169, *221*

S

Sachs, J. S., 270, *276*
Saffran, E. M., 66, *87*, 263, 270, 271, *276*
Saltz, E., 152, 160, 162, 163, *165, 166*
Samuels, S. J., 55, *59*, 303, *325*
Saraga, E., 66, *88*
Scarborough, H. S., 347, *364*
Schank, R. C., 64, 67, *88*
Schauer, R., 84, *88*
Schneider, W., 80, 81, *88*
Schnur, P., 160, *166*
Schulman, A. I., 160, *166*
Schulz, R. W., 294, *327*
Schvaneveldt, R. W., 44, *59*, 78, *87*
Schwartz, M. F., 66, *87*
Schwartz, M. S., 249, *254*
Scribner, S., 318, *327*
Segal, M. A., 307, *327*
Selfridge, O. G., 82, *88*
Selz, O., 317, *327*
Shaffer, L. H., 83, *88*
Shaffner, K. F., 204,*221*
Shallice, T., 66, 81, *88*, 263, 264, 265, 266, 267, 268, 269, 270, 271, 272, 273, 274, *275, 276, 277*
Shashoua, V. E., 229, *245*
Shaw, R. E., 25, *34*, 171, 182, 186, 187, 190, 192, 204, 205, 207, 212, 213, 214, 215, 216, *221*
Shepherd, J., 371, 375, 379, *387*
Shiffrin, R. M., 23, *33*, 47, 49, *58*, 80, 81, *88*, 258, 260, 264, *274*, 310, 322, *324*, 348, *364*
Shoben, E. J., 52, 56, *60*
Shortliffe, E. H., 69, 75, *86, 88*
Shulman, H. G., 272, *276*
Siegel, A. I., 361, *365*
Siegel, E., 361, *365*
Signoret, J. L., 266, *276*
Silverstein, J. W., 111, *118*
Simmonds, D. C. V., 376, 378, *388*

Simon, H. A., 38, *60*, 63, 70, *88*
Skinner, B. F., 41, *59*, 169, *221*
Skinner, B. R., 170, *221*
Sloman, A., 72, *89*
Smith, D. H., 67, *89*
Smith, E. E., 52, 56, *60*
Smith, R. G., 84, *89*
Smith, S. M., 149, *165*
Snyder, C. R. R., 44, *60*, 302, *326*
Speelman, R. G., 269, 270, *277*
Spelke, E., 78, 83, *89*
Sperling, G., 258, 269, 270, *277*
Squire, R., 78, *89*
Starr, A., 266, *277*
Steiger, R., 67, *86*
Stein, B. S., 161, *164*
Stenman, U., 78, *89*
Sternberg, S., 107, 111, *119*, 259, *277*
Stettner, L. J., 21, *33*
Stevens, S. S., 30, *34*, 335, *365*
Stevenson, R., 270, *275*
Stone, G., 335, *365*
Streby, W. J., 338, 343, 348, 356, *365*
Strong, D. R., 185, 186, *221*
Sully, J., 330, *365*
Sussman, G. J., 84, *89*
Svedelius, C., 282, 285, *289*
Sykes, M., 79, 82, *89*

T

Tallman, O., 108, *119*
Teuber, H.-L., 260, *277*
Thomson, D. M.,159, 160, *166*, 305, 307, *327*
Thomson, N., 270, *274*
Thorndike, E. L., 331, *365*
Tieman, D., 306, *325*
Toulmin, S., 29, *34*
Treisman, A. M., 78, 79, 82, *89*, 146, *166*
Trimble, V., 189, 196, *221*
Tsetlin, M. L., 188, *220*
Tulving, E., 117, *119*, 150, 153, 159, 160, 161, 163, *164*, 257, 258, 266, 272, *277*, 305, 306, 307, 308, 309, 312, 318, *325, 327*
Turner, A., 341, *365*
Turvey, M. T., 25, *34*, 82, *89*, 94, 96, *103*, 126, *144*, 168, 171, 174, 182, 186, 187, 188, 204, 207, 208, 212, 214, *220, 221*
Tversky, B., 384, *388*
Tzortzis, C., 263, 267, *277*

U

Uexküll, J. von, 210, *222*
Underwood, B. J., 24, *34*, 44, 45, *60*, 294, 317, *327*
Uttal, W. R., 108, *119*
Uttley, A. M., 76, *89*

V

van Dijk, T. A., 360, 361, *365*
Verbrugge, R. R., 219, *222*
Victor, M., 262, *277*
Vignolo, L. A., 270, *275*
von Wright, J. M., 78, *89*

W

Wald, G., 196, *222*
Wall, S., 80, *86*
Waltz, D., 76, *89*
Wanner, E., 270, *277*
Wardlaw, K. A., 78, *89*
Warren, N. T., 78, *89*
Warren, R. E., 78, *89*
Warrington, E. K., 260, 261, 262, 263, 264, 265, 266, 267, 268, 270, 271, 272, 273, 274, *276, 277*, 379, *388*
Waterman, D. A., 68, *89*
Watkins, M. J., 50, *59*, 149, 159, *164*, 308, 310, *325, 327*
Watkins, O. C., 159, *166*
Watson, J. B., 332, *365*
Waugh, N. C., 25, *34*, 258, 264, *277*, 310, *325*
Weiskrantz, L., 260, *277*
Weiss, P. A., 202, 204, *222*
Welch, L., 320, *327*
Wentworth, K. L., 227, *245*

Wescourt, K. T., 265, *274*, 298, 303, *324*
Westlake, P. R., 110, *119*
Wheeler, J. A., 189, 196, *222*
Whitaker, H., 66, *89*
Whitaker, H. L., 66, *89*
Wickelgren, W. A., 44, *60*, 113, *119*, 152, *166*
Wickens, D. D., 24, *34*
Wigner, E. P., 192, 193, 196, *222*
Wilks, Y., 65, 67, *85, 89*
Williams, G. C., 170, *222*
Willies, G. H., 229, *245*
Willows, D. M., 78, *89*
Wing, A., 66, *89*
Winograd, T., 67, *85, 89*, 124, 132, *143, 144*
Winston, P. H., 84, *89*
Wood, B., 78, *86*
Woodhead, M. M., 376, 378, *388*
Woodward, A. E., Jr., 50, *60*, 149, *166*, 295, 298, 310, *327*
Woolf, C. J., 229, *245*
Worden, P. E., 294, 312, 313, *326*
Worden, P. E., 294, 312, 313, *326*

Y

Yanagihara, T., 230, *245*
Yoblick, D. A., 386, *388*
York, C., 229, 233, *245*
Young, R. M., 68, 70, 84, *89*

Z

Zangwill, O. L., 263, *277*
Zayas, V., 229, 233, *245*
Zedler, J., 20, *34*
Zomzely-Neurath, C., 229, 233, *245*
Zuckerman, J. E., 241, *245*

Subject Index

A

Affordance, 205–209, 217–219
Amnesia, 84, 260–263, 265–266, 285
Analysis, 134–140
  conceptually driven, 134–138
  data-driven, 134–138
  schema-driven, 136–140
Aphasia, 285
Applied research, 367–369
Artificial intelligence, 61, 64, 66–67
Attention, 70, 77–79, 83–84, 146–149, 322
  allocation of, 322
  division of, 83
  inattention, 84
  preattention, 70, 77–79
  selective, 146–149
Attuned organism, *see* Stage setting

B

Behaviorism, 21–23, 168–170, 317
Brain, 229–244, 247–253, 262–263, 286
  abnormal, 251–253
  biochemical changes, 229–244
  cerebral ideogram, 247–254
  lesions, 262–263, 286
  normal, 249–251
  proteins, 230–235, 238–244
Brown–Peterson paradigm, 47–50, 264

C

CADAM, 111–118
  associative information, 114–115
  item information, 112–114
  serial-order information, 115–116
Capacity, 152–153, 272–273, 322–323,
  358–359
Cerebral ideogram, *see* Brain
Cerebral image, 185
Coding, 24, *see also* Encoding
  analogical and propositional, 123
Comprehension, 340–364
Computational paradigm, 63–64
Consciousness, 142, 249–250, 322–324
Constancy, 176, 178, 184
Convolution, 105–118
  applications to memory:
    holography, 110–111
  applications to perception:
    brightness, 109
    optomotor responses, 108
    pattern recognition, 109
    pitch perception, 110
  definition of, 105–106
Correlation, 105–118
  applications to memory:
    holography, 110–111
  applications to perception:
    optomotor responses, 108
    pattern detection, 108

Correlation, applications to perception *(contd.)*
    pattern recognition, 109
    pitch perception, 110
  definition of, 106

D

Default values, *see* Schema, characteristics of
Dementia, organic, *see* Brain, abnormal
Depth of processing, 149–150, 308–310, *see also* Levels of processing
  index of, 147–148, 152–153
  relation to elaboration, 152, 308–310
Description, 124, 127–133
  structure of, 132–133
Dissociation, 284
  double, 260–262
  temporal and spatial, 80
Distinctiveness, 151, 159–160, 163
Distributed memory, 44–45, 111–118
Dualism, animal–environment, 168–179

E

Ecology, 189–190, 227
Econiche, *see* Environment
Ecosystem, 206–209
Education, 7–8, 329–333
Effectivity, 205–206
Encoding, 147–161
  phonemic, 147–150
  and retrieval, 153, 156–161
  semantic, 147–150
Encoding specificity principle, 158–161, 305–310
Engram, 44
Environment, 9, 199–205, 211–213, 227
  as an affordance structure, 205
  and econiche, 199
  and mutual compatibility, 189–190, 193–199, 205–206
Environmentalism, 169–170
Empiricism, 173–178, 180–182
Episodic memory, 145–164, 266
Epistemic mediators, 171–173
Evolution, 13, 185–189
Expectancy, 72–75
Explanation, 28, 42–57

F

Face recognition, 369–387
  encoding, 379–380
  disguises, 380–382
  and reproduction, 370–376
  semantic memory, 382–385
  training, 376–379
Forgetting, 29, 159, 310–315
  instructions for, 310–315
Fourier transforms, *see* Convolution
Fractionation, 260, 263–266
  long-term vs. short-term memory, 263–266
  other types, 266

G, H

Gestalt psychology, 4, 293, 317
Holography, 44–45, 110–111

I

Information processing, 4–9, 24, 257–259, 273
Inheritance, *see* Schema, characteristics of
Integration, 79–82, 294–304
  and elaboration, 294–304
  perceptual, 79–82
  and primary memory, 81–82

K

Knowledge, 65, 68, 71–72, 81, 123–124, 320
  declarative and procedural, 123
  extrinsic and intrinsic, 123
  perceptual, 124

L

Law of Existence, 194–198
Law of Potentiality, 198
Law of Subordinate Existence, 198
Levels of processing, 24, 47, 148–163, 265, 379–380, *see also* Depth of processing

Logic, 190–193
  adjunctive, 190–199
  causal, 190, 192–193
  hypothetical, 190–191
Long-term memory, 24, 51–57, 235, 253,
    314, 347–353, 356

M

Macrostructures, of text, 360–362
Memory, *see also* Episodic memory, Long-
    term memory, Semantic memory,
    and Short-term memory
  ecological reformulation, 216–219
  functions of, 8–10
  and perception, 11–12, 62, 93, 97–98, 101,
    124–126, 145–149, 167
  productive, 4
  reconstructive, 157, 282
  reproductive, 4
  as stage setting, 25, 161–162
  tacit, 62
  trace, 43–46, 156, 162
    strength, 44
Metaphor:
  computational, 63
  economic, 169
  spatial, 5, 7, 20
  storage, 25, 62
Messenger RNA, *see* RNA
Modus tollens, 190–191

N

Nativism, 182–189
Neurogram, 44
Neuropsychology, 257–288
  method of, 273–274, 280–288

O

Organization, 293–324
  dimensions of, 294–304, 308
    elaboration, 294–296, 299–304, 308
    integration, 294–304
  and learning, 320–324
  and repetition, 310–315
Organizational structure, *see* Schema,
    characteristics of

P

Perception, 93–102, 167–216
  conscious, 77–84
  direct and indirect, 213–216
  as an ecosystem property, 208–213
  event, 93–100
  illusions, 180–181
  incomplete specification, 181–182
  visual event, 93, 97–98
  motion, 93–95
    and time, 95
Photo-fit technique, 371–376
Principle of Mutual Compatibility, 189–190,
    193–199, 205
Procedural information, *see* Schema,
    characteristics of
Processing:
  control structures, 133
  elaborative, 151, 294–296, 299–304,
    308–310
  integrative, 294–304
  maintenance, 50, 149, 308–310
  models of perception, 125–126
  reconstructive, 157, 282
  resources, 133
Production systems, 67–76
  integration, 71–72
  modularity, 67
  rules, 70–71

R

Rationalism, 179–182
Readability, 333–340, 356–362
  formulas, 334–335
  limitations, 335–336
Recall, 154–156, 251, 263–266, 268–273,
    304–308, 338–340
  and recognition, 306–308
Recognition, 154–156, 304–308, 369–387
  and recall, 306–308
Rehearsal, 149–151
  elaboration, 308–310
  maintenance, 50, 149, 308–310
Reinforcement, 170, 297
Repetition, 150–151, 297, 310–315
Representation, 123–124, 207
Retrieval, 24–25, 62, 156–161, 303
  and encoding, 156–161
RNA, 226, 229–230, 241–244

Rote learning, 315–324
  as a human ability, 317–320

S

Schema, 4, 124, 128, 130–138
  active, 134–138
  characteristics of, 131
Schizophrenia, chronic, *see* Brain
Science:
  cognitive, 141–142
  normal, 6
  preparadigmatic, 28, 257–258
  revolutionary, 6
Semantic memory, 51–57, 161–162, 266
  models for, 51–57
  role in perception, 77
Semantic processing, preattentive, 77–79
Short-term memory, 24, 47–51, 70, 101, 253,
    263–273, 298, 347–353, 356, 358
  auditory vs. visual, 267–273
  properties of, 267–273
  a reorientation, 49–51
Simulation, 38
Stage setting, 25, 161–162
Storage, 24–25, 62
Strong inference, 31
Synergy, animal–environment, 167, 199,
    202, 206–210

Systems, 8–9, 25, 65–67, 202–205
  classification:
    episodic vs. categorical, 25
    episodic vs. semantic, 25
    primary vs. secondary memory, 25
  cognitive, 8–9
  interactions, 65–67
  partial and total, 202–205
S-100 protein, 230–244

T

Text comprehension, 341–356
  coherence, 344–346
  control processes, 353–356
  a processing model, 346–353
  representation of meaning, 341–344
Theory, 5, 41, 57–58
  construction of, 57–58
  functions of:
    description, 41
    explanation, 41
    prediction, 41
  general vs. miniature, 5

V

Vectors, 45–46, 98–99, 112–116